# SYRIA AND SAUDI ARABIA

# SYRIA AND SAUDI ARABIA

## Collaboration and Conflicts

### in the Oil Era

Sonoko Sunayama

Tauris Academic Studies
LONDON · NEW YORK

Published in 2007 by Tauris Academic Studies, an imprint of I.B.Tauris & Co Ltd
6 Salem Road, London W2 4BU
175 Fifth Avenue, New York NY 10010
www.ibtauris.com

In the United States of America and Canada distributed by Palgrave Macmillan
a division of St. Martin's Press, 175 Fifth Avenue, New York NY 10010

Library of International Relations 31

ISBN: 978 1 84511 302 5

A full CIP record of this book is available from the British Library
A full CIP record is available from the Library of Congress

Library of Congress Catalog Card Number: available

Printed and bound in India by Replika Press Pvt. Ltd
From camera-ready copy edited and supplied by the author

# CONTENTS

# PREFACE AND ACKNOWLEDGEMENTS

'How does Syria, far from a self-sufficient state by any standards, attract enough overseas economic and political aid to ensure its survival?' It was over a decade ago that the question first entered my mind and gripped my thoughts. I was soon introduced to the rich literature on Syrian-Soviet relations, written by scholars of diverse nationalities, providing answers to one piece of the puzzle, but leaving more questions to be asked about how Syria used relations with the neighbouring states to its advantage. Years passed before I set out to study Syrian-Saudi relations—another set of bilateral relations which Damascus relentlessly attempted to tap for its benefit. Only now, after the further passage of time, have I arrived at *an* answer to the question, while making other discoveries along the way, all to be tested and challenged by scholars in the future.

Many institutions and individuals have assisted me in this path, namely: Ito International Foundation for Education Exchange, Matsushita International Foundation Research Fund, the Nihon Ikueikai Award, Institut Français d'Études Arabes de Damas (IFEAD) and the Gulf Research Centre (GRC)—some of which provided me with generous funding while others made available their facilities. At the London School of Economics and Political Science (LSE), to which the first version of this work was submitted as a doctoral thesis, my two supervisors, the late Mr. Philip Windsor and Professor Fred Halliday, generously shared their thoughts on the subject with formidable patience and much-appreciated humour.

I have been looking forward to writing this page in part because it gives me the opportunity to acknowledge the guidance and friendship of ever-dependable Hiroyuki Aoyama (Institute of Developing Economies, Tokyo), to whom I am most indebted. I would also like to thank: Ghassan Mukahhal, Hassan 'Abbas, Hussain Musa, 'Abd al-'Aziz al-Saqr, F.

Tarabulsi, M. Kilu, R. N. el-Rayyes, P. Seale, C. Tripp, J. al-Zein, G. Armanazi and K. Shihabi to name but a few. Some of the other experts and specialists who have kindly given me their time and insights at different stages of this research prefer to remain unnamed for the purpose of their own security and convenience; I thank all collectively.

The limited space will not permit me to acknowledge all those who have offered moral and practical support or sometimes just made themselves readily available to listen. I am grateful in particular for the friendship of: Simon Williams, Maartje Houbrechts, Chieko Shindo, Kiriko Tokura, Yoko Takahashi, Deborah Hawkes, Victoria Robson, Susanne Buckley-Zistel, Ayşegül Keçeciler, Osman Çatı, Özgür Çatı, Steven Colling and the Kleins.

However, the project would not have even come close to completion, had it not been for my parents' understanding and Ross Everson's patient encouragement and sacrifice. I would like to dedicate this book to them.

Transliteration of Arabic words has been kept to the simplest with minimum usage of the extra symbols and letters so as to maintain the readability of the text. More detailed distinction of Arabic alphabets would deem the text cumbersome to read for those with no knowledge of Arabic, while others should be able to deduce the original. Preference is given to an anglicised term, whenever it is widely understood—i.e. House of *Saud*, but *Sa'ud* al-Faisal, and Aleppo, instead of *Halab*. Quoted texts have not been modified to a unified method, and names of authors maintain the spelling as in the original publication.

# INTRODUCTION

An old dictum among Middle East observers reads, 'There can be no [Arab-Israeli] war without Egypt, and no peace without Syria', to which some have recently come to add, 'no normalisation without Saudi Arabia'.[1] The adage attests to the centrality of the so-called Damascus-Riyadh-Cairo tripartite axis in shaping the Arab regional order; it briefly materialised in the mid-1950s and the mid-1970s but collapsed with the foundation of the United Arab Republic in February 1958 and the then Egyptian President, Anwar al-Sadat's visit to Jerusalem in November 1977, respectively. The theme was revisited more than a decade later upon the 6 March 1991 proclamation of the Damascus Declaration or the '6+2' formula, in which the six states of the Gulf Co-operation Council (GCC) plus Egypt and Syria committed to play a central role in securing Gulf security, thereby linking the Gulf issues to the wider Arab concerns, especially the Arab-Israeli sector (Hollis, 1995: 37). Most recently, further evidence of the triangle at work was reported between December 2005 and January 2006, when Syrian President Bashshar al-Asad found himself under heavy international pressure to co-operate fully with the United Nations International Independent Investigation Commission (UNIIC) in its investigation of the ex-Lebanese Prime Minister Rafiq al-Hariri's murder case. Saudi King 'Abdallah bin 'Abd al-'Aziz and Egyptian President Husni Mubarak embarked on joint diplomatic campaigns, promising Asad of their support while seeking to persuade him to fulfil all requests from UNIIC (*Daily Star*, 9 and 14 January, 2006).

Despite its undisputed weight in shaping Middle East regional events, the relationship between Damascus and Riyadh—one side of the triangle—is commonly noted as a 'paradox', in which, 'On the one hand, [the two capitals] differed on almost every major policy issue in the [Middle East]; on the other, both conveyed the impression that there existed some kind of an *alliance*, albeit an uneasy one' (*MECS*, 1984–

1985: 602, emphasis added). This study is an attempt to shed light on the
dynamics of what appeared to be at least an enduring entente[2] if not a
formal alliance—its origin, occasional tension and longevity—which has
over time developed into a defining element in inter-Arab politics.

In order to unveil the 'paradox' of how the two countries, despite their
differences, maintained outwardly amicable relations throughout their
recent history, it is best to detail their behaviour towards each other during
the period of sharpest disagreements, i.e. when their policy aims on key
regional issues were diametrically opposite. That period of acute difference,
be it in international, regional or even ideological orientations, started with
the signing of the Camp David Accords in September 1978 and
definitively closed with Iraq's invasion of Kuwait in August 1990. Syria,
one of the most heavyweight Middle Eastern allies of the Soviet Union
during Hafiz al-Asad's rule, formalised this tie in the Treaty of Friendship
and Co-operation in 1980. Meanwhile, during this period, Saudi Arabia
singularly refused to establish diplomatic ties with the Communist Soviet
Union based on, amongst others, religious considerations (Abu Talib,
1992: 84-85); the Saudi perception of mistrust became that of imminent
security threat after the latter's invasion of Afghanistan in December 1979.
In contrast, Saudi Arabia has been firmly entrenched since World War
Two under the United States' security umbrella. Regionally, Syria stood
behind revolutionary Iran throughout the latter's eight year-war against
Iraq, while Ayatollah Ruhollah Khomeini intermittently called on the
masses to overthrow the Saudi monarchy, destabilising the Kingdom's
internal and external security environment (Wilson and Graham, 1994:
103-104). Moreover, after the Israeli invasion of Lebanon in 1982, Syria
played a key role in purging the al-Fath wing of the Palestine Liberation
Organisation (PLO) from Lebanon, when the latter was the only
Palestinian resistance movement publicly supported by Saudi Arabia.[3] In
the ideological sphere, Syria, according to the official line, has been a
secular, socialist, Arab nationalist state, governed by a President from a
heterodox minority sect, the 'Alawis, or the Nusairis. In contrast, the
House of Saud embraces conservative Wahhabi Islam—renowned for its
unitarism and rigidity—as the backbone of its legitimacy and has been
deeply suspicious of the revolutionary messages of Arab socialism as well
as of the 'Alawi sect.

Such marked contrasts and seemingly incompatible policy goals are
deemed even more remarkable, when seen against the background of
visibly amicable relations and persistent diplomatic efforts to co-ordinate
policies throughout the rocky period of the 1980s. Joint Syrian-Saudi
efforts in resolving the Lebanese civil war, to be crowned with the lasting
observance of the 1989 Ta'if Accord by the Lebanese parties concerned,

could be named a primary example of their co-operation. Furthermore, when, by the mid-1980s, other Arab leaders had exhausted their patience with Damascus' regional policy, Riyadh stood alone in fully honouring the 1978 Baghdad Summit financial commitment to frontline states, among which Syria was the foremost stated beneficiary (*Financial Times*, 2 July 1987). It would be difficult to over-state the uniquely consistent relations between Damascus and Riyadh during the 1980s, when, in contrast, the former's seemingly idiosyncratic regional policy resulted in vicious exchanges of slander and reprimand with most Arab capitals.

Existing studies on inter-Arab relations merely mention in passing these contradictory aspects of Syrian-Saudi relations without seeking to analyse them in detail. The absence of a scholarly contribution to its analysis is not, however, an indication of the marginality of the subject. Safran, for example, goes so far as to say: 'In the Arab-Israeli arena, Saudi policy at the end of [King] Khaled's reign and the beginning of Fahd's was almost completely enthralled to Syria's basic policy' (1988: 453). *MECS* endorsed this view as applicable also to a later period: 'The thread running through...most Saudi inter-Arab policies...was the Syrian factor and its role in the shaping of Saudi policy' (1984-1985: 602). Today, even after Egypt, Jordan and the Palestinians have concluded separate peace with Israel, the Saudis explicitly support Syria's 'steadfastness' and are unlikely to follow in the others' footsteps until an agreement materialises on the Syrian and Lebanese frontlines. The absence of serious studies on the subject may reflect in part the complexity arising from the fact that neither of the two actors has occupied a central place in the other's primary security concerns (Chalala, 1988: 119). Paradoxically, however, neither has been able to realise its own regional objectives without being concerned about what the other does. In order to understand such curious *indispensability*, this study argues that the normative functions of Arabism and, to a lesser extent, of Islam must be brought in to complement interest-focused observations.

Various authors have touched on the key factors which brought Damascus and Riyadh together. For some, the lack of a solution to the Arab-Israeli conflict has sealed the Saudi obligation to frontline Syria (e.g. Kienle, 1990: 93; Perthes, 1995: 32-33); Syria's incentive to mobilise all Arab resources for the anti-Israeli struggle easily converged with the Saudis' commitment to the Arab cause, or at the very least, with their interest in *appearing* committed to it (Drysdale and Hinnebusch, 1991: 85). Others may emphasise the trade-off of Syria's military might and Saudi financial power—the interdependency formula of Arab 'Rich and Poor states' as proposed in the work of Kerr and Yassin (1982). Even in the Gulf arena—where Syria's support for revolutionary Iran amounted to treachery in some Saudi eyes—it could be argued that Riyadh came to appreciate the balancing role of Syria; due to its historic rivalry with the Iraqi Ba'th, Damascus could keep a check on Iraqi expansionist ambitions (e.g. Chalala, 1988: 119; Kienle, 1990: 151) while it could potentially mediate between Iran and the pro-Iraqi Arab camp (Marschall, 1991: 69).

In another vein are arguments involving historic and cultural factors. Many Syrians, for example, have argued—with a mix of sentimentality and melancholy—that the closeness of the two countries was a 'natural' extension of a long-standing historical, social connection which existed through the centuries (personal communications, Damascus, 1999). Some tribal federations and families such as the Ruwala, have lived for centuries along both sides of the Syrian Desert, grazing and trading in the territories stretching across what is now divided into Syria, Jordan and Saudi Arabia (Lancaster, 1981). The Shammar tribe, to which Saudi King 'Abdallah's maternal lineage is traced, is also such an example. All of these themes allow nuanced approaches to primary factors which influence Syrian-Saudi relations, but no definitive attributes of cause can be made. These disparate building blocks of the bilateral ties will be revisited throughout this study to assess the validity and limitations of their explanatory power.

Theoretical debates on alliance and alignment formations also offer clues to understanding different aspects of Syrian-Saudi relations. An acclaimed work by Walt, *The Origins of Alliance,* draws theoretical conclusions on alliance formations through extensive case studies on Middle Eastern states. When Walt treats the term *alliance* as interchangeable with loose *alignment*—'a formal or informal arrangement for security cooperation between two or more sovereign states' (1987: 12)—his theory acquires direct relevance to discussion on Syrian-Saudi relations. He addresses two main factors as 'origins of alliance', which are *balancing/bandwagoning* on the one hand and ideological similarities on the other. However, his conclusion is firmly in support of the realist approach in international relations theory, when he asserts that *balancing* external threats is by far the most dominant cause of alliance formation (1987: 147-180). This position, with regard to Syrian-Saudi relations, is represented by those who profess that Syria's primary value to Saudi Arabia rested on its ability to counter-balance Iraq or to restrain Iran. *Bandwagoning,* which according to Walt is less common than *balancing,* would explain why Riyadh was obliged to assist Damascus' confrontation with Israel in the form of financial as well as political aid. These are valid points in understanding some aspects of the bilateral relations. They fail, however, to explain why, for instance, Riyadh repeatedly attempted to reconcile Baghdad with Damascus during the Iran-Iraq war or why Syria went largely unpunished for sabotaging Riyadh's high-profile initiatives to

resolve the Arab-Israeli conflict, as will be examined in Chapter Three.
Walt also investigates the utility of economic aid as a tool to influence
alliance formation. He concludes, as much Middle Eastern history shows,
that economic aid is a relatively ineffective measure in influencing
decisions of the targeted state (1987: 218-261). Brand, however, challenges
Walt's conclusion through her inspiring case study on Jordan; she asserts
that economic factors which include not only aid but also trade relations
can be a primary *source* of alliance making (1994: 20-21, 29-30). She
specifically points out the possible applicability of her model to Syria and
its pursuit of alliance with the more endowed Arab neighbour states (1994:
299). However, it is noteworthy that the policies of Syria and Jordan
towards Saudi Arabia, despite both being beneficiaries of the latter's
economic aid, are not always identical. For example, Syria's boycott of the
1981 Fez Summit is held largely responsible for the abortion of the Fahd
Peace Plan, while Jordan's position in the summit, in Brand's words, 'not
surprisingly, was one of continuing support for its primary patron's plan'
(1994: 96). What accounts for the lack of comparable submissiveness on
Syria's part? There is no question that Saudi financial aid has constituted a
major incentive for Damascus to maintain cordial relations with Riyadh.
Nonetheless, whether this Saudi financial power was transformed into
political leverage is a point of contention. The analyses of the following
chapters will examine individual incidents in which Riyadh attempted to
utilise financial aid as a tool for influencing Syrian policy. One of the
findings is that these attempts met with little success. As will be argued
below, why this was so can only be better understood when informed by
the role of 'shared identities' in foreign policy.

Furthermore, Walt's discussion on *penetration* in alliance
formation—defined as the ability of one state to influence the
decision-makers of the other—is also useful when widened to encompass
a state's ability to implement *any* cross-border activity, including acts of
sabotage and ideological campaigns against the neighbouring state or
appeals to the sympathy of the neighbour's mass public. For Walt, the role
of such cross-boundary operations does not merit separate analysis from
*balancing* because they are 'not all that different from the external threats'
(1987: 216). This factor, however, is a significant and complex one in
Syrian-Saudi relations. Drysdale and Hinnebusch claim that Saudi Arabia
feared Syria's ability to instigate domestic instability in the Gulf region
(1991: 85), exercised through its self-proclaimed role as the 'throbbing
heart of Arabism (*qalb al-'uruba al-nabid*)'. Acharya argues along a similar
vein that Saudi Arabia has been especially vigilant about Syria's influence
over the Palestinians residing in the Gulf region, who, for their significant
number, can form active anti-House of Saud groupings (1992: 160-161).

This Syrian influence in the Gulf is complicated by the rival claims in the past of pro-Iraqi Ba'thism, Nasirism and, after 1979, pro-Iranian Islamism.

The above views, which emphasise *penetration* as a determining factor in Syrian-Saudi relations, presume the existence of a mass national sentiment whose appeal traverses state boundaries in the Arab region. In this case study of Syrian-Saudi relations, Arabism and Islam—intertwined and partially over-lapping, and hence not necessarily competitive—are the two main identities, arguably shared by the two states. The presumption here is that *penetration* is caused by the existence of identities appealing to individuals in more than one state—or 'transnational' identities. This allows one political message to have an appeal to a community larger than that defined by state borders, and thereby to blur the distinction between a state's *external* and *internal* affairs. Even Walt allows for the role of, in his term, 'ideological similarities' when he deviates from his essentially realist stance: 'In the Arab world, the most important source of power has been the ability to manipulate one's own image and the image of one's rivals in the minds of other [Arab] elites' (1987: 149).

The difficulty of establishing a causal relationship between foreign policy decision-making on the one hand, and mass national sentiment and public opinion on the other, has been widely acknowledged in the literature of international relations theory (e.g. Bloom, 1993: 77). Some dismiss the public opinion as an irrelevant factor in Middle Eastern politics because the prevalence of Bonapartist states does not allow political space for it (Ehteshami and Hinnebusch, 1997: 65, 201). Nevertheless, as Bloom asserts, 'Governments...do have to be sensitive to the general *will* of the mass national public...acknowledging the practical consequences of pursuing unpopular policy' (1993: 77) and that 'the political attractiveness...of the mobilisation of mass national sentiment is that it is the widest possible mobilisation that is available within a state. It theoretically includes the total national population, transcending political, religious, cultural and ethnic factions' (1993: 81). In Middle Eastern politics, the latter observation is further complicated by the fact that such national sentiments may mobilise not only masses *within* a state, but also those *across* the state boundaries.

The question of national sentiments necessitates definition of two key concepts around which the main arguments of this study focus: identity vs. ideology and their relations to the notion of 'state interests'. When discussing *identity* in social sciences, it is useful to revert to Anderson whose landmark contribution solidly established that it was a socially constructed, fluid variable (1983). Not only does a person hold multiple identities and the degree of his or her attachment to them shifts according to environment and experience, but the meanings and practices associated with these identities are also constantly redefined (Telhami and Barnett, 2002: 17); in other words, a person's commitment to Arab nationalism may change over time and grow weaker or stronger according to the situation, and the components and values of Arab nationalism have undergone significant revisions over the last century. For instance, Sharif Hussain of Mecca's Arab nationalism in the 1910s espoused different aspirations and core values to Gamal 'Abd al-Nasir's in the 1950s. The fluidity of identities helps explain in part why political actors attach great priority in winning the contest over identities; because identities are not fixed, and because the values and norms attached to them are subject to alteration, these actors found considerable advantage as well as necessity to be able to control them and shape them to suit their own interests and their needs of mass mobilisation. When the community encompassed by a particular identity is larger than that delineated by state boundaries, the contest of identity by extension developed into a foreign policy issue between multiple states.

This, however, is not to say that *identity* in foreign policy is a mere political instrument to be manipulated by practitioners; in this respect, it is distinguished from *ideology* (Telhami and Barnett, 2002: 11). *Identity*—the sentiment of belonging to a community and norms associate with it—should be understood as more than just a weapon for contesting over material *interests*; it is also an important *source* of concrete *interests* at the same time. *Identity* and self-interest are, in other words, both socially constructed, informed by each other, mutually constitutive rather than exclusive, and affected by all walks of political actors ranging from elites, social voices and international influences.

*Identity* can create certain shared expectations within a community, generating definable *norms*—i.e. 'expectations that constrain action within a specific social contest' (Barnett, 1998: 30). Such expectations define what is a permissible or commendable action for the community member/leader, although their power to 'constrain' may fluctuate and their expectations revised with the progression of time. In the Arab context, the history of Arab nationalism conditioned that non-alliance or anti-imperialism, for instance, developed into a vital component of its norms, while anti-communism was often a concomitant of an Islamic identity. It is only natural for a political actor's perception of interests and preferences to be influenced by these norms, and even if he or she remains aloof from the mass sentiments, *appearing* to cater to such shared expectations would constitute a vital self-interest. Consequently, *identity* informs self-interests in such a way that: 1) it defines the norms of what is, and is not, permissible behaviour for a leader or a state; 2) conformity with these norms ultimately defines the legitimacy of the leadership or the state itself; and as a result, 3) defined norms impose a regulatory constraint on each regime whose failure to tailor its policy along the line of accepted norms can cost it dearly in the form of lost prestige or even material sanction (Saideman, 2002).

When certain identities 'appeal to individuals in more than one state', they can be called 'transnational' or 'shared' by many states (Saideman, 2002: 184). Advocates of constructivist approaches to Arab politics argue that the existence of such a transnational identity 'can be tied to conflict *or cooperation*' (Telhami and Barnett, 2002: 5, emphasis added), but their empirical narratives have concentrated heavily on the question of its rivalry-generating function. Aforementioned Walt (1987: 181-217) also focuses on the divisive role of Arabism or Islam—i.e. to its alliance-*breaking,* instead of alliance-*making,* function—and as such, he sheds little light on how Damascus and Riyadh maintained their seemingly co-operative relations despite acts of *penetration,* including support for opposition groups of one another. Other studies on Middle East politics have also concentrated on the curious sharpening of antagonism among states which compete on identical ideological turf instead of building harmonious relations (e.g. Chubin and Tripp, 1988: 147-148; Kienle, 1990; Halliday, 1990).

Saideman critically notes:

> When do shared identities cause cooperation or rivalry?...we need to address both halves of the question with the same theoretical apparatus to understand what conditions lead to conflict, cooperation, or something in between. This should be the next question for the identity research agenda. (2002: 182)

This account of Syrian-Saudi relations, therefore, aims to contribute to the above debate by exploring the conditions in which 'shared identities' have led if not to co-operation, then, at the very least, to 'something in between'.

'Transnational' or 'shared' identities can, under certain conditions, create a situation in which a member of the 'sharers' either: 1) derives maximum benefit by imposing its own view of the ideological norm on other members; or 2) gets cajoled into obeying ideologically-driven rules defined by other member of the 'sharers'. In either case, a member state, or more accurately its regime, is unlikely to see much benefit in publicising its bitter disagreement with a fellow member. If the ultimate aim is to impose its own version of 'permissible behaviour', this regime will only win its prestige from the success in winning acceptance from other members. If, on the other hand, it is seeking to avoid troubles that might tarnish its domestic and regional reputation, the best strategy is to appear complacent and supportive of other members who command elevated credibility on ideological turf. In either scenario, the outward appearance of bilateral relations between the concerned actors can be quite possibly amicable, and this has been a pattern in Syrian-Saudi relations at times of tension.

Central to the study that follows, two hypotheses can be drawn from the above theoretical discussion. Firstly, Syria and Saudi Arabia succeeded in maintaining a working relationship during the period of 1978–1990, because their *chief* sources of legitimacy, or their *priority* identities, rested on related, but non-identical, foundations, one based on a concept of 'Arabism' and another, on 'Islam'. Instead of entering competition, they have largely succeeded in averting head-on clashes. This contrasts, for instance, with the Syrian Ba'th's struggle with the Iraqi Ba'th over the mantle of Arabism/Ba'thism or the House of Saud's conflict with Iran after 1979 over leadership of the Islamic world.

Related to this first point, most strikingly, each actor's affiliation to opposite sides of the global Cold War competition served to complement rather than to compete with each other. Indeed, when two actors belonged to opposite camps in the global and regional divides, mediation became one of the most prominent tools for survival. The key to understanding mediation in this context is that it was sometimes more important to *appear* to be mediating—thereby acting in the interest of, for instance, Arab solidarity—than to deliver a lasting and substantive reconciliation between actors in conflict. Hence, Riyadh continuously mediated between Damascus and Baghdad, even though consolidation of a powerful Ba'thi axis would pose a significant threat to itself. Syria also expended tremendous efforts to publicise its role as a go-between in the conflict between Iran and the Arab Gulf states with the aim of averting criticism that it was siding with the Iranians who were at war with fellow Arabs in Iraq.

Secondly, the appearance of cordial relations between Damascus and Riyadh masked an abundance of behind-the-scenes coaxing and cajoling; for instance, as Syria used the symbolic coercion of appeals to 'Arabism' to extract more political and financial support from Saudi Arabia, the latter reluctantly went out of its way to accommodate Syrian position with the naked aim of diverting criticism against its Arab or Islamic credentials. In this setting, Saudi financial aid could be expected to perform, at best, a defensive function of fending off attacks from the poorer, hard-line neighbour, but not to influence its policies. Supporting political opposition groups of neighbouring states was another tool to influence or apply pressure on those 'sharers' of the same identity; thus, Syria gave haven to Saudi leftist opposition figures, such as Nasir al-Sa'id, while some of Syria's Islamic groups took refuge in Saudi Arabia.

These fabrics of 'shared identities' have created a normatively-bound setting in which neither Syria nor Saudi Arabia could achieve its primary foreign policy goals without obtaining some degree of understanding and co-operation from each other. This was despite the fact that—never to be forgotten in the discussion that follows—neither saw each other as its primary foreign policy concern. In this respect, one may argue that *because of*—rather than *in spite of*—their diametrically opposite standing in their global orientations and regional affiliations, Syria and Saudi Arabia were faced with greater need than otherwise to be mindful of each other's interests and to seek, at the very least, mutual acquiescence in their own controversial policies.

This study, therefore, explores how in the late 1970s and the 1980s the existence of 'shared identities' conditioned the manner in which Syria and Saudi Arabia formulated their policy towards each other. It does not rule out the explanatory power of the *balancing/bandwagoning* formula, nor does it assert that concerns related to identity and legitimacy were the *chief* motives behind these states' foreign policy-making at *all* times on *every* issue. Nevertheless, through the examination of the Syrian-Saudi case, this study argues that, the regulatory, or normative, function of 'shared identities' are informed by realist interests as well as shape and constrain those interests at the same time. It reinforces the relevance, albeit qualified, of bringing back identities to explaining foreign policy of the Arab states, even though the *norms* and *practices* associated with such identities may not be identical to those from half a century ago.

The outline of this book is as follows: Chapter One gives a historical overview of the period from Syria's independence until 1978 to document the emergence of the bilateral relations. It highlights the existence of contacts between Syrian and Saudi societies both at the societal and at the leadership levels. The detailed case study starts with Chapter Two, which begins with the 1978 Camp David Accords. They marked a dramatic destruction of the Arab regional order that had dominated much of the 1970s in the form of the trilateral axis of Damascus-Riyadh-Cairo. In the two years following Camp David, other momentous regional events followed—the Iranian Revolution of January 1979, Soviet invasion of Afghanistan in December 1979 and internationalisation of the Lebanese civil war in tandem—all of which created further divisions in the Arab world. From October 1978, the lines of these divisions roughly converged into a single framework which polarised the Arab world into two camps, one headed by Syria and another by Saudi Arabia. In this respect, Chapter Two serves as an introduction to the following case study chapters by laying out the sources of Syrian-Saudi controversy albeit one masked by an outwardly smooth appearance.

Chapter Three examines the first two years of the period in which Damascus and Riyadh emerged as dominant leaders of the two opposing camps in the region. This period was unique in that it observed an uncharacteristically pro-active and assertive Saudi foreign policy, while Syria was largely on the defensive in the region, mainly because of its domestic insecurity and Israel's intervention in Lebanon. The bilateral relationship, nevertheless, was a relatively balanced one in which Damascus maintained its ability and willingness to veto major Saudi initiatives. Thus, examination of this period underscores the leverage which Damascus held over Riyadh—or in other words, the reasons behind the former's indispensability to Riyadh—even at the time of relative Syrian weakness.

By October 1982, Saudi primacy had quickly begun to wane, as Riyadh failed to convert the success of the Fez II summit into a lasting diplomatic gain. Chapter Four investigates the subsequent eighteen months during which time Lebanon occupied the central place in Middle East political debate; when an Arab state's prestige rests in part on its agenda-setting ability to define the most important issues in the regional politics, Syria was set to make a comeback as *the* most important player in Lebanese and, by extension, Arab politics. The discussion on this period also highlights how the two superpowers' policy towards the region could potentially develop into a determining factor in Syrian-Saudi relations.

Chapter Five concentrates on the Iran-Iraq war, one of the bitterest sources of disagreement between Damascus and Riyadh. This was particularly so because the centre of Arab debate swung heavily towards the Gulf, as a result of the outbreak of the Tanker War in April 1984. Here again, however, the two actors had to negotiate closely with each other, and both went out of their way not to antagonise the other. The conclusion of this Chapter covers the interim period between the end of the Iran-Iraq war in 1988 and Iraq's invasion of Kuwait in 1990. In this period, the sources of Syrian-Saudi disagreement, as outlined in Chapter Two, gradually disintegrated, or were resolved. The final conclusion of this book builds on the discussion of this interim period by reviewing in brief the new era of the 1990s and beyond. In this framework, it draws thematic conclusions about the role of 'shared identities' in foreign policy in the Syrian-Saudi case.

The methodology adopted in this study would be deemed as 'historical' based on its chapter breakdown and the extensive documentary. An obvious alternative would be to identify landmark events in Syrian-Saudi relations and then to extract a thematic pattern through their analyses.

Although either approach would have perhaps allowed the narrative to reach the same theoretical conclusion, the choice was consciously made in favour of 'time frames' as definitive units of analysis. As the following chapters would amply demonstrate, an event in one corner of the Arab region has, more often than not, been inextricably connected with another in the opposite corner in unexpected manners, and the same could be said of its connection to certain global developments. The complex interlinkage of events was such that singling out any particular event for analytical purposes was doomed to be an artificial exercise and risked placing undue importance to one over another. Analysing a time-defined unit, in contrast, has an advantage of being able to examine a set of events as data on an interconnected 'whole' and then to derive thematic conclusions for each 'phase'. This approach permits a more subtle understanding of how 'shared identities'—as well as other factors—conditioned Syrian-Saudi relations in different *ways* at different *times* with different *degrees* of force.

The regimes of both Syria and Saudi Arabia are particularly renowned for their secretiveness, even by Middle Eastern standards. The resulting difficulty of access to sources has typically created such challenging obstacles to research on the region's contemporary history that it could be at best provisional if not an informed guesswork. This study also has faced difficulty in finding reliable sources to substantiate its assertions, when access was largely limited to secondary sources and media reports from the region and worldwide. While each of these reports may not always provide the most balanced account of an event, comparing those from various Arab countries, Israel and the West—which invariably cover a topic from different angles—is a useful exercise for deciphering the motives and concerns of the publications' host states. Reliance on such reports and the lack of official archives have not enabled the author to answer such a question as, 'what exact amount of economic aid did Syria receive from Saudi Arabia after each Arab summit meeting?'. They do, however, permit discussion on not only speculated figures from different sources but also the context in which aid was brought to the Syrian-Saudi negotiation table and its implications to the bilateral relations. Wherever possible, the findings were supplemented by oral communications, sources of which must remain undisclosed for the reason of their security.

In view of the complexity of Syrian-Saudi relations and the existence of ties at countless levels of society from time immemorial, there is no doubt that innumerable theoretical questions can be addressed through studying the topic, and not one account would perhaps be *the* authoritative one. The thematic questions raised and conclusions reached in this study are also just a few of the many possibilities, and the approach adopted here is an outcome of an attempt to find an opening within the constraints of scarce sources—i.e. seeking questions that can be sufficiently substantiated using available materials—while avoiding arbitrary choice or logical inconsistency.

# 1

# SYRIAN-SAUDI RELATIONS
# BEFORE CAMP DAVID
## Historical background (1946–1978)

Time and again, the Syrian-Saudi connection has been referred to as one of the keys to understanding the dynamics of major political events in the Middle East. Before opening a detailed examination of the turbulent decade of the 1980s, this chapter attempts to examine the evolution of the Syrian-Saudi relationship from Syria's independence, isolating its key determinants and their changes according to the transformation of regional and domestic environment.

Arab nationalist ideas emerged as the major source of inspiration and means of legitimisation for many Arab leaders, especially after the imposition of mandatory regimes in much of the Arab world. In the Arab East, the objective to unify the Arab world was temporarily shelved, taken over by the anti-British/French campaign for independence; as a result, independence was achieved as separate states, defined by the borders largely adopted from the colonial experience. However, the rulers found themselves presiding over countries in which the majority of the population had little sense of identification with the territorial states, whose borders as well as the political structures were believed to be illegitimate constructs of the imperial powers. The states were thus 'territorial' rather than 'national', as political allegiance easily shifted across these borders.

Where the state was so 'alien' (Korany, 1987) to the existing sense of political community, or the national identity, the rulers' domestic legitimacy was constantly threatened from forces within and without the state. The prevalence of Arabist messages at the time meant that this challenge had to be countered by presenting themselves as the most committed representatives of the Arab cause, while their rivals bid for the same title. One of the means to present this commitment was a unity proposal with other Arab states. However, the fact that regime consolidation was the underlying interest behind such schemes reflected the regime's internal vulnerability or its hegemonic aspiration towards a weaker neighbour (Kienle, 1995). In the Arab East, the Greater Syria plan of King 'Abdallah and the Fertile Crescent scheme of Nuri al-Sa'id were early examples of such unity proposals. The Hashemites' hegemonic aspirations stirred much suspicion and fear among other states, especially when these states' nation building was still at an embryonic stage. Thus, Egypt, despite its geographic and historical distinction from the rest of the Arab world, became a willing competitor for the Arab nationalist title. As to the House of Saud, Wahhabi Islam (al-Yassini, 1983: 3-5), tribal loyalties (Kostiner, 1990) and proven military competence had provided the cornerstones of its legitimacy since its first realm in the eighteenth century. The emotional appeal of Arabism was thus originally secondary to the Saudis' concern, but they entered the contest of Arab rivalry all the same, mainly with the aim of frustrating the hegemonic aspiration of the Hashemites, their traditional archenemies. Territorial borders no longer defined the distinction between domestic and inter-state politics, granting Arab regimes a license to interfere in their neighbours' internal affairs under the banner of a common Arab nation. When each regime equally pursued the monopoly of the Arab nationalist language, it appeared to degenerate into a tool to serve the regimes' hegemonic aspirations over the Arab land and to consolidate their domestic rules against the neighbours' interference (Kienle, 1990; Ayubi, 1995: 135).

The ensuing competition among the Arab regimes was, allegedly, fought over Syria, as each state recognised that the key to dominating the Arab Middle East was to control it or at least to ensure that it was not controlled by a rival regime. This centrality of Syria was partly derived from its strategic position in the heartland of the Arab world—not only geo-politically (Seale, 1986) but also economically and ideologically (Binder, 1967)—and partly from the fragility of its domestic political foundation, inviting the neighbours to sponsor rivalling political factions. The countless coups d'état in the early years of independence demonstrated the turbulence and the fragility even by Arab standards. Moreover, this special position as the focus of Arab rivalries made Syria a plane of wider international competition of the East and the West, as will be explored later in the discussion of the Eisenhower doctrine and the Soviet encroachment in the late 1950s.

The period between the 1940s and the 1960s was, in Ajami's words, the time when:

pan-Arabism could make regimes look small and petty: disembodied structures headed by selfish rulers who resisted the sweeping mission of Arabism and sustained by outside powers that supposedly feared the one idea that could resurrect the classical golden age of the Arabs. (1978/1979: 355)

This chapter aims to analyse the development of Syrian-Saudi relations in the context of the Arab states' desperate quest to achieve legitimacy, played out in the form of outbidding rival Arab nationalist claims and denouncing each other's connection with the 'imperialist' powers or the Eastern bloc. During this process, both Syria and Saudi Arabia experienced rapid modernisation, and, in the case of Saudi Arabia, a dramatic increase in its oil wealth. Domestically, both states enhanced their capabilities, on the one hand, to develop their security apparatuses, and on the other, to cater to the interests of politically dominant groups, thereby each consolidating the state and its leadership through a mixture of coercion and tutelage without resolving the 'national' question. Their regional stature also improved dramatically. As a result of these changes, the 1970s—in Ajami's term, the era of 'the end of pan-Arabism'—observed the consolidation of 'the Arab system of sovereign states'. However, the fact that the *national* question remained unresolved suggests that the underlying source of regime insecurity may have been passed on to the later decades. This chapter analyses Syrian-Saudi relations in the three phases of 'the struggle for Syria', the polarisation of the Arab world, and the subsequent period of regime consolidation in the Arab world that provided a foundation for the establishment of the Damascus-Riyadh-Cairo tripartite axis; by so doing, it attempts to underline the basis of comparison with the period after the 1978 Camp David, the main focus of this study.

## 'The Struggle for Syria', 1946–1961

When Syria gained formal independence from France in 1946, the Arab East was roughly divided between the Hashemites in Iraq and Transjordan on one hand, and Egyptian-Saudi co-operation on the other. For Iraq and Jordan, controlling Syria was a prerequisite to achieving a strategic position that linked the northern tier countries, the Arab states and the West (Lesch, D.W., 1992: 47). For Egypt, the most populated and powerful of the Arab states, such a scheme meant its isolation and automatic reduction of its status to a mere secondary actor in the region. Egypt's interests somewhat overlapped with the Saudis' in a sense that both favoured the federation of Arab states as means to foil the Hashemite plans of administrative Arab unity. In this context, the formation of the Arab League in March 1945 was the first Egyptian victory and Saudi gain, as it formally recognised the sovereignty of individual Arab states.

For the Saudis, who founded their kingdom through the conquest of the Hashemite Hijaz, the prospect of having a hostile Hashemite bloc on their northern border was more than an anathema. Their sense of threat emanated not only from geopolitical calculations, but also from their economic dependence on the Arab East for secure consumer goods trade and oil export transit routes (Al-Rasheed, 1991: 117). There may also have been a psychological factor at play on the part of King 'Abd al-'Aziz, commonly known as Ibn Sa'ud, the founder of the modern Saudi state. During his quest to unify what is today Saudi Arabia, co-operation extended by the tribes in the Syrian Desert from the north was instrumental in defeating his main rival, the Rashidi dynasty in the northern Arabian Peninsula.[1] Such a memory is likely to have prompted him to hold the control of Syria dear to his heart, which perhaps provided the grounds for the popular legend about his deathbed speech; he is said to have summoned his sons and advised them in his last breath to 'keep an eye on Syria' (Seale, 1986: 294; personal communications, Damascus, 1999). Another saying goes that Ibn Sa'ud went so far as to plead with Winston Churchill to give his Kingdom a common border with Syria, when the territorial borders of Transjordan were being delineated (personal communications, Damascus, 1999).

In the period between 1946 and 1961, Saudi Arabia strove to influence Syrian politics through scores of secretive means, as will be detailed below: by bribing Syrian political factions or individuals, by funding Syrian newspapers to manipulate the dominant propaganda and election results and by encouraging coup attempts or terrorist acts if more violent means were required. More publicly, Saudi Arabia devoted its petro-dollars to finance lucrative inter-state loans, in the hope that they would cement friendly relations with Syria's governing body. When conditions were favourable, Saudi cash bought them some leverage over Syria's regional and domestic policies.

As for the Syrians, the political scene after independence was dominated by the traditional ruling class, or in their enemies' terms, 'the collaborators of French imperialism'. They were drawn almost completely from some fifty families (van Dusen, 1975: 123), representing the large-scale landowners and merchants ('Ayan). This class ruled uneasily over the ambiguous and deeply divided entity called Syria. Sectarian divisions, coupled with economic stratification, were brewing discontent among the minority groups against the Sunni-dominated ruling class (van Dam, 1978; van Dusen, 1972). To represent the variety of views, political parties were formed, ranging from Arab nationalist, socialist, communist, Syrian nationalist, Islamic and others. Another source of rivalry within the country's political scene was that between the military and the civilian politicians, both of whom blamed each other for the disaster of the 1948 Arab-Israeli war. Furthermore, the ruling class could not even maintain its own cohesion. Geographical division of the north (Aleppo) and the south (Damascus) later developed into rivalry between two main conservative parties, the People's Party (*Hizb al-Sha'b*) and the National Party (*al-Hizb al-Watani*) respectively. This division also roughly corresponded with the opposing political affiliation towards the other Arab powers; since Aleppo region historically enjoyed economic and social ties with Iraq, it was natural for the People's Party to align itself with Hashemite Iraq, while Damascus had established extensive links with Palestine and the Arabian Peninsula. This debate over Syria's regional policy involved a wider international dimension—that of policy towards the West. In other words, the Hashemites' open collaboration with Britain entailed that Syria's choice between the two Arab camps automatically defined its policy towards 'imperialism'.

Such was the fragility of Syria's domestic environment that its affiliation to other Arab powers swung from one extreme to another. It was both a victim and a determinant of regional and international competition in the Arab East (Seale, 1986). Against this background, Saudi Arabia's courtship of Syria, or in other words, the Saudi 'struggle for Syria' went through three distinct phases: a) 1946–1953, b) 1954–1957 and c) 1958–1961.

### The Saudis vs. the Hashemites, 1946–1954

In this initial phase of 'the struggle for Syria', the line of conflict which cut across the Arab world was drawn relatively clearly between the Saudi-Egyptian camp and the Hashemites. Saudi Arabia was in the final years of the reign of Ibn Sa'ud. In Syria, the traditional elites were on their last legs, upholding their dominance, while the military was growing ever more reluctant to return to the barracks after numerous successful coups.

Saudi policy in this period concentrated on removing Syria from the Iraqi orbit. Ibn Sa'ud did not have any ambitious design to annex Syria, but strove to maintain an independent Syria, governed by friendly statesmen who would preserve the balance of power in the Arab world (Khoury, 1987: 587). A friendly regime in Syria was also crucial to Saudi Arabia's economic policy, as it was eager to pass an oil pipeline through the Syrian Heights—or the Golan—to the Lebanese port of Sidon, carrying much of Saudi oil for export (Holden and Johns, 1981: 148). This Saudi policy had already born some fruit when Shukri Quwatli, the leader of the National Bloc (*al-Kutlah al-Wataniyyah*), was elected in 1943 the first president of Syria, still nominally under French rule. Despite all the factional divisions, the lack of unifying principles and rampant corruption, Quwatli's National Bloc was, at this stage, the most organised political group among those that led Syria's independence struggle. His election symbolised the victory of the Damascus-based wing of the National Bloc over its Hashemite-affiliated counterpart whose stronghold was in the northern city of Aleppo. Quwatli's family had long served as commercial agents for the Saudis, and Quwatli himself catered for Ibn Sa'ud by sending him a number of talented Syrians since the 1920s (Seale, 1986: 26; Rathmell, 1995: 9), the most prominent examples being Yusuf Yasin,[2] Ibn Sa'ud's chief adviser on foreign affairs, and Rashad Fira'un, a physician-turned adviser, who went on to serve as chief of the council of advisers to Kings Faisal, Khalid and Fahd. The Saudis' role in Quwatli's election was significant. It was they who offered him haven in 1941, when the Allies and the Axis powers forced him to leave the country during their Syrian battle. It was they who, furthermore, persuaded the French and the British in early 1942 to allow for his return (Seale, 1986: 26; Rathmell, 1995: 9) and convinced the British that he was an acceptable candidate for presidency (Khoury, 1987: 597).

Thus, Quwatli's election marked the initial success of Saudi policy in installing a friendly government in Syria, and once this was done, Saudi Arabia embarked on a diplomatic mission to protect it. In January 1947, for instance, when Hashemite King 'Abdallah's aggression against Syria intensified, the Saudis, assisted by the Egyptians, threatened to revive the Saudi claims to the Jordanian territories of Aqaba and Ma'an unless he withdrew his Greater Syria scheme. Also, in the same year, Ibn Sa'ud allegedly aided Quwatli's attempt to suppress the uprising of his chief domestic opposition, the Druze (Seale, 1986: 133). During the next decade, Saudi Arabia's Syrian policy concentrated on upholding Quwatli's authority. Even after numerous coups turned against his fortunes and overthrew him from the pinnacle of political power, Riyadh repeatedly attempted to reinstall him throughout the best part of the 1950s.

Various other Syrian forces had also courted Ibn Sa'ud since the 1920s; his popularity rested mainly on his support for Syria's (nominal) independence and on his untainted reputation in dealings with the 'imperialist' powers, while the Hashemites, in contrast, were often seen as British puppets (Khoury, 1987: 229). His military victory over the Hashemites also gave added credibility, and his religious reformist orientation appealed to some preachers of the Islamist brand of nationalism. The commercial tie with the Arabian Peninsula was another incentive for southern Syrians to court Saudi friendship. Traditionally, the tribes from Saudi Arabia and Jordan travelled across the desert to Syria in order to purchase daily commodities, the business which contributed substantially to the financial income of the Syrian small-scale merchandise and manufacturers. In the 1930s Syria's economy still depended largely on this transit trade between the Mediterranean ports and the Peninsula due to modest domestic demand. Moreover, after the creation of Israel, all goods from the Mediterranean had to pass through Syria, giving it considerable revenues from taxes and levies (Petran, 1972: 83-84). At a time when the Gulf societies were steadily increasing their purchase power from their oil income, Syria's business interest also began to look more towards the south than the east.

The brief honeymoon of Saudi Arabia and independent Syria came to the first test in March 1949 with Colonel Husni al-Zaim's coup d'état, the first of the countless coups which marked Syrian politics for the next two decades.[3] This was because the event raised Hashemites' hopes that the Syrian officers would translate their admiration for Iraq's well-trained military into pursuit for political alliance with Baghdad; these officers, in turn, lamented the low-keyed Saudi military role in the 1948 defeat and doubted the ready availability of unconditional Egyptian help in the event of an Israeli aggression. Within a month, however, Za'im began to respond favourably to Egyptian and Saudi overtures to such an extent as to call for 'a consolidated union between Syria, Egypt, and Saudi Arabia [that] will create a strong front against the Greater Syria Plan' (Rathmell, 1995: 30). As a reward, Saudi Arabia promised a $6 million loan to Za'im, at the time when Saudi Arabia itself was requesting American and British military aid to balance the Hashemites (Holden and Johns, 1981: 149).

The Iraqi camp was determined not to let this unfavourable situation continue, and in August of the same year, it struck back by actively encouraging Colonel Sami Hinnawi's coup attempt, which was concluded with his assassination of Za'im. The general election following the coup resulted in domination of the Syrian Chamber by the People's Party, which was founded by the pro-Iraqi, Aleppo-based branch of the National Bloc. It brought Syria ever closer to joining the Fertile Crescent unity scheme with Iraq, a development which induced blatant Saudi bribing of sympathetic Syrian politicians and its stirring of discontent among Syrian tribes (Rathmell, 1995: 56). The People's Party's gravest weakness, however, rested in its contradictory policy; it called for a unity with Iraq, while its nationalist commitment forced itself to denounce Nuri al-Sa'id and King 'Abdallah's British connection.

In December, Colonel Adib al-Shishakli, an anti-unionist committed to the republican system of government, carried out the third coup of the year. In the formation of the new government, Saudi Arabia, together with Egypt, manoeuvred to buy a friendly government by offering loans of up to $36 million (Rathmell, 1995: 63). In January 1950, it succeeded in formalising the long-awaited Tapline agreement between the Syrian government and the Trans-Arabian Pipeline Company, enabling Aramco (Arabian-American Oil Company) to pipe oil from Saudi Arabia across Syria to the Mediterranean. The following month, Saudi Arabia granted a $6 million interest-free loan (Seale, 1986: 92; Rathmell, 1995: 63). Under the new cabinet of Khalid al-'Azm, Saudi Arabia and Egypt came to terms with the new political framework in Syria, temporarily shelving their attempts to bring back the former president, Shukri al-Quwatli. However, by May of the same year, 'Azm's cabinet had run into several difficulties, most notably the economic crises and the division in the ruling coalition (al-'Azm, 1973; al-'Azmah, 1991).

When, consequently, Nazim al-Qudsi, the People's Party secretary-general, was asked to form a government, the Saudis saw a window of opportunity to reinstate Quwatli and co-operated with the Egyptians whose officers had established a close link with him during his exile in Alexandria. One of the new means that Saudi Arabia adopted was the use of the Arab Redemption Phalange (*Kata'ib al-Fida' al-'Arabi*), Syria's first state-sponsored subversive organisation, which allegedly planned various assassination attempts against Nuri al-Sa'id of Iraq, King 'Abdallah of Jordan, and Shishakli.[4] Such an undisguised involvement in subversive activities soured Saudi relations with the ruling Syrian government. The relations suffered a further setback when fighting broke out between Syria and Israel in the demilitarised zone near Lake Hula. In contrast to the swift Iraqi support of sending military units to Syria, Saudi Arabia and Egypt remained reticent towards the crisis.

In November 1951, Shishakli launched his second coup d'état to establish a more thorough military dictatorship for the next two years (Seale, 1986: 130-131). The relative durability of his reign was attributed partly to Syria's agricultural boom in the late 1940s and the early 1950s and partly to the foreign support he enjoyed. Shishakli was committed to improving relations with the neighbouring countries, particularly Egypt and Saudi Arabia, but was not prepared to sacrifice Syria's sovereignty in line with the Iraqi proposal. His associates in the new government, notably Akram al-Hawrani of the Arab Socialist Ba'th Party (*Hizb al-Ba'th al-'Arabi al-Ishtiraki*), were staunch neutralists, uncompromising in any dealings with the imperial powers or with the Western-oriented Hashemites. Economically, the upwardly mobile Damascene industrialists preferred the Saudi market to the Iraqi one (Petran, 1972: 103). Also, Shishakli personally looked towards Cairo for military assistance.

Under this general principle of inter-Arab orientation, Syria's relations with Iraq soured. When an anti-Shishakli, exile government—the Free

Syrian Government—was formed in Baghdad by Muhammad Safa', evidence suggests that Saudi personnel were personally involved in distributing bribes to encourage anti-Safa' movements (Rathmell, 1995: 90). As pressure mounted on Shishakli from Iraq and Lebanon, Saudi Arabia's Yusuf Yasin directed more oil revenue to Syria (Holden and Johns, 1981: 148; Seale, 1986: 140), and the Saudi ambassador in Damascus mediated between Syria and Lebanon in February 1954. However, Shishakli was overthrown shortly afterwards by another military insurrection and fled to the Saudi embassy in Beirut. Even after Shishakli's escape from Damascus, Saudi Arabia channelled up to 300,000 Syrian Lira (LS) to pro-Shishakli elements in order to protract resistance (Lesch, D.W., 1992: 57; Rathmell, 1995: 90).

With the fall of Shishakli, the initial phase of 'the struggle for Syria' ended. Saudi Arabia achieved much of its modest goal of preserving Syria's nominal independence and establishing a beneficial economic relationship through the Tapline and trade. Although Quwatli—the House of Saud's best friend—failed to consolidate his rule, Saudi Arabia remained more successful in buying the loyalty of other Syrian individuals than at any other time. For Syria, this was a period in which the chain of numerous coups undercut its ability to establish a constitutional political system, instead leading to the ascendance of military. The Syrians interpreted these coups as product of blatant Western involvement (often through Hashemite channels), and as a result, the radical anti-imperialist forces began to increase their support, threatening to override the traditional ruling class. In the next phase, the new protagonists of Syrian domestic politics emerged, at a time when the global superpowers was beginning to conspire for more explicit regional designs for Middle East defence. As a result of this introduction of the East-West dimension to the inter-Arab power struggle, Saudi Arabia gradually lost its ability to manipulate Syrian affairs.

## Syria amidst the Global Cold War, 1954–1958

The 1952 Egyptian coup d'état was initially a genuinely domestic occurrence, but it soon triggered the rise of both Arab nationalist and communist forces in the Arab world, which, in consequence, invited East European arms sale to the region. These new developments, all sending alarming signals to the Western powers, introduced a new dimension to the already fierce inter-Arab rivalry—that of the East-West conflict. The previous period did see some British, French and American covert actions, attempting to increase their regional standing and to buy a friendly government for specific economic reasons or for stable regional environment in general. The significance of the mid-1950s, however, is that these powers began to introduce a defence design, assigning the Arab governments a specific task of containing the Soviet influence in the Middle East. Ironically for these powers, this was the period when Arab socialists and non-alliance advocates were reaching a new height in their political activism.

Saudi Arabia faced this new era under the new leadership of King Sa'ud. He largely continued his father's anti-Hashemite strategy with Egyptian help and his pursuit of close military co-operation with the US. Saudi Arabia's interest partially overlapped with the United States' anti-Communist campaign. To the pro-status quo House of Saud, the communist revolutionary messages and its atheistic belief were a major threat. However, maintenance of friendship with both Egypt and the US was a policy with inherent contradiction, because Gamal 'Abd al-Nasir's version of Arab nationalism was coloured with an anti-imperialist and socialist outlook. This contradiction was to surface gradually in Syria, as will be elaborated, where the House of Saud continued to support its traditional allies through bribing personnel and media and stirring opposition campaign against the enemies. Just as the Hashemites' British connection hindered them from controlling Syria, the US connection became a major liability for the Saudis in their 'struggle for Syria'.

In 1954, Syria returned to the pre-Shishakli multi-party political system, but this time the leftist parties—the Ba'th Party under the leadership of Michel 'Aflaq, Salah al-Din Bitar and Akram al-Hourani and the Communist Party of Khalid Bakdash—began to challenge the monopoly of political power by the traditional upper class. In September 1954 a general election was held and the Ba'th advanced its position at the expense of the People's Party's retreat. The People's Party had appeared to be too complacent of foreign, especially American and British, involvement in Syrian affairs. The symbolic meaning of the election result, therefore, was the end to Syria's old social order and the confirmation of Syria's commitment to neutralism (Seale, 1986: 184-185). As a result of this change in power configuration, the Iraq-initiated union schemes of this period were again unsuccessful. Many prominent Syrians had come to appreciate the economic benefit of being courted from all directions, and found no apparent benefit in abandoning this lucrative position by linking Syria to any particular union. Furthermore, the junior army officers were opposed to a union with Iraq, whose better-trained and better-equipped army would hinder any prospect of their promotion in the united army (Lesch, D.W., 1992: 46).

The most threatening regional defence scheme for Saudi Arabia and Egypt was the one in which the Hashemites managed to enlist the British and American support—the Baghdad Pact. Beyond the common denominator of the competition for regional influence through controlling Syria—the logic of 'the struggle for Syria'—the Hashemites had additional reasons to seek Syrian participation in the Pact (Kienle, 1993: 362-363). Since the largest part of Iraqi oil came from the Kirkuk area in the north, it was vital that a government in Damascus was tied to Baghdad by a treaty, ensuring co-operation in oil-transit to the Mediterranean. Also, although the Pact's proclaimed aim was to contain *Soviet* influence in the Middle East, the logical outcome of Syria's entrance would be curtailment of the growing domestic communist movement in the country—a much desired outcome from Nuri al-Sa'id's standpoint. Some in Baghdad, particularly in the Iraqi military, also assumed that Damascus' participation in the Pact would deter Israel from initiating hostility against Syria.

King Sa'ud and Egypt's Nasir both viciously opposed the Pact because it signified British-Iraqi dominance in the region. Iraq's emerging co-operation with Iran in the framework of the Pact—an aberration in the history of their relations before and after—also threatened to tip the regional balance of power in favour of Baghdad (Hunter, 1990: 100). The Saudis perceived the Pact as a resurgence of the old Hashemite threat; using the Northern Tier as a springboard, Baghdad would, so the Saudis pictured, reignite its aspiration to engulf Syria, Jordan and Lebanon into the Hashemite-dominated Fertile Crescent scheme. Or, the Hashemites' fresh access to superior Western military equipment and technology might prompt them to renew their claim for their lost homeland of Hijaz (Safran, 1988: 78). As to Nasir—who believed, according to Muhammad H. Heikal, that 'the answer to communist infiltration did not lie in joining Western-sponsored alliances with their "imperialist" overtones but rather in prompting internal economic and social development and in affirming the spirit of nationalism and independence' (Hasou, 1985: 55)—the Pact gave him an additional incentive to counterbalance the Western design by promoting the 1950 Arab security pact under his leadership; in so doing, he manipulated pan-Arab sentiment for the purpose of maximising Egypt's regional role.

Thus, Saudi Arabia and Egypt joined forces to launch a concerted effort to foil the US-initiated security pact, and one of Riyadh's measures was to stop Syria from joining the Pact since the signature of Syria occupied the key to the Pact's success (Safran, 1988: 79; Rathmell, 1995: 93). First of all, it increased the channelling of funds to Syrian politicians and Syrian press to this end. Second, in January 1955 when Faris al-Khuri's government in Damascus failed to show a decisive opposition to the Turkish-Iraqi pact, Saudi Arabia and Egypt exerted pressure to bring his government down and to reinstate Quwatli (Kimura, 1983: 59). The Syrian President Atasi claimed that 'Saudi agents [were the] most troublesome' (Rathmell, 1995: 96). One report alleged that they had spent LS600,000 in this operation (Rathmell, 1995: 97). This Saudi policy was successful as it persuaded the next Syrian cabinet of 'Asali—this time dominated by leftists—to announce the establishment of an anti-Baghdad Pact union of the Egypt-Syrian-Saudi (ESS) Pact. By summer of that year, the Saudis had rallied support for their old friend, Quwatli, as the National Party candidate of the presidential election. In the campaign, Quwatli promised Syria's neutrality between Egyptian-Saudi camp and Iraq, but this was no more than cosmetic, when at the same time, Saudi agents were distributing LS10,000 a month to sympathetic Syrian newspapers (Petran, 1972: 113; Rathmell, 1995: 106). On 18 August, Quwatli won the election against Khalid al-'Azm, an independent candidate with leftist inclination, as the Saudis bought off the People's Party members at the last minute to close ranks behind the former (Kimura, 1983: 59). As a result of the election, the ESS Pact was strengthened, and Saudi Arabia promised to buy more Syrian industrial goods, postponed repayment of its 1950 loan and offered another $10 million loan (Petran, 1972: 114). The fact that the Saudis gained some leverage over the Syrian government in this course of events was apparent in such an occasion as when King Sa'ud pressured Quwatli to relegate the prominent leftist officers (Petran, 1972: 119).

Saudi policy towards Syria began to face serious obstacles in 1956, when the United States changed its policy towards Saudi Arabia. It began to court Sa'ud as the regional counterpoise against Nasir's growing influence, at a time when the neutralist 'Azm, together with his Ba'thist associates, was beginning to enjoy their Golden Age. The Saudis, already encountering difficulties with Egypt, grew wary of Syria's arms purchase from Czechoslovakia and Soviet Union. In this insecure environment, the United States' argument that the leftist axis of Egyptian-Syrian connection would be threatening for Saudi Arabia sounded ever more convincing, and Washington's offer to assign King Sa'ud a central role in the US Middle East design, ever more attractive. An expanded regional role was such an over-sized ambition for a secondary power of Saudi Arabia's capacity that his predecessor, Ibn Sa'ud, would perhaps have cautiously avoided. By 1956, Saudi Arabia had converted from the neutralist camp to the American cause, the most significant gesture of which was the *rapprochement* with Iraq. This decision to side with the US predestined the defeat of Saudi Arabia in the 'struggle for Syria'.

In Syria, the rising tide of leftist Ba'thism and communism swept across the country, and public opinion grew extremely critical of the Saudi connection with the US, especially after the discovery of American plots in 1956 and 1957 to overthrow the Syrian government (Lesch, D.W., 1992). Under strong domestic pressure, even Quwatli was left with little choice but to forsake the Saudi connection (Petran, 1972: 121). This fallout between Syria and Saudi Arabia was manifest in the event that the leading Saudi opposition leader, Nasir al-Sa'id—a chief instigator of the 1956 uprising in Hasa and a participant in the formation of the Arabian Trade Union Association—was given haven in Syria following his uprising. Later in 1958 he founded a pan-Arab, Nasirist organisation, the Union of the Peoples of the Arabian Peninsula (*Ittihad Shu'ub al-Jazirah al-'Arabiyyah*) (Abir, 1988: 76; Salamé, 1993: 600n9). Gamal 'Abd al-Nasir initially attempted to mediate between Damascus and Riyadh, but when this *rapprochement* materialised, Saudi Arabia ironically became a potential threat to Nasir's leadership in the Arab world. When King Sa'ud visited Damascus in late September 1957, his prestige had risen to such an extent that he was hailed as the only leader who could bring the divided Arab World together—much to Nasir's distaste. The ensuing pattern of rivalry between Egypt and Saudi Arabia was consolidated by the landing of Egyptian troops in Syria the following month.

By this stage, the political disintegration of Syria had become a very real possibility, partly because of the excessive intensity and frequency of foreign conspiracies which supported different domestic factions. In the domestic front, the authority of the traditional ruling classes, who were committed to preserving Syria's independence, was being encroached on by the rising middle class leftists and the army officers. The army officers were also factionalised, and there was no indication that a sufficiently authoritative political group was to emerge and maintain cohesion any time soon. To rescue Syria from this chaos, a group of army officers, with support from the Ba'th party, requested Nasir to form a Syrian-Egyptian union in the hope that this would be the solution to Syria's predicament. The Ba'th and Nasir's fierce dislike of the expanding communist influence made them welcome partners for the equally anti-communist officers. The bargaining power was on the side of a reluctant Nasir, and the union was formulated entirely on his terms. In February 1958, Syria and Egypt announced the formation of the United Arab Republic (UAR) with Cairo as the capital.[5]

After more than a decade of overtures from various outside actors, Syria chose to side with Egypt, crowning it the victor of the 'struggle for Syria'. What is telling about Saudi Arabia in this period is the early sign of US factor in shaping Saudi Arabia's regional standing. The US connection was—and continues to be to this day—a double-edged sword which could, on one hand, grant military, economic and diplomatic assistance, but on the other, create a major tender spot for the recipient regime. The cause of this dilemma is found in the fact that the Saudi regime sought legitimacy through its reliance on anti-imperialist ideologies of Islam and Arabism.

As to Syria, the development of this period demonstrated the origin of its characteristic foreign policy orientation in the post-1970 era; it is a policy of locating itself in the special position of being wooed by all sides in regional and international conflicts, thereby capitalising on their 'political donation'. It is worth emphasising that this foreign policy conduct became a more pronounced feature of Syria's orientation in the Asad era.

### The United Arab Republic (UAR), 1958–1961

The UAR was the first experiment in a complete merger between two Arab states. Egypt's prestige as the champion of the Arab world was boosted in the aftermath of 'the struggle for Syria'; meanwhile, the Syrian leaders soon realised that they had surrendered what little political power and few organisation they once commanded. The reality of Arab unity seemed no more than political and economic exploitation by the larger, more powerful Arab state, which was a direct outcome of the Arab nationalists' obsession with foreign policy, unable to divert discussions to constructive policy on administration, social and economic issues, or geographical diversity of the Arab world (Lacquer, 1961: 12). The limitation of Arab unity was also manifest in the fact that it triggered bitter antagonism among other Arab states, with Yemen as an exception. For Saudi Arabia, Jordan, Lebanon and Iraq, it was a serious disturbance to the existing balance of power. Even after the 1958 Iraqi revolution had overthrown the conservative Hashemite monarchy and had brought a radical regime to power, Iraq did not seek to join the UAR, a move which dealt a blow to the relevance of Egyptian-Syrian union.

Saudi Arabia regarded this development with considerable unease. It was a serious setback for its traditional foreign policy objective of maintaining friendship with Egypt and exerting influence over Syria. It seemed a real probability that Nasir, by now the most popular Arab leader in the entire region, was to dominate the Arab world and consequently encircle the kingdom with hostile regional environment. In March 1958, immediately after the formation of the UAR, Nasir announced the discovery of King Sa'ud's plot to assassinate him. Observers hold different views on the validity of this allegation (cf. Holden and Johns, 1981: 196; Abir, 1988: 81; Rathmell, 1995: 148), but whatever the truth may have been, it had an unmistakable effect of discrediting Sa'ud in the entire Arab world. Domestically, Saudi Arabia for the first time turned to the defensive against cross-border operations from Syria. The Saudi branch of the Ba'th Party was founded in 1958 with the blessing of the Syrian Ba'thists, and a number of other leftist and Arab nationalist groups were founded with the support of Egypt and Syria. In response, Riyadh attempted to threaten the union by rallying opposition groups against it.

For instance, the Muslim Brotherhood (*Al-Ikhwan al-Muslimun*) members from Syria and Egypt were given refuge in the Kingdom to attack the UAR's secularisation policies and its closeness to the atheist Soviet Union (Abir, 1988: 88). When the Syrians became disillusioned by the reality of the union, Saudi Arabia, together with Jordan, was more than happy to support the secessionist coup (Petran, 1972: 150). By giving support to the Syrian traditional ruling class who succeeded in their coup in September 1961, the Saudis might have hoped to re-establish the old pattern of influencing Syrian politics through personal ties and injections of cash. However, Syrian social patterns and political structure had undergone dramatic change in the fifteen years after its independence, and Syria was no longer receptive to the old method of external control and influence.

## The Polarisation of the Arab World, 1961–1970

The demise of the UAR did not translate to the abandonment of Arab nationalist ideals by Arab politicians and public alike. Instead, Gamal 'Abd al-Nasir and his sympathisers across the Arab world blamed the failure of the first unity attempt upon those Syrian leaders who called it off and the conservative outside powers that supported it (Hasou, 1985: 115-118). In the years that followed, little effort was made to investigate the inherent weakness of the ideology, while both the Syrians and the Egyptians continued to preoccupy themselves with blaming outsiders for all the shortcomings of Arabism, be they 'reactionary' Arab regimes, Israel, or imperial powers. This ideological warfare divided the Arab world along the line of 'progressives/revolutionaries' and 'reactionaries' who fought their battle on the soil of the Arab periphery. Increasingly, therefore, the new alignment began to take the characteristics reminiscent of the East-West conflict, tempting some to call the period 'the Arab Cold War' (Kerr, 1971). In light of this new development, the relationship between Syria and Saudi Arabia also underwent fierce confrontation, culminating in the period of Salah Jadid's rule between 1966 and 1970. The period can be divided roughly into two phases: 1) 1961–1966 and 2) 1966–1970.

### *'The Arab Cold War', 1961–1966*

The temporary confusion and lack of direction that followed the UAR plunged the Arab world into turmoil. For Syria, the subsequent five years was a period of repairing the psychological and political damage caused by the ideological setback and the dissolution of political parties under Nasir's order. Syria's leftist leaders intensified their Arab nationalist campaign by on the one hand actively courting Egypt and Iraq for another union (Kienle, 1995), and on the other, keeping in line with Egypt in denouncing the conservative kingdoms of Saudi Arabia, Jordan and the Gulf shaikhdoms.

Saudi Arabia experienced two major developments, the consolidation of Crown Prince Faisal's leadership and the embroilment in the Yemen war. By 1961, Faisal had expelled the 'Liberal Princes' of the royal family, who called for the establishment of constitutional monarchy and promoted expanded political freedom in the kingdom as the path to modernisation. As Faisal emerged as the victor of this intra-family dispute, he paved his way to establish a thoroughgoing dictatorship not only politically but economically by launching the first five-year plan. Regionally, Saudi Arabia faced the escalation of war in Yemen. In 1962, the Yemeni Free Officers proclaimed a Republic after overthrowing the Zaidi Imam. Meanwhile, Imam Muhammad al-Badr escaped to his stronghold in the mountain area, and, with Saudi assistance, organised a royalist resistance against the Republic. Although the Yemen war initially flared up as a civil war, it was soon internationalised, because of its coincidence with the period of high tension in the wider Arab world; since Nasir decided to interpret the war as a symbolic confrontation of 'revolutionary' vs. 'reactionary', he placed utmost importance on a republican victory as a way to punish the 'reactionaries' and to reassert his claim for Arab leadership. This determination of Cairo to be directly involved in the war provoked an equally resolute response from Riyadh; the Kingdom perceived the encroachment of radicalist influence in Yemen and the Egyptian military campaign as immediate security threats to itself.

When Syria broke away from the UAR, the most pressing political questions to be answered were: 1) who to hold responsible for the failure of the union; 2) what to do with the socialist measures, such as nationalisation of the major industries, once enforced during the UAR period; and 3) what role the army officers should play in politics (Kimura, 1983: 85-88). Since the traditional elites were the actual figures who signed the memorandum for secession and consequently formed the new secessionist cabinet, most Ba'thists and Nasirists were quick to discredit them as enemies of Arabism. The Ba'thi military coup d'état of March 1963 seemed to give answers at least to the first two of the above questions. The 'guilty' secessionists were purged and Arabism was to be pursued through imposition of strict socialist measures. It was not long before the military wing of the party had ousted the intellectual party founders and had consequently assumed an expanded role in politics—the answer to the third question. This definition of Syria's economic, social and political reorientation under the Ba'th was to shift dramatically its policy towards Saudi Arabia.

In the name of Arabism and socialism, Syria proposed another unity scheme with Iraq and Egypt to form a 'progressive' bloc against the Arab monarchies. As an important component of this defensive strategy to redefine the country's political goals, Damascus consequently intensified its anti-Saudi campaign by aiding the opposition forces in Saudi Arabia and the republican groups in Yemen. The Ba'th launched propaganda campaigns through radio stations and supplied military aid. Syria, together with Egypt, supported the anti-Saudi organisation called the Arab National Liberation Front (ANLF)—formed in Cairo by 'Liberal Princes'—and Saudi Nasirist and leftist organisations. Radio Damascus broadcast subversive messages calling for the overthrow of the Saudi regime (Abir, 1988: 92; Holden and Johns, 1981: 250). Also, during the Yemen war, Syrian personnel flew Mig-19s and Ilyushin bombers in aid of the republicans (Safran, 1988: 127).

For Saudi Arabia, the major Arab threat came from Egypt, but it did not underestimate the Syrian role behind Egyptian clout. Saudi Arabia countered the 'revolutionary' attacks with a combination of diplomacy, expulsion of Syrian workers from its soil, suspension of financial aid to frontline states. First of all, in August 1962, Saudi Arabia announced the formation of a joint command with the Hashemite Jordanian monarch, an unthinkable development five years before. Faisal also established the World Islamic League (*Rabitat al-'Alam al-Islami*) under his leadership to mobilise Islamic support against Arab nationalist campaigns. To some extent, it was for domestic consumption to discredit the Saudi opposition by strengthening the religious legitimacy of the Saudi monarchy. The fact that the language of Islam, another supra-state ideology, was manipulated to counter the dominant cross-border ideological appeal of Arab nationalism revealed the embryonic state of the Saudi national identity. Second, between 1961 and 1964, Syrian workers, together with Palestinian and other non-Saudi Arab workers with leftist inclinations were expelled on several occasions (Holden and Johns, 1981: 256-271). In tandem with this policy of tightening its grips on Arab foreign residents, the Saudi authorities also arrested hundreds of Saudi Shi'as in the Hasa region, the Aramco workers, and others who were suspected of having connection with the Ba'th. Third, Faisal announced his refusal to continue paying subsidies to the Arab frontline states and the Palestine Liberation Organisation (PLO) (Abir, 1988: 98). Finally, some note the Saudi financial support for the Syrian Muslim Brotherhood during this era (e.g. Hinnebusch, 1990: 290).

The five years between 1961 and 1966 present a marked contrast in the pattern of interaction between Syria and Saudi Arabia. Although Syrian politics remained to be characterised by factionalism and instability, the successive governments were more or less in agreement on one issue—hostility to Saudi Arabia and the 'reactionary' regimes. Display of antagonism towards those regimes constituted an essential tactic for recovering from the setback of the failed union. Also, as the power of the pro-Saudi, conservative politicians was steadily curtailed in the new Syrian political scene, Riyadh's means to influence domestic power-struggles in Syria accordingly became limited. In other words, Syrian-Saudi relations became more balanced than the unequal one in the 1950s, both adopting assertive policies towards the other actor, although in both cases, the assertiveness was more a reflection of fundamental regime vulnerability than a display of renewed strength. This phase, however, was a mere prologue to the further exchange of hostility in the next few years.

### Syrian-Saudi Ideological Warfare, 1966–1970

By 1965 Egypt and Saudi Arabia had gradually begun to open a dialogue over the Yemen issue, although skirmishes continued to occur until the 1967 June War. The ideological warfare between Nasir and Faisal began to recede accordingly, and it was now Damascus and Baghdad that rose to represent the 'revolutionaries'. In February 1966, Salah Jadid founded the most radical socialist government in Syrian history, menacing the pro-Western Arab regimes. The new regime of the so-called Neo-Ba'th was dominated by the army officers of minority sects, such as the 'Alawis, the Isma'ilis and the Druze,[6] committed to socialism and secularism. The narrow base of public support for these officers' rule partly accounted for the radicalism in foreign policy, which was intended to serve as means to deflect internal conflict (Bar-Siman-Tov, 1983: 147). Thus, Syria openly claimed war against the 'imperialist' camp (in contrast to the neutralism of the 1950s) and allied itself with the Soviet Union and the Eastern bloc. With the help of Soviet aid, Jadid carried Syria through the most comprehensive development programme to date to transform Syria into a modern state. In the region, outward appearance notwithstanding, the Neo-Ba'th's immediate and primary aim was not the annihilation of Israel, but rather the destruction of the Saudi and Jordanian monarchies (Kerr, 1971: 127).

The Syrian strategy against Saudi Arabia took a variety of forms, ranging from support for the Saudi opposition and diplomatic campaigns, to economic sabotage. Diplomatically, Jadid strongly protested against Faisal's project to create a federation of the Gulf states (Petran, 1972: 252), and even after the debacle of 1967 War, boycotted the Arab summit in Khartoum, as a sign of his refusal to engage in any form of dialogue with the 'reactionaries' (Holden and Johns, 1981: 254). Bar-Siman-Tov's quantitative analysis observed an intensification of Syria's hostile propaganda campaigns against the conservative regimes; 'verbal attacks on Arab "reaction"', as he counted them in official declarations, had increased from 125 cases in the three years between March 1963–February 1966 to 533 under the first year of the Neo-Ba'th's rule between February 1966–May 1967 (1983: 152). The economic campaign was as intense, for Jadid restricted trade with Saudi Arabia, banned Saudi Arabian overflights of Syrian territory, and refused to repair the Tapline, which had broken down and disrupted the flow of Saudi oil (Petran, 1972: 252; Holden and Johns, 1981: 285). When in June 1970 the loss incurred by the Kingdom reached as high as $200,000 per day, the Syrians officials allegedly hinted that they might repair the pipeline in exchange for an American pledge not to supply Israel with additional F-4 fighter-bombers and a 25 percent increase in Tapline transit fees. Furthermore, Syria intensified its campaign to support not only the opposition groups within Saudi Arabia but also the revolutionary forces in neighbouring Eritrea, Yemen, Oman, and other Gulf countries (Abir, 1988: 112). In the Peninsula, Damascus broadcast Voice of the Arabian Peninsula to encourage revolutionary forces and offered sanctuary to Saudi leftists (Petran, 1972: 252). In North Yemen, reports suggest that the Syrians actively cultivated the Ba'thist connection and especially after 1967, aided the republican side by supplying military planes and pilots (Gause III, 1990: 76).

Subject to such hostility, the Saudi monarchy reacted decisively. First of all, Faisal, now crowned King, further tightened domestic security, by arresting hundreds of Shi'as on suspicion of being members of the Ba'th Party and deported foreign Arabs (Abir, 1988: 110). As retaliation against Syria's economic sabotage, he banned imports of Syrian goods (Holden and Johns, 1981: 285) and hinted that he would redirect the future flow of oil to other outlets. Furthermore, the dominance of heterodox Muslim sects in the Syrian regime provided Saudi Arabia with a convenient topic for its propaganda campaign against the 'non-believers'—in stark contrast to the Asad era to follow. In ideological debates, the Saudi government propagated that socialism was 'an alien ideology aimed at the destruction of Islam and Muslims' (al-Yassini, 1983: 12) and that Arab nationalism only served to divide the Islamic world. The Grand Mufti, Shaikh 'Abd al-'Aziz bin Baz, had proclaimed in a mid-1960s publication:

> It is known in Islam that the call to Arab nationalism, or any other form of nationalism, is false and a grave mistake. It is an assault against Islam and its followers.[7]

Despite the concerted effort to discredit Arabism in the face of Islam's pre-eminence, the irony of the matter was that Riyadh still did not distance itself from the obligation imposed by the notion of Arab solidarity. At the Khartoum Arab Summit in July 1967, Saudi Arabia continued to endorse the summit's decision to grant £5 million a year to Syria as a subsidy for the war damage, despite Syria's boycott of the summit itself and despite the Kingdom's own economic troubles. This Saudi reticence could largely be attributed to the domestic instability following the 1967 War, when the public's frustration and despair were directed more against its own regime and the United States than the frontline states. Perhaps, in the eyes of the Saudi public, the oil-rich financiers were an easier target to place the blame on than the leaders of those Arab states whose people were heroically, though unsuccessfully, standing up against the 'Zionist enemies'. It is also worth-mentioning that King Faisal personally felt an unprecedented humiliation when East Jerusalem—home to the al-Aqsa mosque, the third holiest place in his faith—was captured by Israel (Holden and Johns, 1981: 252-253). Hence, until it was recaptured, it was not the time to cut back on aid to the frontline states. Furthermore, there were potentially some advantages for the Kingdom in subsidising the reconstruction efforts of Syria and its Arab war partners, thereby keeping them preoccupied with Israel instead of diverting their hostility to the conservative Arab states (Kerr, 1971: 139). The final point was to bear increasing relevance in observation of the post-1967 Saudi policy. In other words, if the 1950s and 1960s Saudi policy were marked by Riyadh's abundant resort to cash injections as a means of buying allegiance of various political factions throughout the Arab world, the strategy of financing the Arab radical states with the modest aim of keeping criticisms and threats at bay developed into a primary feature of Saudi petro-diplomacy in the 1970s onwards.

Thus, in both Syria and Saudi Arabia, the political trends in the late 1960s indicated the lasting effects of domestic and external insecurity, in no small part derived from the fact that their 'national' questions remained unresolved. In the period that followed, each actor, aware of the other camp's strengths and weaknesses, set out to exploit them. In Syria, politics entered a new era under the leadership of Hafiz al-Asad. Yet, in the fashion of Syrian politicians in the 1950s and the 1960s, he manipulated the banner of Arabism to define the core component of his regional policy as mobilisation of all *Arab* resources—i.e. oil-producing states' petro-dollars—for the benefit of his own localised interests (Perthes, 1995; Kienle, 1990). Saudi Arabia in turn aspired to influence the unruly Syrians through a variety of methods, some of which constituted use of financial leverage and clandestine support of anti-Asad forces in Syria or Lebanon. Although the year 1970 did open a distinctly new era in Arab politics, the remnants of such old rules of the game continued to play a defining role in the inter-Arab relations in general and Syrian-Saudi relations in particular.

### Regime Consolidation and Pragmatic Foreign Policy, 1970–1978

In 1970, the era of ideological warfare in Arab politics came to a close, and with it, the vicious hostility between Syria and Saudi Arabia subsided. It was the year which saw the death of President Nasir—personification of a driving force behind Arab nationalism in the 1950s and 1960s—which marked Egypt's turn towards a relative decline as the Arab socialist centre. The Arab world was not to experience another time when one hegemonic country, or one charismatic leader, commanded such passion and authority across the entire region. Malcolm Kerr eloquently and dismissively captured the end of the era: 'There could hardly be a competition for prestige when there was no prestige remaining [in the aftermath of the 1967 June war]' (Kerr, 1971: 129).

His death coincided with another historical development in the region, which opened the way towards multi-polarity in Arab politics. On that very day of 28 September 1970, two international oil 'majors', Esso and British Petroleum, agreed to the Libyan government's demands for higher revenues, setting a new precedent and preparing fresh grounds for the rise in the influence of the Organisation of Petroleum Exporting Countries (OPEC) (Holden and Johns, 1981: 287). This decision was soon to transform not only the economic fortunes of Arab oil-producing states—and most notably of Saudi Arabia with the largest proven reserve—but also their political weight within the region and beyond.

The Saudi leadership, who received the news of Nasir's death with 'unabashed jubilation' (Holden and Johns, 1981: 287), was thus presented with a golden opportunity to elevate the country's position in the region. Combined with their increasing wealth, other factors allowed the Kingdom to feel generally more confident in its regional environment. King Faisal's dominant personality placed a lid on the intra-royal family feuds and strengthened leadership cohesion, while the country's apparatus of internal repression had become more sophisticated under his reign. In the autumn of 1970, Saudi Arabia launched a five-year economic development plan, aiming to defuse some of the socio-economic tensions. Externally, the end of the Yemen war on humiliating terms for Egypt gave additional confidence to Riyadh. Also, Nasir's death brought an end to the war of attrition between the Arabs and the Israelis, while King Hussain's decided military assault on the Palestinian fighters in Jordan promised a temporary calm in its northern vicinity. Reduction in external and internal vulnerability allowed the Saudi regime to pursue more pragmatic and open policy towards previous 'radical' enemies, such as Egypt and Syria. Concurrently, Arab nationalism was now reinstated as a 'complement' to the religion in Saudi discourse (Piscatori, 1983b: 53n34). Consolidation of the state made Riyadh less vulnerable to externally-initiated cross-border operations and propaganda campaigns which had been prevalent in the preceding twenty-five years. At the same time, such operations had become increasingly costly for Saudi Arabia to pursue, when its neighbouring regimes were also strengthening their grip on power, including the one in Damascus.

Similar dynamics were also at work in Syria, which was going through profound political changes in late 1970. In November, the idiosyncratic Salah Jadid was replaced by another 'Alawi, a more pragmatic Hafiz al-Asad, in an intra-Ba'th Party coup—or what Asad preferred to call 'Corrective Movement' (al-Harakah al-Tashihiyah)—which opened a chapter of unprecedented political stability in the turmoil-stricken history of the country. The Movement introduced a cosmetic change to the Ba'th Party's preponderance by forming a ruling coalition, the Progressive National Front (al-Jabhah al-Wataniyyah al-Taqaddumiyyah), [8] under the banner of political 'pluralism (ta'addudiyyah)'. The establishment of the Front was at once an attempt to co-opt potential oppositions and to deprive them of autonomy and political activism while simultaneously improving the image of the regime as enjoying broader support than under a single-party rule. Asad also launched a new economic policy to remedy the country's battered economy, a legacy of the radical socialist measures imposed by the Jadid regime. Asad's open-door policy, or Infitah, served a political aim of cultivating support among the entrepreneurs who had previously been alienated by the Neo-Ba'th rule and had also felt religious distance from the ruling circle; that those merchants were predominantly Sunnis made their alienation susceptible to developing into a sectarian conflict—Asad's minority-dominated regime against the majority population. It is noteworthy in this regard that the first incident of political unrest after Asad's ascendance broke out in February 1973 over the issue of the constitutional treatment of religion, and the riot quickly opened another question of whether the 'Alawi faith is part of Islam—severely testing the President's Islamic legitimacy. The new economic policy was to help Asad cement an alliance with a selected group of entrepreneurs and, in the following years, led to the creation of a new economic class, or the 'state bourgeoisie', whose survival and welfare depended on the regime.[9]

One of Asad's first missions after taking over the Presidency was to end Syria's acute diplomatic isolation from 1966; especially urgent was the need to mend ties with fellow Arab states. According to Perthes, an authority on Syrian political economy, even those new economic reforms had a secondary political aim of impressing the Gulf countries with his new orientation; some of the new measures were:

> primarily declarations of principle and good intention, aimed more
> at a realignment with conservative Arab states and probably at
> attracting some public sector investments from wealthier Arab
> countries, than at encouraging private Arab investors to freely test
> their entrepreneurial skills in Syria (1995: 50).

Both Saudi Arabia and Syria were now ready to play an expanded role
in inter-Arab politics of the 1970s which were characterised by an
unprecedented level of co-operation and solidarity achieved among the
major players. Taylor was one of the many who used the term 'the
trilateral alliance' to refer to the emerging tripartite axis of
Damascus-Riyadh-Cairo, underpinning this extraordinary stability of the
Arab system (1982: 49). In fact, this triangular relationship has been a
repeated theme in Arab politics to this day: in 1955 the three formed an
anti-Baghdad Pact; in the 1990s, it was revisited in the form of '6+2'
formula in the aftermath of the second Gulf crisis; and throughout the
1990s, the triangle exerted a predominant influence over Arab debates, be
they on the peace process or the question of Iraqi sanctions. However,
when the discussion of this trangle is accompanied by a sense of nostalgia,
it is mostly the trilateral axis of the 1970s that is being referred to, because
it seemed to promise the Arabs expanded influence on world political
scenes with newly consolidated Arab solidarity as its backbone; according
to such a sentimental view, the triangle crystallised in 1973 when Egypt
and Syria jointly launched an attack on Israel, while Saudi Arabia took the
helm of the the Arab oil embargo, buttressing the Arab war efforts.

The euphoria which surrounded the triangle gradually eroded, and the
developments in the mid-70s—most notably the eruption of civil war in
Lebanon and Egypt's responsiveness to the US-led initiative of separate
peace—already signalled the precariousness of the solidarity,
foreshadowing the post-1978 period. With the 1977 Jerusalem visit by
Egyptian President Anwar al-Sadat, all hopes of sustaining this 'golden'
triangle were shattered. This section, the last of the historical background,
surveys the co-operative relationship of the triangle with special emphasis
on the foundation of Syrian-Saudi relations before the difficult period of
1978-1990, when the two disagreed on every conceivable key issue in Arab
politics. The conclusion deals with the effect of Sadat's Jerusalem visit as a
prologue to the new phase characterised by acute polarisation of the Arab
world—the main interest of this study.

### The Birth of Damascus-Riyadh-Cairo Axis and the 1973 War (1970–1975)

The most immediate and dramatic display of King Faisal's diplomatic reorientation was his entente with Egypt (Holden and Johns, 1981: 296-297). Aware of his country's limited capabilities—demographically, militarily, industrially and even culturally—he saw partnership with Egypt as a key to establishing the Kingdom in the mainstream of Arab politics and also as an insurance against attacks of hostile radicalism, be it from the Yemens in the south or Iraq in the north (Safran, 1988: 126). In order to consolidate this relationship with Cairo, he swiftly moved to reconcile it with Washington, the Kingdom's superpower ally. When the *rapprochement* materialised most sensationally in the form of Sadat's July 1972 decision to expel the Soviet advisers—partly through Saudi encouragement—the King felt doubly rewarded: it had gained a diminution of Soviet influence in the Middle East region and greater freedom in pursuing closer ties with Washington at a smaller risk of being censured by the 'radicals' (Holden and Johns, 1981: 292; Safran, 1988: 150).

Under this new partnership, Saudi Arabia was offered Egyptian mediation to ease the tensions with Syria. As a result, in May 1971, Saudi Minister of State on Foreign Affairs 'Umar Saqqaf and Syrian Foreign Minister 'Abd al-Halim Khaddam met in Kuwait, followed by Khaddam's visit to Jiddah, which in turn was reciprocated by Defence Minister Prince Sultan's to Damascus by the end of the year. In tandem, King Faisal offered the Syrians economic aid of $200 million (Holden and Johns, 1981: 299), and in April 1972, the two countries signed an economic and trade agreement.[10] Although he was said to have been suspicious of Asad's lineage as a member of the heretical 'Alawi sect and was unforgiving of his performance as the Defence Minister at the 1967 war, he could not help noticing the positive signals emanating from Damascus.

Indeed, Hafiz al-Asad made several significant decisions that were specifically targetted at the Saudis. Soon after his accession to the throne, Asad closed down the Damascus-based broadcasts of Voice of the Arabian Peninsula, refrained from assisting radical groups in Arabian Peninsula, gave a green light to repair work on the Tapline without demanding an increase in transit fees, and removed the trade barriers and air space restrictions which had been imposed by Jadid (Petran, 1972: 250-255; Safran, 1988: 144). To top up the goodwill, Syria participated in an Islamic Conference Organisation (ICO) foreign ministers' conference in Jiddah in 1972 (Piscatori, 1983b: 53n20). Aside from the conciliatory gestures, Saudi Arabia also needed to take into consideration the very fact that friendly Damascus could be a useful counterweight to its radical neighbour in Baghdad.

Thus, a major reorganisation took place in the pattern of alignments in the Arab world in the build-up towards the 1973 October War, in which Syria and Egypt launched a co-ordinated attack on Israel to regain the territories captured in the 1967 war. From the frontline states' point of view, Saudi Arabia's unleashing of the oil weapon, which caused a quadrupling of world oil prices, marked the first in the history of the Arab-Israeli conflict that Riyadh actively assisted their war efforts.

It is unclear to what extent King Faisal was informed in advance of the war plan. One source maintains that he was taken completely by surprise (Holden and Johns, 1981: 334-337), while others believe that without his foreknowledge and perhaps even endorsement, Cairo and Damascus would not have proceeded with their missions (e.g. Halliday, 1979: 72). In any case, by the time the war erupted, the Kingdom had been for months hinting at the possibility of using the oil weapon as a means to pressure the western powers, particularly the United States, to modify what the Arabs conceived as unbearably biased views in favour of Israel and to adopt a more balanced approach to the Middle East conflict. His religious conviction that Jerusalem should be liberated as a matter of utmost urgency helped to shape this decision (Piscatori, 1983b: 45). By late 1972–early 1973, he had revised his previous belief that oil and politics should remain separate. His proteges began to issue warnings on an oil production freeze, partly because of his utter frustration with the seemingly endless US concessions to the Jewish state but also because such concessions were exposing Riyadh to growing criticism of its own ties with Washington (Safran, 1988: 152). By the October of 1973, the Kingdom had thus prepared itself to unleash the oil weapon.

In view of the unconvincing overall performance by the Syrian and Egyptian armies, it is fair to say that the international attention the war generated was mostly due to the success of the oil embargo in manipulating world energy supplies and prices, sending shock-waves across the globe. Saudi Arabia had become an active party to the conflict, in which it had strenuously avoided direct involvement in the previous decades, at the risk of unprecedented tension with its most important global ally, the United States; the decision was a clear testimony to the growing confidence in Riyadh as a major regional power. Furthermore, the Kingdom assisted the Arab warring parties by bilateral means as well. Within a week of the outbreak of fighting, the Kingdom dispatched a force of 2,000, or one brigade, to assist the defence of the Golan Heights (*Al-Nahar*, 13 October 1973). Although it accidentally saw some action, its value, from the Syrian viewpoint, was more a symbolic one as an expression of solidarity.

After the war, Riyadh promised an increased flow of financial grants and loans to Syria as well as to the other frontline states and the Palestinians, and at the October 1974 Arab summit in Rabat, Faisal played a leading role in formalising the oil-producing states' collective pledge to contribute $2.5 billion annually to the less endowed confrontation states (Safran, 1988: 176). Seale narrates an interesting anecdote which highlights the informal, unsystematic (and unaccountable) method in which Saudi aid was granted:

> Muhammad Haydar, [Syrian] vice-premier for economic affairs at the time [in the early 1970s], recounted that he had gone to Saudi Arabia after the 1973 war and King Faysal had asked him what Syria needed. 'Give me a list of your projects with some figures', the king said. Haydar who had come unprepared spent the night working on his pocket calculator to produce some sort of a document (1990: 448-449).

As an example of such loans and grants, the Kingdom announced a $ 50 million loan to Syria in June 1974 (*Al-Nahar*, 12 June 1974). In 1975, it pledged another $200 million for Syria to purchase weapons. As a result of these fresh commitments, Arab oil states' grants to Syria rose from $45 million in 1972 to a staggering $1,143 million in 1977[11]—enough to turn political rent seeking into an important component of Damascus' regional strategy (Perthes, 1995: 36).

There was another positive ramification of the new Arab oil wealth on Syria's economy; the Syrian workers' migration to Saudi Arabia and other Gulf countries started in the early 1970s and increased dramatically, bringing an injection of remittances to the economy at the rate of $600-900 million per year towards the end of the decade, when it peaked (Perthes, 1995: 36). The significant wage and salary differentials between Syria and Saudi Arabia made work opportunities attractive for the Syrians.[12] Some observers suggest that the Kingdom imported foreign labourers in a quota system by nationality, and that this 'national' quota was manipulated according to Riyadh's foreign relations with the labour-exporting countries.[13] According to this view, the subsequent decline in the number of Syrian workers in the Kingdom had a direct co-relation with the diplomatic tensions that developed between the two states from the early 1980s. However, it is important to stress that, at least in Syria's case, the fluctuation in the number of Syrian workers in the Kingdom has not been a useful indicator of the state of diplomatic relations—and will therefore, not be treated with undue attention in the rest of this study. The decline in figures was foremost a product of a *Syrian* government policy to restrict emigration during the second half of the

1970s and the early 1980s. The underlying reasons for this were the authorities' fear of population drainage and their reluctance to rely excessively on remittances as a source of foreign revenue (Winckler, 1997: 112-115). For the purpose of this discussion, it suffices to mention that the 1970s Syrian economy did get some boost from the extra foreign currency inflow in the form of remittances.

Finally—and most importantly—the 1973 war accelerated the process of diplomatic co-operation between Damascus and Riyadh in the peace process. After the 1973 war, the United States renewed their interests in sponsoring a negotiated peace in the Arab-Israeli dispute, and King Faisal was best placed to act as a go-between in the American diplomatic initiatives that targeted Cairo and Damascus in particular. Egypt secured itself a disengagement agreement with Israel as early as January 1974 and subsequently pleaded with King Faisal to lift the oil embargo—much to Asad's anger. Asad was grateful for the King's initial decision to maintain the sanction until the Syrian agreement was signed but was then disappointed when it was lifted two months later. Damascus and Riyadh maintained constant communication on every step of .US diplomacy (cf. *Al-Nahar*, 25 March 1974), while Secretary of State Henry Kissinger conducted his well-known shuttle diplomacy in late 1973–early 1974 until his efforts led to the 29 May 1974 Syrian-Israeli disengagement agreement. The agreement fell far short of Asad's aim to recover the whole of the Golan, but at least returned him a token piece of land around Qunaitra, which was just enough to save his face after the loss of 1967.

Later in the year, Asad and Faisal joined their efforts in one of the most significant Arab summits in history: the October 1984 Rabat summit. Together—though for different reasons—they pushed for a decision which recognised the PLO as the 'sole legitimate representative of the Palestinian people,' with the aim of foiling Jordanian King Hussain's ambition to represent the Palestinians at any future international conference on Middle East peace.[14] The Damascus-Riyadh realignment culminated in King Faisal's four-day visit to the Syrian capital in January 1975, which was by any standard an exceptionally celebrated event (*Al-Nahar*, 15 January; *Times*, 15 January 1975). At the end of the visit, the two signed a joint-communiqué—something of a rarity in the entire history of their relations—in which Syria's insistence on comprehensive Israeli withdrawal from all occupied territories, guarantees of Palestinian rights and the need to assist Lebanon in overcoming its political troubles were enshrined.[15] The King also promised $350 million in aid (*Al-Safir*, 18 January 1975; Seale, 1990: 255). A month later, Syria's Khaddam toured Saudi Arabia and Kuwait, following Kissinger's visit to Damascus and Riyadh (*Al-Nahar*, 17 February 1975). In Saudi Arabia, he discussed the expansion of US-Saudi co-operation and the US' progress towards the second Israeli-Egyptian disengagement agreement. However, King Faisal allegedly shared Asad's concerns and anger that Kissinger's policy aimed at nothing but division of the Arab world by removing Egypt from the Arab-Israeli equation of conflict and allowing Israel to direct all their military threats to the remaining confrontation states (Seale, 1990: 263). This, in tandem with growing US-Israeli security co-operation, appeared to reinforce the Jewish state to an even more dangerous level.

It was no surprise then that the news of King Faisal's assassination on 25 March 1975 was received in Damascus with deep sorrow. The reaction of Asad, who personally led a delegation to attend his funeral (*Al-Nahar*, 26 March 1975), was depicted by Seale:

> Asad felt lonely and exposed—and lonelier still when King Faysal of Saudi Arabia was assassinated...The austere Faysal, a stalwart nationalist, had been a staunch Asad supporter during and after the October War. It was he who took the lead among Arab producers in pumping money into Syria's war-ravaged economy (1990: 263).

It is, however, misleading to conclude from such an observation that the exceptionally high degree of amicability in Syrian-Saudi relations between 1970 and 1975 was attributable solely, or even primarily, to the closeness of personalities at the leadership level—a relationship which itself had been transformed only in the last years from suspicion to confidence. More accurately, King Faisal reigned in an environment which was conducive to cultivating Syrian-Saudi reconciliation, and his assertive leadership at best served to maximise the opportunity for it. His death coincided with regional developments outside the control of either Riyadh or Damascus, and they introduced destabilising factors to Arab solidarity and endangered co-operative equilibrium between the two capitals.

### The Triangle Strained: Sinai II and the Lebanese Civil War (1975–1977)

Inter-Arab differences which began to surface in the two years following Faisal's death foreshadowed the era of acute polarisation that was to come after the 1978 Camp David agreement. In this period, however, Saudi Arabia under the new leadership of King Khalid and Crown Prince Fahd was relatively successful in holding together the crumbling Arab solidarity. That Riyadh expended tremendous amount of effort in avoiding Arab polarisation accentuated the importance it placed on regional cohesion and stability in general and on the trilateral axis in particular. To this end, the Saudi leadership had to polish their skills in enticing, coaxing and pressuring Damascus.

The first difficulty Riyadh faced was the breach in the Cairo-Damascus axis over Sadat's engagement in negotiations for Sinai II, the second disengagement agreement. Riyadh first attempted to bridge the rift between Sadat and Asad on the occasion of King Faisal's funeral, and then summoned them to Riyadh a month later for a fully-fledged summit.[16] Syria favoured an international peace conference at Geneva, with all Arab representations or none at all, and sponsored by both superpowers together. The latter point particularly disturbed Sadat and the new Saudi leadership who were opposed to a Soviet role in such a conference. The Saudi effort to find a middle ground between Damascus and Cairo suffered a setback when Sadat finally signed Sinai II in early September 1975, which was only a small step short of a peace treaty. When Saudi Arabia expressed unenthusiastic, yet unmistakable, support for the agreement, Damascus was predictably displeased but refrained from public criticism of Riyadh, as it valued the benefit the Saudis could bring to Damascus' quest for a leverage over Washington and for more solid alliances with the other confrontation states. In addition, by having close relationship with the Kingdom, Asad's minority regime hoped to benefit from Riyadh's 's Islamic credentials and its financial capabilities (Safran, 1988: 244-245).

As the Damascus-Cairo side of the strategic triangle was collapsing, Riyadh launched another mediation initiative between Damascus and another powerful Arab capital, Baghdad. Iraq had treated the Syrian regime with contempt after the ideological split in the pan-Arab Ba'th Party in the late 1960s and had stepped up the campaign of hostility against it in the aftermath of the disengagement agreement. In May 1975, Saudi Arabia set out to mediate between Baghdad and Damascus, particularly on a very concrete dispute—the sharing of the Euphrates water (Kienle, 1990: 100). It enjoyed some success, when Damascus agreed to divide the water on a relative scale (*Al-Nahar*, 12-13 August 1975). Although the *rapprochement* was short-lived, the success of Riyadh's efforts testified to its regional influence and leverage over Damascus in the mid-1970s—all the more remarkable when compared to the serial failure of comparable mediation efforts in the next decade.

The greatest challenge Riyadh faced both in maintaining a semblance of Arab solidarity and in co-ordinating policies with Damascus was in Lebanon, where a civil war broke out in April 1975 between a leftist-PLO alliance and the Christian coalition forces. The Asad regime was particularly alarmed at the emerging instability on its doorstep which could potentially generate spill-over effects into neighbouring Syria—particularly relevant in this context was Syria's own precarious sectarian balance—as well as the increased risk of inviting Israeli intervention. Saudi Arabia, in comparison, saw Lebanon as outside its immediate sphere of interests, but its conception that the Kingdom's security depended on Arab regional stability and solidarity made it imperative to contain the conflict. Apart from the major role played by the growing Palestinian population in the conflict, the prevailing propensity among all Lebanese political factions to accept patronage of external regional powers destined the civil war to occupy a central place in Arab political debates (Bannerman, 1979: 123).

At the initial stage of the war, the interests of Riyadh and Damascus roughly overlapped in their principles: both desired immediate restoration of stability particularly in fear of the risk of all-out Arab-Israeli war; neither wanted a change in the status quo which allowed the mosaic state to fall under overwhelming dominance of a single confessional authority, be it of radical leftists or conservative Christians; and both believed that the Palestinian presence should be accepted but not at the expense of Lebanese sovereignty (Bannerman, 1979: 123-125). As other Arab capitals—notably Cairo and Baghdad—threw their weight behind different factions, there was a renewed sense of danger that the Lebanese conflict was turning into a platform for wider inter-Arab rivalries.

When the disagreement between Riyadh and Damascus surfaced, it was more about the *means* of achieving the above goals rather than the goals themselves; or more precisely, it was less about Lebanon than the effect of Sinai II. Riyadh insisted on devising an agreement between the warring parties strictly in the framework of the Arab League, in accordance with which the Saudis volunteered to mediate a cease-fire in the autumn of 1975. Syria, however, snubbed the initiative chiefly because it was unwilling to sit at a League conference with Sadat; Sadat, it maintained, became a 'traitor' when he signed Sinai II and abandoned the other Arab states in ruins.

Saudi Arabia approached the problem with a classic use of 'carrot and stick'. On the one hand, the Saudis responded to Syrian defiance by suspending their $ 700 million annual subsidy of the Syrian economy and freezing the investment projects totalling $500 million (Dawisha, 1980: 113). On the other hand, it understood that the core of the issue was to reconcile Damascus with Cairo. Therefore, on King Khalid's first official visit to the Syrian capital in December 1975 (*Al-Nahar*, 27 December 1975), he communicated his willingness to facilitate the reconciliation, based on the understanding that Saudi Arabia was behind Damascus' policy on Lebanon—no small assurance when the rest of the Arab world seemed to be against Syrian policy (Deeb, 1988a: 168). He is also said to have approved of Damascus' decision to deploy pro-Syrian Palestinian Liberation Army units, assuming it to be a temporary measure

(Bannerman, 1979: 125). For the next five months, the King continued to voice support for Syrian-sponsored initiatives to bring about a cease-fire, and the fact that Damascus and Washington were in agreement on Lebanese issues reduced the cost of Saudi endorsement.

By May, Syria had become aware that on the one hand, its controlled intervention had hitherto only prolonged the violence in Lebanon but on the other, that direct military intervention with the aim of salvaging the struggling Christian forces could isolate Damascus. Therefore, it embarked on a concerted diplomatic offensive to explain its intentions to Arab capitals, Lebanese leaders and Washington (Dawisha, 1980: 134). Damascus' warnings notwithstanding, when in early June Syria's regular army units rolled into Lebanon in full force, the intervention stirred uproar in the Arab world, including within Syria itself.

When Foreign Minister Sa'ud al-Faisal visited Damascus in May, the Saudi leadership learned of Syria's intention to intervene on the side of the Christian forces and shared with Asad the desire to prevent a total destruction of Christian political authority. However, King Khalid was placed in an uncomfortable position when the Syrian forces turned against the Palestinian camps in an operation which Yasir 'Arafat called the 'new massacre' (Safran, 1988: 250). As no Arab leader could afford to be branded as unsupportive of the Palestinian cause,[17] Riyadh had no choice but to intervene. In October, Khalid's envoy presented Asad a strongly-worded message, which summoned him to a mini-summit in Riyadh for talks with the leaders of Egypt, Kuwait, Lebanon and the PLO (Dawisha, 1984: 24). By withdrawing the Saudi contingents from the Golan, where they had been stationed since the October War of 1973, King Khalid made sure the message was understood by Asad (Deeb, 1988a: 170).

The October 1976 Riyadh summit did deliver a long-awaited cease-fire, and in later years, time and again its success was referred to as the pinnacle of Saudi influence on Lebanese affairs. It is ironic then, that the primary motives behind Saudi pro-activeness in Lebanon from the outbreak of the civil war to the Riyadh summit had little to do with the Lebanese themselves; the underlying factors were Riyadh's preoccupation with restoring the crumbling Damascus- Riyadh-Cairo axis and its desire to be engaged in any decision which concerned the fate of the Palestinian cause (Deeb, 1988a: 171). One analysis went further: 'The Saudis believed that peace in Lebanon rested with a Syrian-Egyptian *rapprochement* more than in Lebanon itself' (Bannerman, 1979: 131). Therefore, when Asad participated in the Riyadh summit, agreed to a cease-fire, and even went so far as to reconcile himself with Sadat, Riyadh was pleased with the result. Some hailed this Saudi performance as a demonstration of 'both Saudi leverage over, and exasperation with, the Syrian government' (Deeb, 1988a: 170) and the Syrian president himself showered the Saudi King with praise (Dawisha, 1980: 153).

The more accurate picture, however, was that Saudi preoccupation with the triangle made them more amenable to pressure from Damascus, and the Riyadh summit made a historic decision in favour of Syria arguably at the cost of the Lebanese—i.e. consolidation of Syria's preponderance in Lebanon. By establishing a 30,000-manned Arab peacekeeping force by the name of the Arab Deterrent Force (*Quwat al-Rad' al-Arabiyyah*)—of which 85 percent were Syrians, the summit decision not only strengthened the Syrian physical presence in Lebanon but even gave it an *Arab* cover, or in other words, an *Arab* legitimacy, and even more, formalised the Gulf countries' commitment to pay for the cost (Safran, 1988: 250-251). In return, thanks to King Khalid's efforts, Syria and Egypt reached an uneasy reconciliation in which Syria traded acquiescence to Sinai II for an *Arab* recognition for its special role in Lebanon. The Kingdom topped up Asad's gain with promises to reactivate the annual financial subsidy and to compensate for the economic loss incurred by the cost of its operation in Lebanon. At the end of 1976, the combined effect of Syria's dominance over Lebanon, its strong grip over numerous Palestinian factions and Asad's cordial relations with King Hussain of Jordan raised strong suspicion and antipathy in Arab capitals—including Riyadh—over Syria's ambition to create a regional bloc in the fashion of the 1940s–1950s Greater Syria scheme. For the first time since the independence of Syria, Damascus' regional power and influence were being feared by rival capitals.

The Syrian-Egyptian *rapprochement* was short-lived, and the Saudis' ability to keep their lines to both was stretched to its limit by the vehemence of their antagonism. In 1977, the new US administration of Jimmy Carter rekindled international interest in the Geneva conference on Middle East peace. However, when Syria's stance obstructed convention of an international conference, one of the most dramatic outcomes of the collapsed US initiative was Sadat's appearance in Jerusalem in November 1977. The visit sent shock waves through the Arab world. The period in which Riyadh hoped to secure a comfortable regional environment by upholding the Damascus-Riyadh-Cairo triangle came to an unmistakable end, and pressures from all directions made Riyadh side with Damascus.

## Conclusion:
### Sadat's Visit to Jerusalem as a Prelude to the New Era

Sadat's visit to Jerusalem was another nail in the coffin of the collective Arab effort to recover lost territories from Israel, and the final nail was to come in the form of the Camp David Accords of 1978. The effect was to accelerate the Arab drift towards internal polarisation, profoundly affecting the dynamics of future Syrian-Saudi relations. Syria reacted by busily fortifying the Eastern Front against Israel; in December 1977, less than three weeks after Sadat's historic visit, Syria, South Yemen, Algeria, Libya and the PLO formed the Steadfastness and Confrontation Front (*Jabhah al- Sumud wa al-Tasaddi*). Iraq was conspicuously absent from the signing of the Front's founding charter, not because the Front was too harsh with Egypt, but rather because it was too lenient. The rift between this camp and Egypt was unbridgeable in anyone's eyes.

The resulting rift was the main reason why the Saudis viewed Sadat's visit with distaste; the visit had 'created a predicament which fortified the Saudi traditional fear that they might be forced to identify with one bloc or group and forfeit the advantage of their mediator's position' (Yegnes, 1981: 108). In the year between the Jerusalem visit and Camp David, Riyadh continued to make half-hearted attempts to mediate between the two positions, but soon it was deprived of the cosy option of neutrality as a balanced mediator. The anti-Sadat camp's hostility was so intense and their influence was growing so overwhelming that the Saudis were forced to take a stand on the side of the rejectionist group—a case of 'you are either for us or against us'. Under pressure, Crown Prince Fahd proclaimed: 'Saudi Arabia is closer to Syria and the Palestinian organisations than to Sadat' (Yegnes, 1981: 113). When the regional environment forced Saudi Arabia into taking sides in the polarised Arab world, the new dynamics of Syrian-Saudi relations emerged, as will be explored in the following chapters.

The history of Syrian-Saudi relations after Syria's independence went through distinct phases. In the first two decades, Saudi Arabia was one of the active Arab participants in the competition to control Syria as a means of either attaining a hegemonic position in the region or preventing another Arab capital from achieving that aim. Syrian politicians, in turn, attempted to exploit such external commitments to further their individual political ambitions. The period was marked by a proliferation of cross-border activities across the Arab world, and Saudi Arabia's main instruments were manipulation of personal contacts with Syrian politicians and cash injection—the remnants of which were amply present in Saudi policy towards Syria in later decades. The dynamics changed in the 1960s after Syria reclaimed its independence from the failed union with Egypt. The chaos in Syrian politics—in terms of both, ideological directions and factional rivalries—and intensification of Saudi-Egyptian conflict as played out in Yemen contributed to increased ferociousness in Syrian-Saudi exchanges of hostile campaigns. The hostility was expressed in terms of ideological disagreement and the methods used were clandestine activities, sabotage and propaganda campaigns. The depth of the Syrian-Saudi rift in the 1960s illuminates, in comparison, the paradox of the 1978–1990 period. The two disagreed on every policy matter, yet, unlike the earlier period, maintained an outwardly amicable relationship in an uneasy entente. To complicate matters, both sides retained in the 1980s some of those 1960s methods as a means of applying pressure on each other; such high degree of cross-border permeability and the weight of personal contacts in the decision-making process continued to highlight a unique feature of inter-Arab politics.

The 1970s opened yet another new phase in bilateral relations, as both actors attained the unprecedented level of stability and consolidated state power. In this respect, the leaders grew more confident of exercising pragmatic and sustained foreign policies and 'led to the development of working relationships across previously rigid ideological divisions' (Noble, 1991: 51-52). The subsiding of ideology—particularly Arabism—from the concern of the leadership level, however, did not correspond with its loss of appeal at the societal level of the masses. It is illuminating in this context that the 1973 'permanent' constitution of Syria—still in force today—defines the Syrian Arab region (*qutr*) as part of the larger Arab nation (*watan*), and its people as those who strive for the realisation of complete Arab unity (Articles 1.2. and 1.3.). As to Saudi Arabia, the regime's dependency on US protection had to be defended not in terms of a purely 'Saudi' interest but an 'Arab' one. It was to remain a tender spot in the House of Saud's legitimacy, not only in the 1970s but well into the twenty-first century.

If the historic events of 1967 did result in the public's disillusionment with the Arab nationalist ideals, they were being replaced, less by the more localised nationalism of individual Arab states, but by another supra-national identity of religion. One of the first major domestic uprisings in the Asad era was over the regime's treatment of Islam in the new constitution. The Islamic political forces were to cause more problems for Asad in the late-1970s and the early 1980s. Thus, in the 1970s, the Arab states in general were still struggling to resolve the 'national' questions, and the embryonic development of national cohesion continued to be a source of security concerns. This insecurity provided the underlying cause of Saudi preoccupation with subversion, ideological warfare, blackmail and propaganda campaigns in the extreme which, in other countries, might be reserved for outright external military threats alone (Quandt, 1982: 7). For the purpose of this study, it is noteworthy that such preoccupation of the Saudis made them particularly prone to manipulation by other regional actors like Syria. The implication, in short, was that until adequate solutions were found to these 'national' questions—or the questions of shared identities—inter-Arab relations were to continue functioning under very different sets of rules from those of other regional systems—as will be demonstrated in the following chapters.

# 2

# DRAWING THE FAULT LINES
The Camp David agreement and its aftermath
(September 1978–October 1980)

The Camp David Accords in September 1978 marked the opening of a new era in inter-Arab politics. As Egypt, the largest and the most powerful Arab country, withdrew itself from the Arab fold, the Arab states felt severely weakened vis-à-vis Israel, and, at the same time, observed the demise of the precarious Damascus-Riyadh-Cairo trilateral axis, which had played a major role in shaping regional events in the mid-1970s. The rest of the Arab world established a short-lived Arab consensus to oppose the Egyptian move, but this consensus quickly crumbled in the wake of the Egyptian-Israeli Peace Treaty, as differences emerged over the degree of sanction to impose against Egypt and ultimately around the overall policies toward the country.

The significance of such a polarisation, however, was not limited to the question of 'what to do with Egypt'. Rather, this question gradually came to have a bearing on more fundamental concerns during the first two years after the Camp David: which country defines the core agenda of Arab political debate; what is to be the most central agenda; and what constitutes an acceptable or legitimate relationship with the two world superpowers, in relation to their policies towards such regional agenda. Seen in this context, Syria and its Steadfastness Front's obsession with the anti-Egyptian campaign can be interpreted as a desperate attempt to keep the Arab-Israeli conflict at the heart of the Arab political debate. In the meantime, political developments in the Gulf region were increasingly causing this very diversion of attention that Syria feared, thereby threatening to sideline Damascus.

The shift of focus away from the Arab-Israeli arena was given additional impetus by the Iranian Revolution and the subsequent war between Tehran and Baghdad, both of which further heightened the sense of regional instability. Moreover, the Soviet invasion of Afghanistan shook the Arab Gulf states, many of which saw it as part of the larger Soviet scheme to encircle the Gulf region. Meanwhile, such a shift of attention tempted Israel boldly to pursue ambitious, militant policies in Lebanon and in the Occupied Territories. The first two years of the post-Camp David era were, thus, a transition period in which main issues of conflict came into full display to polarise the region for a decade to come. As the fault line for each issue became clearer, all began to converge roughly along one line, dividing the Syrian-led camp from the Saudi-Iraqi axis and its protégés. Before opening the in-depth investigation into the dynamics behind Syrian-Saudi co-operation—sustained in spite of their disagreements over every conceivable policy matter—it is vital to single out the key issues on which the disagreements emerged and to compare one actor's policy goals with the other's. This chapter, in this respect, is a prologue to the analyses of the following chapters which aim to uncover how the Syrian-Saudi differences were bridged—or, at the very least, sufficiently regulated—and why either of the two actors was cornered to find a compromise, or sometimes, even voluntarily chose to do so.

## Conflicting Attitudes toward the Camp David
### (September 1978–November 1979)

On 17 September 1978, Egyptian President Anwar al-Sadat and Israeli Prime Minister Menachem Begin signed the Camp David Accords, which prepared the grounds for the first formal peace treaty between Israel and an Arab country. Egypt's epoch-making decision deprived Syria of the partner with which it had fought wars and allowed Israel to concentrate military forces on its Eastern Front, of which Syria was the most vital component. This challenge to Syria's regional position came at a time when the Asad regime was facing a number of difficulties both abroad and at home. Ever since its military entanglement in the Lebanese civil war, Syria had had uneasy relations with the Lebanese leftists and the PLO. In the meantime, Syria's former Christian allies were increasingly looking towards Israel as their more credible backer, the courtship responded to with great enthusiasm as was demonstrated by the latter's military incursion, the March 1978 'Litani Operation'. Syrian President Hafiz al-Asad's decision to send his troops to the Lebanese battlefields also triggered widespread opposition within Syria, as people were increasingly rallying around the Muslim Brotherhood. This dissatisfaction came to be expressed through violent means, with the opposition groups accusing the Asad regime of sectarian orientation and corrupt practices. The fact that the Brotherhood was allegedly receiving military or financial support from the neighbouring Arab states—namely Jordan, Iraq, Saudi Arabia and pro-Iraqi elements in Lebanon—amplified the regime's vulnerability. In such a critical setting, Syrian policies following Egypt's 'defection' were guided by the following aims: 1) to find other Arab partners to counterbalance Israeli military capability; 2) to persuade Egypt to abandon its pursuit for unilateral peace, and failing that, to isolate Egypt so as not to allow other Arab states to follow in Egypt's footsteps; and 3) to enlist further military and political support from the Soviet Union.

These objectives largely ran counter to the needs faced by the Saudis in the wake of the Camp David Accords. Unlike Syria, Saudi Arabia's initial reaction to the Accords was ambivalent, reflecting its dilemma. On the one hand, Egypt and the United States, the ultimate protagonist behind the peace negotiation and the superpower ally of Saudi Arabia, had been assuming automatic Saudi approval as soon as the deal materialised (Quandt, 1986: 212, 265). The American assumption was derived from several factors which characterised Saudi regional policies hitherto: the long-standing alliance between Sadat and the Saudi leadership, Saudi support for US involvement in resolving the Arab-Israeli conflict, and a Saudi commitment to peaceful solution to the conflict (Salamé, 1980: 557-558). The fact that the Saudi reaction to Sadat's 1977 visit to Jerusalem was at most bewilderment rather than condemnation was also an encouraging signal for the parties of the Camp David Accords. Hence, the pro-Camp David camp expected Saudi Arabia to endorse the agreement, if not to follow suit. On the other hand, the Saudi leadership was under heavy pressure from other Arab states that violently condemned the agreement. From the viewpoint of those Arab states, Saudi Arabia, with all its wealth and the ensuing political influence, was *the* state, which could not be lost to the pro-Camp David camp if the Arabs were to maintain any significant weight in their anti-Israeli struggle.

Under the threat of re-polarisation of the Arab world, it was a matter of time before Saudi Arabia was forced to take sides. Consequently, Saudi Arabia forfeited its previous attempt to reconcile Damascus with Cairo, which had been a dominant objective in Saudi regional policies since the 1973 war.[1] The initial Saudi objectives in the wake of the Camp David agreement can be summarised as follows: 1) appeasing the radical anti-Camp David Arab bloc, while resisting any pressure to incur a heavy political or economic burden, most importantly, the use of oil weapons, while simultaneously 2) avoiding outright confrontation with the US, while opposing its key policy on Egyptian-Israeli peace and 3) obstructing any Soviet attempt to intervene in Arab and regional affairs.

In view of these contrasting objectives, Syria and Saudi Arabia were bound to encounter a conflict of interests. On one hand, each actor was vigilant of any move by the other side adopting policies that ran counter to its own interests, and whenever possible, each took precautionary measures against such an eventuality. On the other hand, each side was cautious not to alienate the other at least by displaying obvious gestures of awareness towards the other's needs.

## The Syrian-Iraqi Unity and the First Baghdad Summit (October–November 1978)

The heightened sense of insecurity Syria experienced in the wake of the Camp David Accords can be observed in its frantic search for a regional partner to compensate for the strategic imbalance caused by the loss of Egypt. The Steadfastness Front, formed in the aftermath of Sadat's visit to Jerusalem in the previous year, was not proving to be an effective or influential alliance to carry out anti-Sadat campaigns and consisted of too unreliable or too peripheral members in the region. In a surprise move, Syria set its eyes on Iraq as the primary candidate for its new regional partner, although Iraq had been its archrival since the 1968 coup brought the anti-Syrian wing of the Ba'th Party to power (Kienle, 1990). In contrast to the total absence of high-level contacts between the two countries prior to the Camp David, the exchange of visits by high-ranking officials promptly resumed in early October. The contacts culminated in the summit meeting in Baghdad between Presidents Hafiz al-Asad and Ahmad Hasan al-Bakr on 24–26 October, which produced the Charter of Joint National Action (*Mithaq al-'Amal al-Qawmi al-Mushtarak*), effectively agreeing on an immediate military union with further plans to follow. On a parallel development, Iraq—eager to fill the vacuum of regional leadership role as abandoned by Egypt—began to assert its hegemony by calling for an Arab summit meeting in Baghdad on 1 October to discuss the challenge of the Camp David. As long as Syrian-Iraqi *rapprochement* was sustained, the new axis was bound to dominate the Arab political scene, and any collective decision was to reflect the wishes of those two states.

Saudi Arabia was also faced with a profound dilemma. Initially, the Camp David agreement was a promising start for the Saudis who had consistently supported the American-sponsored settlement of the Arab-Israeli conflict. The Kingdom held some hopes that the agreement would either create a ground for a comprehensive settlement (Holden and Johns, 1981: 492), or that, otherwise, it would fail on its own accord before a formal treaty was signed (Salamé, 1980: 558)—the end result of which would not be any worse than the pre-Camp David situation. Also, with Egypt neutralised, any future eruption of military confrontation was likely to be smaller in scale than the previous wars, hence, less likely to drag the Kingdom into undesirable military conflicts (Safran, 1988: 261).

With the above factors considered, the 19 September communiqué of the Saudi Cabinet gave an implicit blessing to the Camp David; it expressed appreciation for the American efforts, maintained that the resolution on the Sinai was no more than an internal Egyptian affair, and downplayed any expression of dissatisfaction to the lack of achievement on the Palestinian issue (Safran, 1988: 262). The Americans, however, wanted a more affirmative, unconditional endorsement from the Saudis. On 22–24 September, Secretary of State Cyrus Vance visited the Kingdom as part of a tour to Amman, Riyadh and Damascus; in a statement that followed the visit, the Saudis publicly endorsed the Camp David process, praising it as 'an initial step toward peace' (*MECS*, 1977-1978: 167).

Nevertheless, Saudi Arabia was soon reminded of the widespread anger the agreement generated among the other Arab parties; not only the members of the Steadfastness Front, but also the Palestinians and even pro-American Jordan were outspoken in their objection. No sooner had Vance left Damascus than President Asad boarded a plane to Riyadh in order to counteract the US pressure on Saudi Arabia. The aim of this visit on 26 September was to persuade Riyadh to denounce the agreement and to participate in the forthcoming Arab summit on the Camp David. A succession of Arab heads of states followed Asad's lead. Four days later, King Hussain of Jordan arrived in Riyadh, followed by the Iraqi Vice-President Saddam Hussain on 2 October, and Yasir 'Arafat, chairman of the PLO on 7 October (Abu Talib, 1992: 178). A similar stream of Arab visitors flooded into the Saudi capital on the eve of the 2–5 November Baghdad Arab Summit; from Syria, Rif'at al-Asad, President Asad's influential younger brother, arrived in the Kingdom on 28 October (*Arab Report and Record,* 16–31 October 1978.) Such a pressure on Saudi Arabia to condemn the Camp David agreement had become all the more irresistible because of the Syrian-Iraqi unity plan published only two days before.

The Baghdad summit meeting marked the beginning of short-lived Iraqi supremacy in the region, and, by extension, the temporary rise in political influence of Syria as its union partner. For those who opposed Sadat's peace, the summit was an overwhelming success, as not only were the states previously supportive of Sadat—Sudan, Oman, Morocco, and North Yemen—fully represented in the conference, but all members of the Arab League unanimously agreed on unqualified condemnation of the Camp David. The first sign of difference emerged, however, when the summit agenda turned towards the question of punitive measures to be applied to Egypt. Iraq, Syria, and the Steadfastness Front members advocated immediate sanctions, but Saudi Arabia and the Gulf states were reluctant. When a compromise was eventually reached, the agreement read that the terms of punitive measures were to be determined at the summit, but they were to be applied only if and when the Camp David eventually produced a formal peace treaty between Egypt and Israel.[2]

Crucially—for Syria's relations with the rich Gulf states in general and with Saudi Arabia in particular—the summit participants also agreed to establish an Arab 'support fund' which would make annual financial allocations to the frontline states for the next ten years in order to combat Israeli threats against the 'Arab nation'. At least on paper, Syria was the largest beneficiary of this fund—promised $1,800 million per annum—and Saudi Arabia, the most burdened financier with $1,000 million to contribute.[3] Hence, the common theme of Arab solidarity was successfully manipulated by the Arab 'have-nots' to justify their claim for shared access to the oil wealth of the Arab 'haves'. In order to secure such a dividend, Asad had made a point of visiting Moscow before the Baghdad Summit (Karsh, 1991: 119). The alarming possibility of a Soviet-Syrian *rapprochement* after the period of chill since 1976 Lebanon intervention, and Damascus' increased dependence on Soviet weapons were sufficient to blackmail the oil-rich countries, notably Saudi Arabia, into granting more aid to Syria. Indeed, before the Baghdad summit, Syria had obtained assurances of significant Arab financial support, as it successfully played on the Saudi fear of inviting Soviet influence into Arab regional dispute (Kienle, 1990: 137). This financial gain compounded Syria's incentive to create an all-Arab, anti-Sadat consensus, and Syria was willing to accommodate at least some demands from the moderate camp, i.e. the postponement of sanctions against Egypt.

On the Saudi side, the rejectionists' call for harsher treatment of Egypt became an irresistible pressure mainly because the formation of the Damascus-Baghdad axis added an extra weight behind their voices. The Saudis had little choice but to agree to the basic demands of the anti-Sadat camp, because the failure to do so would preclude the Baghdad summit from creating a consensus; and the collapse of the summit would be blamed mainly on the Saudi position. The inevitable consequence of this scenario would be that the Damascus-Baghdad axis would embark on an anti-Saudi campaign as priority, be it in the form of propaganda or aiding Ba'thist and Palestinian elements within the Kingdom and its vicinity. This threat came at a time when the US and Egyptian administrations' explicit criticism towards Saudi passivism appeared to confirm Riyadh's suspicion that the pro-Camp David group was totally oblivious to the Saudi leadership's sensitive position and were lacking in appreciation for Riyadh's painstaking effort to minimise the Arab punishment of Egypt. As a result, the Saudi leadership, although internally divided on the question of the Camp David (Salamé, 1980: 558-559; *MECS*, 1977–1978: 738-739), had little choice but to go along with the dictates of the radicals, who came to represent the most influential trend, not to speak of the numerical majority. One of the most significant marks that the Summit left was a quiet attempt by Saudi Arabia and Iraq to replace its latest tension with efforts at co-operation (*MECS*, 1978–1979: 216).

### The Interim Period (December 1978–March 1979)

By the start of 1979, the Saudi government had become consumed by other regional developments which compounded the pressure from the Damascus-Baghdad axis. Saudi domestic opposition forces of all colourings, be they leftists or Islamists, were showing signs of activism at the time when the Iranian Shah was increasingly losing control over his own domestic security. The Soviet-backed regimes in Ethiopia and Afghanistan appeared to be an ominous proof of the Soviet design to encircle the Kingdom, and this in turn gave added significance to the Saudi reading of the tensions mounting between its southern neighbours, the two Yemens.

The conflict in Yemen was a decisive point when the Saudis were reminded of the growing influence of the Damascus-Baghdad axis. The border between the YAR (Yemen Arab Republic) and the PDRY (People's Democratic Republic of Yemen) had been volatile since the latter half of 1977 and had exploded into a full-scale war by February 1979 (Halliday, 1990: 123-126). In contrast to months of failed attempts by Saudi Arabia to mediate a cease-fire, Syrian and Iraqi mediators, supported by Jordan and Algeria, persuaded the two Yemens to agree on a cease-fire as soon as the low-flame skirmishes erupted into a full-scale war. Furthermore, on 6 March the two Ba'thist regimes submitted a set of proposals to the Arab League Council meeting of Foreign Ministers to facilitate the resumption of the North-South unity dialogue, which had begun after the 1972 Yemeni war. In order to bring about a cease-fire at a time when the PDRY's military advances were showing enough momentum to reach the heart of the YAR territory, Syria and Iraq sent a crucial warning to Aden that 'export of revolution' to the North was impermissible. The two also supported the Saudi call to stop the PDRY's advance on Ta'iz, the second city of the YAR.[4] The Ba'thists' motives behind their eager undertaking of mediation are succinctly summarised by Gause III, and they were closely linked to the Camp David:

> Saudi Arabia was, along with Jordan, the key to Iraqi and Syrian efforts at this time to build a united Arab front against Egypt and the peace process. Baghdad and Damascus recognized that the fighting in Yemen highlighted Saudi vulnerability, and could push

Riyadh into closer security arrangements with the United States and Egypt. The *quid pro quo* in such a scenario would certainly be Saudi support for Sadat and Camp David (1990: 134).

It was a considerable relief for Saudi Arabia that the conflict in Yemen was contained before it reached a point of threatening the security of its southern border. Especially because its own initiative was rejected by the protagonists, the Kingdom was perhaps to an extent grateful to the intervention of Syria and Iraq, both of which had watered down their hitherto pro-Aden position to adopt a more balanced approach. The fact that the massive airlifting of US arms to the YAR government failed to secure an end to the fighting also contrasted with the Syrian-Iraqi success. The Syrian Vice-President 'Abd al-Halim Khaddam had reasons to sound haughty when he proclaimed that Saudi Arabia 'knows the role Syria and Iraq have played in bringing the Yemen dispute to an end, thereby contributing to the stability and security of the Arabian Peninsula' (*MECS*, 1978–1979: 260n92). Nevertheless, by the same token, Riyadh grew suspicious and wary of the omnipotence of the Damascus-Baghdad axis. The Ba'thists had already demonstrated in Yemen their ability to dictate the shaping of regional events, and this influence could potentially work against Saudi interests; in the context of the Yemeni issue, a creation of a united Yemen—ruled by a leftist government hostile to Riyadh and allied to progressive regimes in the north of the Kingdom—would be just such a scenario (Safran, 1988: 293). In short, returning to Gause III's analysis, the Saudis were aware that 'those [Syria and Iraq] who could bring about such a desired end could also create enormous problems for the Kingdom' (1990: 135).

Not unrelated to the Yemen crisis, the overwhelming superiority of the anti-Camp David Arab camp was such that Saudi Crown Prince Fahd chose to make a gesture of postponing his planned official visit to the United States. The announcement was first made on 24 February 1979 (*BBC/SWB/ME*, 26 February 1979), followed by the final decision to cancel the visit altogether (*MEI*, 2 March 1979). The decision reflected a multitude of concerns: Saudi suspicion towards US commitment to deploy the F-15 fighter planes in the Kingdom; Saudi-US disagreement over Saudi oil strategy in the aftermath of the Iranian Revolution which brought chaos to the oil market; and Saudi mistrust towards the US Gulf policy when it failed to protect the Iranian Shah (Holden and Johns, 1981: 498-502). Nevertheless, the core of Saudi disappointment continued to be over US policy on the unilateral peace between Egypt and Israel and over the continued US insistence on acquiring Saudi blessing for the coming formal peace treaty without taking into account the Saudi requirements—first and foremost, the incorporation of the Palestinian question into the peace plan. The mounting tension in Saudi-US relations at this time was such that Saudi Arabia flirted with Soviet overtures (*MEI*, 2 March 1979; Quandt, 1982: 69). For instance, Sa'ud al-Faisal referred to the 'positive' Soviet role in the region, and Crown Prince Fahd to its 'importance' (Quandt, 1982: 69). In fact, throughout the period of 1970s and 1980s, such friendly signals from Riyadh to Moscow almost always indicated less an improvement of bilateral relations between the two capitals but more a deterioration in the Saudi-US ties.

The evidence that Saudi Arabia succumbed to the dominance of Syria, backed by the Damascus-Baghdad axis, can be detected in the field of economic aid, in the interim period between the two Baghdad Conferences. On 21 December 1978, approximately a month after the Baghdad Summit, the Saudi Development Fund signed an agreement with the Syrian government under which the Fund would grant soft loans of 84.2 million Saudi Riyals (SR; $25 million) for development projects. Furthermore, the Fund also increased from SR40 million ($11.9 million) to SR75 million ($22.3 million) its contribution to developing roads in the country (*BBC/SWB/ME*, 2 January; *MEED*, 5 January 1979). In addition, in February of the following year, Saudi Arabia fulfilled the terms of the 1976 Saudi-Syrian agreement by delivering 1.2.million barrels of crude oil to Syria (*MEED*, 2 February 1979). Furthermore, by March, a feasibility study of the Hijaz Railway project, an attempt to revive the train connection from Saudi Arabia across Jordan to Syria, had been commenced by a German company, which may be interpreted as a gesture to encourage improved social and economic ties among the countries concerned (*MEED*, 16 March 1979).

As to Syria, the leadership took great care not to alienate Saudi Arabia by reassuring it that the axis with Baghdad was not a threat directed against the Kingdom, or at least to keep it informed on any developments which touched on Saudi sensitivity. The first of these gestures was 'Abd al-Halim Khaddam's visit to Saudi Arabia on 11 December 1978, just before the announcement of the Saudi Development Fund loan (*Arab Report and Record*, 1–15 December 1978; *MECS*, 1978–1979: 244). Two months later on 1-2 February 1979, a similar visit was undertaken by Khaddam, a day after Asad and Saddam Hussain met in Damascus to conclude a follow-up agreement to the Charter of Joint National Action, and the visit was reciprocated by Prince 'Abdallah, Second Deputy Prime Minister and Commander of the National Guard (*Al-Nahar*, 3 February; *Arab Report and Record*, 28 February 1979).

By this stage, its vocal commitment to unity notwithstanding, Damascus had become resistant to moving forward with the Iraqi plan for fear of total entrapment into the Iraqi sphere of influence; Iraq, after all, was the dominant half of the unbalanced relationship with its stronger economy based on oil income, larger military capability and more efficient security services and party organisations. With Iraq still a potential rival rather than a trustworthy partner, it was only natural that Syria was keen to stay in the Saudis' good books.[5] Thus, when Syria was met more than half way by Saudi Arabia in resolving their differences, the former at the very least displayed some sensitivity to Saudi interests; this pattern of behaviour became an oft-seen feature in the bilateral relations.

### The Second Baghdad Conference Meeting (March–July 1979)

As late as March 1979, Saudi Arabia was still hoping that the US-sponsored initiative on Egyptian-Israeli peace held some chance of accommodating wider Arab concerns by linking the Palestinian autonomy issue to the Egyptian-Israeli agreement. This hope, however, was shattered by the conclusion of a formal peace treaty in Washington on 26 March 1979. On the very next day, an Arab Foreign and Economy Ministers' meeting was convened in Baghdad to discuss the peace treaty and possible countermeasures against it. This conference was marked by critical disagreements, proving the unanimous consensus at the earlier Baghdad Summit meeting to be short-lived.

Syria, together with Iraq and members of the Steadfastness Front, led some of the most extremist voices. It called for suspension of all diplomatic ties with Egypt and immediate application of sanctions against it including an oil embargo; it was also a rare occasion, in which Damascus singled out Saudi Arabia in cautioning against leniency towards Egypt (*MECS*, 1978–1979: 819-820). The PLO was alone in its demand for an even more extreme measure, which involved sanctions against the United States. Another group led by Saudi Arabia, on the contrary, called for the most limited of the punitive measures and strongly opposed the severing of diplomatic ties with Egypt. After some dramas, with representatives threatening to walk out at the height of the discussion, agreement was finally concluded three days later on 30 March.[6] As was the case in the previous Baghdad Conference, Saudi Arabia bent under pressure from Syria and Iraq and decided to concede on the issue of diplomatic relations with Egypt (Safran, 1988: 279-281).

However, the rocky attempt to maintain a Damascus-Baghdad axis faltered amidst the domestic and regional upheavals; on 28 July, the Iraqi authority announced the discovery of a Syrian-backed plot against Saddam Hussain (*BBC/SWB/ME*, 31 July 1979), who had become the head of state after Ahmad Hasan al-Bakr's resignation less than two weeks before. Although the Syrian side insistently denied any knowledge or involvement in such a plot, the bilateral relations deteriorated steadily to such an extent that a complete break-off of diplomatic ties was announced the following year. The event marked the end of the brief *rapprochement* between the two Ba'thist states, which was an aberration in the history of their hostile relations. The marriage of convenience had been forced on each party by the sheer necessity to adjust to the new power balance in the Middle East strategic map, brought about by the Camp David Accords. When Syria and Iraq failed to resolve their deep-rooted differences in the course of events, Saudi Arabia and other conservative Arab states were relieved of pressures from a potentially powerful radical axis. When the union formally failed, Saudi Arabia swiftly consolidated a new partnership with Iraq, leaving Syria increasingly isolated and vulnerable in the region. As a result, Damascus manoeuvred to recruit new partners with whom to countervail the emerging Riyadh-Baghdad alliance. The ensuing fragmentation in the Arab region more or less consolidated into a pattern of inter-Arab rivalry which prevailed for the following decade.

### Riyadh-Baghdad Axis vs. Syria (August–November 1979)

It did not take long for Syria and Iraq to return to hostility after the failure of their unity scheme, and this in turn created a more favourable balance for Saudi Arabia as far as its relations with Syria were concerned. This time, it was Saudi Arabia's turn to take Iraq to its side and to challenge or at least counterpoise Syria, which had by then cultivated ties with the revolutionary regime of Iran in anticipation for such an undesirable outcome. As early as 17 September, Saudi Minister of Interior Prince Na'if presented an agreement with Iraq on security co-operation. Simultaneously, it was announced that Foreign Minister Sa'ud al-Faisal was to stop by Damascus en route to Baghdad the following day, presumably to brief Syria on this development (*BBC/SWB/ME*, 19 September 1979), although the actual visit appears not to have taken place until a few days later on 23 September (*Al-Nahar,* 24 September 1979). Just as his Syrian counterpart, Khaddam, used to frequent Riyadh whenever any progress was made on the Damascus–Baghdad co-operation, it was the Saudis' turn to make gestures not to alienate Syria while pursuing closer ties with Baghdad. The talks may also have covered the latest disagreements between Syria and Saudi Arabia at the regular Arab League Council session in Tunis on 18–19 September; the Saudi representative sharply opposed Syrian and Libyan attempts to push for stricter sanctions against Egypt in the forthcoming Tunis summit (*MECS*, 1979–1980: 171). Riyadh's new *rapprochement* with Iraq was thus giving the Kingdom extra confidence in handling inter-Arab diplomacy.

All the signs of polarisation in the Arab camp were visible even before the Tunis Arab summit meeting began on 20–22 November 1979. The preparatory meetings of the summit were most extraordinary for the fact that two mutually exclusive groupings held separate meetings; Saudi Arabia headed one, and Syria another. On 16 October in Ta'if, the Saudi camp held a meeting of Foreign Ministers from six Gulf countries excluding Iraq to co-ordinate their position at Tunis on Gulf security matters. The Syrian-led grouping met in Algiers on 1 November with Libya, Algeria, the PDRY and the PLO, marking the revival of the Steadfastness Front, which had been temporarily eclipsed by the overwhelming rallying power of the Damascus-Baghdad axis. The proceedings in the Tunis summit also reflected the same line of division and the change in the regional balance of power. Syria's proposal, supported by other members of the Front, to step up the sanctions against Egypt was overruled by majority decision. Furthermore, its request to give the Iranian delegation observer status was rejected due to strong objections from Saudi Arabia and Iraq (*MECS*, 1979–1980: 174).

Thus, by late 1979, Saudi Arabia and Syria had firmly established themselves as leaders of opposite Arab camps, regarding the question of Camp David, or more precisely, Egypt's position in the Arab world. In the initial confusion after Camp David, the two actors engaged in this battle for regional influence by competing for one prize—Iraqi allegiance. When Iraq was 'won' first by Syria, and then by Saudi Arabia, their weight in the inter-Arab political platform changed accordingly. The status of the Riyadh-Baghdad axis was elevated, and with it, the importance of Arab/Persian Gulf security issues in the Arab political debate. This rearrangement of political allegiance in the region, in turn, threatened to shift the focus of debate away from the Arab-Israeli conflict, thereby reducing Syria's weight in Arab regional politics. The emerging fault line which cut across the Arab world was further consolidated when troubles erupted in Iran and in Afghanistan.

## The Iranian Factor: Siding with the Opposites
### (February 1979–September 1980)

The Camp David Accords may have been a significant landmark in the contemporary history of the Middle East, but its significance was quickly overshadowed by another major event, the fall of the Pahlavi dynasty in Iran. The Iranian Revolution of February 1979 redrew the political and strategic map of the Gulf region, if not of the entire Middle East, as the new government of Iran resorted to hostile interventionist measures against its neighbours and upset all sense of mutual confidence cultivated over decades by the previous Iranian regime. This sudden and dramatic change in the orientation of one of the most powerful regional actors provided another source of friction between Syria and Saudi Arabia. In fact, amongst the four factors identified in this chapter as those that contributed to the deepening of the Damascus-Riyadh rift, none other than Syria's support for Iran's new government so astounded or even baffled Saudi Arabia. Yet, as this section will illustrate, both Syria's strategic alliance with Iran and Saudi Arabia's open support for Iraq were founded on shaky grounds, afflicted with contradictions. As with the policy towards the Camp David, there were ample reasons why the two capitals could not disregard each other not only as an obstacle but also as a potential asset.

*Contrasting Policies towards Iran (February–December 1979)*
During the Shah's rule, Saudi Arabia shared with Iran close ties with the West—which in turn meant antipathy towards the Soviet Union, mistrust for Iraq and support for the legitimacy of the monarchical character of leadership. The uneasy partnership, with an undercurrent of suspicion, was maintained between the two, despite some marked disagreements over oil policies, Saudi opposition to Iran's support for Israel, and the rivalry over leadership in Gulf security arrangements. The partnership was strong enough to mislead the Saudis into endorsing the Shah's rule and pledging their support as late as only a few days before the triumph of the revolutionaries—not a good start for the relations with Iran's new regime (Wilson and Graham, 1994: 103). The fall of the Shah and the establishment of the Islamic Republic seriously shook the Saudi leadership for numerous reasons: 1) the Saudis feared that the popular revolution in Iran could give fresh inspiration and impetus to other dissenting groups under dynastic rules, particularly among the Shi'as in Saudi Arabia and other Arab Gulf countries; 2) the new Iranian regime began to challenge the very core of the Al-Sa'ud's legitimacy, its Islamic credentials, by claiming to speak for a universal Islamic authority; and 3) the fall of the Shah put in question the reliability of the US as the protector of its loyal regional allies (Chubin and Tripp, 1996: 4). Khomeini not only argued that Islam and hereditary kingship were incompatible, questioning by name Saudi Arabia's form of governance, but also contested the latter's claim to the guardianship of the Holy Cities of Mecca and Medina (Quandt, 1982: 39-40). With regard to foreign policy, the new regime in Iran adopted an anti-US position in the extreme—by extension, antagonistic to pro-US regimes in the region— and was set to 'export the revolution' throughout the Muslim world (Freedman and Karsh, 1993: 7).

Facing these outspoken attacks, the Saudis initially adopted an appeasing posture, praising the new Iranian regime for its Islamic principles. Prince 'Abdallah, went so far as to call for bilateral co-operation with religion as its basis (*BBC/SWB/ME*, 24 April 1979). Nevertheless, such a show of goodwill did not induce any change in the hostile propaganda campaigns from Iran, which continued to fan outbreaks of anti-Al-Sa'ud discontent.

On 20 November 1979, Juhaiman 'Utaiba, a member of a prominent tribe which led the *Ikhwan* rebellion fifty years before,[7] proclaimed himself a *mahdi* (messiah) and led several hundred armed religious zealots to seize the Grand Mosque of Mecca, the holiest shrine in Islam. That such a seizure took place at all caused an unprecedented loss of face for the Saudi leadership both domestically and internationally. Worse still, the Saudi National Guard took as long as two weeks to subdue the rebels at the cost of heavy casualties, and allegedly with the help of foreign troops (*BBC/SWB/ME*, 11 December 1979). This incident, widely covered by the Arab and international press, was only a prelude to the expression of discontent from a variety of other forces in the Kingdom.[8] The Grand Mosque event triggered an explosion of mass demonstrations not only challenging the religious credentials of the Al-Sa'ud but also protesting against social injustice. There were widespread suspicions that tribal land was unjustly appropriated by the House of Saud, and a privileged few exploited the skyrocketing of real estate prices (Salamé, 1985: 16).

In such a turbulent period in Saudi domestic politics, the Iranian experience came to be viewed as an promising example of a successful popular uprising, particularly amongst the Saudi Twelver Shi'as, some 200,000 of whom resided in the oil-rich Eastern provinces. Emanating partly from the socio-cultural ramifications of hasty modernisation, and partly from inspiration from the Iranian experience, anti-regime disturbances broke out among these Shi'as first in late November 1979, eight days after the start of the Grand Mosque seizure, and again in February 1980 (Abir, 1988: 152-158; cf. Munadhdhamah al-Thawrah al-Islamiyyah fi al-Jazirah al-'Arabiyyah, 1980). Unlike the Shi'i assertiveness of the following years, they were less a product of Iranian manipulation than a genuinely popular expression of discontent and of communal solidarity, but they nonetheless received public support from the Revolutionary government of Iran (Kostiner, 1987: 179). Other examples of Saudi organisations that were receptive to Iran's revolutionary messages were the Islamic Revolution Organisation in the Arabian Peninsula and the Saudi Organisation of the Islamic Revolution. In the decade following the Iranian Revolution, Shi'i protests, with indisputable involvement of the Iranians, became a recurring theme in Saudi politics particularly during the *Hajj* pilgrimage months.

If the Saudi leadership, or at least many members of the ruling circle, had any hope of ostracising the extremist Iranian regime by creating a pan-Arab front, such a hope was quickly shattered by Damascus. Syria was only second to the USSR in recognising the new Iranian regime and congratulating the Iranians on the success of the revolution. In fact, the Asad regime had been cultivating its ties with the religious elements in Iran since the early stage of its rule. In the early 1970s, the Iranian-Lebanese cleric, Musa al-Sadr rescued the Asad regime with a *fatwa* (legal opinion) which officially recognised the 'Alawi sect as a branch of Shi'ism.[9] He subsequently became a bridge that linked Syria, Iran and the Shiite community in Lebanon. Besides this personal network, Syria had every reason to be hostile to the Shah, who was essentially pro-US in orientation, a long-term ally of Israel and a supporter of Sadat's initiative. Syria's support for the Iranian oppositions was exemplified by its offer of asylum to Khomeini in October 1978 when he was expelled from Iraq, where he had been commanding in exile an anti-Shah movement.[10]

Hafiz al-Asad's sustained support for the Iranian opposition paid off when the success of the Revolution promised the Syrian regime additional benefits. First, at a time when the newly emerging Riyadh-Baghdad axis was isolating the Syrians, Damascus badly needed a strong alliance with one of the major regional players, and Tehran helped alleviate some of the pressures. The alternative option of bandwagoning with Riyadh and Baghdad was not an attractive prospect; had Asad joined the anti-Iranian coalition led by these two capitals, the logical consequence would have been an undesirable deference to Iraqi or Saudi hegemony and an acceptance of the downgrading of the Arab-Israeli conflict in Arab political agenda (Ehteshami and Hinnebusch, 1997: 102).

Second, its association with Tehran helped counter the domestic troubles with the Islamic oppositions. The prelude to the showdown between the Syrian Islamists and Hafiz al-Asad's regime was the killing at the Aleppo Artillery Academy on 16 June 1979. As a majority Sunni Muslim's statement against the sectarian nature of the minority-dominated Asad regime, the Islamists singled out 'Alawi cadets, killed thirty two of them and injured more. The event in Aleppo triggered major escalation in the government's retaliation campaign leading to the 1982 Hama massacre. The Syrian Muslim Brotherhood, which formed the core of the Islamist opposition, initially looked towards the new Iranian regime with great expectations that its call for the 'export of revolution' would target Syria before long and help to oust the secular regime. The Brotherhood sent delegations to Tehran to this end, but they were received with indifference at first, and later, with open contempt,[11] outmatched by Asad's comparably eager attempt to divert Tehran from supporting the Syrian Islamists (Lobmeyer, 1995: 270). Although Asad's domestic concern was unlikely to have been the paramount reason for his association with

Tehran, L. Robinson goes so far as to assert:

> Asad hoped that supporting Iran would preclude that country from
> lending aid to the [Islamic] revolt, while at the same time serving to
> shore up the Syrian president's Islamic credentials at home...In
> response to the *Ikhwan*'s challenge, the Asad regime was forced to
> support actively the Iranians in order to refute its secular,
> anti-Islamic image at home (1996: 45).

Many of Syria's Arab neighbours, particularly Saudi Arabia, despised
Syria's pro-Iran policy, at times branding it 'treason to the Arab cause'.[12]
Nevertheless, Saudi Arabia, at the time of the Iranian Revolution, was in
no position explicitly to criticise Syrian policies towards Revolutionary
Iran. The Damascus-Baghdad axis was still dominating Arab political
debates—as was exemplified in the Yemen cease-fire in March
1979—while Riyadh was at a loss; it had no major regional ally with whom
to form a matching axis, while its superpower friend appeared to be either
oblivious to Saudi interests or simply incapable of meeting Saudi needs.

Syria attempted to defend its position by consistently adopting the
language acceptable to most of the fellow Arabs—that of the anti-Israeli
rhetoric. Among Revolutionary Iran's foreign policy objectives,
destruction of Israel was placed at the forefront from the very inception
of its rule. Syria would argue, when facing a suspicious Arab audience, that
antagonising Iran would be counter-productive to the Arab struggle
against their true enemy, Israel (Agha and Khalidi, 1995: 10-13; Ehteshami
and Hinnebusch, 1997: 49, 88-91). When Khaddam visited Tehran in
August 1979, his interview with Iranian *Kayhan* primarily focused on Iran's
positive role in the Arab-Israeli conflict and even its potential to substitute
for Egypt's defection (*BBC/SWB/ME*, 21 August 1979).

Another strategy Syria adopted was to present itself as a mediator in
disputes arising between Iran and the Arab Gulf states. Whether Syria did
indeed play any significant role as a mediator is doubtful in these early
days of tensions, but the number of reported incidents at least testifies to
Syria's effort to *appear* to be mediating. As early as June 1979, Kuwaiti
daily *Al-Siyasah* reported that President Asad mediated between Iraq and
Iran over the tensions rising in Khuzestan/Arabistan (*BBC/SWB/ME*, 4
June 1979). It is unclear whether this mediation effort did in fact take
place; ten days later, Iran announced that it would, *in the future,* welcome
such mediation (*BBC/SWB/ME*, 15 June 1979). In October, Damascus
home service reported on Syria's 'successful' mediation between Iran and
unspecified Gulf States, who share the common 'imperialist-Zionist
enemies' (*BBC/SWB/ME*, 18 October 1979). Furthermore, on 4

November, the day the US Embassy in Tehran was seized by a group of mobs, the Kuwaiti News Agency reported that the Kuwaiti Deputy Minister and the Saudi Foreign Minister were to accompany Asad on his visit to Iran—scheduled at the end of the month but never materialised.

Annoyed as they may have been, the Saudis did not resort to open criticism of Syria's new Gulf policy, perhaps because they perceived it—wishfully and wrongly—to be a temporary tactical manoeuvre, rather than a seed of emerging long-term alliance, and also because the ensuing crack in the Damascus-Baghdad axis would not be an unwelcome development in their perspectives. Saudi frustration was to grow, however, when the tension between Iran and Iraq began to intensify in 1980.

### *Towards the Iran-Iraq War: Consolidation of the Inter-Arab Rift (January–September 1980)*

If the hosting of the two Baghdad conferences in November 1978 and March 1979 reflected Saddam Hussain's ambition to position Iraq as the pivotal Arab state, his effort reached its peak at the publication of the Pan-Arab Charter in February 1980.[13] The Charter, to which most Arab states subscribed, was primarily aimed at strengthening internal cohesion of the Iraqi state as well as at countering the Iranian challenges against Iraq. Syria, together with the PDRY, made a point of rejecting not only the Charter itself but also Iraq's call for a special Arab Summit dedicated to this agenda. The special summit was never convened despite the majority support the Charter enjoyed. According to *MECS*, the failure of the Iraqi manoeuvre is attributable to both Syria's refusal to take part and Saudi Arabia's reluctance to attend a summit which was boycotted by Syria (1979–1980: 196). From the spring of 1980, it became clear that Syria's open defiance against Iraq was no passing event. Syria, for instance, turned the April 1980 Tripoli conference of the Steadfastness Front into a vehicle of rallying support for Iran against Iraq, while, simultaneously, Damascus intensified high-level contacts with the Iranian leadership (*BBC/SWB/ME*, 11 and 28 April 1980).

What remained of Syrian-Iraqi *rapprochement* came to a formal end in late August 1980, when large quantities of arms and ammunition were allegedly discovered at the Syrian Embassy in Baghdad (*BBC/SWB/ME*, 20 August 1980). Although Syria promptly denied the charges, the two countries expelled each other's diplomatic missions. Against this background, Syria began a renewed search for a friendly regional partner, and as a result, responded favourably to Libya's call for unity; President Asad visited Tripoli on 8 September and agreed on the unity scheme (*BBC/SWB/ME*, 10 September 1980). Saudi Arabia expressed its 'delight' with the news of the unity, partly because it had traditionally felt disturbed by the fragmentation of the Arab world—or because it had to *appear,* at the very least, to be supporting any step which might lead to wider Arab unity (Qindil, 1980c), and partly because it did not wish to damage the bilateral relationship with Syria (Abu Talib, 1992: 197). The unity scheme was, yet again, no more than a hypothetical programme which indicated the protagonists' weaknesses and desperation (Kienle, 1995); the Steadfastness Front was hardly functioning as a coherent unit, the anti-Sadat bloc was crumbled and the Saudi-Iraqi axis[14] was gaining strength by the prospect of inviting in Jordan.

The shifting of alliances and their consolidation were a prelude to Iraq's adventurism. With Saddam Hussain's dramatic gesture on 17 September of publicly abrogating the 1975 Algiers agreement with Iran, sporadic military campaigns began against the Iranian military targets. When full-scale war broke out five days later on 22 September, this action of Iraq—based on gross miscalculation—fundamentally altered the strategic map of the region for years to come. Three days after the outbreak of the war, King Khalid telephoned Saddam Hussain to express the Kingdom's full-support for Iraq.[15]

The Syrian and Saudi leaderships also conferred with each other on a number of occasions around this period.[16] It soon transpired, however, that Saudi Arabia's hope of establishing a united Arab front against Iran was doomed from the outset as Syria—much to Riyadh's surprise—continued to support Iran even after the outbreak of the war, which Saddam Hussain preferred to call a revival of an ancient animosity between Arabs and Persians. Saudi frustration with the Syrian position was to grow substantial as, later in the conflict, the possibility of Iranian victory began to pose a grave threat to the Kingdom's security; in such a scenario, Saudi Arabia would be the first target of Iranian reprisals as the main financier of Iraq's war efforts. On the other hand, the historical mistrust between Iraq and Saudi Arabia also made the Saudi leadership wary of an outright Iraqi victory. It was here that Syria's value—sometimes as a counter-weight to Iraq and other times as a potential intermediary to pacify Iran—could not be ignored The Saudis' vision of Syria during the eight years of the Iran-Iraq war was consequently coloured with ambiguity.

**The Superpower Factor (December 1979–October 1980)**

Sources of disagreements between Syria and Saudi Arabia were not limited to regional issues. Their relations with the two world superpowers also displayed a stark contrast, but in this formative period of the post-Camp David regional order, disagreements chiefly concerned the Soviet Union in two major events, the Soviet invasion of Afghanistan and the signing of the Syrian-Soviet Treaty of Friendship and Co-operation. In this section, the analysis will focus on the following questions: what were the sources of friction between Damascus and Riyadh in these events?; and how and why did the two states attempt to isolate those sources of friction from wider issues in the bilateral relations?

Ba'thist Syria had maintained a cordial relationship with the Soviet Union even throughout the difficult times of the 1970s when Syria, much to its paymaster's distaste, went half-way with Henry Kissinger's disengagement initiative. It further annoyed Moscow by pursuing an independent Lebanese policy and striking a damaging blow to the pro-Soviet PLO. Nevertheless, in the wake of the Camp David Accords, which left Syria to stand virtually alone against the military threat from Israel, Syria became increasingly dependent on the military and political support from the superpower, especially in its quest to achieve 'strategic parity'[17] with Israel. By 1979, Syria had not only become solely dependent on military aid from the Soviet Union but also had hosted more than 2,500 Soviet military and technical advisers in its army.[18]

Saudi Arabia, in contrast, officially rejected any revival of diplomatic relations with the Soviet Union since their lapse on the eve of World War Two, despite the latter's occasional wooing. It also consistently criticised Soviet policy towards the Arab-Israeli conflict by drawing, in its own logic, a direct link between international communism and Israeli interests.[19] By the late 1970s, the Saudis came to fear the threat of the 'red peril', approaching its southern doorsteps (e.g. *BBC/SWB/ME,* 22 February 1979; Qindil, 1980a). In December 1979, South Yemen and the USSR signed the Treaty of Friendship and Co-operation (Halliday, 1990: 193-194), and even North Yemen was drifting towards *rapprochement* with the latter, as it received large shipments of Soviet arms accompanied by military advisers (*MECS*, 1979–1980: 698). As discussed previously, South Yemen was periodically launching military campaigns against North Yemen, at a time when Ethiopia, backed by Cuban and Soviet forces, was waging war against neighbouring Eritrea and Somalia. As if this was not enough, the Saudi communists were gaining a boost in their morale from the above events as well as from the Saudi regime's troubles with the Islamists and Shi'a oppositions.

With the aim of containing this grave situation, Saudi Arabia adopted some measures of moderation towards the Soviets, allegedly with establishment of diplomatic relations in sight. In fact, only two days before the Soviet invasion of Afghanistan in December 1979, Crown Prince Fahd was quoted as favouring such ties (Qindil, 1980a; *Washington Post*, 28 January 1980). However, the Saudis perceived the invasion as yet another Soviet design against the Kingdom, this time from the north. The

momentary hopes for improved relationships between the two were
shattered by the event, and the Saudis reverted to their traditional
approach by viewing the invasion as part of a larger scheme of
international communism, encircling the Kingdom and its oil wells. In
consequence, weakening of the Soviet presence in the Middle East became
an obsession for the Saudis, which ran exactly counter to the Syrian
intention of drawing closer to the USSR. The Saudis, therefore, saw
Syrian-Soviet relations as the constant source of irritation and even a
threat to its regional policies.

Syrians, on the other hand, perceived Saudi Arabia's frantic objection
to the Soviets as yet another diversion of attention away from the
Arab-Israeli conflict, as was also the case with Saudi exaggeration of the
Iranian threat. As the Syrians saw it, the USSR was the only world power
which could support the Arabs against the US-backed Israel, and
antagonising Moscow, therefore, was counter-productive to the main Arab
struggle against the Jewish state. As a result, Syria made its co-operation
with Saudi regional policy contingent on raising the profile of the
Arab-Israeli discussions. Also, an increased amount of Saudi financial aid
did not come amiss in securing such a co-operation from Damascus.

### The Soviet Invasion of Afghanistan as a Threat to Saudi Security (December 1979–March 1980)

On 27 December 1979, more than 80,000 Soviet combat troops rolled
onto Afghan soil to overthrow the defiant leader, Hafizullah Amin, and to
replace him with a Soviet protégé, Babrak Karmal. [20] One of the
consequences of the invasion for the Saudis was that the Soviet air forces
in Afghanistan were now firmly established at Shindand, within
fighter-bomber range of the Straits of Hormuz and a crucial outlet for
Gulf oil. The Saudi government was quick to issue a statement on 29
December criticising the invasion as a 'flagrant interference in the internal
affairs of Afghanistan and a violation of international law and practices'
(*BBC/SWB/ME*, 31 December 1979). Various Saudi papers also reported
on the invasion with strong words of criticism, citing its 'bestial and
savage objectives, the primary one being to strike the Islamic faith of
Afghanistan' (e.g. *BBC/SWB/ME*, 31 December 1979).

In the coming months, Saudi Arabia, first of all, strenuously denied
rumours that it had been on the verge of establishing diplomatic relations
with the superpower (e.g. *BBC/SWB/ME*, 23, 24 and 28 January 1980),
and second, took a concrete political measure of protest by announcing on
6 January 1980 its intention to boycott the coming Moscow Summer
Olympic (*BBC/SWB/ME*, 7 January 1980). It became the first country to
do so and called on other Arab and Muslim countries to follow suit. The

more ambitious step for the Saudis was to achieve a unified Islamic front in condemnation of the invasion. They rallied to summon an emergency session of the Islamic Conference Organisation (ICO) Foreign Ministers meeting in Islamabad, Pakistan, to deal with the Afghan issue. Significantly, Saudi Arabia took the precaution of notifying the Syrians of its scheme in advance. In the midst of this anti-Soviet campaign, Sa'ud al-Faisal made a surprise visit to Damascus on 9 January to discuss Afghanistan and the Saudi intention to summon an ICO Foreign Ministers conference (*Al-Nahar*, 10 January 1980).

Damascus, however, was defiant towards such Saudi gestures, although privately, the Syrian leadership was said to have been unhappy with the Soviet invasion (*Washington Post*, 22 February 1980). Only three days after Saud al-Faisal's visit, Asad received the Soviet ambassador in Damascus, who delivered a message from Leonid Brezhnev. Asad stressed his eagerness to strengthen bilateral ties, while reiterating his praise for the Soviet support for the Arab cause against Israel and the Camp David agreement (*BBC/SWB/ME*, 14 January 1980). Furthermore, on 14 January in an emergency session of the United Nations (UN) General Assembly on Afghanistan, not only did Syria go against the overwhelming majority and abstained from the resolution to condemn the Soviet action but its diplomats also reportedly lobbied in support of the Soviet cause prior to the voting (Karsh, 1988: 51). The only other Arab states which refrained from voting in favour of the condemnation were members of the Steadfastness Front. Two days later, Syria summoned a meeting of the Front's Foreign Ministers Conference in Damascus in order to discuss means to confront Saudi Arabia's efforts in condemning the USSR's invasion of Afghanistan in the forthcoming Islamabad Conference.

The Damascus meeting of the Steadfastness Front focused on the Saudi-initiated ICO meeting. Reflecting each member's discomfort with the Soviet action, the resolution avoided outright boycott of the Islamabad Conference, but instead laid down two impossible conditions for their attendance, virtually predestined to be rejected: 1) the conference venue be moved from Islamabad to Mecca, a suggestion calculated to discomfort the Saudis so soon after the Grand Mosque incident; and 2) the date be changed from 26 January so as not to coincide with the start of Egyptian-Israeli diplomatic relations, or in other words, the exchange of Egyptian and Israeli ambassadors (*Washington Post*, 23 January 1980). To accentuate the second point, the final statement of the Steadfastness conference also called for the widening of the Islamabad agenda to include the Egyptian-Israeli normalisation, Palestine, Jerusalem, and the US 'schemes' in the region (*MECS*, 1979–1980: 180). When these requests were predictably rejected by the ICO Secretary-General, the Front members announced their boycott, although only Syria and the PDRY adhered to the decision. The Syrian act of defiance towards Saudi Arabia seemed more pronounced when during the Damascus meeting, pro-Syrian Beirut newspaper *Al-Sharq* played up reports of instability in Saudi Arabia in the aftermath of the Grand Mosque seizure. The report mentioned the massive capital flight from Saudi Arabia and of arms smuggling into the vast and uncontrollable territory (*Washington Post*, 23 January 1980).

The convening of this Front meeting marked a break from its period of eclipse when its significance had been overshadowed by the short-lived dominance of the Damascus-Baghdad axis. In this revival, the Front became less of an anti-Sadat bloc than a 'club of Soviet faithfuls' (*MECS*, 1979–1980: 181). Syria's overt pro-Soviet action was, first of all, underlined by its need to secure continued flow of Soviet arms supplies in the wake of its domestic troubles and Israeli adventurism in Lebanon.[21] Secondly, in a more general context, there was a genuine concern in Damascus that Arab attention was being diverted away from the 'struggle' against Israel and the Egyptian-Israeli accords; a special conference on the Afghan issue would only serve to consolidate this ominous trend. Thirdly, Asad feared that the ICO meeting was going to be used as a platform to further the Carter Doctrine, the new US policy on the Middle East; on 23 January, President Carter expressed the US' readiness to use military might against external threats which undermined stability in the Persian Gulf (*Washington Post*, 24 January 1980); to Asad, the statement read as a clear evidence of American hegemonic aspirations in the region (Safran, 1988: 319).

As a token gesture to the Steadfastness Front's demands, the ICO decided to postpone the opening of the Islamabad Conference to a day after the original date, 27 January, and to widen the agenda to include Palestine and Jerusalem. On 26 January, Asad made an emergency visit to Riyadh as a last-minute attempt to make his positions heard and to convince the Saudis not to submit to the American designs (Safran, 1988: 320). Hopes were raised that Syria might change its decision to boycott the ICO meeting if Asad's Riyadh visit produced a compromise arrangement (*Al-Nahar*, 27 January 1980). In his twenty-four-hour visit, Asad conferred with King Khalid and Crown Prince Fahd, but the two sides failed to see eye-to-eye. According to pro-Syrian Lebanese daily *Al-Anwar*, Asad stressed that the 'enemy of Islam' and the immediate threat to Syria were always the West, the Camp David and Israel, not the Soviet Union, while the defence of Islam should begin with Al-Aqsa mosque of Jerusalem, not Kabul. The report further read that Asad confided that Syria could not consider use of its Soviet-equipped forces against the Russians (29 January 1980). Riyadh's response was clear; the

Saudi leadership maintained that all Muslims, including Syria, should stand on the side of the fellow Afghani Muslims, although—it cautiously added—that was not to say that the Kingdom had preference over the US or the USSR. Although unsuccessful, Asad's last-minute efforts, according to *MECS,* 'indicated Syria's interest in preventing too visible a polarisation along East-West lines in the Arab world, and, more specifically, in allowing such a split to affect Syria's own relations with Saudi Arabia' (1979–1980: 181).

Failing in his mission, President Asad flew back to Damascus and counteracted against the Islamabad Conference by receiving Soviet Foreign Minister Andrei Gromyko on the very day of the Conference. The joint communiqué, issued two days later, expressed strong support for Soviet policies towards the Middle East region, including Afghanistan, while sharply criticising those of the 'imperialist circles' led by the United States (*MECS*, 1979–1980: 779; Karsh, 1991: 124).

While Asad was receiving Gromyko, the ICO meeting in Islamabad opened without participants from Syria and the PDRY. Saudi Arabia actively manoeuvred to steer the conference towards harsh condemnation of the Soviets, and reportedly, even asked the members to break diplomatic ties with Moscow (*Washington Post*, 28 January 1980) as well as calling them to follow its own footstep of boycotting the Moscow Olympic. Nevertheless, the conference ended in a milder tone than what Saudi Arabia originally envisaged, because only with some moderation in the language, Riyadh was able to achieve unanimous endorsement of the final resolutions. The participants with close connections to Moscow attempted to water down resolutions of condemnation, and the Arab states in particular frustrated the Saudis by putting pressure to broaden the conference agenda to include the Egyptian-Israeli peace treaty. The ensuing resolutions emphasised neutrality between the USSR and the US and also narrowed the criticism of the former to the Afghan issue alone.

The conference did, however, bring some qualified but significant gains for the Saudis. Its leading role in the ICO, essentially an organisation of its own creation, was particularly crucial for demonstrating its Islamic credentials at the time when they were tarnished by the latest Grand Mosque incident, and when the Islamic debate in the region was fuelled by political developments in Iran on the eve of the creation of the Islamic Republic. Not unrelated to this issue was the Conference's contribution in justifying the Saudi connection to the US, albeit indirectly. Although this connection had always constituted the core of Saudi security designs since its inception, it had, at the same time, been the Kingdom's point of vulnerability, not only questioned by the domestic audience but often by radical Arab states like Syria. Safran opined:

The Saudis wanted the Soviet Union to be condemned [at the ICO meeting] for some of the very reasons that worried Syria. They wanted precisely to destroy its image as a selfless friend of Arab and Muslim peoples and at least put those who would cooperate with it in no better position than those who cooperated with the United States. The implication was that if the higher interests of Syria justified its cooperation with the Soviet Union, similar interests justified Saudi cooperation with the United States (1988: 320).

This political gain was a consolation for the Kingdom, as the two boycotting countries, Syria and the PDRY, appeared as if they were forming an anti-Saudi axis. According to an unverified report in Cairo weekly *Akhir Sa'ah*, the two countries were supporting anti-royal family covert operations in the Kingdom, particularly those by the Saudi Shi'a population ('Azmah Samitah bayna al-Sa'udiyyah wa Suriyya', 20 February 1980). The report also referred to Palestinian sources, according to which Nasir al-Sa'id[22]—a Saudi dissident who had been a resident in Syria and was now operating in Beirut—had planned to kidnap one of the Saudi ambassadors in the Gulf or a member of the royal family with Syrian and South Yemeni consent. The Saudis, in turn, reportedly threatened the Syrians with curtailment of its financial aid for the Arab Deterrent Forces (ADF; *Quwat al-Rad' al-'Arabiyyah*) in Lebanon. It is difficult to cross-check this information, and it is also highly questionable if the Saudis were in a position to threaten the Syrians on the ADF issue at the time when the Kingdom was virtually on their knees, requesting the Syrians to reconsider their redeployment decision. However, such a report at least conveys the atmosphere of Saudi paranoia concerning the Syrians and the PDRY.

In the following month, Syria reacted cautiously so as not to allow its Soviet connection to undermine its reputation as the committed 'vanguard' of the Arab cause, especially because of the Asad regime's growing domestic troubles and its regional isolation. On 20 February 1980, Syrian Prime Minister 'Abd al-Ra'uf al-Kasm reiterated Syria's reasons for absenting itself from Islamabad that it was only a matter of priority with anti-Israeli concerns coming first. He added, 'The fact that we did not go to Islamabad does not mean we accept the Soviet intervention in Afghanistan'—one of the first expressions of Syria's indirect denouncement of the Soviet policy. He also assured that the Soviets would 'not go beyond Afghanistan to other neighbouring states' (*BBC/SWB/ME*, 22 February 1980), a statement clearly aimed at easing anxiety among the Saudis and other Gulf Arabs. A similar line was repeated the following month by Information Minister Ahmad Iskandar

Ahmad (*BBC/SWB/ME*, 7 March 1980).

Syria and Saudi Arabia's dealings on the Afghan issue highlighted both the conflict of interests in the global arena and the ensuing regional competition. The pattern of some gesture of consultation and acknowledgement of the other side's interests is consistently displayed. The issue also brought to light the fact that the two countries' relationship with the superpowers was a crucial element for their regional and domestic legitimacy, and that was specifically the reason why the debate became so heated between the two. Following the initial reaction to the invasion, increasing Syrian dependence on Moscow and the Saudi fear of expanding Soviet influence in the region accordingly became one of the major points of contest between the two countries.

### *Towards the Syrian-Soviet Treaty of Friendship and Co-operation: The Global Cold War and Syrian-Saudi Relations (April–October 1980)*

The Treaty of Friendship and Co-operation was a standard security pact, which Moscow concluded with its Third World allies.[23] It is less binding than the USSR's defence pacts with the Eastern European allies, and the commitments are somewhat vaguely defined.[24] This partly explains the reason why Moscow's signing of the Treaty with Egypt in 1971 did not stop Sadat from expelling the Soviet military advisers from the country the very next year. Nevertheless, Asad had throughout the 1970s turned down the Soviets' proposal of such a treaty in fear of compromising Syria's independent course of action and tarnishing its image in the non-alignment movement. In fact, Syria was outspokenly critical of both Egypt and Iraq when they signed such treaties with Moscow in 1971 and 1972, respectively. By 1980, the Treaty had come further to alert the regional allies, since the Soviets had cited the mutual security clause in its Friendship Treaty with Afghanistan to justify the invasion. Therefore, the fact that the Syrians began to alter their position on the issue of the Treaty was a clear sign of troubles surrounding Damascus.

By April 1980, Syria's regional and domestic troubles had compelled the Asad regime to abandon its decade-long strategy of guarding its autonomy from Moscow and to seek closer and formalised ties with the superpower. Prominent Syrian officials, including President Asad, began to hint at the possibility of signing a Friendship and Co-operation Treaty with the Soviet Union in public speeches (Karsh, 1991: 125-126). Some ten official visits were exchanged between Damascus and Moscow between April and October 1980, when the Treaty was finally concluded.

In the context of Syrian-Arab Gulf relations in general, and Syrian-Saudi relations in particular, a new trend in Syria's propaganda campaign became noticeable; the frequent allusion to the Syrian-Soviet bilateral treaty went hand-in-hand with verbal attacks against the oil-rich Arab countries' unwillingness—according to Syrian depiction—to commit to the common Arab 'struggle'. In the April summit of the Steadfastness Front, for instance, Prime Minister Kasm explicitly called for more Arab aid to be provided to the principal frontline states, the point reiterated in Khaddam's interview with *Al-Nahar al-Arabi wa al-Duwali* (cited in *MECS*, 1979–1980: 775). Khaddam claimed that the Arab states were making Syria carry the burden of 'confrontation' alone and that Arab aid covered less than a fifth of the burden. He also deplored the shift of interests to Iran and Afghanistan as a sign of abandonment of the anti-Israeli and anti-Camp David 'struggle'. Syria, thus, launched a propaganda campaign of using the 'Soviet card' to serve two related aims: firstly to justify Damascus' new treaty with Moscow as an inevitable consequence of the Gulf Arabs' action, namely the absence of their commitment to the common Arab cause; and secondly to draw out increased sum of financial aid from states like Saudi Arabia, who might consider coughing up an extra contribution as a necessary cost of keeping the Soviet influence in the Middle East further at bay.

The first high-level Arab meeting that accentuated this Syrian tactic was the Amman meeting of Arab Foreign, Economy and Finance Ministers conferred on 6–10 July 1980. To display its confrontationist position, Syria suddenly imposed a new regulation for Arab citizens who wished to travel to the country. According to a broadcast from Riyadh, the Syrian authorities, as of the very day of the Conference, banned Saudi citizens from entering Syria, unless equipped with a valid entrance visa. Hundreds of Saudi holidaymakers found themselves strangled at the Syrian border to their dismay. [25] Meanwhile, at the Conference, Khaddam led the Steadfastness Front and delivered a speech, which called for undivided Arab attention to the Arab-Israeli affairs—or more specifically, the sanction against Egypt—and as an extension, demanded annual military assistance of $5 million to enable Syria to balance the military strength of Israel (*Al-Nahar*, 7 and 16 July 1980). The difference erupted between the Steadfastness Front on the one hand and the camp led by the full-fledged Saudi-Iraqi axis on the other. The harshest criticism towards the Syrian position came from Iraq; Saudi Arabia could happily hide behind its back and kept the lines to the Syrians open (Safran, 1988: 321). After a dramatic gesture of contempt by Khaddam, who at one point 'threatened to slam the doors shut' (*MECS*, 1979–1980: 176; *BBC/SWB/ME*, 7 July 1980), the Saudis advocated a concession to the Syrians by supporting the proposal of setting up a $1.5 billion fund 'for less developed parts of the Arab homeland' (*MECS*, 1979–1980: 218-220).

Immediately after the Amman Conference, on 12–14 July, Rif'at al-Asad visited Saudi Arabia. According to *MECS*, this visit was a 'vigorous attempt at fence-mending' with the Kingdom (1979–1980, 207), but Syrian sources claimed that it was for the purposes of expressing disappointment that no military aid was promised to Syria at the Amman Summit and of briefing the Saudi leadership on President Asad's forthcoming visit to Moscow. When daily *Tishrin* reported on Rif'at's visit on 13 July, a separate article in the same paper called for an upgraded relationship with the USSR (13 July 1980). Referring to Khaddam's speech at the Amman conference, the paper also claimed that there was a clear distinction between those who are 'friends who support us' and those who 'side with our enemies'. By the former, it referred to the USSR, and the latter was a threat against the Gulf states which failed to fund Syria in its 'struggle' against the 'enemies'. During Rif'at's visit to Ta'if, he reportedly expressed Syria's intention to 'qualitatively' develop its relationship with the USSR 'in the near future' (*Al-Nahar*, 15 July 1980). At least on the surface, the visit ended in as amicable a tone as usual, and Prince Fahd stressed Saudi Arabia's objection to Camp David and its support for Syria's role in the confrontation with 'the Zionist enemy'; in his words, 'support for Syria was a duty for all sincere Arabs' (*BBC/SWB/ME*, 16 July 1980). Although *MECS* deduces that 'no significant Syrian-Saudi rapprochement was achieved in the wake of the visit' (1979–1980: 207), Syria might well have won some economic reward through this visit; on the day Rif'at departed the Kingdom, the Syrian authorities abruptly announced the cancellation of its latest regulation that demanded entry visas from Saudi holiday makers as well as a few other Arab citizens.[26]

In the following month, Syria stepped up its effort to strengthen its relations with the USSR, despite the Saudi warning to all Arabs 'to evaluate their relations with the world's great powers' (*BBC/SWB/ME*, 12 August 1980). One of Damascus' gestures towards the Soviets was its promise to restore diplomatic ties with pro-Soviet Ethiopia, an initiative realised by South Yemeni mediation (*BBC/SWB/ME*, 28 August 1980). Furthermore, President Asad took the care to congratulate President Babrak Karmal of Afghanistan on the Afghan National Day on 17 August (*BBC/SWB/ME*, 19 August 1980).

By this stage, it had become clear that Syria's conclusion of a bilateral treaty with the USSR was imminent, and once the decision was fixed in Damascus, the Syrian leadership began to display great care to mitigate the anger and concern of its paymasters in the Gulf. In early September, 'Abd al-Halim Khaddam toured a number of Arab capitals to obtain at least a tacit acquiescence for the treaty, while at the same time Damascus restrained its propaganda campaign against the Gulf countries, especially

Saudi Arabia (*MECS*, 1979–1980: 774, 779). To accentuate Syria's sensitivity to the Saudi opposition, President Asad himself undertook a visit to Saudi Arabia, shortly before he travelled to Moscow on 7 October to sign a twenty-year Treaty of Friendship and Co-operation (*MECS*, 1979–1980: 775). The gesture was reminiscent of Asad's trip to Riyadh earlier in the year on the eve of the Islamabad Conference.

The immediate Saudi reaction to this Syrian move was ambiguous. It is almost impossible to imagine the Saudi leadership to have bought the Syrian argument that the treaty would be beneficial for the wider Arab cause, especially in the 'Arab struggle against Israel' (*BBC/SWB/ME*, 13 October 1980). Curiously, however, the Saudi-based Islamic Development Bank agreed on 8 October, the very day of the signing of the treaty, to provide a loan of $6.4 million for Syria's Aleppo water project (*BBC/SWB/ME*, 21 October 1980). Displeased as they may have been, the Saudis were at least not taken by surprise, having received the high-level visits as well as warning signals from Damascus over several months.

The superpowers' policy towards the Middle East, though by no means the sole determinant factor in Syrian-Saudi relations, constituted one of the core concerns for both parties. The contrasting orientation of Syria and Saudi Arabia—the former inching ever closer towards the USSR, while the latter upheld the long-term strategic ties to the US, sometimes enduring severe criticism from abroad and at home—was further accentuated at the time of the Soviet invasion of Afghanistan. The two publicly led anti- and pro-Soviet camps in the diplomatic scenes of the Arab and Islamic worlds. The relations with the superpowers were sensitive issues for both states. Security was the primary reason, when both states steadily deepened dependence on their respective superpower allies for their arms supply and military co-operation. For Saudi Arabia, which was terrorised by the idea of the Soviet 'encirclement', Syria's position on the Afghan invasion and later its pursuit for the Friendship Treaty could not have been more ill-timed. For Syria, by the same token, how far the Kingdom would allow the US military presence in the Middle East region was an objectionable issue, as will be discussed later on the question of Lebanon and the Iran-Iraq war.

Nevertheless, the superpower factor in Syrian-Saudi relations betrayed the simplistic notion that high politics of global power distribution would determine the dynamics of conflicts and co-operation; for Syria and Saudi Arabia, another key element was at play, the question of legitimacy; the political traditions and the ideological appeal of Arabism and Islam, coloured with the legacy of non-alignment, rendered excessive association with any outside power illegitimate. Hence, Saudi Arabia perpetually struggled to justify its close alliance with Washington, and whenever Washington's policy was seen as harmful to the Arab cause or Muslims' interests, Riyadh's legitimacy was put in question. For the same reason, Syria had striven to maintain a healthy distance from Moscow to avert censure from the Arab camps as well as from the domestic oppositions.

Thus, the question of legitimacy and the notion of 'acceptable' relations with the superpowers complicated the Syrian-Saudi relations. For Saudi Arabia, amicable relations with Syria, one of the most virulently anti-American states and self-styled champion of Arabism, was hoped to exempt it from charges of collaboration with the 'imperialists' in Washington, and Riyadh also attempted to take advantage of Syria's ties with Moscow as a useful channel of communication.[27] Syria, by the same token, at times counted on Riyadh's influence over Washington. Thus, both Riyadh and Damascus despised each other's close alliance with the respective superpowers, but under the circumstances in which these alliances were unlikely to go through tremendous changes, each sought to capitalise on the other side's access to the superpower in the opposing camp. Controversially, Syria's relations with Moscow and Saudi Arabia's with Washington provided all of the following in the post-Camp David era: a source of friction, a basis for co-operation, as well as a weak point where the opponent could needle on.

### Internationalisation of the Lebanese Civil War: Simmering Differences between Damascus and Riyadh (October 1978–October 1980)

Throughout history, Lebanon has held a special place in the Arab world for its cosmopolitanism, for its centrality in Arab cultural activities and intellectualism and at times even as a financial and commercial centre. What happened in Lebanon was bound to have tremendous regional and international ramifications, and the activism of its press, widely circulated throughout the Arab world, made sure this remained the case. In political terms, the significance of the country was further elevated after the 1970 Black September in Jordan; a mass exodus of the Palestinians into Lebanon began, radically altering the delicate sectarian balance in their new host country, whose integrity as a state was at best on precarious foundation. The introduction of the 'Palestinian factor'—the most central question of the Arab-Israeli conflict—into Lebanon, the ensuing outbreak of the civil war and Israel's military ambition towards this divided neighbour, coupled with the Lebanese factions' propensity to invite external patrons, all contributed to assign Lebanon a principal place in the Arab political debate.

The intensification of fighting in Lebanon since the autumn of 1978 and the subsequent growth of Arab interests in the war were, in a limited sense, by-products of the Camp David Accords. When the Accords failed to stipulate for a Palestinian state in any form, it dawned on the Christian Lebanese factions that their unwelcome guests were to stay in their country for the foreseeable future and no external power was extending any help to resolve the Palestinian issue in Lebanon. With this ominous realisation, the Christians stepped up their war efforts from sporadic fighting into deadly prolonged battles (Snider, 1979a: 205). In addition, Camp David directly fed Israel's ambition towards weak and divided Lebanon; now that the most powerful Arab country was neutralised, the Likud government could confidently pursue its aim of subjugating the northern neighbour. Since the March 1978 operation in South Lebanon—Israel's biggest military campaign since the eruption of the civil war in 1975, Menachem Begin's government had steadily consolidated its control of the South, establishing a 'security belt', in its own terminology. In this strip of land, there was no stopping of the Maronite Major, Sa'd Haddad, Israel's local protégé, from massacring Lebanese Muslim and Palestinian civilians despite the new deployment of the United Nations Interim Force in Lebanon (UNIFIL). Also, the Israelis began to strengthen their ties with the rightist Lebanese Front in Beirut with the aim of concluding a formal alliance. The deepening of Israeli involvement in Lebanon marked the start of internationalisation of the Lebanese conflict after Camp David.

As discussed in the Introduction, Lebanon did not fall into Saudi Arabia's traditional sphere of influence—unlike, for instance, the smaller states of the Arab Gulf or Yemen—but the ramifications of the Lebanese conflict on inter-Arab relations had made the Saudis act decisively in the early years of the civil war. This diplomatic activism was facilitated by their close relations with traditional Lebanese notables, particularly those from the Sunni Muslim families. For decades, the Saudis had been cherishing their relationship with Sa'ib Salam, a Beiruti Sunni notable and several times prime minister of Lebanon, who was said to be enjoying the deepest friendship with the Saudi leadership figures.[28] Personal connections between the Saudi and Lebanese leaderships were not limited to the Sunni Muslim circles. Among the Maronite Christians, with whom the Saudis shared the adherence to rigid conservatism, Pierre Jumayyil maintained especially close ties with the Saudis. Even Kamal Junblat, whose leftist revolutionary orientation in general and his periodic criticism of Saudi policy in particular were despised by Riyadh, was always welcomed there on his visits and allegedly enjoyed genuinely warm relationship with some Saudi princes (Bannerman, 1979: 117-120). When the Palestinians—namely Yasir 'Arafat and other al-Fath leaders, who had long cultivated amicable relations with the Saudi leadership—entered the Lebanese political scene as principal players, the Saudis' stake in the Lebanese conflict rose sharply. To this day, close personal connections with leading figures in Lebanese politics have served as one of the main tools of Saudi Arabia's Lebanese policy. The two countries also maintained strong economic ties; in the mid-1970s, Saudi Arabia was the primary destination of Lebanon's industrial and fruit exports. It also accounted for the bulk of Lebanon's tourist income and overseas employment (Petran, 1987: 151).

For Syria, in comparison, a strong interest in the Lebanese affairs was a matter of inevitability. As Seale put:

> Syria's interest in Lebanese affairs did not arouse surprise in either country, for in the general perception Syria and Lebanon were members of the same body...In culture, religious diversity, ethnic background, spoken dialect, even in what they ate and drank, Syrians and Lebanese were much of a piece. The populations of the two countries were thoroughly intermingled, with countless families straddling the French-drawn frontier...by and large Syrians and Lebanese knew that they belonged together (1990: 268-269).

Thus, for both Saudi Arabia and Syria, the exacerbation of the Lebanese conflict was no marginal concern. Lebanon was destined to develop into one of the core agenda in Syrian-Saudi relations and when it did, the two countries supported opposing groups and each envisaged very different pictures of future Lebanon. Saudi Arabia had traditionally supported the conservative Maronites and the Sunni notables, as it interpreted the Lebanese conflict to be one between the right and the international left (Yegnes, 1981: 109-110; Petran, 1987: 169). The tie with the former, however, was to undergo tremendous strains in the 1980s, as the bloodshed between the Christian militia and the Palestinians increased in scope and frequency. Riyadh cherished its relations with the PLO, particularly with Yasir 'Arafat's al-Fath faction, but it also had to manipulate the PLO with great care; the Saudis did not, for instance, wish to see the PLO hijacking Lebanon's politics altogether—one of the fewer points on which the Saudis agreed with Damascus, but for different reasons. Riyadh wanted the PLO moderate but sufficiently disgruntled with their situation in Lebanon so as to be able to steer them into accepting a separate peace agreement with Israel as a follow-up to Camp David—a scenario which would jeopardise Syria's interests.

Syria's strongest Lebanese connection, in contrast, was with the Shi'a community, now mobilised by cleric Musa al-Sadr's Amal (acronym for

*Afwaj al-Muqawamah al-Lubnaniyyah*) movement. Among the Palestinian groups, Damascus not only fostered al-Saiqah, a group essentially of Syrian creation, but also the leftist PLO factions—such as Na'if Hawatimah's Democratic Front for the Liberation of Palestine (DFLP) and George Habash's People's Front for the Liberation of Palestine (PFLP). Although the alliance between Syria and various factions shifted dramatically throughout the civil war, as a general trend, the progressive forces were Damascus' more natural allies; meanwhile, its relations with the Christian militias and 'Arafat were to deteriorate to the level of open military clashes, as will be examined thoroughly in later chapters.

Not only did Riyadh and Damascus ally with opposite sides of the warring factions in Lebanon, but they disagreed on what role these two capitals should play in resolving the civil conflict. On the surface, the two capitals appeared to be complementing each others' role: Syria maintained an overwhelming military presence in Lebanon with endorsement from the Arab League under the name of the ADF; Saudi Arabia undertook to finance Syria's military operation; and both played pivotal roles in sponsoring cease-fire negotiations between the warring factions. In reality, however, Riyadh was growing uneasy about Syria's role. It was frustrated by the Syrians' inability to bring a quick end to the fighting despite the enormous size of their military presence in the country, reaching some 35,000 by the late 1970s. Despite their ineffectuality, Syrian monopoly of Lebanese affairs was reaching a dangerous level, allowing no other Arab capital to balance Damascus. One of Saudi Arabia's long-term aims in Lebanon, therefore, was to curb Syria's influence, which in essence meant restoration of Lebanon's sovereignty and stability and withdrawal of all foreign troops from the country—both Israeli and Syrian.

Damascus, on the other hand, had no intention of relinquishing its overlordship, and, in its view, turning this sister country into a de facto protectorate only served the higher cause of Arab unity. According to this logic, it was a pan-Arab responsibility to finance Syria's military contribution in keeping Lebanon intact, especially at a time when the Jewish 'enemy' was extending its reach into the country. In the late 1970s, Syria's aim, in relation to the Saudi role in Lebanese affairs, was to extract as much financial support from the Kingdom without allowing the paymaster to translate the financial muscle into political leverage.

Thus, Lebanon was destined to be a factor of contention in Syrian-Saudi relations—as was the case with the aforementioned questions of the post-Camp David regional order, Gulf security and the relationship with the superpowers. In later years, however, Lebanon came to epitomise what these two states were capable of achieving through their co-operation; the road to the 1989 Ta'if Accord, which officially marked the end of the fifteen-year civil war, was by no means smooth, or even amicable, but its conclusion was a monument to a Saudi-Syrian joint effort. This section outlines the roots of Syrian-Saudi differences on Lebanon in the first few years of the post-Camp David era and the dynamics which forced the two actors to work together despite those differences.

In the post-Camp David era, the first occasion in which Syria and Saudi Arabia were compelled to co-ordinate their Lebanese policy arrived in the Bait al-Din Conference on 15–17 October 1978. Lebanese President Elias Sarkis and his solely Christian delegation turned to the Gulf states—the paymasters of the ADF—for assistance in convening an Arab conference dedicated to the latest crisis in Lebanon. The call brought together the Foreign Ministers of all states whose troops participated in the ADF: Syria, Saudi Arabia, Kuwait, Sudan and the United Arab Emirates as well as Lebanese representatives of the main political parties. The resolution of the Conference endorsed the decisions reached in 1976 Riyadh summit and established a 'follow-up (*mutaba'a*)' committee comprising Syria, Saudi Arabia and Kuwait—replacing the four-sided one, which included Egypt and established at the 1976 Riyadh summit. Thanks to Saudi persuasion, the Lebanese Front observed a truce at least while the conference was held (Petran, 1987: 248), although the final outcome of this Conference never went beyond an agreement on paper. Sa'ud al-Faisal—who stopped in Damascus on the way to and from Bait al-Din—must have been confident enough of the Saudi achievement when he expressed 'optimism' in his private meeting with Asad (*Al-Nahar,* 18 October 1978). The event highlighted the indispensability of the two countries, Syria and Saudi Arabia, in bringing about any dialogue between the Lebanese factions, a reminder of which repeatedly appeared in later years. Also, Saudi Arabia attempted to prevent Syria from having a free hand in Lebanon through an increase in the other Arab countries' troop contribution to the ADF (*Arab Report and Record,* 16–31 October 1978). To start with, the Saudi contingent replaced the Syrians in sensitive areas in East Beirut, where clashes between Syrian and Maronite forces were the fiercest prior to the Bait al-Din Conference (*Arab Report,* 14 March 1979; Fisk, 1990: 144).

The Saudi manoeuvre to prevent total Syrian dominance on the Lebanese ground ended in miserable failure shortly afterwards; non-Syrian forces of the ADF, including the Saudis, began withdrawing from Lebanon—despite the exacerbation of the conflict in mid-January 1979, triggered by Israel's biggest incursion into South Lebanon. By April, Syria had emerged as the sole Arab state assigned to maintain order and security in the country. The nominal purpose of Arab withdrawal was to put pressure on the Lebanese government to carry out the army reforms as defined in the Bait al-Din agreement and to re-establish its authority over the entire country (Petran, 1987: 250), but, in the Saudi case, there was an additional reason; the 1,500-man Saudi contingent was recalled on 28 February and repositioned to strengthen the Kingdom's southern border as preparation for countering the advancing PDRY forces (Holden and Johns, 1981: 501; Safran, 1988: 277). The announcement was received not unfavourably by the Syrians, who saw a window of opportunity to obtain a free hand in the military operations, and even better, to have their costs shouldered by others. After the withdrawal of all non-Syrian Arab forces and the Arab League's extension of the ADF mandate from April to June, the Syrian Prime Minister, Muhammad Ali al-Halabi, promptly made a press announcement that the ADF forces should remain in Lebanon, i.e., that the *Syrian* forces should (*BBC/SWB/ME*, 20 April 1979).

The conclusion of the Egyptian-Israeli Peace Treaty in March 1979 fuelled Israel's ambition towards Lebanon, and Syria's militancy increased accordingly, resulting in what is known as the aerial war over Lebanon. By the time the Lebanese President had called on the Arab League for a summit meeting to discuss the Lebanese crisis, however, the entire region was consumed with the other, wider affairs of Egypt and Iran. Syria, although displeased by the degree of autonomy the Lebanese President displayed, saw the summit as an opportunity to press, yet again, for broadening its agenda to anti-Sadat measures. Saudi Arabia, on the other hand, was keen to avoid just that and it was also anxious not to be caught up between warring sides on the Lebanese issue itself. Hence, Saudi Arabia made its attendance of the Tunis summit in November 1979 conditional on prior understanding among the PLO, Syria, and the Lebanese government (*MECS*, 1979–1980: 171; Safran, 1988: 315). This assurance was most likely sought first during Sa'ud al-Faisal's meeting with President Asad on 23 September 1979 when he also met PLO and al-Fath representatives in Damascus, and it was most probably granted upon Saudi Prince Abdallah's surprise visit to Damascus on 10 November, the day the Saudi government announced its willingness to attend the summit (*Al-Nahar*, 11 November 1979). In this state of disarray, it was no surprise that the Tunis Summit Conference on 20 November bore little fruit as far as the Lebanese issue was concerned. The PLO presence in Lebanon was implicitly endorsed much to the disgruntlement of the Lebanese government; the latter's gain was limited to a grant of $2 billion over a five-year period, half of which was to finance reconstruction projects in the South. Saudi Arabia, yet again, was the primary financier of this 'appeasement' (Safran, 1988: 317).

By the end of 1979, Syria had lost credibility in the Arab world because of its inability to contain the Lebanese crisis, notwithstanding the massive Arab funding. As a result, Damascus grew keener to distance itself from the military and political quagmire in Lebanon (Avi-Ran, 1991: 108). This change in Syrian strategy was chiefly out of the necessity to counter the worsening domestic crisis, where the Islamic oppositions' military campaign against the regime was gaining momentum. Furthermore, the Lebanese crisis by this stage posed a possibility of direct military embroilment with Israeli forces, which the Syrians had been desperate to avoid. Consequently, from January 1980, Syria began removing some of its forces from the coastal strips and Beirut and concentrating them in the Biqa' valley, which would enable it to withstand a possible Israeli military action against the Syrian mainland and to rapidly deploy them to quell the domestic oppositions if necessary (Rabinovich, 1985: 113). Accordingly, the Lebanese army and the Palestinian militias were assigned to fill the vacuum left by the Syrian forces (Avi-Ran, 1991: 108).

Although the withdrawal was a sign of Syrian weakness, ironically its announcement resulted in added legitimacy to its military presence in Lebanon and, by extension, dramatic improvement on Syria's standing in Lebanon and, more generally, in the Arab world. The sudden announcement from Damascus was met with dismay and fear for further breakdown of order, even by the harshest critics of Syrian policy (Rabinovich, 1985: 101; Fisk, 1990: 141). On 13 February, after Syria had informed the UN of its intention of redeployment, Saudi Prince 'Abdallah travelled to Damascus to discuss this issue (*Al-Nahar*, 14 February 1980). Asad remained adamant on his decision, but Saudi Arabia pledged to grant whatever financial aid was needed for Syria's continued presence in Lebanon (*MECS*, 1979–1980: 773). By then, Syria's decision on redeployment began to take an appearance of diplomatic brinkmanship, aimed at rescuing the legitimacy of its presence in the neighbouring country and at obtaining additional material aid to maintain the presence. The improvement in Syria's bargaining position can be seen, for instance, in Khaddam's interview on 12 April 1980 after Syrian forces began returning to previously assigned stations. He took the occasion to complain about the insufficiency of Arab aid and demanded, not only moral support, but also increased material and political aid: 'This [Arab] aid, although important, does not constitute a fifth of the military burdens and their economic requisites that are endured by Syria…We feel that all the Arabs must support us' (*BBC/SWB/ME*, 15 April 1980). The whole incident surrounding Syria's withdrawal was one of the first displays of Syrian-Saudi tug-of-war over the ADF; Saudi Arabia aspired to use its funding as a leverage to discipline Syria, while Syria repeatedly complained of the insufficient commitment by the financiers (Qindil, 1980d).

Lebanon began to unveil another worrying aspect for Saudi Arabia with the outbreak of the Iran-Iraq war. On 5 October, a bomb exploded in the

Saudi Embassy in Beirut. An organisation which called itself 'Martyr Abu Ja'far Organisation' first claimed responsibility for the incident, followed by another secret organisation in support of Iran. The latter group threatened that unless Saudi Arabia declared complete neutrality in the Iran-Iraq war, further attacks would follow against Ambassador Ali al-Sha'ir and Crown Prince Fahd (*BBC/SWB/ME*, 8 October 1980). Three days later, more explosions took place outside the Saudi Embassy, at the office of Royal Jordanian Airlines and the Swiss ambassador's residence. An Organisation calling itself 'the Iraqi Mujahidin Movement' claimed responsibility.[29] Although these military campaigns in Lebanon had more to do with the Gulf affairs—i.e., the protagonists' displeasure with the Saudi support for Iraq, the fact that they concentrated in Lebanon had some implications on the Syrian-Saudi relations. There are suggestions that the culprits, presumably from the Shi'a, carried out these campaigns of violence with Syrian acquiescence if not active endorsement (personal communications, Damascus, 1999). As far as Riyadh was concerned, even if the Syrians had no prior knowledge, they were the only forces in Lebanon who could have prevented it, and therefore, they were at least partially responsible for the damage caused. They came to question what the Saudi gains were in funding the ADF if the Syrians were not going to co-operate to safeguard minimum Saudi interests in the country. Thus, the weight of the Lebanese factor steadily increased in Syrian-Saudi relations partly through its linkage to the wider developments in the Gulf.

During the first two years after the Camp David agreement, the civil war in Lebanon intensified, and, in tandem, points of Syrian-Saudi differences surfaced. The roots of disagreement were complex and intertwined: Damascus and Riyadh each supported various Lebanese factions and the Palestinians, who were at odds with each other, although the local conflict never bore the appearance of a 'pro-Saudi camp vs. pro-Syrians' conflict. The relationship with the PLO in Lebanon later developed into a particularly sensitive subject between Damascus and Riyadh, as will be discussed in the following chapters. The most heated debate between the two capitals in the early years of the post-Camp David era was conducted over the question of the ADF funding and the Syrian military role in Lebanon. When the then Saudi ambassador to the UN, Jamil Barudi, was quoted as saying that the Syrian troops in Lebanon were being 'misused' and that President Hafiz al-Asad was a 'crook', those words may have reflected the majority feeling of the Saudi leadership.[30]

Although the Saudis were clearly apprehensive of the Syrian supremacy in Lebanon, they made no attempt to contend with the Syrian influence, in stark contrast to the other Middle Eastern states—such as Egypt, Iraq and later Iran. Instead, Riyadh merely promoted the Bait al-Din follow-up committee in hope that it would somehow keep a tight rein on Syria's activities in Lebanon. For the Syrians, the committee at times served as a useful tool when they needed an Arab cover to legitimise their Lebanese operations, but the rest of the time, they laid obstacles one after another before the committee's tasks with the aim of eliminating its efficacy. As a result, Saudi Arabia opted to co-operate with the Syrians sometimes at the expense of its own policy goals. It mostly failed to translate its financial leverage to political influence, and, as a result, displayed its willingness to bend over backwards to meet Syria's needs.

Syrian-Saudi co-operation in Lebanon—which was achieved in large part through Saudi compromise—rested on several related factors: 1) Syria's overwhelming military might on the ground; 2) Saudi Arabia's inability to replace Syria's role or to appoint a more suitable actor should the Syrians withdraw from Lebanon; 3) Syria's ability to manipulate local Lebanese political actors; 4) absence, in contrast, of a solid alliance between Riyadh and any local political group; 5) Syria's appeal to the 'pan-Arab' obligation in countering the Israeli threat; and 6) curtailment of Saudi influence in the wider Arab region in the aftermath of the Camp David, due to the rise in status of the anti-Camp David voices. In the following decade, leading towards the Ta'if Accords, these conditions, as well as the sources of Saudi-Syrian differences, were to undergo considerable changes, as will be discussed in the remaining chapters.

## Conclusion

Throughout the 1970s and the 1980s, Syrian and Saudi Foreign Ministers, 'Abd al-Halim Khaddam and Sa'ud al-Faisal frequently held meetings, and on one such occasion, they were described as '[p]hysically, emotionally and politically…a diplomatic odd couple,' in reference to their markedly contrasting mannerism and personalities (*Time,* 2 August 1982). The statement could not have been truer regarding not just the foreign ministers but more generally, the orientation of the two capitals, Damascus and Riyadh, in the aftermath of the Camp David Accords. The two states held incompatible viewpoints on all major issues of significance to the Arab region during the first two years of the post-Camp David era, each issue further deepening the gulf that roughly divided the Arab world into two camps, one led by Damascus and the other by Riyadh.

Syria and Saudi Arabia both entered the post-Camp David era of inter-Arab politics with an acute sense of crisis. The fluidity of the regional situation engulfed the two into worrisome uncertainty, while the regimes of both states, against the background of regional turbulence, were faced with the most serious domestic opposition. Amidst the confusion, nevertheless, the issues which were to dominate the Arab regional concerns and, by extension, the Syrian-Saudi relations, gradually began to shape the post-Camp David regional order in the first two years; those issues were the question of Arab-Israeli conflict, position of Egypt in the Arab world, instability in the Arab Gulf, the Soviet incursion into Afghanistan and the intensification of the Lebanese civil war. With the aim of isolating the core issues surrounding Syrian-Saudi relations, this chapter outlined how these specific issues were central to the dealings between the two states, why the two adopted mutually conflicting positions on them, and how, in consequence, the entire Arab world became polarised into two camps.

As an introduction to the remaining chapters—which will demonstrate the dynamics in which neither of the two actors could dispense with co-operation from the other side despite their apparent differences—the analyses in this chapter introduced decisive factors that induced the two to work together or, at the very least, to avoid burning bridges. At an apparent level, Syrian-Saudi differences surfaced over concrete issues of the Camp David Accords, status of Egypt in the Arab world, relationship with Iran's revolutionary government, alignment to the global superpowers, and approach to the Lebanese Civil War. At a closer look, however, there were more fundamental, underlying dynamics at play which conditioned the two states policy towards each other; they were the political significance of Arab financial aid to non-oil-producing states, the precariousness of regime legitimacy and profusion of cross border acts of sabotage in the Arab world. All of these elements, in a distant way, were by-products of the existence of shared political identities in the Arab world, however illusionary the 'commonality' might have been.

One of the apparent reasons why Damascus desired an amicable relationship with Riyadh was its need to secure a regular flow of cash from the oil-rich state. At the Baghdad Summits and conferences on Lebanon, as well as on occasions of formal visits by prominent personnel, speculations abounded as to how much aid Damascus extracted from Riyadh. Salamé elucidates the role of oil aid in Arab politics, a suggestive reading of Damascus' calculation and apparent success in cultivating the financial channel, much to Riyadh's apprehension:

It is only natural for a state, or a group of states, to seek some influence over neighbouring, well-endowed and poorly defended ones, *especially when cultural and other themes could be manipulated to this effect*. It is as 'natural' to see the latter trying to limit, as far as possible, this pressure. A 'natural' result of the whole process is a certain amount of frustration and misgivings. How non-Gulf Arabs view Gulf oil is indeed a very sensitive issue in contemporary Arab politics (1988b: 240, emphasis added).

In the case of Syrian-Saudi relations, the key question lies in the extent to which Riyadh succeeded in translating its ability to 'finance the Arab cause' into the political leverage it endeavoured to acquire over unruly aid-recipients like Syria. The answer in the immediate aftermath of the Camp David was next to none, although, as the following chapters will explore, the two countries' economic situation later raised the importance of economic factor in the bilateral relations.

Thus, whether Riyadh fulfilled its commitment to the 'Baghdad Summit stipend' or the ADF funding came to be seen as a reasonably reliable index—as opposed to a key determinant—of the health and balance of the bilateral relations. The fundamental concerns for both actors lay as much in the question of agenda setting in Arab politics as in financial or economic matters. Numerous questions were being asked in the Arab world in the turmoil of the new Camp David order: should the political development in Iran be considered a greater threat to stability in the Arab world than Israel's incursion into Lebanon?; is an alignment with Soviet Union more legitimate for an Arab regime than that with the United States?; and what constitutes a reasonable relationship with Egypt, who 'betrayed' the Arab cause? In short, an Arab state which was capable of imposing on the wider Arab world its preferred answers to these questions was placed in the strongest position in the regional order.

The peculiarity of the post-Camp David era lay in the fact that Damascus and Riyadh, for the first time in the history of Arab politics, became the two rival centres in Arab divisions. Previously, Cairo or Baghdad performed such roles, and Damascus and Riyadh merely strove to maximise their influence and self-interest by aligning with one or the other of the more powerful regional actors. The period after September 1978, in contrast, was an era of power vacuum in Arab politics; as Egypt withdrew itself from the Arab ranks and Iraq immersed itself deeper into the conflict with Iran, '[n]o single state had the capacity to engage in extensive revisionism or achieve a hegemonic position' (Noble, 1991: 51-52). A rare condition was thus created in which the strife for regional leadership slid into the hands of second fiddles: Riyadh and Damascus. The two were undoubtedly major regional actors in the emerging multi-polar structure of the Arab system, but their strengths were restricted and qualified in their individual way—the limitations ranging from a precarious economic base and an absence of domestic legitimacy to troubled foreign relations with countries outside the Arab region. Burdened by their weaknesses, Syria and Saudi Arabia, instead of opting for open competition, chose to continue to work with each other, *albeit* uncasily—an option available to them largely because their sources of power, both material and ideological, were more complementary than competing. This chapter, seen in this light, was a tale of how Syria and Saudi Arabia were elevated from the position of second-rank in the Arab regional system, and, in the process, sharpened the differences over the most dominant issues of contest in the region.

# 3

# HEADING OPPOSING CAMPS
## The primacy of Saudi Arabia
## (October 1980–September 1982)

With the outbreak of the Iran-Iraq war in September 1980, polarisation of the Arab world in the post-Camp David era became consolidated after the initial two-year transition period. By October 1980, Saudi Arabia and Syria had each established themselves as leaders of the two major rivalling camps, the former in the context of Saudi-Jordanian-Iraqi axis and the latter by heading the Steadfastness and Confrontation Front. Although this overall pattern was to prevail roughly throughout the 1980s with varying degree of disagreement, the period of October 1980–June 1982 stands out in that it observed uncharacteristically pro-active and assertive Saudi foreign policy-making.

Saudi Arabia has historically favoured a low-keyed and detached approach to regional disputes for fear of being drawn into such conflicts against its will. In the 1970s, this stance was gradually abandoned, partly because of the strong personality of King Faisal, but more importantly due to the Kingdom's sudden growth in wealth, which ensued greater political influence (Dawisha, 1979: 129-130). During the first two years of the Iran-Iraq war, manifestation of Saudi Arabia's growing confidence culminated, not only in its mediation efforts between the warring actors but also in its assumption of a leadership role in the resolution of a broader regional conflict, namely the Arab-Israeli conflict. Several factors contributed to this development. With Egypt still isolated in the Arab world, Iraq consumed in its war effort against Iran, and Syria embroiled in the Lebanese quagmire, a rare window of opportunity opened for Saudi Arabia to fill the vacuum of a regional leadership role. Coincidentally, the new US administration of Ronald Reagan was only too glad to see Riyadh do so at the time when it lost its precious Gulf ally as a result of the Iranian Revolution. Reagan was famously quoted: 'I believe the Saudis are the key to spreading peace throughout the Middle East' (*MEI,* 13 November; *Business Week,* 16 November 1981). Finally, an attempt to create a Gulf security alliance headed by Saudi Arabia, a scheme which theoretically existed since King Faisal's era, was steadily taking concrete shape, to be materialised in the creation of the GCC in May 1981.

In contrast, Syria's position in the region was significantly weakened by its inability to overcome regional isolation. The Steadfastness Front, which in the previous period coalesced around anti-Sadat policies, was displaying signs of disintegration. It had become highly questionable whether the Front would ever mature into an effective unitary bloc. Outside the Front, Syria's support for Iran in the war against Iraq was considered 'un-Arab', while its growing association with the USSR, an 'aggressor' in the Afghan conflict in the majority Arab view, was branded as 'un-Islamic' (*MECS,* 1980–1981: 242). Furthermore, its inability to bring a swift end to the conflict in Lebanon—despite its persistent demands for Arab financial commitments—severely cast doubt on its credibility as a frontline state. The bellicose Likud government of Israel was growing ever more confident in the backdrop of Arab divisions, thus threatening to expand its operation in Lebanon at Syria's doorsteps. Domestically, the Asad regime was encountering the most organised and widespread opposition it had known, mainly led by the Islamists.

Thus, in the period under review, the power balance tipped in favour of Saudi Arabia against Syria. This, however, is not to say that the aforementioned clash of interests could be contained solely through total surrender of the weaker actor to the will of the more dominant. The tug-of-war between Riyadh and Damascus was a delicate and complex manoeuvre. Curiously, in the major issues of contest in this period, Saudi Arabia's ambition was frequently hindered by Syria's 'nuisance' power, or its ability to sabotage joint Arab action, and if Syria were to comply with Saudi wishes, it would often be rewarded. When, however, Syria over-stretched Saudi patience, it incurred a heavy loss; it was left to its own devices to confront Israeli aggression. Ironically, such isolation only pushed Syria to closer alliance with Iran, the main source of security threat for the Kingdom. When Iranian hostility against Iraq and its supporters—namely Saudi Arabia and Kuwait—gained momentum, Riyadh had to adopt a policy of 'carrot and stick' towards Damascus, the only potential window of communication with Iran. The investigation of this period will, therefore, highlight aspects of Saudi dependence on Syria, even at a time when the Kingdom enjoyed unprecedented political influence in the region. By so doing, the value of Syrian-Saudi relations in the Saudi eyes will be underlined, which emanated not so much from dynamics of their own, but from the developments outside their control, especially in Israel or Iran. The fact that Syria and Saudi Arabia, nevertheless, were indispensable to each other in pursuit of their individual policy goals was witnessed in the consistent absence of explicit criticism of each other even at the high point of disagreements.

This chapter will first examine the role of Syrian and Saudi opposition groups in Syrian-Saudi relations with special emphasis on Saudi Arabia's relationship with the Syrian Muslim Brotherhood. These Islamists' campaign nearly brought down the Asad regime during the period under review in this chapter, and in tandem, overseas support for this Syrian opposition group became a determining factor in the Asad regime's regional policy. This latter point was never more prevalent than in the Amman Arab Summit in November 1980 and the subsequent Syrian-Jordanian border crisis, the next two topics of discussion in this chapter. During the border crisis and the ensuing Syrian-Israeli Missile Crisis, Saudi Arabia undertook the role of a mediator and left a mark as an emerging regional leader. Such newly gained confidence incited the Kingdom to launch its own version of a Middle East peace plan, an ambition that surpassed its capability. No other than Syria's veto led to the abortion of the first Saudi peace initiative in Fez, which served to confirm the limitation of Saudi regional influence. The chapter closes with the examination of the 1982 Israeli invasion of Lebanon and the second Fez Summit as the peak of Saudi prestige and the lowest point of Syria's regional influence; the analyses of these events elucidate the building blocks of Saudi and Syrian regional power and the two actors' expectation of each other.

### The Domestic Opposition Groups and Syrian-Saudi Relations

The ascendance of Islamic opposition in Syria under Hafiz al-Asad era gained momentum in the mid-1970s, when the regime's unpopular intervention in the Lebanese civil war, rampant corruption, stagnation of economic growth, unpopular support for Soviet invasion of Afghanistan all contributed to brewing discontent in the wider public. The Islamists' most oft-used rhetoric against the Asad regime was on its sectarian nature; they claimed that power was concentrated in the hands of 'Alawi minority. The majority Sunnis' suspicion of Asad's sectarian orientation heightened with the first signs of the regime's support for Khomeini and his movement. When the regime continued to side with Khomeini after the Iranian Revolution—notwithstanding the outbreak of the Iran-Iraq war—the Sunni Muslim-led opposition consolidated its conviction that denominational sympathy governed Asad's decision-making.

The Syrian government had at various times accused Jordan, Iraq and the US of being the main foreign patrons of the Syrian Muslim Brotherhood (*Al-Safir,* 2 March 1982; Seale, 1990: 331-337), which constituted the core of the Islamists' alliance against the regime. These countries allegedly supplied weapons, offered the use of military training camps and haven to those who fled Syria. Another source adds to this list of supporters, the Egyptian Muslim Brotherhood, Kuwait and Saudi Arabia (Hinnebusch, 1990: 290).

As to Saudi Arabia, abundance of reports testify to the financial channel linking it to the Brotherhood (e.g. Qindil, 1980d), but the extent of support has not been documented, and Syria rarely finger-pointed at the Kingdom in public statements. This is partly due to the fact that the Saudi government did not enact an official government policy of funding the Syrian oppositions, but rather, merely turned blind eye to private Saudi donations.[1] One group of such donors came from the Syrian community in Saudi Arabia who had immigrated in thousands since the 1960s. It consisted mainly of traditional landowners and entrepreneurs who had not only suffered material losses under the Ba'thi nationalisation measures but also political persecution for their affiliation to the Muslim Brotherhood, which, together with the Nasirists, formed the Bath's chief political opponent in the 1960s (Hinnebusch, 1982a: 157-161). The most exemplary of such Syrians is the *al-Khumasiyyah,* a group of five industrialists who established their names in Saudi textile industry (*MEI,* 13 February 1981). Ma'ruf al-Dawalibi, one of the five and ex-Prime Minister from the People's Party, for instance, was known for strong Islamic inclinations.[2] He later became known for his Muslim activism and affiliation to the Brotherhood. In the Kingdom, where he became a pillar of the expatriate Syrian community, Dawalibi has served as an adviser to the royal court and allegedly engineered covert operations against the Syrian Ba'th with Saudi help (Hinnebusch, 1988: 42). In the mid-1970s, he temporarily returned to Syria to seek a political role amongst the oppositions; one account goes so far as to claim that Saudi Arabia made an unsuccessful attempt to convince Asad to appoint Dawalibi Prime Minister in the 1977 cabinet reshuffle (Salamé, 1980: 667).

The second group of Muslim Brotherhood supporters in Saudi Arabia consisted of Saudi nationals who had relatives in Syria through marriage or extended family connections,[3] while those in the third category were simply driven by their religious commitments; they allegedly ranged from members of religious authority[4] to conservative royal family members, but the details are not known. There have been rumours that illegal publication of the Brotherhood was allowed to circulate in the Kingdom (e.g. Abd-Allah, 1995: 110) and that some members of the Saudi government participated in the Brotherhood's conferences held in Europe,[5] but few conclusive reports are available on these subjects.

Such Saudi policy of supporting the Syrian Muslim Brotherhood was a complex operation with numerous motives. The fact that the flow of aid took place through private channels allowed the Saudi regime to divert direct criticisms or reprisals from Asad. At the same time, Riyadh sought to translate its Brotherhood-connection into leverage over Asad; it was one of the means to remind Asad of Riyadh's political weight, when he adopted policies harmful to Saudi interests. The ability to finance oppositions of neighbouring countries has been an important foreign policy tool in Saudi thinking (Salamé, 1980: 660), although the success of this strategy in yielding political influence has not always been clear-cut. At the very least, the strategy of maintaining open communication with opposition groups of neighbouring countries has allowed Riyadh to diversify its options and minimise the element of surprise in the event of a coup d'état or an equivalent change in neighbour governments.

Also, the Saudi connection to the Brotherhood can be seen in part as a balancing act against Damascus' fostering of the Saudi oppositions; the Saudi communists and Shi'a oppositions were based in Damascus until the early 1990s when they moved to London—a development which reflected the stability in Syrian-Saudi relations after 1990. The examples are Saudi Hizbullah, the Organisation of Islamic Revolution in the Arabian Peninsula (*Munadhdhamah al-Thawrah al-Islamiyyah fi al-Jazirah al-Arabiyyah*), re-named in 1991 the Reformist Movement in the Arabian Peninsula (*Al-Harakah al-Islahiyyah fi al-Jazirah al-'Arabiyyah*) [6] and various communists.[7]

The Syrian oppositions' Islamic credentials appeared to have been secondary in Saudi considerations; the Saudis were extending aid to Syrian leftist oppositions as well,[8] which was hardly surprising in view of the fact that they had for years been funding the Christians and the Palestinians alike in Lebanon. Even in terms of concrete policies, there was little co-ordination between Riyadh and the Syrian oppositions. Thus, Saudi policy towards the Syrian opposition groups was essentially a product of tactical calculations within the overall strategy towards the Asad regime.

Nevertheless, when Asad's conflict with the Islamists intensified, the Saudi leadership was faced with a dilemma; co-operation with Asad was imperative for regional stability—and by extension the Kingdom's own security—but overlooking his regime's brutality against the Islamists might cast doubt on the Saudi regime's commitment to Islam, its major pillar of legitimacy. Saudi Arabia, thus resorted to publicly maintaining friendly relations with the Asad regime, but behind the scenes, applying pressure on Damascus to change its policies towards the Islamic opposition. For

instance, when the Brotherhood exploded a bomb in al-Azbakiyyah area
of central Damascus, taking some two hundred lives, King Khalid sent a
public message of condolence to Asad (*Al-Nahar*, 5 December 1981).
Meanwhile, when King Hussain visited Damascus in August 1979, the
King reportedly passed on to Asad messages of Saudi dissatisfaction with
'what is befalling the Sunnis, and particularly the Muslim Brotherhood at
the hands of the Syrian government.'[9]

The conflict with the Brotherhood culminated in a bloodbath in
February 1982 in Hama, the fourth largest city in the country. As the
militants entrenched themselves within the old city walls of Hama, the
government elite forces, led by Rif'at al-Asad's Defence Brigades (*Saraya
al-Difa' 'an al-Thawrah*), subjected the city to indiscriminate bombardments
by artillery and helicopter gunships and the levelling to the ground of
whole sections of the northern and eastern parts of the city. The siege of
Hama lasted over two weeks, leaving an estimated death toll ranging from
5,000 to as high as 20,000. After the showdown in Hama, Saudi Arabia
struggled to control media reports on the issue (Safran, 1988: 340). It
reportedly sent the Gulf Arab leaders messages concerning the Hama
event with the aim of co-ordinating their positions, although the allegation
was denied by a Saudi official source.[10] In essence, the Kingdom avoided
taking a public position on the issue.

After Hama, *al-Mu'assasat al-'Ammah* or the International
Brotherhood—the most moderate of the three branches of the
Brotherhood—fled to Saudi Arabia for safe haven. The faction was led by
'Ali Bayanuni and Shaikh 'Abd al-Fattah Abu Ghuddah[11]. The Saudi offer
to host this wing did not seem to have produced friction between the
Saudi and Syrian regimes for two reasons: 1) the Saudi regime was
providing Asad with a service of keeping a lid over the Brotherhood
activity; and 2) it created an opportunity for the Saudis to play their
favourite role as mediators. As early as 1983, Saudi mediation facilitated
Asad's reconciliation with the International Brotherhood; Asad sent 'Ali
Duba, head of the Military Intelligence, as an envoy to Saudi Arabia for
negotiations (Raad, 1998: 94). A tangible progress in the reconciliation,
however, was reported only after Abu Ghuddah was granted amnesty by
the Asad regime in 1995 (Aoyama, 1998).

Thus, Syria had reasons to be relatively lenient with Saudi Arabia's
support for the domestic opposition, in contrast to those by other
neighbouring governments, namely Iraq and Jordan. This leniency partly
stemmed from Syria's awareness of the political and economic cost of a
fall-out with the oil-rich Kingdom and partly because the nature of Saudi
aid to Syrian oppositions was financial and not military. The contrast,
however, may have also stemmed from a more fundamental, underlying

factor—that of legitimacy and ideology. R.N. el-Rayyes asserts, in reference to Iraqi-Saudi relations, that the former capitalised on the Islamic credentials of the latter to strengthen its legitimacy, while Saudi Arabia in turn could fend off criticism against its Arab nationalist commitment by cashing on close association with Ba'thist Iraq (el-Rayyes, 1998: 218-220). The same could be induced of the Syrian-Saudi relations that cordial relations with 'the guardian of the Holy Cities' could be publicised as implicit endorsement and approval of Asad and his domestic policies (al-Rayyis, personal communication, Beirut, December 1999). Such a trade-off of legitimacy created a curious compatibility, while history of inter-Arab politics has shown that governments competing over monopoly of the same ideological doctrine became the fiercest rivals. One needs to look no further than the two Ba'thist regimes of Iraq and Syria to illustrate this point. Similar states repel and opposites accommodate—even if they may not *attract*—each other, a phenomenon which partly explains the grounds for co-operative relations between Syria and Saudi Arabia.

### The Amman Summit and the Syrian-Jordanian Border Crisis (November–December 1980)

The Amman Arab Summit of November 1980 was the first arena in which the newly consolidated pattern of polarisation in the Arab world unfolded itself. The majority camp led by the Saudi-Iraqi-Jordanian axis was joined by other Arab Gulf states, North Yemen, Sudan and Morocco. The opposing camp was the Syrian-led Steadfastness Front consisting of Libya, Algeria, South Yemen and the PLO, while Egypt was still withdrawn from the Arab political scene. The two blocs disagreed on almost every issue of preoccupation for the leaderships, ranging from policies towards Iran, the superpowers and Egypt, to the future of the Middle East peace process. The gap between the two camps was further deepened as Saudi Arabia severed diplomatic relations with Libya on 29 October 1980, following Colonel Mu'ammar Qadhdhafi's anti-Saudi propaganda campaigns.

By the time the Amman Summit was convened, the polarisation had become conclusive and pronounced, as Syria succeeded in bringing together all the members of the Steadfastness Front to boycott the summit, unlike the previous attempt at the Islamabad Islamic Conference Organisation (ICO) meeting. Worse still for the Saudi camp, while the summit convened in Amman, Syria sent an unmistakable signal of objection to it by mobilising some 30,000 troops and 500 tanks along its border with Jordan. This was the first occasion since 1970 when Syria and Jordan literally came to the verge of military confrontation—a scenario most dreaded by the Saudi leadership. Such a war would inevitably force them to take sides between the belligerents, exposing them to attacks from at least one side—if not both—in the event that Saudi support was deemed insufficient by the recipient, which often seemed to be the end result. Hence, annoyed as they might have been with the development, they were left with little choice but to embark on a highly publicised campaign of mediation between the two countries with the aim of securing withdrawal of both forces from the Syrian-Jordanian border.

In this episode, Syria appeared to have succeeded in imposing its own will over other Arab states by a dramatic display of its 'nuisance' power, most probably also winning additional windfall of 'appeasement' bounty. Syria, however, was not the real victor, since the negative reputation it earned through this bold move resulted in costly regional isolation. Saudi Arabia, on the contrary, may have on the surface succumbed to Syria's 'tantrum', but it gained prestige as the moderating and influential actor in Arab politics. This new prestige became a springboard for scoring more diplomatic wins in the following months. The examination of this period will highlight Saudi preoccupation with Arab solidarity, the use of financial aid and mediation as means to achieve it, and Syria's exploitation of such Saudi sensitivities. By so doing, the analyses highlight the peculiar phenomenon in Arab politics, wherein diametrically opposed interests and policy goals can bring two actors to co-ordinate policies.

### The Summit Preparation and Syria's Boycott
### (Mid-November 1980)

Syria formally proposed postponement of the annual summit meeting through Foreign Minister Khaddam's official letter to the Arab League Secretary-General. The main reason given was, in short, unsuitable 'timing', by which he meant that the Arab nation was too divided for a summit to formulate co-ordinated policies (*BBC/SWB/ME*, 13 November 1980). The real motives were more complex. First, Syria feared that the summit discussion would predominantly focus on the recent outbreak of the Iran-Iraq war, against Syria's determination to maintain the Arab-Israeli conflict as the region's core concern. In such an eventuality, Syria would be cornered because of its support for Iran against the majority backing for Iraq (Qindil, 1980d; Safran, 1988: 323). Second, the Syrians were growing increasingly suspicious of Jordan's anti-Camp David commitment. They were convinced that King Hussain was attempting to hijack the Palestinian agenda and follow Egypt's path in signing a separate peace deal. Thus, to signal their objection to a possible expansion of Jordan's role, Syrians requested a change in the venue from Amman to Mecca. Third, it was also fearful that the summit would provide the opportunity for the Arab oil states to review the Arab funding to the frontline states (Qindil, 1980e).

Safran claims that Saudi Arabia departed from the past practice of avoiding confrontation with Syria and pressed for holding the meeting on schedule (1988: 323). However, closer examination suggests that such a role was played more by Jordan, while the Saudis merely succumbed to the joint Jordanian-Iraqi pressure. Saudi *Al-Majallah* in early November raised the possibility that the summit might not convene, largely because of King Hussain's 'stubbornness' in insisting that the summit be held exactly on the appointed date and that its resolution should support Iraq against Iran (8 November 1980 cited in *MECS*, 1980–1981: 231). Another Saudi commentary hesitantly called for the convention of the meeting: 'it is vital…to clear all obstacles in the way of holding any [Arab] meeting on whatever level' in order to counteract the 'infiltration' of (unspecified) 'big powers' in the Arab region (*BBC/SWB/ME*, 13 November 1980).

A delicate Saudi position as a go-between was also observed in: 1) its active diplomatic effort to persuade Syria to attend the summit; and 2) the delay in making an official announcement of its own attendance. In fact, the announcement came only after a delegation headed by the Saudi Foreign Minister, Sa'ud al-Faisal, had visited Damascus on 17 November (*MEED*, 21 November 1980). His task in Damascus was deemed crucial, as it had become apparent by then that Syria's boycott was likely to take the entire Steadfastness Front with it—a sure prescription for failure of the summit.

Of particular significance was a possible boycott of the PLO. The PLO's dilemma was acute, as on the one hand, it needed to maintain cordial relationship with Riyadh, its main financier. Furthermore, its absence from an Arab League leaders' meeting—the first ever since it joined the 21-nation organisation in 1964—carried the risk of strengthening those voices which preferred Jordan as the main spokesman for the Palestinians in future peace negotiations (*New York Times*, 25 November 1980). On the other hand, pressure from Syria was tangible; the PLO head offices as well as Palestinian camps in both Syria and Lebanon were hostages to the Syrian army units, security services and the elite paramilitary (Qindil, 1980e). The PLO chairman, Yasir 'Arafat met with Hafiz al-Asad on 13 November (*BBC/SWB/ME*, 15 November 1980). According to an Egyptian source, 'Arafat delivered to the Syrian President, a message of explicit threat from Saudi leadership against 'those who were receiving Saudi funding, yet were inclined to boycott the summit.' 'Arafat was told during his prior visit to the Kingdom:

We will not allow Syria to twist our arms and to oblige us to postpone or boycott the Amman summit. We will not tolerate overt threats from the PLO and the Palestinians...As a price for any attack on the Saudi position, we would cease to pay for and to support the PLO. Libya suffered that as our diplomatic relations were cut, and that will apply to Hafiz al-Asad, too (Qindil, 1980e).

Also, Syria was allegedly warned of a possible curtailment of Saudi financial aid and a review of the budget for the Syria-manned Arab Deterrent Force (ADF) (Qindil, 1980d).

Such a strong-worded message from the Saudis may have been reiterated by Sa'ud al-Faisal during his Damascus visit. On 18 November, the day after the visit, Khaddam appeared in Amman to participate in the preparatory Arab Foreign Ministers conference despite his earlier indication to boycott it. His reluctance to be present was all too clear; at one point he threatened, 'if this summit takes place over our objections, it may be the last summit held by the Arab League,' and the following day, he abruptly departed for Damascus (*New York Times,* 20 November 1980 cited in *MECS,* 1980–1981: 231). Back in Damascus on 20 November, he met the representatives of the Steadfastness Front and then returned to Amman on the same day. When his fresh proposal to hold a series of 'mini-summits' before the full one was rejected, he announced Syria's boycott of the forthcoming summit (*New York Times,* 23 November 1980).

On 24 November, the day before the summit, Crown Prince Fahd flew to Damascus to make the final effort to convince Syria at least to send lower-level representation to Amman (*MECS,* 1980–1981: 233). The Saudi persistence testifies to the indispensability of Syria's acquiescence for Saudis' regional policy—attributed in part to Damascus' ability to mobilise other key Arab actors, especially the PLO. Syria's co-ordination of policies with the PDRY, which the Saudis saw as a hostile Marxist regime at its southern border, also alarmed them. Indeed, the Amman summit was the high point of Steadfastness Front's co-ordination since its inception, as no member defected to the other camp or even adopted a neutral position. Thus, after Syria's announcement of boycott, the Saudi press began to criticise not only the boycott itself but Syria's 'pressure on others' (*Al-Jazirah,* 23–26 November 1980 cited in *MECS,* 1980–1981: 233).

It is not clear whether the Saudis, in retaliation, played their trump card of cutting financial flows to Syria and its allies. Sources indicate that threats to cut off aid were made by several participants during the Amman conference proceedings (*Daily Telegraph,* 1 December 1980; *MECS,* 1980–1981: 235), but these threats, according to Saudi *Al-Jazirah* were not acted upon but instead aimed merely to publicise Saudi impatience (*MECS,* 1980–1981: 235). In fact, the Saudi Foreign Minister swiftly denied such rumours by declaring that his country would continue with the financial aid pledged in the Baghdad and Tunis summits, in addition to honouring the new commitment made at the Amman Summit (*BBC/SWB/ME*, 28 November 1980). Such a gesture to spare Syria tangible punishment paid off. The consideration was reciprocated by the Syrians in the midst of their virulent propaganda campaign against Jordan and its associates (e.g. *BBC/SWB/ME*, 29 November 1980). The range of targets at times widened to include Iraq, Oman, Sudan or Somalia, but Saudi Arabia was not in the list, or at least spared mention of its name. Such concerns shown by both Syria and Saudi Arabia not to jeopardise bilateral relations, if only reluctantly, played a crucial factor in defusing the Syrian-Jordanian border crisis, a direct by-product of the summit.

### The Syrian-Jordanian Border Crisis and Saudi Mediation (Late November–December 1980)

Despite its absence, or rather because of it, Syria dominated the Amman summit proceedings. By the second day of the conference, Syria had deployed 20,000 troops and 400 tanks near Dara', three miles from the border with Jordan (*New York Times*, 27 November; *BBC/SWB/ME*, 28 November 1980). The number was increased to 30,000 troops within a week, while Jordan responded by mobilising two armoured divisions (*BBC/SWB/ME*, 2 December 1980; *MECS*, 1980–1981: 238-239). Syria's official reasons for this deployment were Jordan's support for the anti-regime activities of the Syrian Muslim Brotherhood and its 'conspiracy' to break Arab ranks by joining the Camp David process (e.g. *BBC/SWB/ME*, 22 November and 2 December 1980). The real reasons, however, can be summarised as follows: 1) intimidating the Amman summit conferees by reminding them what Syria was capable of doing if its demands were disregarded; 2) deterring Jordan from sending troops to Iraq against Iran (Safran, 1988: 324); 3) cutting the weapons supply routes from the port of 'Aqaba to Iraq; and 4) deflecting attention from Asad's own domestic troubles—particularly the conflict with the Islamists (Qindil, 1980e).

Although Saudi Crown Prince Fahd, representing the Kingdom at the Amman summit conference, was described as 'very upset' at Syria (*New York Times*, 27 November 1980) and the Saudi press conducted a rare outspoken attack on Syria's 'defeatist stand' (*Al-Jazirah*, 25, 26 and 29 November 1980 cited in *MECS*, 1980–1981: 743), the Saudis saw to it that the conference resolutions did not deviate from the previous agreements in Baghdad and Tunis. The final statement refrained from explicit condemnation of Syria—despite its openly menacing conduct. Furthermore, the text reaffirmed that the PLO, not Jordan, was the sole representative of the Palestinian cause.[12]

The eventual defusing of tension on the Syrian-Jordanian border was also largely accredited to the Saudis (*MECS,* 1980–1981: 238)—complementing the Soviet pressure on Damascus (*Al-Nahar,* 3 December 1980). Once the summit was closed, Saudi Arabia launched a campaign of mediation between Syria and Jordan. Saudi Prince 'Abdallah first appeared in Damascus on 30 November (*BBC/SWB/ME,* 2 December 1980). On 2 December the Prince flew to Amman to confer with King Hussain and then again to Damascus the following day. After his first visit to Damascus, 'Abdallah expressed his optimism and satisfaction with Asad's 'great understanding and good intention towards Arab solidarity,' although reports circulated on the difficulties his mission was encountering (*Al-Nahar,* 2 December 1980). On behalf of Damascus, 'Abdallah allegedly delivered to Jordan two conditions for withdrawing forces: 1) a written commitment from Jordan that it would not support the activities of the Syrian Muslim Brotherhood and 2) continued acceptance of the PLO as the sole, legitimate representative of the Palestinian cause (*Al-Nahar,* 3 December 1980). Although the Jordanian Information Minister promptly denied receiving such conditions, let alone accepting them (*Al-Nahar,* 3 December 1980), 'Abdallah, upon his return to Damascus on 3 December, hailed the success of his initiative. He secured an agreement from Syria gradually to withdraw its forces as the above conditions were accepted (*BBC/SWB/ME,* 5 December 1980) and invited both Asad and Hussain to Riyadh to work out an agreement on mutual troop withdrawals (*Newsweek,* 15 December 1980).

What 'carrots and sticks' had to be employed in order for Saudi Arabia to secure this agreement from the Syrians are not documented. However, messages carried by 'Abdallah on his tour reportedly contained threats against Damascus, most likely those on the financing of the ADF or other bilateral transactions (*Al-Nahar,* 2 and 3 December 1980; *MECS,* 1980–1981: 238-239). As for the 'carrot', by most accounts, Syria received a pay-check of $500 million for responding favourably to the Saudi initiative (Qindil, 1980f; *MECS,* 1980–1981: 743; personal communication, London, June 2001), although these allegations were denied by 'Abdallah who expressed his 'deep sorrow' over publication of such 'false' reports (*BBC/SWB/ME,* 16 December 1980).

The mediation might have turned out to be an expensive operation. What matters for the Saudis, however, was that a military showdown was prevented and, even better, it was accredited to Saudi Arabia's effort—the *Arab* prestige they were eager to cherish. The Saudi press 'went out of its way' (*MECS,* 1980–1981: 798; cf. *MEED* and *BBC/SWB/ME,* 5 December 1980) to praise Abdullah's efforts. Encouraged by this success, the Kingdom, together with the Arab League Secretary General and

Algeria, formed a fraternal good offices committee (*lajnah masa'i akhawiyah*) with the aim of realising reconciliation between 'some Arab countries' (*BBC/SWB/ME*, 30 December 1980). Its first mission visited the Syrian, Jordanian and Iraqi capitals in late December. In tandem, there was also another small gain for the Saudis in this manoeuvre; Damascus announced on 2 December—in the midst of 'Abdallah's shuttle diplomacy—its willingness to resume the pumping of Iraqi oil across its pipeline to the Mediterranean, a welcome gesture for the Saudis.[13]

Thus, examination of Syrian-Saudi dealings in the Amman Summit and the Syrian-Jordanian border crisis underlined some key aspects of the bilateral relations. First, Syria's regional policy was preoccupied with erecting the Arab-Israeli conflict—and not the Gulf conflict—as the core agenda in all-Arab debate, where it was able to claim central position. Furthermore, in this debate, no actor—except the PLO, which was subordinate to Syrian pressure—was to have an authoritative voice on the future of Palestine. As for Saudi Arabia, this event highlighted typical usage of mediation and financial aid to achieve Saudi foreign policy goals. Financial aid had been the most important foreign policy tool for the Kingdom, as was demonstrated in the $500 million to Syria. The aid might not have swayed the Syrians, but as R. S. Porter summarises, the Saudi political rent was not an entire failure:

> [A]id commitments were entered into response to particular events and pressures and were designed to ward off possible threats from within the Arab region [rather than to achieve clearly defined foreign policy objectives of a fairly long-term character]. Looked at from this point of view the effort might be counted a success so far (Porter, 1988: 202).

### The Syrian-Israeli Missile Crisis (January–May 1981)

If the turmoil of the Amman Summit were resolved partly through appeasing the Syrians, the Saudi effort paid off at least for the first few months of 1981 when the Syrians refrained from what had become a customary act of 'sabotage.' For instance, President Asad headed the Syrian delegation to the ICO summit meeting, convened in Saudi Arabia between 25-28 January. At the conference, and in stark contrast to the previous meeting in Islamabad, a rare air of amicability prevailed much to the pride of Saudi Arabia, which took over the Presidency of the Organisation (*MECS*, 1980–1981: 239). This tranquillity, however, was short-lived as another trouble was brewing in Lebanon. The escalation of violence in Lebanon was an issue the Asad regime did not desire at a time of regional isolation and domestic troubles with the Islamists. Syria was forced into hostility by escalation of violence between the local factions, coupled with the growing Israeli ambition to take advantage of the Arab divide and to gain a foothold in Lebanon (*MEED*, 5 December 1980; Seale, 1990: 369). As Syria became embroiled in the worst fighting since the Lebanese civil war first broke out in 1975, Saudi Arabia attempted to exploit the opportunity to 'discipline' Syria.

Syria, for the first time since the 1973 October War, stood on the brink of direct and full-scale military engagement with Israel. In the absence of support from Egypt or Iraq—to whom Syria turned in the previous wars against Israel—Syria counted on Saudi Arabia in finding a diplomatic breakthrough. Its main ally, the Soviet Union, despite extension of economic and military support to Syria, had limited value as a mediator, because it had no channel of communication with Israel (Karsh, 1991: 132-133); hence, Syria looked towards Riyadh for political support, in hope that it would help persuade the US to apply pressure on Israel for restraint. If successful, the Kingdom were to be able to gain some leverage over Syria and prestige as an able mediator and to win credibility with the US as a competent regional ally. At a time when Riyadh was pressing for an airborne warning and command systems (AWACS) purchase, it was imperative to prove to Washington its capability to bring out desirable settlement in regional disputes.[14] Despite its relative position of strength vis-à-vis Syria, Saudi Arabia still had to tread carefully in this manoeuvre not to appear too close to the 'imperialist' superpower in the Arab eyes. In order to avoid accusation that it was acting on behalf of the US interests in the region, Riyadh first had to secure endorsement from Syria (and the Palestinians to a lesser extent) for its mediation. The Missile Crisis and the international efforts to resolve it highlighted the dynamics in which alliance with opposing superpowers—or, in other words, affiliations to opposite camps in the global Cold War—did not necessarily hinder Syrian-Saudi communications, but instead enhanced mutual understandings at times.

### The Background of the Missile Crisis (April 1981)
The Missile Crisis of April 1981 erupted as Bashir Jumayyil led his Maronite Phalangist militia blatantly to challenge the Syrians by attempting to expand territories under Christian control. Emboldened by the backing from his Israeli ally, he deliberately provoked the Syrians, first by capturing the strategic town of Zahlah in the Biqa' valley, killing Syrian soldiers there and shelling Syrian army headquarters in Shutura (Petran, 1987: 258-259). When the Syrians retaliated against the offensive and successfully dislodged the Christian forces from the highest peak of Mount Sanin, Israel saw a danger to its vision of establishing a

protectorate over Lebanon. Israel, thus, expressed its protest by shooting down two Syrian helicopters on 28 April, which in turn prompted a Syrian response of installing surface-to-air missiles (SAM) in the Biqa'. When Israeli Prime Minister Begin made clear that he was prepared to remove the Syrian missiles by force, Damascus called on other Arab states to fulfil their 'pan-Arab responsibility' and stand behind Syria.

Syria had enough reasons to be anxious about the extent of support it could rally amongst the Arab countries. Considerably annoyed by Syria's bellicose behaviour at the time of the Amman summit and its pro-Iranian stance in the Iran-Iraq war, Saudi Arabia and other Gulf states had since been quietly expressing their disapproval of Syria's regional policies (Robinson, L., 1996: 49; Nonneman, 1988: 99). Most importantly, shortly before the Missile Crisis, Saudi Arabia and Kuwait disclosed that they had been withholding the subsidy for the *Arab* Deterrent Force for the past four months because its makeup had become exclusively *Syrian* (*MEI*, 8 May 1981; Evron, 1987: 92). The aid, according to *MEI* (8 May 1981) and *New York Times* (20 May 1981), amounted to $180 million a year, although Asad himself quoted it at under $10 million.[15] At the same time, Saudi Arabia led the calls for the ADF to be diversified by returning to the original multi-national composition, thereby ending Syrian monopoly (*MEI*, 8 May 1981; *MECS*, 1980–1981: 242-243).

Furthermore, Syria perceived disturbing signs that Saudi Arabia might be growing responsive to the US-Camp David camp's courtship. US Secretary of State Alexander Haig unveiled a new Middle East policy, entitled 'strategic consensus' in March—in short, a design to mobilise local support against Soviet incursion into the region. Haig toured Saudi Arabia, Egypt, Israel and Jordan the following month to win support for this scheme. Despite the Saudis' strenuous effort to distance themselves from the scheme,[16] Damascus remained suspicious of the Saudi intention and publicly warned against collaboration with the US. Immediately after Haig's visit to Riyadh on 7–8 April, Asad stated:

I do not object to any of our Arab brothers wanting to build friendship with the United States. Everyone has his own point of view. It is not harmful if some of us manage to establish a real friendship with the US. After all, it is a major power. But the friendship that exists between the US and certain Arab sides cannot be beneficial. The US has no friends among the Arabs at all; no Arab can be true friends of the US (*BBC/SWB/ME*, 14 April 1981).

What Asad perceived as ominous signals from the Gulf came at a time when his unity plan with Libya was already on the rocks (*BBC/SWB/ME*,

7 February 1981), and he had clashed repeatedly with the USSR over his policy on Lebanon since his forces entered the country in 1976.

### Saudi Mediation Efforts (May 1981)

Once the crisis erupted, Saudi Arabia dealt with Syria and the Missile Crisis on two levels. On the public level, it expressed firm support behind Syria. This position was essential in furthering its own aim to contain the Crisis as a mediator, while upon doing so, avoiding accusation of collaboration with the US. Also, once Syria successfully hindered the Phalangist advance, Damascus, once again began to enjoy greater respect from the wider Arab public (*MEI,* 8 May 1981) and among its usual Steadfastness allies and Iran (e.g. *BBC/SWB/ME,* 9, 11 and 15 May 1981). Behind the scenes, however, the Kingdom responded to the Crisis with detachment and implicit criticism towards Syria.

The first official contact between the two countries was Deputy Commander of the National Guard, 'Abd al-'Aziz al-Tuweijiri's visit to Damascus on 30 April (*Al-Nahar,* 1 May 1981) and confirmed Riyadh's position of standing by Syria in the confrontation with the Israeli 'enemy'. On 4 May, after receiving 'Arafat who had travelled to Riyadh via Damascus, King Khalid sent an 'important' message to Reagan on Lebanon (*BBC/SWB/ME,* 6 May 1981). The following day, Reagan announced the dispatch of a special envoy, Philip Habib, to the region in order to defuse the Missile Crisis and to stop the fighting in Lebanon. After touring Tel Aviv and Damascus, Habib arrived in Riyadh on 17 May. It is most probable that the Syrians discussed with Tuweijiri the possible US role in restraining Israel. The Saudis are unlikely to have enlisted direct US mediation without prior consent, if not a request, from the Syrians. In the meantime, Damascus radio reported on 16 May Saudi Foreign Minister Sa'ud al-Faisal's declaration of 'absolute support' for Syria (*BBC/SWB/ME,* 18 May 1981), while King Khalid sent another message to Asad the following day to report on Habib's Riyadh visit (*Al-Safir,* 24 May 1981). Habib carried a modified proposal from Riyadh to Damascus which allegedly contained resumption of Arab aid to the ADF and the diversification of its troop composition (*New York Times,* 20 May 1981).

In tandem with Habib's mission, Saudi Arabia actively pursued the convening of all-Arab meetings to resolve this crisis. The first of such meetings was the Tunis conference of Arab army chiefs of staff in the first week of May, which pledged to close ranks behind Syria (*New York Times,* 8 May 1981). Two weeks later, on 22 May, the Arab League Foreign Ministers met in Tunis for an emergency session on Lebanon. The conference resolution promised Syria 'the required aid to repulse Israel's aggression' and also implicitly agreed on the resumption of the ADF funding, but at the cost, for the Syrians, of relinquishing monopoly over the Lebanese affair; not only was the ADF composition expanded to include troops from other countries, but the conference reactivated the Follow-up Committee as a forum for settling Lebanese disputes, thereby 'Arabising' the conflict (*New York Times*, 24 May 1981; *MECS*, 1980–1981: 244).

Intense contacts continued between Syria and Saudi Arabia as the Lebanese conflict escalated towards June with renewed Israeli-Palestinian fighting. Rif'at al-Asad arrived in Saudi Arabia on 23 May as soon as the Arab League Foreign Ministers meeting was closed (*Al-Safir*, 24 May 1981). He carried a hand-written message from the President, allegedly urging Saudi pressure on the US to urge moderation on Begin (*New York Times*, 24 May 1981). The Saudi aim in the meeting was to induce Syria to return to the pre-Missile Crisis state of affairs, which involved removal of the missiles, cessation of attacks on the Phalangists and withdrawal of forces from Mount Sanin, in return for the Phalangists' surrender of Zahlah to the Lebanese Army (*New York Times*, 28 May 1981). The meeting was a disappointment for Philip Habib who was waiting in Tel Aviv for several days for positive news from Riyadh on the above points. On 28 May, Tuweijiri undertook his second visit to Damascus in ten days (*Al-Nahar*, 29 May 1981), and the visit was reciprocated by 'Abd al-Halim Khaddam to discuss the Arab Follow-up Committee meeting, scheduled for 7-8 June in Bait al-Din (*Economist*, 6 June 1981; *MECS*, 1980–1981: 244-245).

The Committee meeting did not produce any agreement, because of differences between Syria and Saudi Arabia. Syrians insisted that the Phalangists' renunciation of ties with Israel was a prerequisite for any peace, while the Saudis wanted to see the missiles taken down first. Also, the entire meeting was largely overshadowed by Israel's dramatic destruction of Iraq's nuclear facilities in Usirak on the same day (Safran, 1988: 330-331; Seale, 1990: 370). In public, as always, Syria and Saudi Arabia both stressed their satisfaction with the progress made and reiterated their commitment to ending the conflict, as Sa'ud al-Faisal, with his Kuwaiti counterpart, travelled to meet President Asad in Damascus the day after the conference (*Al-Nahar*, 10 June 1981). The Saudi Foreign Minister was particularly cautious not to be blamed for the failure of the Conference; to give the Saudi role an Arab legitimacy; and to avert suspicion that the his country might be acting on behalf of the US. Before the Damascus meeting, he had issued a statement asserting: 'Saudi Arabia was part of the wide Arab move, and it did not have a separate role or private contacts with America or anyone else about this matter' (*BBC/SWB/ME*, 4 June 1981). In Damascus, he reiterated that there was no *Saudi* initiative, but only an *Arab* one (*BBC/SWB/ME*, 8 June 1981).

The Arab Follow-up Committee Conference was followed by a succession of meetings before a peace deal could be concluded. The Foreign Ministers met in Jiddah on 23-24 June as a preparatory meeting for the 4 July conference. The sticking point, according to Khaddam, was the Phalangists' refusal to severe ties with Israel, and because this issue was not resolved in the first meeting, another meeting had to be scheduled for 25 July (*BBC/SWB/ME,* 7 July 1981). In the meantime, the Arab League meeting on 23 July extended the ADF mandate for further six months without change in its composition, although this issue was re-examined in a number of subsequent follow-up committee meetings (*MECS,* 1980–1981: 244-245). The funding for the ADF also was reportedly resumed (*MEED,* 9 July 1981). In the end, a cease-fire was reached on 24 July through a compromise among Asad, Begin and 'Arafat, and the agreement was largely attributed to Habib's efforts (Seale, 1990: 371). This American-Saudi achievement was based on the understanding that the observance of a cease-fire agreement between Israel and the PLO would be guaranteed by their respective sponsors—the understanding which unravelled in less than a year (Petran, 1987: 262).

Despite the seemingly close co-ordination between Syria and Saudi Arabia in the resolution of the Missile Crisis, the latter used the occasion to criticise the former's policy, mostly only implicitly, but on occasion, through media commentaries. In the first days of the Crisis, Radio Riyadh referred to Syrian actions as 'mistakes which provide the Israeli enemy with excuses and justifications to invade Lebanon' (30 April 1981 cited in *MECS,* 1980–1981: 744). When the first official statement on the conflict was issued by the Saudi Foreign Ministry, its call to respect 'sovereignty, independence and unity' of the Lebanese entity implicitly raised objections to Syria's large presence in the country (*Al-Riyadh,* 18 May 1981). Contributors to *MECS* analysed the statement as follows:

It began by saying that the Kingdom 'wishes to reaffirm its position by the side of Lebanon' (not, that is, by the side of Syria around whose missiles the situation was revolving). It made a reference to the ADF operating 'under the orders' of Lebanon's 'legitimate authorities' (i.e. of President Sarkis)—a reminder to Syria that, despite its *de facto* authority, the ADF was not formally a Syrian preserve. The ADF, the statement continued, was responsible for the '*pan-Arab* role entrusted to it…of which sister Syria shoulders a *large share*' (yet no more than a *share*). The implication was that Syria's task in Lebanon was to act on behalf of the Arab countries who had given the ADF its mandate, and not to establish a Syrian power monopoly there (*MECS,* 1980–1981: 244).

Statements by other prominent Saudi figures also repeated their support for 'Lebanese sovereignty' (e.g. *BBC/SWB/ME*, 20 May and 5 June 1981) and attributed the latest Israeli aggression to the deplorable 'state of minimum Arab solidarity' (e.g. *BBC/SWB/ME*, 22 May and 6 June 1981). With the memories of the Amman Summit vivid and the Syrian support for Iran still staunch, there was little doubt that the Saudis held Syria primarily responsible for this lack of 'Arab solidarity'.

Syria was tremendously disappointed by the cold Arab reaction to the Missile Crisis. It did not receive even an official statement of support from the Arab Gulf states during the first days of the crisis, not to speak of Jordan and Iraq, which maintained their anti-Syrian stance throughout the Crisis (*MECS*, 1980–1981: 798). In stark contrast to the 1973 War, there was no talk of contributing forces for the defence of Lebanon or Syria except from Libya and South Yemen. What Syria received was essentially limited to verbal backing and the resumption (rather than an increase) of financial contributions for the ADF. Syria's bitter complaints were expressed through press reports and interviews of official figures. Official daily *Tishrin* condemned the 'silence maintained by some of the Arabs' at a time when Syria was 'waging a pan-Arab battle' (12 May 1981 cited in *MECS*, 1980–1981: 244). Also in mid-May, Khaddam, in his interview with London-based Saudi daily *Al-Sharq al-Awsat* blamed unnamed Arab states who were withholding the ADF contributions as directly responsible for the escalation of tension in Lebanon (*BBC/SWB/ME*, 16 May 1981). Despite its bitterness, Syria had to content itself with a qualified readmission to the Arab fold after suffering from acute regional isolation (Seale, 1990: 372).

The Missile Crisis was illustrative of Saudi Arabia's new confidence in its attempt to twist Syria's arms. It must, however, be noted that were it not for the aggressive Israeli policy, a development outside control of either Syria or Saudi Arabia, Riyadh could not achieve this relative supremacy. Also, Saudi prestige pre-supposed its ability to influence Washington—the connection badly needed by Damascus—but this presumption became questionable at later times. Thus, the limits of Saudis' ability to shape events and regional power balance were evident. When the Kingdom's confidence grew disproportionate to its capability, it launched an ambitious project, the Fahd Plan, which backfired at the Fez Arab Summit in November 1981.

### The Fahd Plan (August 1981–January 1982)

Regardless of whether the Arab governments committed genuine support to any given Palestinian political grouping, sentiment for Palestine has remained a constant source of inspiration and rallying point in Arab societies; Palestine has become, by extension, a crucial source of legitimacy for Arab governments (Hudson, 1977: 115-119). Legitimacy here is not restricted to domestic acceptance granted to the regime but stretches further to regional recognition of the state itself. To obtain leadership in the Arab world, therefore, an Arab state must demonstrate its commitment to the Palestinian cause. It was a matter of time, therefore, that Saudi Arabia was to launch a new peace initiative, with Palestine as the core agenda, in this period of unprecedented assertiveness and confidence. In Kazziha's words:

> Thus the role of political leadership in the Arab world finally fell to Saudi Arabia. And with that role, Saudi Arabia inherited the responsibilities of meeting the challenges which were facing the Arab world. First among these challenges was the Palestine cause. In short, Saudi Arabia had to give the Palestine question top priority by virtue of its new role as the leader of the Arab world.[17]

As early as mid-May 1981 at the height of the Missile Crisis, Prince Faisal al-Turki reportedly made clear the Saudi strategy of 'first Lebanon, then Palestine'—in other words, extension of a Lebanese settlement towards a wider peace process—during his meeting with President Reagan in Washington (*MEI*, 5 June 1981). The success of the Lebanese cease-fire talk in July 1981, for which the Kingdom took credit, gave further boost to its confidence in launching its own proposal for a comprehensive peace. In addition, the latest Israeli aggression confronted Saudi Arabia with renewed sense of urgency in improvising a peace settlement for the region; when Israel destroyed the Iraqi nuclear reactors on 7 June, the bombers violated Saudi air space before reaching Usirak in Iraq. The Saudi leadership felt that the Kingdom was no longer just another *peripheral* state in the conflict with Israel but could potentially be dragged into a *frontline* or *confrontation* line-up (Kazziha, 1990: 307).

This was the context in which the Saudi Middle East peace plan—also known as the Fahd Plan, notwithstanding Prince Fahd's public disapproval of the title—was first published in August 1981. It was intended to mark the new phase in Riyadh's leadership role in the region (*MECS*, 1981–1982: 221). By the same token, the failure to achieve at least a broad Arab consensus on the plan (if the actual peace were beyond reach) was to testify to the limits of Saudi power and influence. It was Syria, yet again, that was directly responsible for the thwarting of this new Saudi diplomatic initiative. This time, unlike the Amman Summit, Syria's long-standing policy of being deliberately difficult was damaging not only to Arab solidarity but specifically to Saudi interests. Saudi inability to stand up against such a challenge even at the height of regional prestige illustrated its fundamental weakness; its stability and security depended on the elusive, and most of the time unattainable, notion of Arab solidarity, and Syria was able to capitalise on the Saudi vulnerability.

### The Proposal (August–September 1981)
On 7 August 1981, Saudi Crown Prince Fahd gave an interview to the Saudi Press Agency, in which he proposed a peace plan as an alternative to the Camp David formula (cited in *BBC/SWB/ME,* 10 August 1981). The essence of the plan was summarised in eight points, mostly derived from the past UN resolutions, familiarly calling for Israeli withdrawal from all occupied territories, dismantling of Israeli settlements on those lands, recognition of Palestinian rights and the creation of a Palestinian state with Jerusalem as its capital. The only controversial point, both from Arab and Israeli points of view, was Article 7 which asserted that 'all states in the region should be able to live in peace.' For the next year, whether 'all states' included Israel became a focal point of Arab debate.

Observers are almost unanimous in their view that the aim of this plan was about attaining not so much peace but rather the broadest possible Arab consensus on the question which preoccupied Arabs—the conflict with Israel (e.g. *MECS,* 1981–1982: 204; Safran, 1988: 332-333). The benefit of achieving such a goal would be multifaceted. Not only would it resolve the perpetual instability created by conflicts between Arab 'radicals' and 'moderates', but it would send the clearest message—crucially towards Washington, not to speak of domestic and regional audiences—of the Saudis' leadership role in shaping regional events and formulating co-ordinated Arab policy towards Israel.[18] In view of the Israelis' immediate rejection of the proposal and the lukewarm American reception, it is indeed questionable whether the Saudis were at any point optimistic enough to believe that the Plan would create a foundation for a comprehensive peace. Hence, how the fellow Arabs would respond was the crucial question for Riyadh.

The evidence of Saudi confidence in assuming the new leadership role could be found in the fact that no Arab leader, bar Yasir 'Arafat, was consulted on the Plan prior to its announcement (*Time,* 19 October; *Washington Post,* 24 November 1981). 'Arafat expressed his positive view towards the Fahd Plan as 'a good starting point' (*BBC/SWB/ME,* 20 August 1981), despite rejection of the Plan by some of the fellow PLO officials. The recent bitter experience of the Amman Summit notwithstanding, the Saudis seemed to have been little concerned with Syria's reaction, as can be inferred from the absence of high-level government contacts in the weeks preceding the announcement. One source assessed that the Saudis 'acted as if they could afford to ignore it [Syrian opposition]' and goes on to say that they 'believed that anything acceptable to the PLO, the party most directly involved, should be acceptable to other Arabs even Syria' (*MECS*, 1981–1982: 203-204). The developments in the next few months were to prove that it was an over-confidence based on misjudgement.

The Syrians initially emitted mixed signals. On the one hand, the media strongly condemned the Plan albeit without mentioning the Kingdom by name (*Al-'Amal*, 21 August 1981); one commentary noted: 'Some of the moderate Arab countries are submitting proposals which aim to serve American designs and to obscure the renunciation of declared commitments in what is related to the struggle against Israel' (*Al-Nahar*, 16 August 1981). On the other hand, government officials were quoted as giving milder comments about the Plan, if not readiness to accept it. The Foreign Minister Khaddam, upon his visit to Riyadh on 18 August, expressed Syria's readiness to attend the forthcoming Arab summit meeting and to approve its agenda with the Fahd Plan as the main item (*MECS*, 1981–1982: 215n46). Although his insistence on discussing the subject prior to the November summit indicated Syria's reservations towards some articles of the Plan, its willingness to negotiate on the matter was a promising gesture for the Saudis. Saudi optimism was surely enhanced by the Syrian ambassador to Saudi Arabia, Muhammad al-Tall, when he claimed: 'Syria always supports the solutions which guarantee the Palestinian rights, as the ones submitted by Prince Fahd' (*Al-'Amal*, 21 August; *MEED*, 4 September 1981).

The Syrian position decidedly tilted from ambiguousness to rejection in September after Menachem Begin travelled to Washington for talks on the US-Israeli bilateral agreement on strategic co-operation, known as the Memorandum of Strategic Understanding. The Memorandum, formally signed two months later on 30 November, was a defence pact which prescribed the signatories to intervene militarily on the side of the treaty partner, should either of them be subjected to military aggression from a third party. To Syria's alarm, it was a far more binding agreement than its Friendship and Co-operation Treaty with the Soviet Union, which merely required the signatories to *consult* one another at times of crises. In the light of the Soviets' unequivocal refusal to accept Syria's persistent request to upgrade their treaty to parallel the Memorandum (Karsh, 1991: 136), Damascus grew increasingly suspicious of the merits in engaging in talks with bellicose Israel from the position of military weakness—be it in the framework of Fahd Plan or otherwise. In its view, bargaining from the position of weakness was the very reason why Sadat's deal with Israel resulted in no more than a 'capitulation' (Seale, 1990: 348).

To combat this new threat, Asad attempted to rally regional support, first by dispatching Khaddam to the Gulf states, who started the tour with Ta'if, Saudi Arabia's summer capital, on 13 September (*Al-Nahar*, 14 September 1981). Khaddam allegedly opposed the Saudi peace plan and stressed the need for military option, reiterating Syria's long-maintained belief that 'it was necessary to restore Arab strategic balance with Israel before talking about any kind of settlement' (Safran, 1988: 334). Concurrently, the Steadfastness Summit convened in Benghazi, Libya, with an additional attendant from Iran as an observer, to co-ordinate a stance on the Memorandum (*BBC/SWB/ME*, 16 September 1981).

Riyadh succumbed to pressure from Damascus partly because the Kingdom was striving at the time to divert Arab criticism for its quest to obtain the American AWACS planes. The Saudi leadership was placed in an even more uncomfortable position when an allegation spread that Fahd had been consulted by US Secretary of State Alexander Haig on the Memorandum during their meeting in Malaga immediately after the Begin-Reagan summit. The day after Khaddam's visit to the Kingdom, an official spokesman for the Saudi government delivered a statement denying the allegation, but it is doubtful whether the statement ameliorated Syria's mistrust for Riyadh's motives. The spokesman went on to criticise the Memorandum for the reason that it would 'hinder the peace process underway in the region' (*BBC/SWB/ME*, 16 September 1981), presumably referring to the Kingdom's own initiative.

The first Saudi attempt to pacify the Syrians—in desperation for Arab consensus on the peace plan—came from Prince 'Abdallah who arrived in Damascus on 27 September to persuade the Syrians to accept the Fahd Plan (*Al-Nahar*, 28 and 29 September; *MEED*, 2 October 1981). The talks with Asad centred on the aforementioned two issues of AWACS deal and the peace plan. In return for Syria's acquiescence to Saudi quest for American arms, 'Abdallah allegedly offered to help Syria acquire arms from the Soviets by underwriting one-third of an envisaged $2 billion deal (*MECS*, 1981–1982: 798; Safran, 1988: 334). It was a classic Saudi tactic to win Syria's approval for the purpose of legitimising the close relations with Washington. As for the Fahd Plan, the Saudis promised to reciprocate Syria's co-operation by considering an establishment of diplomatic relations with the Soviet Union. Such Saudi support for the Soviet role would have been a significant gain for the Syrians, not only in securing a Soviet role in any future Middle East peace negotiations, but, more immediately, in legitimising Asad's growing dependence on the Soviet connection. It was one of the most favourite points of attack for the Syrian Muslim Brotherhood, who after temporary calm following the

Missile Crisis, resumed and stepped up its anti-regime campaign in the summer of 1981. Much to the regime's embarrassment, the opposition campaign of violence specifically targeted Soviet interests at times, such as the Soviet national carrier Aeroflot office in Damascus and Soviet military advisers (*Washington Post,* 28 January 1980).

Syria began to calcify its hard-line rejectionism, by then a familiar stance. In mid-October, a senior Ba'th Party official, Muhammad Haidar, voiced the most explicit rejection of the Fahd Plan on behalf of the Party's Regional Command. In an interview with Lebanese daily *Al-Safir,* he criticised the Plan as 'a mistake from the outset' for 'its timing, the [Saudi] single-handedness in its publication, and its content, i.e. the recognition of Israel.'[19] Syrians were annoyed by the Plan's 'unilateral' publication, or in other words, exclusion of Syria from its formulation and publication. Damascus criticised it as contrary to the 1978 Baghdad agreement, which, upon deliberation on Sadat's 'treachery', conditioned that no Arab League member state should publicly submit a peace proposal without prior presentation to other member states (*Washington Post,* 26 November 1981). Furthermore, the Council of the Conference of Arab Oil and Mineral Workers, which met in Damascus between 12–16 October, condemned the Plan, called Fahd an 'agent' and incited Saudi workers to bring down their regime (*MECS,* 1981–1982: 861).

Whether Article 7 of the Fahd Plan—the rights of all states to live in peace—applied to Israel was the most (and only real) controversial point in the entire Plan. Other contentious issues which had, in the past, been included in numerous different peace proposals were carefully excluded, such as those on normalisation of relations and methods of negotiations (*MECS,* 1981–1982: 203). Even the Saudi government itself had difficulty in presenting a co-ordinated position on the article's definition. One affirmative statement that it did imply recognition of Israel would quickly be overturned by another press report or a high-ranking official's interview (*Washington Post,* 6 November; *Time,* 16 November 1981; *MECS,* 1981–1982: 203). From the Syrian point of view, 'recognition' was the only trump card left to the Arabs against Israel, especially at this moment in time, when they are militarily weaker than its opponent. One observer endorses the Syrian conviction: 'there is only one thing of importance that the Arabs *can* offer to Israel, namely recognition, in word and in deed, of its right to live in peace' (*MEI,* 11 December 1981). So why relinquish it gratuitously, the Syrians argued. In Asad's words:

> Peace cannot be attained in the absence of a comprehensive strategic balance between the two combatant sides, us and the enemy, nor between the strong and the weak. A peace concluded

between the strong and the weak is bound to dictate a state of capitulation, not a state of peace (*Tishrin*, 13 December 1981).

### Towards the Fez I Summit (October–Mid-November 1981)

Thus, the root cause of disagreements between Syria and Saudi Arabia on the Fahd Plan appeared fundamental, touching at the very core of their national security concerns. Yet, Saudi Arabia persisted in its quest to launch the Fahd Plan at the highest level of the Arab League meeting, the forthcoming Fez summit, scheduled for 25 November. Various elements contributed to the resurgence of interests in the Plan, once waned in the wake of the US-Israeli Memorandum. The most dramatic push to the Saudi appetite for a leadership role came from the assassination of Sadat on 6 October, which cast doubt on the future Egyptian commitment to the Camp David agreement, thereby giving additional relevance to the Fahd Plan as an alternative. Furthermore, at the end of the month, the long-awaited AWACS deal was approved by the US Senate.[20] A successful conclusion of the deal gave a boost to Saudi aspiration to become a central regional player with influence on Washington. As for the Arab support for the Fahd Plan, a crucial endorsement was publicly made by Yasir 'Arafat, although other pro-Syrian PLO factions maintained their rejection (*BBC/SWB/ME*, 19 and 22 October; *New York Times*, 31 October 1981). 'Arafat, encountering yet again the dilemma of being sandwiched between Syria and Saudi Arabia—one a politico-military backer on the ground, and the other a financial and political patron—shuttled between Damascus and Riyadh during the month of November (*BBC/SWB/ME*, 4, 5 and 24 November; *Al-Nahar*, 24 November 1981).

In tandem with 'Arafat's diplomatic efforts, Saudi Arabia and Syria directly engaged in intensive consultations with no less than five high-level exchanges in the final weeks leading up to the Fez Summit meeting. On 15 November, Khaddam made a brief visit to Riyadh (*Al-Nahar*, 16 November 1981). His discussions with the Saudi leadership allegedly dealt not only with the forthcoming Fez summit but also with the US-Israeli Memorandum, US 'designs' in the Middle East and need for strategic parity with Israel. After the meeting, Khaddam stated in an interview with Syrian daily *Al-Thawrah*, 'the doors are closed to any settlement in the region' and emphasised the need for the military option as an alternative (cited in *MECS*, 1981-1982: 205). Two days later, Sa'ud al-Faisal arrived in Damascus to persuade Asad to give the Plan 'whatever chance it stands (fursah ma)' (*Al-Nahar*, 19 November 1981).

Syria's position hitherto had been that there should be no open debate or vote on the Fahd Plan at Fez, but rather, a special committee should be set up to consider the proposal at a later date, in private meetings (as opposed to formal sessions of the Arab summit), and together with other peace plans (*Washington Post,* 20 November 1981). This formula, perhaps the Syrians thought, would be a face-saving compromise for both Damascus and Riyadh, but it was incompatible with Saudi Arabia's aim to obtain public recognition for its leadership rather than the behind-the-scene progress in peace negotiation. Despite Sa'ud al-Faisal's exaggerated comments on the success of his visit (*Al-Nahar,* 21 November 1981), all the signs indicated that the two countries were not seeing eye-to-eye on the matter. Even during Sa'ud al-Faisal's presence in Damascus, Syrian officials issued statements which were implicitly critical of the Fahd Plan. For instance, the Syrian Premier, 'Abd al-Rauf al-Kasm, delivered a speech, reaffirming Syria's adherence to the slogan of 'no recognition, no settlement and no negotiation' with Israel and its opposition to American designs (*Al-Nahar,* 18 November 1981). He further criticised the Fahd Plan as 'ineffective' (*Time,* 23 November 1981). Concurrently, Faruq al-Shar', the Syrian State Minister on Foreign Affairs, was at the Steadfastness Front's meeting in Aden and issued an ambiguous statement—conciliatory but implying reservations and warnings against the Saudi initiative. He promised that Asad would personally attend the Fez I Summit and that Syria would discuss the Plan 'in a fraternal spirit … particularly since our brothers in Saudi Arabia will not stick to this plan if it is not approved by the Arab summit conference' (*Al-Nahar,* 24 November 1981). The Aden meeting's final statement called for a military option to complement the political option, accurately reflecting Syria's position (*BBC/SWB/ME,* 20 November 1981).

There was no breakthrough in Syrian-Saudi negotiations before the Arab League Foreign Ministers met in Fez on 22–23 November for a preparatory meeting of the actual summit. Despite the outwardly positive and friendly comments from both sides, Khaddam refused to back away from opposition to the Fahd Plan, and Sa'ud al-Faisal, equally unyielding, insisted that the Kingdom would seek acceptance of the Plan in the original form intact (*MECS,* 1981-1982: 226; Safran, 1988: 337). An uncompromising position adopted by the Saudis convinced the critics that they were more interested in asserting their own supremacy. In addition, the fact that the Saudis ruled out Soviet involvement raised suspicion that the Plan was no more than a Saudi project to win credit with the Americans.[21] This was a game that the hardliners were not willing to play.

To break this cyclic pattern of deadlock, efforts were underway behind the scenes. On 22 November, 'Abd al-'Aziz al-Tuweijiri arrived in Syria for the second time in two weeks (*BBC/SWB/ME,* 23 November 1981). The very next day, Rif'at al-Asad arrived in Riyadh to reciprocate the visit

(*Al-Nahar*, 24 November 1981). In the discussion, Syria allegedly demanded as much as $4 billion of aid as a condition for accepting any Plan implying recognition of Israel—although the allegation was denied by Asad in a customary fashion (*Tishrin*, 13 December 1981); the sum was to be used for fortifying the Syrian military against the Jewish state (*Washington Post*, 26 November 1981). The talks achieved some success, or so the Saudis must have concluded; on the morning of 25 November, a black limousine was waiting at Fez Airport for the arrival of President Asad.

### The (Brief) Summit Proceedings (Late November 1981)

The Saudis, as well as the other Summit participants, were in for a major surprise. At the very last minute, Asad announced that he was not attending the summit after all. Other absentees included the heads of state of the Steadfastness Front[22] and Iraq, but Syria held the key to the summit's disarray and its subsequent collapse. Any Arab consensus without the signature of the main remaining frontline state would be rendered meaningless, especially when the Palestinians, yet again, chose to toe the Syrian line despite 'Arafat's earlier endorsement of the Fahd Plan (*MEI*, 27 November; *Washington Post*, 27 November and 8 December 1981). Syria was instead represented by Khaddam who was in no conciliatory mood. From the outset, he attacked the notion of 'recognition' in the Saudi peace plan, although he was careful not to sound as if he was against the Plan outright (*Time*, 7 December 1981). He argued that if the Arabs tacitly accepted Israel's existence at this point, there would be little incentive for Israel to return the captured Arab lands or grant Palestinians self-determination. After the 'shouting match' between Khaddam and Morocco's King Hassan, the summit host, Crown Prince Fahd offered to withdraw the Plan from the agenda, but was discouraged to do so by King Hassan and King Hussain of Jordan (Safran, 1988: 337). The summit was adjourned five and a half hours after the opening and was postponed indefinitely (*BBC/SWB/ME*, 28 November 1981).

Defiant the Syrian action might have seemed to the Saudi leadership, a more accurate picture was that Syria strove to obliterate signs of disagreement with the Kingdom. Indeed, even Asad's decision to absent himself from the summit was not intentionally confrontationist or slanderous towards the Saudis; to the contrary, it was more an attempt to avoid a damaging personal confrontation with Prince Fahd in the high-profile public arena (*MEI*, 11 December 1981). After the summit, Asad quickly embarked on damage-limitation propaganda campaigns, stressing that the summit was not a failure and the relations with the Kingdom was 'close and fraternal' (*Tishrin*, 13 December 1981; *MECS*,

1981–1982: 226).

Saudi Arabia was also busy averting criticism that the Kingdom's imposition of self-centred views was responsible for the summit's break-up. To recover from the loss of regional prestige, it embarked on a face-saving campaign, coupled with attacks on Syria, whose endorsement the Saudis actively sought and falsely believed they had secured. Asad's last minute declaration of a boycott, therefore, was deemed not only mainly responsible for the summit's collapse but a personal breach of promise. Immediately after the summit, chains of commentaries criticising Syria was published in Saudi daily *Al-Riyadh*, although official government sources refrained from singling out Syria as the culprit. One article, without mentioning Asad by name, charged that his boycott was an effort to extract more financial support from the wealthy Arab states—an effort which backfired since a review of all Arab financing was now in order. The editorial went on to say that Syria had believed it could afford to stay away because it counted on 'continued support for the confrontation, which it is no longer exactly known, aimed at confronting whom' (cited in *MECS*, 1981–1982: 226, 798). Even criticisms of the PLO, though it had equally disappointed the Saudi leadership, were implicitly directed more against 'those outside powers' who were exerting pressure on the Organisation (i.e. Syria) (cited in *MECS*, 1981–1982: 226).

### The Aftermath of Fez I: The Israeli Annexation of the Golan (December 1981–January 1982)

A mere five days after the Fez I Summit, the US-Israeli Memorandum of Understanding was formally signed. To add to this provocation—and to the earlier events of the bombing of Lebanon, the attack on Iraqi nuclear reactor and uncompromising opposition to Fahd's peace initiative—the Israelis further displayed their confidence by annexing the Golan Heights; on 14 December, the Israeli Knesset adopted a bill, which applied Israeli laws to the area which Syria had governed until June 1967 (*BBC/SWB/ME*, 16 December 1981). This move added another nail to the coffin of the Saudi peace plan and was partly intended to create a wedge between the US and its Arab allies, namely Saudi Arabia. It also served to test the extent of Egypt's commitment to the Camp David process before the formal return of Sinai, scheduled for April 1982 (*MEI*, 21 December 1981).

Syria reacted angrily to the Israeli announcement and launched extensive diplomatic campaigns, one in the United Nations (Safran, 1988: 338) and another targeting specifically its 'Arab brothers' (*BBC/SWB/ME*, 13 February 1982). Fully aware of the blame directed against them for the Fez Summit's collapse, the Syrians implied that their hard-line position at the summit was vindicated by the latest Israeli aggression; it was, in their logic, no time to talk peace (*BBC/SWB/ME,* 18 December 1981). Damascus radio commented that the prerequisites for peace simply did not exist, implicitly questioning how the Saudis could now ask the Syrians to change their position on a plan which recognised Israel (*MEI,* 21 December 1981). After achieving some success in the UN, President Asad began a Gulf tour on 22 December, starting with Riyadh with the aim of rallying support on the Golan issue. No details of this visit were officially issued, but the fact that 'Abd al-Halim Khaddam and Faruq al-Shar', the two top portfolios in foreign affairs, accompanied Asad indicated the importance he placed on this tour (*Al-Nahar,* 23 December 1981). As it later turned out, this meeting with Fahd and Khalid produced significant reconciliation in bilateral relations which, at least behind the scenes, had undergone much strain since the 1980 Amman Summit.

At the Riyadh summit meeting, the two countries agreed on a barter deal. As Syria's gains, first of all, Prince Fahd made a gesture of 'indefinitely' postponing his visit to Washington, which was scheduled for 19 January 1982, after having been rescheduled once already from 10 December as a form of protest against the Memorandum (*BBC/SWB/ME,* 24 December 1981). Second, the Saudis announced that they would reconsider the establishment of diplomatic relations with the USSR and confirmed their willingness to support Syria's quest to acquire Soviet weapons (Safran, 1988: 339). They also promised to resume their mediation efforts in Lebanon and to re-establish diplomatic relations with Libya. As for the crucial question of the Fahd Plan, Fahd publicly denied that the discussion dealt with the issue at all (*Al-Nahar,* 24 December 1981). However, the Saudis allegedly assured Syria that it would be consulted more closely on any future discussion on such peace initiatives, in turn asking Damascus not to torpedo the Plan again (Safran, 1988: 339). To top up these good gestures, Fahd proclaimed in public full backing for Syria's efforts to nullify the Golan annexation and warned that if 'peaceful means' failed, the Arabs would collectively consider other appropriate measures to take (*New York Times,* 24 December 1981).

The Saudis, also, were set to exploit this opportunity to settle scores with the Syrians. In fact, the only reason why the Saudi leadership was lenient on the Syrians as evident in the aforementioned conciliatory agreement was because, in the meantime, developments in Bahrain precluded Saudi Arabia from taking an overtly high-handed position. The fighting in the Iran-Iraq war was steadily intensifying, and the odds were in favour of Iran. What concerned Saudi Arabia most was the discovery in early December of plots to subvert the Bahraini, and subsequently Saudi, regimes, involving some 75 former Gulf nationals (13 Saudis, one Kuwaiti, one Omani and some 60 Bahrainis) (Kostiner, 1987: 180). Two days after the Golan Heights annexation, the announcement was made that they had been arrested in connection with the plot which bore hallmarks of Iranian involvement (Safran, 1988: 339). Manama and Riyadh immediately proceeded to sign a security pact; the Kingdom announced that 'any attack on a Gulf Co-operation Council member state is an attack on Saudi Arabia itself' (BBC/SWB/ME, 22 December 1981). As a measure to keep this threat at bay, Saudi Arabia cautioned Syria against supporting Iran and induced Syria to use its good offices to moderate Iran's aggressive position. Furthermore, Riyadh demanded Syria to reconcile its differences with Iraq and Jordan, and reasoned that the cordial relationship with those two states would be an advantage for Syria in retrieving the Golan (New York Times, 30 December 1981; MECS, 1981–1982: 798). Indeed, only hours after Asad's return from the Gulf tour, the Syrian press agency announced that contacts were to be made with the Iranian government (MECS, 1981–1982: 865). Furthermore, Damascus made a symbolic gesture to Baghdad by reopening one of the two pipelines carrying Iraqi oil to the Mediterranean (MECS, 1981–1982: 231). As for the Fez Summit, there is no doubt that Fahd and Khalid twisted Asad's arms on the issue to obtain the latter's support for the Fahd Plan (Al-Majallah, 6–7 January 1981). Fahd remarked: 'Asad's visit is the first of further visits aimed at ensuring excellent results for the Fez summit, should it reconvene' (Radio Riyadh, 23 December 1981 cited in MECS, 1981–1982: 798).

Thus, it appeared that the tension in Syrian-Saudi relations had been resolved 'in a comprehensive understanding at the highest level' (Safran, 1988: 339). The agreement allegedly was accompanied by a generous financial package as usual.[23] Also, Riyadh agreed to pay for additional Soviet arms shipment to Syria, when Khaddam visited the Kingdom on his way to Moscow in early January 1982 (Financial Times, 14 January 1982). Following Asad's visit, Saudi Information Minister blamed the US and Israel's negative attitude to the Fahd Plan as the main reason for Syria and the PLO's rejection of the plan. He further claimed that all of the Golan must be returned as a pre-condition for the Fahd Plan.[24] Furthermore, Prince Talal bin 'Abd al-'Aziz was quoted as saying 'even Syria began to understand the significance of the Fahd Plan' (Al-Nahar, 8 January 1982). Shortly, however, the agreement was put to a severe test, yet again by the unfolding of events in the Gulf, outside Saudi or Syrian control.

## The Iran-Iraq War (October 1980–May 1982)

During the period under review, the Iran-Iraq war as a determinant of Syrian-Saudi bilateral relations was much overshadowed by developments in the Arab summits and the Arab conflict with Israel, especially until the autumn of 1981. In this early phase of the war, the fact that Syria and Saudi Arabia sided with opposing sides did create a source of conflict between the two, but largely in conjunction with other related regional developments. For instance, Syria's support for Iran was much disapproved of by the Saudi leadership, not so much for the amount of Syrian aid *per se,* but more because such support created a deep rift in the Arab world, namely by pitting the Syrian-led Steadfastness Front against the Iraqi-Jordanian axis. Such a rift, or more precisely a deliberate attempt by Syria to destroy the Arab consensus, touched the heart of Saudi security concerns, as has been discussed. The turning point in this state of affairs arrived later with the change in the situation on the ground; when the Iranian effort to repel Iraqi advances began to show success, and concurrently Syria's commitment to Iran intensified, Saudi Arabia became more embittered by Syria's backing for Tehran.

Saudi leniency with regard to Syria's position on the war partly stemmed from the ambiguity over its own policy. Saddam Hussain's war against Iran was initially welcome news for the Saudi leadership, so long as the war was won swiftly enough to induce a collapse of the newly established revolutionary regime. The war would have had a dual blessing. Saddam, for one, was willing to do the dirty work in eliminating a hostile Shi'i regime which explicitly stated that the overthrow of the Saudi regime was one of its primary foreign policy aims. Furthermore, the fact that his attention was focused on the eastern border meant that he would modify, at least for the time being, his adherence to 'radicalism' and hostility to conservative—or in his term, 'revisionist'—Arab states. All it had to do, Riyadh expected, was to be prepared to bankroll Saddam's enterprise. If the war had gone according to Saddam's plan and had ended in a few weeks with an overwhelming Iraqi victory, Saudi Arabia would have had to count on Syria to play its traditional role of checking on Iraqis' expansionist ambition.

Defying all expectations, however, the new Iranian regime proved itself to be far more resilient than anticipated, and the conflict became a war of attrition. Stalemate was, to an extent, even more convenient for the Saudis. With Saddam's hands tied in the war, Egypt isolated and Syria perpetually exposed to imminent threat from Israel, Saudi Arabia launched a peace initiative to claim a central role in regional politics. Moreover, to encounter the period of uncertainty, Saudi Arabia reviewed its defence policy. First of all, it requested American military co-operation and involvement in the Kingdom's defence, as was manifest in the persistent pursuit for AWACS and F-15 planes. Second, it successfully founded in May 1981 the GCC, a collective Gulf security scheme, under its own leadership and excluding the two belligerents.[25] In tandem with the new defence policy, the Kingdom manipulated the ICO to mediate between the two sides.

For Syria, in contrast, the war threatened its regional standing by diverting Arab and world attention away from the Aran-Israeli issue—where Syria is undoubtedly a core player—to the Gulf arena at a time when concerted Arab effort against the Israeli 'enemy' was most needed. From the onset, Damascus was unambiguous in its judgement that it was a 'wrong war'; unlike the Shah, it argued, the new Iranian regime vociferously supported the Palestinian cause. Hence, Syria began to aid Iran militarily (*BBC/SWB/ME,* 15 October; *Newsweek,* 20 October 1980) and diplomatically at the cost of isolating its own standing in the Arab. Syria's support for Iran was a significant part of the reason why it received considerably little Gulf backing in the Golan annexation issue and the conflict in Lebanon. Nor did its proclamation to act as an effective mediator in the Iran-Iraq war rid the other Arab states of their suspicion towards Syria's strategy.

Saudi displeasure with Syria's closeness to Iran became increasingly pronounced in the latter half of 1981 as the Iranian counterattack began to achieve success, pushing back the Iraqi army from the land occupied in the initial stages of the war. What was even more disturbing for the Saudis was that Iran, after scoring some victories, unambiguously spelled out that in the event of a decisive victory over Iraq it intended to march further to liberate Jerusalem and the Holy Cities of Mecca and Medina. To prove its point, in October 1981, the Iranian air force raided Kuwaiti oil installations, followed by more attacks on northern Kuwait on 12 and 16 November. Furthermore, in early October, Iranian pilgrims arriving in Mecca for the annual pilgrimage, or the *Hajj,* clashed with the Saudi security police, making the event, as *MECS* described, 'the most unsettled pilgrimage in nearly sixty years of Saudi guardianship over the holy cities of Islam' (1981-1982: 286). Two months later, the Iranian-backed plot to overthrow the regime in Bahrain, mentioned above, was discovered, as further testimony to Iran's incentives towards the Arab Gulf states; the threat appeared to have reached the doorstep of the Kingdom.

By the end of 1981, Saudi Arabia reiterated to Asad that the Kingdom would not view kindly his support for Iran. As discussed above, when he visited Riyadh to rally support against Israel's annexation of the Golan, he had to concede to Saudi demands by promising to improve relations with Iraq and Jordan and to mediate the end of the war. This agreement in Riyadh, however, was short-lived. Syrians were disillusioned by the lack of Riyadh's pressure on Washington to change the latter's pro-Israeli policy, as was evident in the US veto of a Security Council Resolution, stipulating sanctions against Israel as a follow-up measure to the earlier resolution which illegalised the Golan annexation. One way for Riyadh to apply such pressure on Washington would have been to improve relations with Moscow, but the Saudis made no such move, notwithstanding Khaddam's urging during his quick tour to the Kingdom en route to Moscow in early January 1982 (*BBC/SWB/ME*, 12 January 1982).

As far as Syria was concerned, Saudi Arabia's attitude towards the Golan issue was not sufficiently supportive—at least, not enough to be reciprocated with a significant concession in the Gulf issues. The Saudi Oil Minister made it clear in early February that the oil weapon was not going to be unsheathed over the question of the Golan, and the GCC Foreign Ministers meeting in Bahrain on 6-7 February also reportedly ruled out anti-American sanctions. Frustration in both capitals, Damascus and Riyadh, began to show in the oblique criticisms exchanged in the state-owned press (*MEI*, 12 February 1982). The Golan issue was to be discussed on 12-13 February at the emergency meeting of the Arab League Foreign Ministers in Tunis (*MEI*, 26 February 1982). At the conference, Syria was expected to submit a working paper calling for severing of political and economic relations with the US and those countries that support Israel.

Saudi Arabia, however, was in no position to openly challenge the US. A few days before the conference, Prince 'Abdallah was promptly dispatched to Damascus (*BBC/SWB/ME*, 10 February 1982), presumably to moderate Syria's proposals. While 'Abdallah conferred with Asad, Khalid and Fahd remained in Riyadh, negotiating conditions for deploying the AWACS with Casper Weinberger, the US Defence Secretary, and explaining the reasons behind the postponement of Fahd's visit to Washington (*Al-Nahar*, 9 February 1982). At the Tunis Conference, the final statement of anti-Israeli and anti-American expression was so watered down—allegedly by Saudi and Kuwaiti intervention—that the points raised in the original Syrian paper were unrecognisable. What remained of it was merely an agreement to establish a committee 'to evaluate the political and economic relations between the Arab countries and the states that support Israel' (*MECS*, 1981–1982: 273n54). Such ambiguity was a typical Arab face-saving tactic when no agreement could be reached, and disagreements needed to be shelved.

Absence of tangible support for Syria from fellow Arabs marked a stark contrast to the Iranians' forthcomingness, who pledged to send a battalion to the Golan at the end of January (*BBC/SWB/ME*, 1 February 1982). Furthermore, Iran remained faithful to Asad even at the crucial moment when he was carrying out the hitherto largest military operation against the domestic Islamic opposition, which had been conducting a campaign of violence since the late 1970s. As discussed earlier in this chapter, the world was shuddered at reports of the showdown in Hama in February 1982, and those Arab and Muslim regimes which were on good terms with Asad were considerably embarrassed. Iran, however, remained loyal to Asad and refrained from criticising the Hama crackdown despite its Islamic credentials. Asad subsequently utilised the Iranian support to de-legitimise the revolt as 'un-Islamic'.[26]

In the meantime, reports began to circulate on a serious effort by the Gulf states to punish Syria for its support of Iran, and possibly even for the Hama incident as an undercurrent.[27] London-based Saudi daily *Al-Sharq al-Awsat* reported on 9 March that the GCC meeting on 7 March was seriously studying proposals to stop aid to Syria (cited in *MEED*, 26 March 1982). According to this report, five out of the six member states backed such a plan, and one unnamed member abstained, although the GCC Secretary-General, 'Abdallah Bisharrah promptly denied the allegation (*BBC/SWB/ME*, 22 March 1982). In the next months, more unverified reports suspected of revision in Gulf states' aid programme for Syria (*Newsweek*, 10 May; *Financial Times*, 25 May 1982; Calabrese, 1990: 189). Whether these allegations were true or not, talks of such suspension must have put significant pressure on the Syrians. After all, the Kuwaiti parliament had already voted in favour of suspension of aid for the Syrian-dominated ADF in Lebanon.

The threats from the Arab Gulf, however, ironically pushed the Syrians further into Iranian arms. Shunned by the Soviets and having few friends to turn to among the Arabs, Syria took a decisive step in formalising the alliance with Iran, a step hitherto most damaging to Iraqi economy. 'Abd al-Halim Khaddam paid a visit to Tehran on 13–17 March which produced a barter-deal with far-reaching implications. Iran was to export 9 million tonnes of oil per year while Syria in return was to supply 1 million tonnes of phosphates and other goods, altogether worth some \$2 billion (*BBC/SWB/ME*, 15 March; *MEED*, 16 April 1982). This agreement freed Syria from dependence on Iraqi oil, in consequence allowing Syria to close the borders with Iraq and to shut the Iraqi pipeline passing through the country. The loss incurred by the Iraqis as a result of this 8 April measure was estimated in one source close to \$6 billion (Kienle, 1990: 163); in other words, it cut Iraq's oil export by 40 percent and reduced its foreign exchange earnings by 25 percent (*Newsweek*, 10 May 1982). Seen in conjunction with Iran's access to Syria's air bases, the shipment of Soviet arms to Iran, and Syrian military pressure on the Iraqi border (Marschall, 1991: 68-69), the new agreement gave the Syrian-Iranian relations a character of a full-fledged strategic alliance (*MECS*, 1981–1982: 866).

The new alliance was heavily criticised by the Gulf Arabs, Iraq's debt to whom was increasing by the day. By March 1982, the debt for the previous year alone was estimated at some $22 billion (*Financial Times*, 26 March 1982). Saudi Arabia and the Gulf states expressed their anger towards Syria's decision, branding it 'hostile to Iraq and Gulf states', although they refrained from accepting Iraq's demands for collective sanctions against Syria (*Al-Safir*, 20 April 1982). The Saudi press became increasingly vocal in its disapproval of Syria's policy (e.g. *Al-Jazirah*, 4 April 1982 cited in *MECS*, 1981–1982: 234). The timing of the Syrian-Iranian announcement was crucial, too. In late March, the Iranians successfully launched a counter-offensive which started the chain of their military victories leading up to the recapture of Khorramshahr in May. To Saudi Arabia's horror, a comprehensive Iranian victory became a real possibility, and Syria's role in realising that prospect appeared instrumental.

High-level contacts with Syria began as usual. Amidst Iraq's angry call for collective Arab action against Syria, 'Abd al-'Aziz Khuwaitir, Saudi Minister of Education who had close contacts with Baghdad, arrived in Damascus on 26 April (*Al-Nahar*, 27 April 1982). On 11 May, Syrian Chief-of-Staff Hikmat al-Shihabi visited Riyadh (*Al-Nahar*, 12 May 1982). May 1982 was the month when the fall of Khorramshahr threw the Gulf states into a state of near panic. On 24 May, immediately after the fall, Sa'ud al-Faisal flew to Damascus as part of a GCC mission, this time most probably to discuss Iranian terms for a settlement and to explore possibilities for Syrian mediation on behalf of the Gulf Arabs (*Al-Nahar*, 25 May 1982). Saudi Arabia, together with other Gulf states, was ready to offer Iran an estimate sum between $10 billion (*Financial Times*, 26 May 1982) and $25 billion (*MEI*, 4 June 1982; *International Herald Tribune*, 2 June 1982) in return for a cease-fire, falling far short of Iran's demand for $50 billion. On top of the reparation, Iran presumably demanded cessation of Arab aid to Iraq, Arab adoption of the hardest of the hard-lines against Israel, continued exclusion of Egypt from the Arab fold, and removal of Saddam Hussein from the Iraqi 'throne'—conditions far too extreme for the Arabs to deliver (*Economist*, 29 May 1982). On the very next day of Sa'ud al-Faisal's visit, the *Financial Times* reported that the GCC states collectively threatened Syria with a withholding of the Baghdad Summit subsidies (25 May 1982 cited in *MECS*, 1981–1982: 234). Although the report was not confirmed elsewhere, a Radio Damascus report reacted angrily against what they termed, 'economic blackmail' by 'American regimes' (1 June 1982 cited in *MECS*, 1981–1982: 234).

Such defiant comments notwithstanding, Syria was careful not to appear as though its support for Tehran was without limits. Syria had been consistent in its objection to widening the war to Arab countries other than Iraq, and on a number of occasions promised the Gulf Arabs that this would not happen. Earlier in October 1981 when the Iranians attacked the Kuwaiti oil installations, Radio Damascus gave publicity to a telephone conversation between Asad and the Amir of Kuwait, in which Asad promised to support Kuwait should it come under Iranian fire again (*MECS*, 1981–1982: 865). Also, when Khaddam signed the economic agreement in Tehran in March 1982, the joint communiqué clearly stated:

> the two sides emphasised the importance and necessity of co-operation between the Islamic Republic of Iran and the Arab countries in strengthening their joint anti-Zionist and anti-imperialist position *on a basis of non-interference in the internal affairs, and respect for the territorial integrity of others* (*BBC/SWB/ME*, 19 March 1982, emphasis added).

By June, reports began to circulate that Asad had personally received fresh assurances from Khomeini that the Iranian forces would not attack other Arab states (e.g. *Al-Ahali*, 2 June 1982).

Syrian gestures were predictable in view of the fact that the Saudis and other Gulf states began to emit strong signals that they regarded the threat from Iran as potent enough to override all other considerations, even those arising from the Arab-Israeli conflict (*MEI*, 21 May 1982). Also, since the Iranian victory in May 1982, the Gulf Arabs, in a state of near panic, began to intensify efforts to reincorporate Egypt into the Arab world. Both were goals to which Syria was viciously opposed (*MEI*, 23 April 1982). Pressures on Syria to review its Gulf strategy were mounting.

Syria's behaviour on the issue of the Iran-Iraq war was most exemplary of its tactics in gaining regional influence through adopting policies deliberately opposed to what was considered majority Arab view—and by extension, attaining leverage over Riyadh which was obsessed with all-Arab consensus. Syria's April 1982 economic deal with Tehran was particularly harmful to Iraq and the Gulf Arabs. At this stage, both Damascus and Riyadh played a carefully calculated game of applying just enough pressure on each other to extract concessions but careful not to alienate each other completely. When the Saudis hoped to utilise Syria's Tehran connection as an only available channel of communication with the Shi'i adversary, the need to limit Syria's isolation in the Arab world became even greater. Finally, the Iranian factor, like all other key issues in Syrian-Saudi relations, was inter-linked with other factors, particularly with developments in Lebanon as will be discussed next.

### The 1982 Lebanon War and the Fez II Summit
### (June–September 1982)

On 6 June 1982, Israeli ground forces embarked on their long-anticipated invasion of Lebanon. Its aims were to install a puppet government, free from Palestinian and Syrian influences and, by extension, to impose another separate peace agreement on a neighbouring Arab state. The army swiftly advanced towards the Beirut-Damascus highway, the lifeline for Syria's access to Lebanon, with the ultimate aim of besieging Palestinian-controlled West Beirut. Through this operation Israel abrogated the so-called 'red line' agreement with Syria—in which the two sides acknowledged each other's sphere of interests in Lebanon—and also the precarious understanding reached after the 1981 Missile Crisis. The right-wing Israeli Prime Minister, Menachem Begin, helped by American complicity (Petran, 1987: 275; Seale, 1990: 379-383; Fisk, 1990: 268), seized the moment when the Arabs were preoccupied with the shock of Iranian victory at Khorramshahr. In addition, Israel had just completed the formal return of Sinai to Egypt and so was now ready to divert its focus against the unstable and small neighbour in the north. A total of 76,000 men, 1,250 tanks and 1,500 armoured personnel carriers crossed the northern border on the first day (Seale, 1990: 376).

The scale of military confrontation that followed was such that it is sometimes referred to as the fifth Arab-Israeli war after the fourth 1973 October War. [28] Unlike the earlier Arab-Israeli wars—in which Syria variably received military as well as political support—assistance from other Arab states to aid Syria's war effort was limited to mere promises of financial aid, and Syria was practically left to its own device. The 1982 War was an unmistakable military defeat for Syria, which cost the country loss of prestige and political weight in the region. As discussed in the opening chapter, some observers conclude that Syria's ability to extract financial support from the Gulf Arab states—an indicator of Syria's leverage over them—largely depended upon its ability to present itself as a credible enemy to Israel (e.g. Perthes, 1995: 32-33). According to this logic, a natural consequence of the defeat of 1982 would be a decrease in the financial commitments from the Gulf and the overall diminution of Syria's significance in Arab politics in general and more specifically in its relations with Saudi Arabia. There is no doubt that Syria's feeble response to the invasion was more than a disappointment to the Gulf states, who had bent backwards to fund Syria's military presence in Lebanon and had long subjected themselves to blackmailing by the front-line state. [29] Counter-intuitively, however, the following analysis illustrates that Syria's military defeat did not halt the financial flow.

The events of June 1982 were significant in Syrian-Saudi relations mainly because Syria's military defeat led to the loss of regional influence; Saudi Arabia leaped into the spotlight of Arab politics at the expense of Syria. The analysis of this event and of the Fez II Summit that followed will help identify each actor's bargaining chips against each other and the expectations one actor holds towards another.

### Conflict of Interests in the Shadow of Diplomatic Co-operation (June–July 1982)

After being utterly outmatched by Israel in military performance, Syria responded positively to the US-negotiated cease-fire proposal on 11 June (*BBC/SWB/ME*, 11 and 12 June 1982). Such receptivity fuelled the anger of Arab states, particularly Jordan, Egypt and Iraq, which launched vicious propaganda campaigns against Syria's sorry military performance (e.g. *BBC/SWB/ME*, 7 and 8 June 1982; *MECS*, 1981–1982: 248, 794). The fact that even Libya, the Steadfastness Front ally, had been questioning Asad's lack of engagement in the first few days of the war indicated the degree of Syria's regional isolation (*BBC/SWB/ME*, 8 June 1982).

In such an anti-Syrian climate, Saudi Arabia stood out for its avoidance of an explicit attack. Before the invasion took place, Riyadh had been criticising Syria and the PLO for giving Israel 'excuses and justifications to invade Lebanon' (Radio Riyadh, 30 April 82 cited in *MECS*, 1981–1982: 793), but in the wake of the catastrophe, responsibility was placed not on any particular actor but on the vague notion of 'Arab dismemberment', i.e. divisions within the Arab world. Since Syria had been the main 'spoiler' of any chance for Arab consensus, there was little doubt that the reference to a lack of Arab solidarity was a roundabout way to blame Syria, but an explicit indictment was strenuously avoided. This restraint was remarkable particularly because, by the summer of 1982, the Iranian victory in Khorramshahr fuelled Arab anger towards Syria, the chief ally of Tehran.

Saudi diplomatic activities also indicated that the leadership was far from indifferent to the Lebanese affair, even though their engagement fell short of what Syria expected of the Saudis—perhaps a military contribution or fresh oil embargoes in the fashion of 1973 October War. Within a few days of the invasion, Sa'ud al-Faisal was in Paris and London, from which he flew to Algeria, calling for an unconditional Israeli withdrawal at each stop (*Al-Nahar,* 12 June 1982). In Bonn, he reportedly warned that the conservative Arab states might in the future have to look to Moscow and its allies in the region (i.e. Syria, Libya and the PDRY) to guarantee their security (*MEI,* 18 June 1982). Although this speech was a reference more to the recent Iranian victory in the Gulf War than the Lebanese crisis, nothing was a clearer signal of Saudi dissatisfaction with

Washington than an invitation to an expanded Soviet influence in the region. Meanwhile, Prince Fahd, soon to accede to the throne, sent a series of urgent messages to Washington, urging the Reagan administration to control Israel. It was allegedly Reagan's Secretary of State, Alexander Haig, who blocked these messages from reaching Reagan until Fahd issued an ultimatum to the President that the Kingdom would within hours withdraw all its investments from the US and impose oil sanctions against the West.[30] This Saudi channel to Washington was given added weight when Riyadh co-operated with Cairo, another heavyweight Arab ally of the United States, to send a joint message along the same line (*MEI,* 18 June; *Washington Post,* 20 June 1982).

In the Arab arena, Saudi Arabia took the helm of the foreign ministers' emergency meeting in Tunis on 26-27 June. Although the meeting itself did not produce a much-desired joint Arab reaction bar the establishment of a special seven-member committee (*BBC/SWB/ME,* 29 June 1982)—classic Arab window dressing to mask a lack of achievement at a high-level Arab League meeting, the committee's first meeting in Ta'if on 1-2 July highlighted the centrality of Saudi Arabia's role. Sa'ud al-Faisal was elected its chairman and attempted to facilitate a discussion between Bashir Jumayyil, the Phalangist leader, and the PLO. One report summarised that the Saudis were 'uniquely placed to influence Washington, and they had a special responsibility towards Arafat and Lebanon's Muslims, a special stake in front-line moderation and a special vulnerability to the repercussions if the massacre went ahead [in Beirut]' (*MEI,* 2 July 1982). These Saudi efforts paid off, as it was spared attack in Syria's counter-campaign against those Arabs who criticised Syria's performance in Lebanon.[31]

In fact, Damascus maintained close diplomatic consultations with Riyadh throughout June. On 5 June, on the eve of the full-scale invasion, Rif'at al-Asad arrived in Saudi Arabia (*Al-Nahar,* 6 June 1982.). Given the sporadic military clashes between Israeli and Palestinian forces, Rif'at most probably urged the Saudi leadership to pressurise the US administration to restrain Israel and possibly to dispense increased financial aid to Syria—which may have been granted, according to the *Financial Times* (9 June 1982). Four days later on 9 June, President Asad received a telephone call from Prince Fahd, following US envoy Philip Habib's arrival in Riyadh via Jerusalem and Damascus (*BBC/SWB/ME,* 11 June 1982). Such telephone communications between Asad and members of the Saudi leadership allegedly took place almost daily at that time (*New York Times,* 2 September 1982). Furthermore, upon King Khalid's ill-timed death on 13 June, Damascus announced that Prime Minister 'Abd al-Rauf al-Kasm would head a delegation to attend the funeral.[32] Kasm was followed by

'Abd al-Halim Khaddam on 19 June, who urged the Saudis to make every effort to persuade Washington to apply more pressure on Israel, while he explained Syria's much-criticised policies on Lebanon (*Al-Sharq al-Awsat*, 23 June 1982 cited in *MECS*, 1981–1982: 248, 862). Khaddam was received by Fahd for the second time in two weeks when he arrived in Ta'if on 1 July to attend the Arab League seven-member committee meeting (*Al-Nahar*, 2 July 1982). The meeting appeared to have achieved very little in view of the fact that, only three days later, President Asad unexpectedly arrived in Ta'if (*Al-Nahar*, 5 and 6 July 1982).

The fact that Asad himself cared to appear in the Kingdom underscored the degree of disagreements between the two states, although the exact sticking points in the negotiations remained unclear. They were undoubtedly no mere procedural matters but rather fundamental issues, emanating from the divergence of Saudi and Syrian long-term aims in Lebanon; the Saudis' main objective was to devise a formula for Syria's removal from Lebanese soil by uniting the Lebanese factions under the central government's authority, while Syria was adamant to stay. Without the massive military presence in Lebanon, now totalling some 40,000 troops, Syria would be stripped of not only its influence over the Lebanese factions and the Palestinians, but consequently much of its political weight in the entire Middle East region. Hence, Damascus had been justifying its military presence by invoking the successive Lebanese governments' 'invitation' and by legitimising their troops as the *Arab* Deterrent Force, although it came to be solely constituted by Syrian forces. Both of these justifications, in Damascus' assertion, had differentiated the Syrian presence in Lebanon from that of any other foreign troops, particularly Israel's. However, the Saudi call for evacuation of *all* foreign forces from Lebanon deliberately fudged such a distinction. To make matters worse, while the Arab Foreign Ministers conference in Tunis was still in session, the Radio Riyadh broadcast an unmistakable objection to Syria's presence in Lebanon and indicated Riyadh's change of heart on the question; it read that 'Lebanon should not be left to the hegemony of one Arab state,' as this would mean 'repeating past mistakes' (26 June 1982 cited in *MECS*, 1981–1982: 794).

From Asad's point of view, another ominous implication of the latest developments was Riyadh's apparent co-operation with Cairo. On the occasion of King Khalid's funeral, President Mubarak visited Riyadh, the first of its kind since his predecessor Anwar al-Sadat's controversial visit to Jerusalem. Mubarak's strongly-worded attack on Israel's aggression in Lebanon was also the first of its kind since 1977; he branded it a flagrant violation of international law and demanded an immediate withdrawal (*MEI*, 18 June 1982). His words were further met by a concrete action of sending joint message to Washington with King Fahd to warn against the grave consequences of continued Israeli bellicosity. Such a return of Egypt in mainstream Arab diplomacy was diametrically opposed to Syria's interest in keeping Egypt isolated and hence upholding a unified Arab objection to the Camp David formula. Egypt had already re-established some link with the Iraqi regime by proposing to support the latter's war effort in the Gulf; a full-fledged return of Egypt was certain to add a strong momentum to anti-Syrian voices in the Arab arena.

Despite the official announcement that the Asad-Fahd meeting had ended amicably with promises to co-ordinate efforts to counter the Israeli aggression, a fundamental incompatibility of interests indicated the rift between Syrian and Saudi positions (*Al-Nahar*, 6 July 1982). The first problem arose only a few days after the summit when a new cease-fire was declared. Saudi Arabia made it public that King Fahd, after talks with Presidents Reagan and Asad, had acted as midwife to this new arrangement (*BBC/SWB/ME*, 7 July 1982). Sa'ib Salam—the former Lebanese Prime Minister who was one of the closest Sunni Muslim politicians to the Saudi regime and also Philip Habib's main intermediary with the PLO—emphasised the prominent role of King Fahd in the cease-fire negotiation; he announced that President Asad had agreed, after talks with Fahd, to accept the PLO fighters evacuating Beirut under the new cease-fire agreement (*New York Times*, 9 July 1982). The very next day, however, Riyadh was slapped in the face as Damascus rejected the idea of receiving the guerrillas; this, despite the fact that the Syrian capital was a host to seven of the fifteen members of the PLO executive committee and the three hundred-member Palestinian National Council, the Organisation's parliament in exile. What caused the change of heart from Asad's earlier acceptance of the Palestinian fighters remains unclear, but suspected reasons were: Saudi rejection of Syria's demand for more financial compensation; the US' refusal to make more concessions; and Soviet objection to the scheme (*Washington Post*, 10 July 1982). According to an Israeli source, Syria demanded from the Kingdom US$ 14 billion as compensation for its agreement to take in the PLO men besieged in West Beirut. The report went on to say that the Saudis had agreed to grant Damascus only half of the requested sum, and that Syria's rejection of the agreement was in response to this deadlock in negotiations with Riyadh over financial aid.[33] On the eve of Crown Prince 'Abdallah's visit to Damascus two weeks after the report was published, an 'authoritative source' in Riyadh denied that there was such a request from Asad (*Al-Nahar*, 25 July; *BBC/SWB/ME*, 26 July 1982).

Another point of contention between Damascus and Riyadh emerged over the convention of the emergency Arab summit on the Israeli invasion. On 9 July, the Tunisian President Habib Bourgiba made a fresh call for an Arab summit meeting on Lebanon, proposing that it meet a week later. A few days later he withdrew the proposal due to a lack of positive Arab responses (BBC/SWB/ME, 15 July 1982), and Saudi Arabia was finger-pointed as the prime culprit for Bourgiba's withdrawal. Indeed, Saudi Arabia discounted the need for a summit at this moment on the grounds that more attention should be focused on the forthcoming visit to Washington by the Arab delegation acting under an agreement at the Tunis Arab Foreign Ministers meeting (BBC/SWB/ME, 15 July 1982). Riyadh was cashing in on the prospective success of its own diplomatic initiative on the Lebanese issue, chiefly through its chairmanship of the Arab committee and its direct contacts with Washington and various Lebanese factions. Another failure of an all-Arab effort after the Tunis Foreign Ministers meeting would be a setback for the Kingdom's scheme to establish itself as an influential mediator of the region.

Syria accused 'those who opposed the Arab summit in Tunis' (implicit but sufficiently unmistakable reference to the Kingdom) of conspiring to aid 'the Zionist-imperialist scheme' against Lebanon (Al-Safir, 16 July 1982; MECS, 1981–1982: 251). This was a clear indication that Damascus was keen to foil any Saudi attempt to assume a manifest leadership role in settling regional affairs—the exact motive behind Riyadh's boycott. It is unlikely that Syria had any other incentive to support the summit and to needle those who did not, in view of the fact that Damascus had been consistently contributing to the aborting of such summit meetings.

On 20 July, the aforementioned Arab delegation, consisting of Sa'ud al-Faisal and his Syrian counterpart 'Abd al-Halim Khaddam, met with President Reagan in Washington. The cruces of the negotiation were the transfer of the Palestinian fighters to other Arab countries, particularly Syria, the US' recognition of the PLO and a demand for increased American pressure on Israel for an immediate withdrawal from Lebanon.[34] Apparently, no breakthrough was produced on any of these issues in Washington,[35] but the visit was a high point in Syrian-Saudi diplomatic co-operation on Lebanon. The fact that the tripartite meeting took place at all, amidst the aforementioned Syrian-Saudi controversy on Lebanon, accentuates the indispensability of such a co-operation for either party. Even more remarkably, their conflict of interests was not restricted to the Lebanese arena at that time; in mid-July, the Iranians launched a major offensive against the Iraqi city of Basra, prompting another unsuccessful mediation tour to Damascus via Baghdad by Saudi Crown Prince 'Abdallah on 25 July (Al-Liwa', 27 July 1982).

## The Fez II Summit and Its Preparation (August–September 1982)

In the first two months after the Israeli invasion, the Arabs were signally incapable of presenting a cohesive and convincing opposition against it. With the aim of reaching the minimum goal of clearing this negative atmosphere, the Presidents of North and South Yemen, uncharacteristically showing signs of receding enmity, jointly proposed to convene an Arab summit. They first visited Saudi Arabia for an audience with King Fahd on 2–3 August, proceeding to Damascus to meet with President Asad (*BBC/SWB/ME*, 5 August 1982). The proposal was received favourably in the two capitals, which were 'virtually at the opposite ends of the Arab political spectrum' (*MECS*, 1981–1982: 262). When other Arab capitals also supported the proposal, Saudi Arabia concluded that time was ripe for making its own call for a summit meeting and proposed the resumption of the Fez Summit meeting, suspended in disarray nine months ago (*MECS*, 1981–1982: 252).

As Syria was held chiefly responsible for the aborted Fez I Summit, Arab diplomatic efforts to prepare the ground for a successful summit concentrated around Damascus for the next month, particularly between Damascus and Riyadh, assisted by King Hassan, the prospective conference host. The Moroccan Foreign Minister, Muhammad Boucetta, was the first to brief King Fahd as early as 13 August on his meetings with the Syrian leadership in Damascus (*Al-Anwar*, 14 August 1982). Two days later, Sa'ud al-Faisal arrived in Damascus (*BBC/SWB/ME*, 18 August 1982). Khaddam in turn reciprocated by making an unannounced visit to Taif on 18 August, where he expressed Syria's readiness to attend the summit (*Al-Safir*, 19 August 1982). He also agreed to the inclusion of the eight-point Fahd Plan in the agenda, although Syria's willingness to *discuss* the Plan at the summit was as far as his endorsement went, stopping short of supporting it; in other words, his reservation indicated that Syria insisted on some amendment in the Plan (*MECS*, 1981–1982: 206). Sa'ud al-Faisal returned to Damascus a week later to secure a guarantee for Syrian participation. Simultaneously, Rif'at al-Asad was on a visit to Washington, amidst speculation that he was holding talks on Lebanon with senior US officials in the presence of a Saudi delegation (*Al-Nahar*, 26 August; *New York Times*, 28 August 1982). Thanks to these Saudi efforts—which were rumoured to contain financial inducements (*New York Times*, 2 September 1982), Khaddam appeared at the preparatory meeting of Arab Foreign Ministers in Morocco on 28 August.

In the week between the ministerial conference and the summit, now scheduled for 6–9 September, the summit agenda had to be revised yet again. On 1 September, as the last ship full of Palestinian fighters was leaving Beirut, President Reagan announced what came to be known as the Reagan Plan,[36] the essence of which was a rejection of both, an independent Palestinian state and Israeli annexation of the West Bank and Gaza, in favour of some form of Jordanian-Palestinian federation. From the point of view of the Saudi leadership, who, together with the Jordanians, had participated in secret discussions on the Plan prior to its publication, any American commitment to halting Israeli settlements and removing them from the occupied territories could not be dismissed out of hand in view of the new balance-of-power created by the Israeli invasion of Lebanon (*MEI,* 17 September 1982).

The matter was very different for the Syrians, who not only were kept in the dark despite Rif'at's presence in Washington at that time, but more importantly, found its content totally unacceptable, perhaps even personally insulting. For Syria—the self-proclaimed 'vanguard' of the Palestinian cause, a Jordanian-Palestinian federation was even greater anathema than an independent state of Palestine. As if that was not enough, the future of the Golan Heights was not even addressed in this new *Middle East* peace process, potentially leaving Syria as the only disgraced Arab state that failed to retrieve the territory lost in 1967. The reason why Syria's initial language of criticism was surprisingly mild (e.g. *BBC/SWB/ME,* 4 September; *Washington Post,* 10 September 1982) was largely because Israel's immediate rebuttal of the Plan had more or less determined its fate, making it unnecessary for Syria to risk another fall-out with Washington over the matter.[37] It was also a reflection of Syria's weakness that it was in no position to press its point of view against the superpower, even though the Plan was presented as a reaffirmation of the Camp David formula.

Consequently, both Saudi Arabia and Syria, for very different reasons, looked forward to Fez II to hatch an *Arab* peace formula. The Saudis were ready to re-launch the Fahd Plan,[38] armed, at the very least, with a US objection to the Israeli occupation of the West Bank albeit a qualified one. Successful adoption of the Plan by the summit participants would be the most glorious moment in Saudi assertion of regional leadership and prestige. As for Syria, whose regional bargaining position had been significantly weakened since June and also completely excluded from the US vision of peace, Fez presented an opportunity to break out of regional isolation and to incorporate its position into a collective Arab initiative as an alternative to the Reagan Plan.

The change in Syria's position from Fez I to Fez II is particularly instructive in delineating sources of its bargaining power against the Saudis and vice versa. In Fez I, Syria could afford to rebuff the Saudi initiative and was capable of doing so successfully, as seen by Asad's pointed absence from the summit. The conditions had changed dramatically in the ten months that followed.[39] Betraying expectations that Damascus was to succeed Beirut as the centre for Palestinian activities (e.g. *MEI*, 3 September 1982), the evacuation of the PLO from Lebanon had ironically loosened Syrian shackles on the Organisation, permitting 'Arafat to voice his eagerness for the Fez summit (Sayigh, 1982: 15-16). Thus, the loss of the 'Palestinian card' reduced Syria's ability to play a 'spoiler' in Arab consensus-building. Also, the balance of power in neighbouring Lebanon had tipped in favour of the Maronites led by a charismatic leader, Bashir Jumayyil, who made no secret of his affiliation and co-operation with Israel. Syria had, thus, lost Lebanon as well as the PLO in asserting its featured rejectionist stance in the Arab arena. Furthermore, Syria's decisive military defeat by the Israeli forces discredited the Soviet Union as a superpower guardian. Opinions are divided over whether the Soviets were indeed indifferent to Syrian losses and inept at supporting its ally during the fighting.[40] However, at least in the eyes of the Arab audience, Syria's oft-proclaimed policy of 'strategic parity' as an alternative to Washington's separate peace lost any credibility. It had become clearer than ever that the only superpower that could moderate the seemingly unstoppable Israelis was the United States, and amongst the Arabs, the Saudis had the strongest channel with Washington. Thus, Syria was in no position to displease Riyadh at this time. Needless to say, its dependence on the infusion of Saudi cash also increased considerably, due to the critical need to rebuild its military machinery (*MECS*, 1981–1982: 777).

The unanimously adopted final resolution[41] reflected the weakness of the Syrian position in the region. The most significant compromise that Riyadh could extract from Syria was on the Iran-Iraq war. Asad reluctantly complied with a statement that read, 'the conference had decided to declare its commitment to defend all Arab territory and to consider any aggression against any Arab country as and aggression against all Arab countries,' which unmistakably outlawed any form of support for Iran, including those extended by Syria thus far. Although some consistency can be observed with Syria's earlier loss of enthusiasm about the alliance with Tehran, particularly since the latter's overt military victory on the Iraqi soil, there is no doubt that this was a difficult position for Syria to take. Its media reports deliberately dropped the Gulf War from the Fez summit headlines altogether (*MECS*, 1981–1982: 256). Furthermore, the moment the summit ended, Damascus had to go through great lengths to reassure the Iranians that its commitment to the alliance had not wavered. As soon as the Fez II closed, Minister of Information Ahmad Iskandar Ahmad visited Tehran to brief the Iranian leadership on the Summit (*BBC/SWB/ME*, 16 September 1982). An end result of the desperation was what could be called a Janus-faced denial. He publicly endorsed Iranian objections to the summit resolution as justifiable, reiterated Syria's support for the Iranian Revolution, denied any future plans for an Asad-Saddam meeting—in total dismissal of King Hassan's announcement of such a plan—and rejected Iraqi calls for improved relationships.[42] After all, of all the countries in the region, it was Iran alone that had come to assist the Syrian forces repel the Israeli advancement into Lebanon—marking the beginning of visible Iranian presence in Lebanon.

Other major concessions from the Syrians came on the topics of foreign forces in Lebanon and the Arab-Israeli conflict. Syria uncharacteristically acquiesced to a direct reference to the termination of the ADF in the final statement, although the language was toned down merely to state the conference's acknowledgement of such a decision by the Lebanese government.[43] Also, on the Arab-Israeli conflict—the item over which 'Saudi Arabia and Syria were the principal adversaries' (*MECS*, 1981–1982: 254)—endorsement of an eight-point plan, which still closely resembled the original Fahd Plan, was in itself more than what Syria was prepared to do ten months before. Upon doing so, Syria dropped its customary call for mobilisation of all Arab resources (including oil weapons) for an armed confrontation with Israel and its demand to include in the summit resolution explicit condemnation of the Reagan Plan. Dishon and Maddy-Weitzman summarise the majority view amongst observers, when they conclude: 'The list of winners was headed by Saudi Arabia,' and '[i]t was Syria, weakened as it was by the [Lebanon] war, which had to bear the brunt of pressures from Saudi Arabia, Iraq, Jordan and Lebanon' (*MECS*, 1981–1982: 257).

Some, on the contrary, stress the modifications and compromises made by Riyadh, 'particularly so as to ensure Syrian consent', and it was such Saudi 'readiness to meet the Syrians more than halfway', which accounted for the passage of Fez II resolution.[44] This view is based on some of the gains Syria made before and during the summit. Prior to the summit, according to Kuwaiti *Al-Qabas*, Syria extracted from Saudi Arabia a financial reward of $600 million for its participation as well as a promise for a continued annual payment of sums pledged at the Baghdad summit (15 September 1982)—in stark contrast to Riyadh's threat to cut aid as recent as May 1982 (*MECS*, 1981–1982: 790). Also, Syria must have been pleased to see that the boycott of Egypt was upheld, despite Cairo's diplomatic attempts until the last minute to gain admission to the summit and despite the moderate Arabs' increasing reliance on Egypt's diplomatic and military weight, be it in Lebanon or in the Gulf (*MECS*, 1981–1982: 253). When the summit opened, it became apparent that Riyadh had modified the original Fahd Plan to accommodate Syria's position—in itself a significant gesture of compromise, when only a few days prior to the summit, the Saudi media was heralding the Plan as 'the only complete solution' for the Middle East (*MECS*, 1981–1982: 279n223). As for the controversial Article 7 in the original Plan, which affirmed 'the rights of all countries of the region to live in peace', it was rephrased to read 'peace for all the states of the region'; the question of recognition of Israel was thus circumvented, as Syria insisted.[45] These 'rights', furthermore, were to be guaranteed by the United Nations Security Council, thereby securing a Soviet role in the future peace talks, hitherto completely excluded. In addition, the fact that the future independent Palestinian state was emphasised as among 'all the states' thwarted Reagan's vision of a Jordanian-Palestinian federation, which Syria bitterly objected to.

Although it is plausible that Syria succeeded in securing some gains, this does not contradict the fact that Saudi Arabia came out as a bigger winner from the conference with boosted prestige. Syria, meanwhile, was sufficiently cornered to swallow more compromises than it ever had so far on some key regional issues—Iran and the Syrian presence in Lebanon. Equipped with financial leverage and the Washington connection—a double-edged sword—Saudi Arabia briefly enjoyed the golden moment of diplomatic victory at the expense of Syria's weakened status. This Saudi prestige, however, rested on precarious ground, conditioned by the elusive notion of 'Arab consensus'. The Fez II resolution, as was often the case with 'Arab consensus', was doomed to be a merely declarative scenario with no practical steps towards implementation.

The 'winner' between those two states 'on the opposite ends of the political spectrum,' can only be determined by assessing the Plan's implementation. Prognosis for the Plan's future was already bleak in the immediate aftermath of the summit, when the Syrian Information Minister, Ahmad Iskandar Ahmad, denied in the audience of the Iranian leadership all points of compromises Syria had made at the summit. He downplayed the significance of the summit itself, and even continued to advocate the most rejectionist line by claiming that the resolution 'did not include recognition of the Zionist entity, not even by implication' (Radio Damascus, 14 September 1982 cited in *MECS*, 1981–1982: 207). Saudi Arabia consequently failed to turn this diplomatic triumph into an established regional influence for itself, allowing sufficient time to the Syrians to put their house in order and make a comeback as the nuisance power, as will be examined in the next chapter. The Kingdom's inability to please all protagonists in conflicts, yet pinning its own security on achieving exactly that, underscored the reason behind its limitation in becoming a hegemonic power in the region.

## Conclusion

This study focuses on the question of how Syrian-Saudi relations have been sustained even at times of acute differences of interests. The reasons for the outwardly co-operative nature of their relations can be found mostly not in the existence of shared goals or sympathies but, counter-intuitively, in their acute differences. The fact that the two actors have been locked in the common Arabo-Islamic system, characterised by exceptionally intense interactions and binding values (Noble, 1991: 55-60), has compelled them to search for a formula for working together, even at times of acute and visible conflicts. Such co-operation with voices of opposite interests from its own was particularly vital to both Riyadh and Damascus because neither was capable of single-handedly imposing a hegemonic order onto the larger Arab world.

When the bilateral relations were founded on such a fragile basis, the co-operation was bound to be a shaky one, in which both sides attempted to maintain as much leverage as possible over the other. The Saudi support for the Syrian opposition groups and vice versa were one manifestation of such attempts by Riyadh and Damascus to retain the cards of threats and manipulation. Furthermore, in their domestic policies, the Asad regime and the Saudi royal family have both gained from the bilateral relations; Asad's cordial relationship with Riyadh helped improve his image in the Islamic light, and Riyadh's hosting of some Syrian oppositions was at times an advantage for Asad. In turn, Damascus' approval of Riyadh's policy and its expression of fraternity with the Saudi leadership served, in a distant way, to dampen anti-Al-Sa'ud critiques against the lack of Saudi commitment to Arabism and the government's reactionary orientation. Thus, such a trade-off of legitimacy created a curious compatibility between the two.

At the Amman Summit of November 1980, Saudi Arabia embarked on mediation between Syria and Jordan largely from fear of instability in the region. The fact that Syria's Khaddam, however reluctantly, participated in the conference after receiving considerable pressure from Riyadh testified to the extent of Saudi leverage, particularly when the 'stick' was accompanied with a 'carrot'—promises of financial aid. Nevertheless, that was as far as Syria's compromise reached; Damascus obstinately refused to revise its policy and demonstrated its centrality in the Arab regional affairs by taking hostage the PLO and the Steadfastness Front member states, a performance repeated more dramatically at the Fez I Summit of November 1981. Saudi Arabia's attempt to use the political rent to dictate Syrian policy failed yet again during the Syrian-Israeli Missile Crisis. Its threat to withhold funding for the exclusively Syrian ADF also proved to be insufficient to tame Damascus.

What the Syrians expected from the Saudis during the Missile Crisis was in fact less the promises of financial support than tangible pressure on Washington to restrain the Israelis, the benefit which the Kingdom repeatedly failed to deliver during the period under investigation. Damascus, as a result, had little reason to follow the Saudi dictate and defiantly went on to sabotage the Saudi Middle East plan announced by Fahd. Such Syrian tactics of gaining regional influence through deliberately jeopardising Arab consensus—and by extension, foiling Riyadh's regional policy—were exemplified in Damascus' behaviour in the Gulf arena. Its April 1982 economic deal with Iran was most damaging materially and symbolically to the interests of Iraq and its Arab supporters. However, Syria's policy of 'being deliberately difficult' came at a cost; by May 1982, its regional isolation had weakened Damascus' standing to such an extent that the Syrians came to fresh realisation that it could not afford to dispense with Riyadh. As a result, Damascus initiated extensive consultations with the Saudi leadership and responded positively to Saudi request for mediation between Tehran and the Gulf Arabs, notwithstanding Tehran's obstinate rejection of such Syrian efforts.

Syria's troubles were further exacerbated in the aftermath of the Israeli invasion of Lebanon. The 1982 Lebanon War and the unmistakable Syrian military defeat in it temporarily removed a major obstacle to Saudi regional dominance, i.e. Damascus' defiance. Aside from a verbal expression of solidarity, the Saudi leadership pointedly refused all Syrian pledges for support, such as the unsheathing of the oil weapon against the US—an accomplice of the Israeli operation—and a symbolic dispatch of Saudi troops to the warfront. That Asad personally paid an unannounced visit to the Saudi capital to enlist more tangible backing highlighted the importance Syria placed on the Saudi role. Riyadh, instead, decided to exploit the occasion to discipline Syria; when official Saudi statements called for evacuation of *all* foreign troops from Lebanon, they were thinly disguised expression of Riyadh's long-term desire to rid the country of Syrian influence, while appearing to be directed against Israel.

Following the announcement of the Reagan Plan in early September 1982, King Fahd's confidence was boosted to such a degree that he was prepared to resubmit his peace plan, soiled only ten months ago. The contrast between Syria's status at the Fez I and the Fez II summits could not have been more stark. Damascus had lost the extensive control over the PLO and the Lebanese affairs, its Soviet ally had been discredited in the Arab eyes, and the need for Saudi cash to rearm its battered armed forces was ever more acute. Thus, the Fez II summit, one of the triumphant moments in Saudi diplomatic history, materialised by momentarily winning Syrian complacency.

This chapter, by focusing on the period of relative Saudi

preponderance vis-à-vis Syria and more generally within the Arab system, explored the dynamics in which Saudi Arabia, even in its moment of strength, could not dispense with Syrian co-operation to achieve any of its major regional policy goals. As Syrian-Saudi bilateral relations were shaped by factors outside the strictly bilateral issues, each actor's bargaining power also fluctuated according to external developments. Decisive factors were: the attitudes of the global superpowers; degree of control exercisable over other Arab actors like the PLO; acuteness of immediate threats from 'enemies' like Israel and Iran; and those enemies' success in achieving their militant goals. Damascus and Riyadh held markedly different bargaining cards on almost all the regional issues, and the tools they possessed in addressing these issues were also diametrical opposites—be it alliance with the superpowers or the military, financial, and demographic capabilities. Yet, locked in the binding constraints of the Arab system—whose link by nature extended beyond physical proximity but defined the norms and values to be observed by the member states, both capitals most of the time strove to co-operate with each other instead of accentuating their differences, thereby taking advantage of the other actors' strength and substituting it for its own deficiency.

# 4

# THE BEGINNING OF THE END OF 'THE SAUDI ERA'
## (October 1982–March 1984)

If the overwhelming success of the Fez II summit, wherein what was virtually a Saudi peace plan was endorsed unanimously, gave an appearance of Saudi prestige and the Kingdom's emergence as a new regional power, the rapid demise of the Fez formula testified to the fragility of the Kingdom's power base. In hindsight, its newly acquired status as a leading Arab and Third World power was hopelessly short-lived and largely illusionary. Indeed, its earlier failure to demonstrate a concerted influence during the Israeli invasion of Lebanon[1]—despite its oil, financial muscle or political leverage in the Western capitals—had marked, in Muhammad H. Haikal's words, the end of 'the Saudi era'.[2] In the period that followed, Saudi Arabia desperately attempted to dominate Arab politics through the following strategies: 1) integration of the Fez resolutions with the Reagan Plan, 2) mediation between contending Arab actors, 3) formulation of national reconciliation in Lebanon and 4) enlistment of broadest Arab support for Iraq in the war effort against Iran. All of the above ended with little positive achievement, if not outright failure, which was in large part, though not exclusively, caused by Syria's return from the lowest ebb to the centre stage of Arab politics and its ability to weld a veto over major Arab decisions.

Syria's comeback was facilitated by a number of factors. First and foremost, a new relationship with the USSR was formed, in which the superpower became more forthcoming in supplying Syria with advanced weaponry albeit under stricter Soviet supervision on its usage. After the near total military defeat in Lebanon, the Soviet stakes in Syria's inviolability had become higher, partly as a matter of safeguarding its prestige and partly as a cornerstone for thwarting the Reagan Plan and the ensuing US domination of the region. To the Syrians, this Soviet change in attitude not only accelerated the rearmament programme to an unprecedented speed and degree, but also meant that Damascus had more room for manoeuvre in defining the scope of confrontation with Israel. Such assistance from its superpower ally was conducive to Syria's ascendancy, amply demonstrated in the control of the PLO and in the restoration of military pre-eminence in Lebanon. In Lebanon, whose control constituted a pillar of Syria's regional influence, Syria managed to maintain its military presence, in spite of the mounting external pressures for a withdrawal. Furthermore, despite the concession made at the Fez II summit to revise the attitude towards the Iran-Iraq war, Damascus successfully avoided tension with the most powerful regional ally, Iran, whose performance at the war fronts was improving day by day. Furthermore, at least until late 1983, the Asad regime was blessed with relative domestic tranquillity, unlike the previous period marked by violent confrontation with the opposition movements.

The decline in Saudi influence was already manifest two months after the Fez II summit, when the Saudi leadership announced the postponement of the forthcoming Arab summit, scheduled to take place in its own capital in November. Riyadh had to concede to the fact that the Arab consensus, which it so dearly assembled two months ago, had been dangerously eroded, so much so that the summit was destined to fail. Such a failure would be, in the short-term calculation of the Saudi government, a further blow to its shaky claim for regional leadership. In the longer term, Saudi obsession with promotion of Arab co-operation and solidarity was underlined by its belief that 'a broad Arab consensus on major issues could keep Arab radicalism at bay, moderate disputes and provide a climate in which a rich, conservative country [like Saudi Arabia] could achieve the tranquillity it sought and prosper' (*MECS*, 1982–1983: 751). The return to the pre-Fez II Arab division meant also the return to Saudi policy of wavering between attempts to win Syrian support for its mediation efforts and yielding to Syria's objections, allowing Damascus to pursue its own exclusive interests. Thus, Damascus came to be named as one of the two capitals, together with Washington, 'whose attitudes most affected [Riyadh's] policy' (*MECS*, 1983–1984: 616).

The Saudi obsession with promoting and securing 'Arab consensus'—at times synonymous with winning Syrian consent (*MECS*, 1982–1983: 744)—was the very reason behind its complacency and co-operation with Syria, the country at the opposite end of the Arab political spectrum to itself. This chapter examines in detail how Saudi Arabia quickly slipped from its moment of triumph, and reverted to the earlier pattern of being compelled to seek Syrian co-operation, even through downright appeasement. First, the Kingdom committed its energy to the implementation of the Reagan Plan as a basis for this elusive 'consensus'. Syria successfully countered by ensuring that the Jordanian-PLO negotiation would fail, and by extension the entire Plan. Second, when the 17 May agreement was signed as a quasi-peace treaty between Lebanon and Israel, the Saudis became sandwiched between two opposing pressures: unrealistic American demands to bring Syria into endorsing the agreement and Syrian obstinacy against it, invoking 'Arab rights'. This Saudi dilemma was further heightened when Washington and Damascus directly exchanged fire after the Lebanese Shuf Mountain war intensified. Finally, Iran's military success in the Iran-Iraq war, *the* major foreign policy concern of the Kingdom at the time, came as a warning to Saudi Arabia that Syria, Tehran's most significant Arab ally, had to be treated with caution and appeasement (*MECS*, 1982–1983: 165).

### The Reagan Plan, the Fez Formula and the Superpower Commitment to Syria and Saudi Arabia (October 1982–April 1983)

In the post-Fez II period, the cornerstone of Saudi regional policy came to be defined as progress towards implementation of the Fez resolutions, thereby maintaining the Arab consensus as achieved at the summit. The biggest missing link between the Fez principles and their implementation was the Likud government's willingness to participate in any peace initiative—to be demonstrated by the freezing of settlement activities and the withdrawal from Lebanon. The Arabs were painfully made aware that the only actor which could potentially deliver Israel to the negotiating table was Washington. Hence, Saudi policy on the Middle East peace came to aim at synchronising the Fez principles with the Reagan Plan, despite the fact that in their key points the two plans were incompatible; for instance, the former explicitly reiterated the PLO's authority as the representative of the Palestinian cause, while the latter called for a federation with Jordan as the solution. Within weeks, however, the Saudi attempt to uphold the Fez principles encountered obstacles mainly due to Syrian objections.

Indeed, it did not take long for the Syrians to show in deeds their defiance of the Fez agreement, sealing its fate to be no more than an agreement on paper. On Iran and Lebanon, in particular, Syria's earlier endorsement of the items concerned was proven to be merely perfunctory. As discussed in the previous chapter, the Syrian Information Minister hastily travelled to Tehran within days after the summit to reassure the Iranian leadership that his country's commitment to the alliance with Iran was unaltered. On Lebanon, top-level officials issued statements which justified continued presence of Syrian forces in Lebanon.[3] On the larger issue of the Arab-Israeli conflict, Syria began to harden its position from the initial ambivalence; it turned bitterly opposed to the central role assigned to Jordan in the Reagan initiative and to Washington's total disregard for the Golan (*BBC/SWB/ME*, 20 and 22 October; *MEI*, 26 November 1982).

Thus, from the outset of the post-Fez II period, the Saudi initiative was circumscribed by the need to reconcile Saudi, Syrian and US interests and to ease the tension between the latter two. The Saudi gesture at the end of 1982 to improve relations with Moscow can be seen in this light. At a time when Sa'ud al-Faisal headed a delegation to Moscow of the Arab seven-member committee to discuss the Fez principles and the Reagan Plan, Saudi papers published favourable remarks on the new Soviet leadership under Andropov (*BBC/SWB/ME*, 3 December 1982), although speculation of imminent restoration of diplomatic ties with Moscow was dismissed by Crown Prince 'Abdallah (*Al-Safir*, 10 December 1982). The friendly gesture can be interpreted partly as a display of responsiveness to Syria's long-standing demand for *rapprochement* between Riyadh and Moscow, while simultaneously pressurising the US to deliver an ever-uncompromising Israel to the negotiating table; otherwise, Riyadh signalled to Washington, the Soviet involvement in the peace initiative would become a real prospect. King Fahd also attempted to rally wider Arab backing in a visit to Algeria, where he conducted a tripartite meeting with the Algerian President and Yasir 'Arafat on Fez II (*BBC/SWB/ME*, 23 November 1982). Although Fahd made a point of briefing Asad on the meeting (*MEI*, 26 November 1982), the PLO's display of autonomy added to Syria's frustration and hardening of its opposition towards the idea of negotiated peace. Also, in the last quarter of 1982, 'Ali al-Sha'ir, the Saudi ambassador to Lebanon, strenuously mediated between the Lebanese government, Damascus and the PLO, and committed a multi-billion dollar fund for the reconstruction of the war-stricken country in order to lure the Lebanese government away from a separate peace agreement with Israel.[4] The Saudis feared that an agreement, as was then emerging, was not linked to the Palestinian problem nor did it envisage an immediate and full Israeli withdrawal, and, hence, would ignore Syria's interest in Lebanon (*Al-Nahar*, 30 December 1982; *MECS*, 1982–1983: 754-755).

Saudi efforts to display concern for Damascus' interests notwithstanding, Syria's position on the Reagan Plan was transformed from initial ambivalence (*MECS*, 1982–1983: 166) to total and irreversible objection; on 14 January, Foreign Minister Khaddam publicly expressed his government's rejection of the Plan and warned that all Arabs should be alert to the American 'intrigues' (Syrian Arab News Agency, 14 January

1983 cited in *MECS*, 1982–1983: 819). The following day, Syrian daily *Al-Thawrah* reiterated the objection, particularly to the Jordanian-PLO federation (cited in *BBC/SWB/ME*, 17 January 1983). The timing of these announcements was particularly significant, coinciding with the arrivals of Soviet arms and military personnel on the very same day. The visit by the Soviets was the latest in a series of meetings since June 1982, and the intensity of contacts continued throughout Andropov's reign. Syrians had successfully exploited the superpower's desire to restore its 'lost honour' in Lebanon and to undermine the Reagan Plan; Moscow agreed to deploy Soviet-manned SAM-5 surface-to-air missiles in Syria—the first time such missiles were deployed outside the Warsaw Pact territory (Halliday, 1987-1988: 57)—and the deal was topped up with \$2.8 billion worth of weapons for the expansion of the Syrian armed forces between June 1982 and early 1984 (Karsh, 1988: 72-73). Based on Soviet aid, Syrian military expanded its capacity from 300,000 soldiers in 1983 to 500,000 in 1985 (Zisser, 2001: 39). Politically, Moscow issued public statements in support of Damascus' special role in Lebanon, an issue which had previously been one of the biggest sources of friction between the two capitals.[5] One immediate consequence of such backing from Andropov, whose reign marked the peak of Syrian-Soviet friendship, was the boost in Syria's self-confidence to frustrate the Reagan Plan and the emerging Israeli-Lebanese accord (*MECS*, 1982–1983: 801-802; Karsh, 1991: 148).

Khaddam's open attack against the Reagan Plan foreshadowed a difficult ride for Crown Prince 'Abdallah, who arrived in Damascus the very next day after the Soviets—a peak of Saudi efforts to build Arab consensus on both the Middle East peace and the Iran-Iraq war (*Al-Nahar*, 16 and 17 January 1983). The visit ended in failure, and subsequently, Saudi Arabia shunned away from publicly initiating talks between adversaries, reverting to reticence towards Syria's hard-line opposition. In early 1983, Syrian officials repeatedly voiced criticisms towards 'deviation from the Fez plan', by which they warned the Saudis of the danger of replacing the Fez formula with the Reagan Plan (e.g. *BBC/SWB/ME*, 24 February 1983). When Damascus home service commentary attacked unnamed Arab rulers' attitudes towards Palestine, it critically referred to a key phrase which King Fahd used in his earlier speech on the need to maintain impetus of the peace process—'the time factor (*'amil al-waqt*)' in bringing the Arabs together (*Al-Nahar*, 19 January 1983). The commentary read:

> Have those Arab rulers really exploited *the time factor* in the real sense of the word in the interest of the Arab people so that they can have the right now to warn this people that it is too late? The time of

which they are afraid seems to be the time of the Americanisation of the Arab world, because they believe that their interests depend on this Americanisation (19 March 1983 cited in *BBC/SWB/ME*, 22 March 1983, emphasis added).

In tandem with these rigorous campaigns in the inter-Arab arena, Damascus strove to promote an anti-'Arafat front within the PLO—an influence Syrians appeared to have lost in the immediate aftermath of the Israeli invasion but subsequently regained (Brand, 1990: 27). After the 1982 invasion, the PLO suffered the most serious challenge to its organisational integrity. In the course of self-criticism, anti-'Arafat revolt broke out among al-Fath forces in Lebanon's Biqa' valley, and subsequently among the wider PLO ranks. Syria took advantage of the split, partially out of an attempt to foil 'Arafat's negotiations with King Hussain, but more generally in undermining any PLO move towards increased autonomy from the Syrian influence. Syria's influence on various Palestinian factions was evident when the Palestinian National Congress's Algiers meeting on 15 February 1983 categorically rejected the suitability of the Reagan Plan as a basis for the solution to the conflict with Israel, although it did not explicitly condemn contacts with King Hussain. In addition, Asad's determination to undermine 'Arafat's position within the PLO hierarchy may also have been tinged with the personal animosity between the two characters (Seale, 1990: 378).

Syria's two-track policy of diplomatic campaign against the Reagan Plan and anti-'Arafat strategy was instrumental in aborting the Jordanian-Palestinian dialogue in April, thereby driving a nail in the coffin of the Reagan Plan (*MECS,* 1982–1983: 753). Prior to Jordan's official announcement of the dialogue's collapse on 10 April, intensive contacts with Damascus were initiated by Riyadh. On 5 April, the very day when the Saudi government issued a statement calling for an emergency Arab summit meeting, presumably for the purpose of resolving the crisis between King Hussain and 'Arafat, King Fahd consulted President Asad by phone (*BBC/SWB/ME*, 7 April 1983). Three days later, Foreign Minister Sa'ud al-Faisal arrived in Damascus via Amman to persuade Syria to participate in the conference but without success (*MECS*, 1982–1983: 229, 812). The collapse of the talks left keen disappointment in Riyadh, but the subsequent attack on Syria was kept mild and implicit.[6]

Saudi Arabia's regional ambition was thwarted by the inability to capitalise on its remarkable diplomatic success of Fez II. Meanwhile, the abolition of the Reagan Plan was a prelude to Syria's return as a regional force to be reckoned with. The comeback was facilitated by the Soviet commitment to Damascus, in stark contrast to Washington's lack of understanding for Riyadh's and larger Arab interests. Also, Damascus' retention of influence in Lebanon and among the Palestinians gave added political weight to Syria's influence in the region. As will be examined later, these factors were compounded also by Syria's alliance with Iran, which by early 1983 was preparing another major offensive. In addition to Syria's sabotage of the Saudi quest for Arab consensus, its hostility to King Hussain's regime was a particular concern for the Saudi leadership; memories of serious tension on the Syrian-Jordanian border were still fresh from the incidents in 1970 and 1980. In the context of 1983, such an outbreak of hostilities could jeopardise not only the Arab consensus as enshrined in Fez but also Iraq's vital supply route via Jordan and thus weaken Iraq in its war with Iran (*MECS*, 1982–1983: 165). As one Saudi official was quoted, 'Our money gets us access, enables us to talk to more people, but not to dictate to governments like Syria' (*'Ukkaz*, 10 May 1983 cited in *MECS*, 1982–1983: 753). The rift between the two countries was to widen further in May 1983 over Lebanon.

### Lebanon (I): The 17 May Israeli-Lebanese Accord
### (May–August 1983)

Had the Israelis immediately converted their sweeping military victory of June 1982 into a diplomatic gain, the Israeli-Lebanese accord, signed almost a year later, might have seen a different fate. The change of tides started in September 1982 with a sequence of events, following Bashir Jumayyil's assassination, the massacre of Sabra and Shatila refugee camps and accession of Amin Jumayyil to the presidency, Bashir's brother with less charisma and a different political outlook. Bashir's death removed from the Israeli plans for Lebanon the most reliable local ally,[7] and the subsequent massacre in the Palestinian camps caused domestic uproar within Israel, casting a dark shadow over the Likud government's Lebanese policy as a whole. Amin Jumayyil, the succeeding brother, attempted from the outset to correct the Lebanese Forces' closeness to Israel and to steer the government away from complying with Israeli demands. In this new climate, Israel's pressure on the Lebanese government to enter peace talks lagged, and the actual negotiation, though finally set in motion in December 1982, faced one deadlock after another.

It took Washington the undoing of the Reagan Plan—as signified by the collapse of the Hussain-'Arafat talks in April 1983—to commit single-mindedly to the Israeli-Lebanese accord. Also, a massive explosion in its Beirut embassy in the same month heightened the sense of urgency to find an early solution to the Lebanese quagmire.[8] US Secretarty of State George Shultz tirelessly shuttled from Jerusalem to Riyadh, Damascus and Beirut, and eventually pushed for the 17 May agreement. Philip Habib, the chief US negotiator, claimed that the agreement was 'a peace treaty in all but name'.[9] Although it did not prescribe for 'total normalisation' as such—which would involve a peace treaty, open borders, a trade agreement and more—a time-line was fixed for negotiations on free movement of people and goods to take place during the first six months after Israel's withdrawal. For the purpose of this discussion, the most significant element of its signing was in fact the secret side-agreement between Israel and Shultz, the US-Israeli Memorandum of Understanding. Wary of the 17 May accord's stipulation for Israeli troop withdrawals, the Likud government requested from the Secretary of State an immunity from the obligation to implement the accord until the Syrians and the Palestinians had redeployed their forces outside Lebanon.[10] By so doing, ironically, the implementation of the Israeli-Lebanese accord became hostage to a factor none of the direct protagonists could guarantee: Syria's compliance (since the Palestinian presence in Lebanon was by then at Syria's mercy). Just as the Fez II had a crucial missing link—how to get Israel to agree on its terms—the accord suffered the major inadequacy of granting President Asad a veto power (Seale, 1990: 408).

Asad was determined not to let the accord neutralise Syria's influence in Lebanon, and by extension, in the region as a whole. When the Lebanese challenge was complicated by heightening tension between Asad and 'Arafat, he simultaneously fought two battles to achieve that goal. The two immediate challenges for Syria in May 1983 were: the possible capitulation of Lebanon to Israel and the on-going battle against 'Arafat—weakened and humiliated, but not deposed. Although the 17 May accord marked the most serious diplomatic challenge to Syria's pre-eminence in Lebanon since the intervention in 1976, on the ground, motion was already underway to re-establish its overlordship.

Against the background of such measured Syrian tactics on the Lebanese battlegrounds, Saudi Arabia gradually abandoned its initial hopes of ridding Lebanon of Syrian influence, but instead succumbed to Syrian pressure. When Amin Jumayyil was first elected, there was an air of hope in the Kingdom that Lebanon was to be the testing ground where its newly gained confidence in the successful Fez II summit could be transformed into regional influence. Under Amin's presidency, Lebanese politics initially returned to the traditional pattern of an alliance between a Maronite President and the Sunni notables of Beirut, who were personally aligned with the Saudi leadership. Sa'ib Salam and his colleagues, who had been eclipsed by the PLO and the militias in the 1970s, were cast once again in the roles of spokesmen for Arabism and Islam, or in other words representatives of Saudi points of view in the Lebanese political arena (Rabinovich, 1985: 155-156). If the failure of Fez I in November 1981 had driven Bashir Jumayyil to abandon the Saudi option and to fall into Israeli arms, the manifestation in Fez II of Riyadh's ability to bring all Arabs together should, by the same token, win new friends, or so the Saudis hoped. Indeed, intense diplomatic contacts were exchanged between Amin Jumayyil and the Saudi government until the end of 1982, compounded with promises of Saudi funds for the reconstruction of Lebanon (*Al-Mustaqbal*, 16 October 1982; *MECS*, 1982–1983: 754).

Riyadh began to voice objection to the Israeli-Lebanese peace treaty negotiation, its underlying concern being that an agreement which was not linked to the Palestinian problem would 1) ignore Syria's interest in Lebanon; 2) legitimise Israel's position; and 3) fundamentally contradict Fez II's spirit of comprehensive approach to peace.[11] Meanwhile within the Jumayyil regime, frustration was growing with the Saudi inability to apply sufficient pressure on Washington to secure prompt Israeli withdrawal. Riyadh was soon running a gauntlet when Washington accused it of lack of co-operation in securing a Syrian withdrawal from Lebanon (*International Herald Tribune*, 24 January 1983), while Syria was ready to strike at the slightest hint of collaboration with the US 'imperialist' schemes (e.g. *BBC/SWB/ME*, 11 January 1983). To make matters worse, Saudi Arabia could not achieve its own desirable solution without co-operation from all the above parties who held incompatible goals. Sandwiched by demands and criticisms from multiple directions, Saudi policy in Lebanon was reduced to virtual paralysis. The examination of Syrian-Saudi dealings on the 17 May agreement underscores how Syria's leverage over Saudi Arabia was upheld by its diplomatic activism, influence in the Lebanese politico-military arena and the grip on the Palestinians.

### Syrian-Saudi Contacts over the 17 May Accord

Despite Asad's unequivocal refusal of the accord, the US administration remained confident that once it was signed, Washington's pressure (*MEED*, 20 May 1983) and Riyadh's financial leverage[12] would suffice to bring him around to endorse it. Washington failed to understand the intensity of Asad's objection and his dramatically improved military standing within Lebanon. The extent of Syria's rearmament reflected the renewed Soviet commitment to the Asad regime in order to avoid another political embarrassment after the US' unilateral success at Camp David and Syria's military defeat in June 1982 (*MEED*, 20 May 1983; Karsh, 1988: 78). More importantly, it also misjudged the Saudi leadership's view on the accord and Riyadh's ability to impose policies on Damascus (*MEED*, 13 May 1983), although the misjudgement can be attributed, at least in part, to confusing signals from Riyadh.

In spite of the initial disapproval of the Israeli-Lebanese negotiations,[13] Riyadh's attitude had turned dramatically positive by early May when the terms of the agreement first became public. There is little doubt that it was a reflection of mounting Saudi frustration with Syria's recent policies on the PLO and the Reagan Plan as well as its continued support for Iran. When Shultz arrived in Riyadh from Damascus on 7 May—after he received hours of Asad's lecture on why the Syrians would not bow to a US-Israeli *diktat*[14]—Sa'ud al-Faisal reiterated Riyadh's commitment to evacuation of *all* foreign forces from Lebanon and indirectly stated that Damascus should support the draft agreement (*BBC/SWB/ME*, 9 May 1983). King Fahd also told him that he did not believe Syria's rejection was final and that he felt Saudi Arabia might change Damascus' stand to America's satisfaction (*Times,* 9 May 1983 cited in *MECS,* 1982–1983: 759). The Saudi state-controlled media broadcast welcoming comments on the agreement, stating that 'the agreement was a success of an US initiative' and demonstration of the US' enormous ability to apply pressure on Israel and to solve or to complicate any crisis (*Al-Nahar,* 10 May 1983). One commentary added that the agreement was an inevitable compromise with reality, which should be endorsed by the Arab world ('*Ukkaz,* 12 May 1983 cited in *MECS,* 1982–1983: 755). Saudi Arabia, thus, attempted its best to avoid being trapped in the crossfire between Washington and Damascus by following its usual policy of urging the Arabs to give in to the American pressure and coating this advice with calls for Arab sovereign rights and solidarity in order to deflect Damascus' criticisms.

Riyadh's tilt towards Washington in the crosscutting pressures from the two capitals did not last long, and it soon revised its stance to keep in line with Damascus. The turning point was the visit to Jiddah by Asad and Khaddam on 8 May only hours after Shultz had departed (*Al-Nahar,* 10 May 1983). Saudi Arabia was the only country the Syrian President himself visited in order to lobby against the agreement, testifying to the importance he placed in Riyadh's role, while cabinet ministers undertook campaigns towards other Arab capitals. Although the contents of the three-round talks between Asad and Fahd were not disclosed, it is believed that the former complained bitterly about the Kingdom's support for the Israeli-Lebanese agreement, while the King also raised the issue of the internal uprising in al-Fath, proposing a 'mini-summit' of Syria, Jordan and the PLO (*MECS,* 1982–1983: 812). A spokesman of the Syrian Presidential Palace, however, emphasised that Syria and Saudi Arabia held 'identical' views on the developments in the region and the dangers of the Israeli-Lebanese agreement (*BBC/SWB/ME*, 11 May 1983).

The high-level contacts with the Syrian leadership seemed to have effected an immediate change in the Saudi position; on the day Asad departed from the Kingdom, Saud al-Faisal asserted that unlike the Israeli forces, 'the Syrians are there [in Lebanon] at the request of the Lebanese,' and, therefore, had a right to remain there until formally requested to leave by the Lebanese government (*Wall Street Journal*, 9 May 1983 cited in *MECS*, 1982–1983: 755). Prince Sultan, the Defence Minister, also told US Defence Secretary Casper Weinberger that Riyadh would not bring pressure to bear on 'any Arab nation' (Saudi Press Agency, 12 May 1983 cited in *MECS*, 1982–1983: 759), followed by another statement that the Kingdom was not a tool in the hands of any big or small power for exerting pressure on any Arab nation (*Al-Hawadith*, 20 May 1983 cited in *MECS*, 1982–1983: 755).

The Saudi dilemma originated in the impossibility of simultaneously pleasing both Washington and Damascus, and the desperation drove the Saudis into a strategy of all-round denial: Prince Sultan first claimed that he had 'not heard' that Syria rejected the Israeli-Lebanese agreement, emphasised that 'the US did not ask us to apply pressure on Syria' to withdraw its forces from Lebanon, rejected the claim that there was a Saudi initiative to mediate a Lebanese solution and then dissociated the Kingdom from the controversy as it was 'neither for nor against the agreement' (*Al-Hawadith*, 20 May 1983 cited in *MECS*, 1982–1983: 199-200). The Saudi pendulum, thus, initially swung between Washington and Damascus but eventually rested closer on Syria's side; Prince Sultan added that Syria's security was Lebanon's security and vice versa and that disagreement with Syria would not be in Lebanon's interests (*Al-Nahar*, 14 and 16 May; *Al-Safir*, 16 May 1983).

The post-Asad-Fahd summit press conference by Khaddam is instructive in underlining Riyadh's soft belly: the US connection, threat of war with Israel, increased Soviet involvement in the event of war (*BBC/SWB/ME*, 11 May; *Al-Safir*, 16 May; *Al-Nahar*, 16 May 1983). In his statement, the Syrian Minister of Foreign Affairs held the United States' 'designs' as ultimately responsible for Israel's aggression towards 'an Arab capital [i.e. Beirut]', thus implicitly warning against Arab compliance with the US policy on Lebanon—a clear signal to Riyadh. When he hinted at an expectation of war with Israel, it was a direct appeal to the Saudi regime's perennial fear of a regional war, an event which usually threatened it with instability and upsurge of radicalism. Indeed, throughout May and June even after the threat of war had faded, the Syrian leadership went to great lengths to maintain an atmosphere of imminent war, in line with its customary attempt to capitalise on Syria's status as a confrontation state (*MECS*, 1982–1983: 795). Khaddam also boasted that the Kingdom promised at the summit meeting to commit its military for Syria's defence in the event of another war with Israel, as was the case in 1973. He also invoked the Friendship Treaty with the USSR in this context, playing on Riyadh's obsession to stave off Soviet involvement in Middle Eastern affairs.

Damascus' diplomatic initiative to win the Saudis on its side was buttressed by Asad's protégés in the following weeks. When the Israeli-Lebanese accord was signed on 17 May, Syria's diplomatic campaign to explain its views started with Saudi Arabia; Interior Minister Ahmad Iskandar Ahmad travelled to the eastern city of Dhahran to meet 'Ali al-Sha'ir, his Saudi counterpart and former ambassador to Lebanon, and then delivered Asad's message to King Fahd on 'Arab viewpoints' of the accord (*Al-Nahar*, 22 May 1983). After the audience, the Minister contended that the King 'fully understood Syria's position' (*BBC/SWB/ME*, 23 May 1983), although Fahd himself no more than called for unity of Arab ranks and efforts (*BBC/SWB/ME*, 25 May 1983). The visit was reciprocated within a few days by 'Abd al-'Aziz al-Tuweijiri, who allegedly discussed with Hafiz and Rif'at al- Asad a possible easing of Syria's opposition to the accord and a gradual Syrian withdrawal from Lebanon (*Al-Nahar*, 25 May 1983). By this time, even some US experts on Middle Eastern affairs were beginning to recognise the limitation of Saudi influence on Syrian policy; Nicolas Veliotes of the State Department, who had previously maintained that the Saudis and other US Arab allies would tame the Syrians (*MEI*, 27 May 1983), came to acknowledge that 'the Saudis remain important but they are not in a position to impose their will on Syria' (*Al-Nahar*, 25 May 1983).

### *Syrian Pressure on Saudi Arabia in the Arab Regional Arena*

The pressure on Riyadh to take a firm supportive position on the 17 May agreement came from the US-supported Amin Jumayyil, who energetically lobbied to counter Syrian campaigns. Although the Kingdom persisted in its mediation efforts to achieve an immediate cease-fire and to contain the dangerous split in the Arab region over the agreement, the extent of its dilemma and confusion was apparent in the self-contradictory statements it issued; caught in the cross-fire between Damascus, Washington and Beirut, it supported and complimented all sides as if there was no contradiction. Exhausted of options, the Saudis attempted to assist Lebanon's call for the emergency Arab summit, in the hope that such an all-Arab forum would endorse their mediator role; they desperately needed the appearance of acting in the wider Arab interests when their slightest diplomatic move in any direction was destined to antagonise at least one of the three capitals.

Such a Saudi effort, however, was bound to be shot down by Damascus, which had in the past years gone out of its way to avoid a summit for fear of isolation and censure when it could afford to do so. Indeed, Syria had been very clear about its uncompromising rejection of the summit as well as any Arab mediation on Lebanon:

> Syria will never accept mediation or a compromise in a principled issue related to the pan-Arab cause and existence. No Arab brother who realises the threats posed by this agreement can be a mediator (Damascus home service, 26 May cited in *BBC/SWB/ME*, 28 May 1983).

In view of such opposition, Riyadh embarked on a customary low-key mediation. Media reports spoke in favour of the summit (e.g. *Al-Madinah*, 19 May 1983 cited in *MECS*, 1982–1983: 227n56), and Fahd promised the Lebanese that his country was 'ready to continue to try and persuade Syria to withdraw its forces from Lebanon and to find a suitable approach that would lead to the withdrawal of all foreign forces from Lebanon' (*BBC/SWB/ME*, 6 June 1983). When Jumayyil eventually made a formal call, the Saudis pinned their hopes on Prince 'Abdallah, who promptly departed to convince the Syrians to attend the summit and to reconcile Damascus with Beirut as well as with Baghdad (Saudi Press Agency, 6 June 1983). Although Saudi sources close to Prince 'Abdallah claimed upon his departure from Damascus that the summit was 'close' (*Al-Nahar*, 8 June 1983), it was evident that the Prince had failed to convince Syria; on the same day as the Saudi statement, Syrian daily *Tishrin* defiantly criticised 'some Arab brothers' for trying to mediate between Syria and the signatories of the Israeli-Lebanese accord, even if their motives 'might be innocent and sincere' (*BBC/SWB/ME*, 9 June 1983).

Prince 'Abdallah was not the only Arab dignitary who arrived in Damascus at that time. Syria's diplomatic campaign towards other Arab states also appeared to be paying off, when the Arab League Secretary-General and the Algerian President also appeared in the Syrian capital almost simultaneously. The latter maintained its reservation towards Syria's position on the accord, but expressed solidarity with Syria 'in good and bad days' (*Al-Nahar*, 6 June 1983). A Syrian broadcast boasted that these contacts 'have shown that Syria's position enjoys broad Arab and international respect and support' (*BBC/SWB/ME*, 9 June 1983), reflecting Damascus' restored confidence as a pivotal state in the Arab East.

Riyadh never raised again the proposal to convene an extraordinary summit on Lebanon and instead, distanced itself from the Israeli-Lebanese agreement; Riyadh subtly signalled the absence of its association, when 'Ali al-Sha'ir's well-publicised private visit to Beirut was carefully timed to take place *after* the Lebanese government's ratification of the accord (*Al-Nahar,* 17 June 1983). Furthermore, Prince Talal bin 'Abd al-'Aziz, a special Saudi emissary to Washington, endorsed the Syrian role in Lebanon—'if the Syrians withdraw now, there would be another war'— although he qualified his statement by emphasising that the Kingdom was doing 'maximum that is possible' to achieve the eventual withdrawal of all forces (*MEED*, 24 June 1983). Thus, Riyadh relinquished the attempts to negotiate Syria's acceptance of the Israeli-Lebanese accord and its withdrawal from Lebanon (*MECS*, 1982–1983: 202), and this was at least in part attributed to Asad's success in rallying wider Arab support.

### Syrian Hegemony in Lebanon:
### Cultivating the Lebanese Opposition

In tandem with diplomatic campaigns centring around Syrian-Saudi dialogues, the Syrians rigorously created new facts on the Lebanese ground to improve their bargaining position. Three days before the accord was signed, Asad mobilised key anti-Jumayyil, anti-accord figures to hold the first of a series of meetings, which in the following month came to establish an opposition coalition, the National Salvation Front (*Jabhat al-Khalas al-Watani*). The Front was led by influential personalities: former President Suleiman Faranjiyyah, former Prime Minister Rashid Karami, and Druze leader and Progressive Socialist Party president, Walid Junblat. The Shi'a movement of Amal did not join the coalition—to signal its independence from Syrian influence (Bailey, 1987: 234n15)—but was closely aligned to Junblat. The implications were: 1) the Front enjoyed a broad, cross-sectarian base; and 2) the Druze occupied a dominant position within the coalition. The Front's link to the Syrians was unconcealed; its Charter was broadcast on Damascus home service on 23 July (Seale, 1990: 517n20) and Junblat announced its official establishment the following day upon his return from Damascus. He hailed it as an alternative Lebanese government to the sectarian 'Phalangist government' (*MECS*, 1982–1983: 808).

With Syrian and Amal assistance, the Druze led the opposition's military campaign against the Lebanese Forces and the Israeli positions and succeeded in pressurising the Israelis to re-deploy their forces from the Shuf mountains to the Awali River line, forty kilometres to the south and forty-five kilometres north of the Israeli border. Approximately a year after the humiliating military defeat against the Israeli forces, the Syrians had reversed the situation in Lebanon completely, and once again, they proved to be the foreign presence whose interest could not be ignored. As Rabinovich summarises:

the assassination of Bashir set in motion a chain of events that neutralised Syria's principal adversaries in Lebanon. Asad excelled in locating their weaknesses and in exploiting them to the full. He understood that in the Lebanese arena it was sometimes better to remain passive and let the contradictions inherent in his rivals' positions work for him (1985: 187).

Within a month of the inception of the accord, the Americans came to realise that their policy of assisting an isolated regime of Amin Jumayyil was doomed and attempted to reopen a channel of communication with Asad through the help of the Saudis. The first of the Saudi mediation efforts took place when a new figure was appointed from within the Saudi royal circle to deliver Fahd's message to Asad: Prince Bandar bin Sultan (*Al-Nahar,* 20 June 1983). As ambassador-designate to Washington and son of the powerful Defence and Aviation Minister, he was well placed to mediate between Washington and fellow Arabs.[15] Press reports quoting diplomatic sources were optimistic that Bandar's visit on 19 June would lead to a convention of high-level meetings between Syria and the US (*Al-Nahar,* 20 June 1983), but Shultz's invitation to Khaddam to visit Washington was declined on the grounds of scheduling difficulties (*MEED,* 24 June 1983); Asad went so far as to deny categorically any knowledge of Khaddam's planned visit (*BBC/SWB/ME,* 25 June 1983). Instead it was Shultz who had to honour his Syrian counterpart with a visit on 5 July after touring Saudi Arabia and Lebanon (*BBC/SWB/ME,* 6 July 1983); according to *MEI,* 'it was as though Washington had scored a break through just by getting to see the man [Asad]' (*MEI,* 8 July 1983). Following Shultz's departure from Damascus, the Lebanese government criticised the shaky American commitment to implementation of the accord, or more specifically, to securing a full withdrawal of all foreign forces (*BBC/SWB/ME,* 7 July 1983).

The Syrians were, thus, comfortably placed to play for time and derive maximum gains from its revived bargaining position. *MEI* observed:

> The new definition of power [in Lebanon] is: who [among Reagan, Begin and Asad] can live most comfortably with the current situation, and who is best placed to pursue his interests? The answer is: Hafez al-Assad by a long way (8 July 1983).

Nevertheless, Syrian realism had always dictated that ultimately they would have to deal with Washington in order to attain a desirable regional order. Asad had always kept the door open for talks with Washington and even agreed to the formation of an American-Syrian working commission to consult on Lebanon (Seale, 1990: 412). Syria's goodwill was most indicative when in mid-July it helped free an American national and acting President of American University of Beirut, David S. Dodge, who was abducted by a pro-Iranian Shi'i group, Islamic Amal, led by Hussain Musavi.[16]

In the light of such direct contacts between Washington and Damascus, the Saudi role in bridging the difference between them may have been less than instrumental. What is evident, however, was that Syria's improved standing and performance in the political and military map of Lebanon imposed changes of attitude in Washington. In consequence, Saudi Arabia also was left with no option but to support Damascus' cause, no matter how disagreeable Syria's tactics may have been.

### Syria's Second Frontline in Lebanon: the PLO

While the 17 May agreement heightened the tension in the Lebanese battlefield, Asad simultaneously confronted another challenger to Syria's key role in the Arab-Israeli conflict as a whole: Yasir 'Arafat (Seale, 1990: 412). Damascus had been quietly backing the anti-'Arafat faction led by Abu Musa within al-Fath since February (*MEI*, 8 July 1983). In May, at the time when the 17 May agreement deepened political crisis in Lebanon, this internal dissent developed into a full-fledged military rebellion, launched from the Syrian-controlled Biqa'. Although Syria vehemently denied involvement, it is unlikely that the uprising was staged without its consent, if not active backing. Damascus had a strong motivation to do so, too; like Syria, the Abu Musa faction was against 'Arafat's 'flirting' with Jordan and the Reagan Plan. Such a tactical consideration was compounded by the long-standing personal animosity between 'Arafat and Asad, and the tension culminated in 'Arafat's expulsion from Damascus on 24 June (*BBC/SWB/ME*, 25 June 1983).

Saudi Arabia, historically a keen supporter of 'Arafat, stood firmly behind the al-Fath leader. It had always preferred dealing with al-Fath rather than with the PLO as a whole, and with 'Arafat in his capacity as the al-Fath leader rather than as PLO chairman (*MECS*, 1982–1983: 199). This was in part because al-Fath in its formative years bore characteristics of an Islamist political movement, while the PLO was comprised of networks of greater diversity, including the Marxists and the Arab socialists. When the intra-PLO feud broke out, Riyadh actively demonstrated its support for 'Arafat (*MECS*, 1982–1983: 199, 226n38), while expressing unmistakable criticism of Syria's policy—although, as always, Damascus was not explicitly censured (*MECS*, 1982–1983: 756). Riyadh's intention to mediate between Asad and 'Arafat was obvious when on the very day 'Arafat was asked to leave Damascus never to return,

Sa'ud al-Faisal arrived in the Syrian capital for talks on 'internal differences in the Palestinian field and how to mend a rift,'(Syrian Arab News Agency cited in *Al-Nahar*, 25 June 1983). The effort was followed up three weeks later by Saudi Minister of Education 'Abd al-'Aziz al-Khuwaytir, following a PLO delegation's visit to the Kingdom three days earlier (*Al-Nahar*, 13 June 1983). Intense consultation continued between Syria and Saudi Arabia, as Khuwaytir's visit was reciprocated within a few days by Khaddam (*Al-Nahar*, 25 July 1983). By the end of July, Bandar was back in Damascus for the second time since the disruption of relationship between Syria and the PLO.[17]

All its mediation efforts notwithstanding, Saudi Arabia failed to change Damascus' attitude towards 'Arafat and his al-Fath followers. Support for the PLO was one cause through which the Saudi regime could safely appear to demonstrate Arab, or even revolutionary, credentials. For that reason, it was originally more assertive in expressing its frustration with Syria's policy towards al-Fath than with other issues related to Lebanon. Yet, in the month after 'Arafat's expulsion from Damascus, the Syrians successfully reasserted themselves as overlords of the PLO. It is important to note that the two superpowers' attitude had much to do with this development; the Soviets abandoned initial neutrality between its two allies and tilted towards Damascus, while Washington weakened the PLO's claim for an independent voice by adamantly adhering to the policy of non-recognition. Thus, the Saudi criticism or pressure did not translate to sufficient influence on Damascus to review its hostile policy towards 'Arafat and his faction within the PLO. In fact, on the contrary, Syria's reassertion of hegemony over both Lebanon and the PLO gained momentum. Before the end of the year, 'Arafat's faction was to be expelled from Tripoli, the PLO's last stronghold in Lebanon, and the Mountain War in the Shuf culminated in the victory of the Syrian-backed Lebanese opposition.

In sum, the Syrian-Saudi dealings surrounding the 17 May accord, most clearly exemplified one aspect of Saudi dilemma: the need to achieve two mutually incompatible goals of falling in line with Washington and keeping Syria sweet, thereby staving off attacks on its Arab nationalist credentials. Significantly, the Saudis altered their policy from initial support for the US-sponsored accord to endorsement of Syria's objection to it, despite heavy pressure from the Reagan administration. Indeed, support for Syria's role in Lebanon was a remarkable departure even from Riyadh's own definition of policy objectives—evacuation of all foreign forces from Lebanon and establishment of an effective central government authority in Beirut.

Syria's success in winning over the Saudis can be attributed to the two-track strategy of active diplomatic campaigns and military build-up. Syria's regional diplomacy, not only its focus on Riyadh as was demonstrated by Asad's visit to Jiddah in early May, pressurised Riyadh when Syria won support from Moscow, Tehran and other Arab capitals. Damascus inched ever closer to Moscow under Andropov, and the closeness of the tie translated into the largest build-up of Syria's arsenals, which resulted in renewed confidence in its military capability. On most of the battle grounds of Lebanon, Syria was able to re-establish its military dominance simply by rallying the opposition forces against the US-backed Amin Jumayyil regime and quietly backing anti-'Arafat factions within the PLO. The fate of the 17 May accord was sealed; *MEI* observed at the time: 'Now that the agreement is there, the beauty of the thing from the viewpoint of the Syrians is that they have to do literally nothing in order to kill it stone dead' (27 May 1983). In this new turn of events, Saudi Arabia came to see little benefit in adhering to its initial compliance with the US policy.

Nevertheless, Damascus did have to play its cards carefully with Riyadh in order for this success to be sustained. This was partly because the latter held a 'swing' vote in determining the moderate Arab states' position on major regional issues. On this occasion, however, another function Riyadh often performs, i.e. an access point to Washington, did not appear to be of much use to Damascus. Also, Riyadh continued to be a main financier for Syria, whose economy had slowed down considerably (*Al-Nahar*, 7 June 1983). Estimates of Saudi aid were, as usual, varied. *MEED* reported that it had shrunk from an estimated $1,200 million a year to $800 million (20 May 1983), but *Middle East Currency Reports* gave a figure of some $1 billion in 1983—most of which was to finance military equipment imports from the Soviet Union (cited in *MECS*, 1982–1983: 820) Furthermore, at the time when Riyadh was attempting to persuade Damascus to accept the Israeli-Lebanese accord, reports circulated that Syria made its withdrawal of forces from Lebanon conditional on $12 billion financial assistance from the Kingdom as well as other requirements (*Al-Safir*, 2 June 1983). Syria's brinkmanship continued in the following months, much to the torment of Riyadh, to demonstrate its pivotal position in inter-Arab diplomacy as the Israeli withdrawal from the Shuf mountain triggered the so-called Mountain War.

### Lebanon (II): From the Mountain War to the US Marines Withdrawal (September 1983–March 1984)

From the very beginning of his presidency, Amin Jumayil attempted to distance himself from direct Israeli tutelage as much as the situation allowed. As he became cornered by the growing, widespread opposition against the 17 May accord, he became, in Israeli eyes, an incapable and also untrustworthy ally.[18] In Israel, the rising military cost and number of casualties made the Lebanese operation an unpopular venture in domestic public opinion, and the Likud government finally announced at the end of August a unilateral decision to withdraw from the Shuf mountains and the area around Beirut. This withdrawal—followed by fierce fighting between the Lebanese Army on one hand, and the Druze and Amal on the other—marked the beginning of latter's ascendancy. It also triggered the United States' direct involvement in the fighting on the losing side of the Maronites, leading eventually to the US force's direct clashes with the Syrian army. The Jumayyil regime, abandoned by Israel, was literally upheld by Washington's commitment alone, and initially, it appeared that Washington was prepared to go a long distance in order to tilt the power balance in favour of the weakened Maronite President. The first US Marines' bombardment of Syrian-held positions in the Shuf Mountain took place in mid-September and continued thereafter, reaching the brink of war with Syria by December.

Saudi Arabia actively undertook its favourite role as a mediator from the very beginning of this conflict between Syria and the Lebanese government as well as between Damascus and Washington—the two capitals whose decision most affected its own standing in the region at the time. In these mediation efforts, however, Saudi Arabia did not go beyond its customary practice of stepping in only when a reasonable chance of achieving a positive result had emerged in the horizon. Its role thus remained largely ceremonious,[19] and such absence of conviction allowed Syria to run the show. Handicapped also by its superpower ally the United States' insensitivity for Riyadh's interests and constraints, Saudi Arabia resigned to endorsing Syria's primacy in the Lebanese affairs. The investigation of the dynamics of events in the Lebanese Mountain War highlights how the superpowers' policy to the Arab region can determine Syria and Saudi Arabia's attitudes towards their bilateral relations. It also identifies the nature of threat from which Saudi Arabia feared, when Syria perceived its core interests were harmed.

### The 25 September Cease-fire (September 1983)

Israel's unilateral withdrawal was to leave a power vacuum in the Shuf Mountain area, and the outbreak of hostilities there between the Lebanese Forces and the Druze-led oppositions was widely foreseen. Riyadh's initiative to mediate between the two took off as early as mid-August when Israel publicised its intention to withdraw. In this context, Prince Bandar bin Sultan visited Damascus on 18 August (*Al-Nahar*, 19 August 1983; *Al-Hawadith*, 26 August 1983), followed by another visit to

Damascus on 1 September within a day after the formal announcement from Israel (*Al-Nahar*, 3 September 1983). Bandar was accompanied by Rafiq al-Hariri on these missions, a Lebanese-cum Saudi national, later to become Lebanon's Prime Minister in the post-civil war era.[20] The person of Hariri is a living example of the long-term Saudi interest and influence over Lebanon at the highest level of human contacts. Meanwhile, Bandar's countless visits to the Syrian capital in the following month underscored Damascus' centrality in the Lebanese dialogues. Damascus was Riyadh's single most important interlocutor on the issue—more than any one Lebanese or Palestinian faction was—and it also provided the venue for Saudi contacts with the Lebanese oppositions (*MECS*, 1982–1983: 755).

Bandar's mediation efforts notwithstanding, the fighting in the Shuf intensified, and reports of massacres committed by both sides were aired daily (Petran, 1987: 320-322). Within days, the Syrian Foreign Ministry presented a memorandum to the Arab League Secretary-General on severance of ties with the Beirut government, because the 17 May accord turned Lebanon into an Israeli 'protectorate' (*BBC/ME/SWB*, 7 September 1983). As Lebanon's Shafiq Wazzan begged for the Saudi efforts to continue, Bandar returned to Damascus on 9 September (*BBC/ME/SWB*, 9 September 1983). He then shuttled back to Damascus from Larnaca, where the Lebanese government's delegation had been on standby, gained approval from the Syrian leadership on the new draft agreement, returned to Cyprus and then back to Damascus before he returned to the Kingdom on 12 September (*Al-Nahar*, 12 and 13 September 1983). Within a day, he departed again for Damascus with another draft resolution, travelled to the Ba'abda Presidential Palace in the outskirts of Beirut to present it to the Lebanese government, but by the end of the Ba'abda meeting, Damascus was issuing its rejection of the draft (*Al-Nahar*, 16 and 17 September 1983).

Although the exact details of these draft resolutions remain unclear, the main point of disagreement between Damascus and Beirut appeared to be over the role and mandate of the Lebanese Army (*Al-Nahar*, 14 September; *BBC/ME/SWB*, 16 September 1983). The Saudi intermediary was apparently extremely frustrated with the high-handed Syrian strategy to the point where twice he came close to abandoning the mission (*MECS*, 1982–1983: 210; e.g. *BBC/ME/SWB*, 15 September; *Al-Nahar*, 17 September 1983). The frustration was conveyed publicly through his father Prince Sultan's mouthpiece. On 7 September, the Defence Minister issued a strongly-worded statement, demanding *all* foreign forces—'whatever they are'—to withdraw from Lebanon and called on the Lebanese and their neighbours to view the 'reality' and higher interests of the Arabs, or else, he threatened that the Kingdom would 'freeze' the mediation efforts (*Al-Nahar*, 8 September 1983). He also discounted the need for Syrian military presence in no obscure terms: 'I believe that the Lebanese Army and the Lebanese people are capable of looking after themselves and that is why it is better that all the forces present in Lebanon withdraw' (*BBC/ME/SWB*, 10 September 1983).

In the meantime, the US Marines were getting increasingly involved in the fighting. When Israel withdrew from the Shuf, the Marines stationed off Beirut were reinforced by 2,000 more troops, now reaching the total of 3,200. Reagan gave the Marines a green light to military action against the Druze-Syrian armies in the event of any threat to the Lebanese Forces, and the order was promptly carried out. Washington made clear to the Syrians that it would not permit the fall of Suq al-Gharb, the last stronghold of the Forces in the Shuf. Thus, the Lebanese Forces' presence was upheld, but at the cost of relinquishing any claim for superpower neutrality; the US was seen to be assisting the Lebanese government's attack against its own people, and all this for the sole purpose of assisting the Jewish state. When the cease-fire was finally reached on 25 September, Reagan naively boasted that the US' enemies accepted the deal essentially in recognition of the superior American naval power (Petran, 1987: 327-329).

It took Bandar and Hariri two more visits to Damascus in the final week before another Lebanese cease-fire was formally announced, symbolically from Damascus.[21] On most issues, the Syrians had their way.[22] In the newly established forum for national dialogue, the National Reconciliation Committee, Syria replaced the original candidates from the Sunni and Shi'i representatives with those of its own choice. Furthermore, it secured a ticket to take part in the Committee as an observer. Once again, it extracted the concession from the Lebanese Christians that a withdrawal of Syrian forces need not precede the opening of the national dialogue. Some rumours circulated that Syria, as was customary, secured some extra financial commitment from Riyadh before agreeing to the terms.[23] Besides the incontestable local superiority on the grounds, additional explanation for Syria's position of strength could be found in the command of international support, namely from the Soviet Union and South Yemen. The Soviets initially opposed the Syrian interference in Lebanon, but came to acquiesce in it, eventually agreeing to sending its own military officers to missions inside Lebanon (Ramet, 1990: 177; Freedman, R.O., 1991: 182-183).

Syria also conceded two significant points: the Lebanese Forces remained in control of Suq al-Gharb—as the Reagan administration obstinately insisted, and the US military continued to be represented in the Multi-National Forces stationed in Lebanon—whose neutrality had been questioned by Damascus (*MEED*, 23 September 1983). There appears to be much truth in the observation that Bandar's mission 'succeeded only when Damascus realised that it could not achieve all its aims in Lebanon at that stage... When its [cease-fire] agreement was finally obtained ... it was only because Damascus had become convinced that because of American pressure it could not realistically hope to make any further immediate gains' (*MECS*, 1982–1983: 813). Although Saudi Arabia also won an observer status at the Reconciliation Committee, it was a token gain in the larger context of overwhelming Syrian superiority. Riyadh's yielding attitude was apparent when the cease-fire announcement was followed by acknowledgement by senior princes[24] that the Syrian military held a distinct role in Lebanon; the statements were in stark contrast to those in the preceding months which had been calling for immediate evacuation of *all* forces.

### The Palestinians in Lebanon: A Test Case for Saudi Credibility (October–December 1983)

Saudi Arabia attempted to compensate for its political retreat in Lebanon in other regional agenda, and the most immediate issues were the hostility between Syria and the PLO and the Iran-Iraq war. The later section in this chapter will examine the Gulf development, but here the question of the PLO will be addressed, since the issue was closely intertwined with the Lebanese settlement. In a parallel development to the Shuf Mountain War, Syrian forces, together with dissident al-Fath commandos, continued their offensives against Yasir 'Arafat's headquarters in Tripoli throughout September (Petran, 1987: 340-344). As was discussed earlier, Riyadh was never complacent with the destruction of al-Fath, nor 'Arafat's personal authority for that matter. Nevertheless, after suffering a curtailment in its role in Lebanon, upholding al-Fath in the face of Syrian hostility developed into a question which put at stake Saudi credibility as a dominant player in the region (*MEI*, 14 October 1983). In early October, Prince 'Abdallah, known for the closeness to the Syrian authorities, issued a strong warning against the destruction of pro-'Arafat faction of the PLO—i.e. Syrian aggression towards it (*Al-Nahar*, 9 October 1983)—and discounted the legitimacy of the dissident Abu Musa faction (Abu Talib, 1984). Simultaneously, King Fahd sent 'Arafat an official invitation to visit the Kingdom, which was accepted by his close advisor, Khalid al-Hassan.[25] Rumours circulated at that time that Syria attempted to trade its *rapprochement* with Iraq for Gulf's acquiescence in the ouster of 'Arafat from the PLO leadership (*Al-Safir*, 12 October 1983; *MECS*, 1983–1984: 150n53).

The warring camps were not pacified by these efforts, but Riyadh initially persisted in pursuing the maximal objective to sponsor a widely supported Arab settlement for the PLO, and, by implication, for Lebanon as well. Assuming that such a successful agreement would win automatic American support (*MEI*, 11 November 1983), the Kingdom ambitiously aimed for a settlement at the Riyadh Arab summit, scheduled for late November. In the context of preparing the grounds for a successful summit, 'Ali al-Sha'ir visited Asad on 17 October (*Al-Nahar*, 18 October 1983), but on that very day, Radio Damascus aired an elaborated commentary against its convention (*MECS*, 1983–1984: 125). Met with such objection from Damascus, Riyadh was compelled to postpone the summit a few weeks before the scheduled date (*MECS*, 1983–1984: 123-125).

Syria had repeatedly sabotaged the summit in the past years for fear of isolation, but this year it had a particularly strong incentive to see it postponed; the time had come to renew the five-year term of the 1978 Baghdad Summit aid commitment to the frontline states, and Syria had enough reason to believe that the amount allocated to Syria would be significantly cut down, should it go through formal revision at the summit.[26] Furthermore, co-operation between Baghdad and Cairo had fully resumed, and there was every indication that Egypt would be readmitted to the Arab fold at the coming Summit.

Riyadh persisted in working on the PLO/Lebanese issues and dispatched 'Abd al-'Aziz al-Tuweijiri to Damascus in early November under the GCC umbrella (*BBC/SWB/ME*, 8 November; *MEED*, 11 November 1983). Then followed a team of Saudi, Kuwaiti, North Yemeni, Tunisian and Algerian ministers (*MEI*, 11 November 1983). There were also rumours that the Saudis had attempted to buy Syria's acquiescence by paying $2 billion, and then $4 billion, which financed the latter's purchase of Soviet armaments (*Wall Street Journal*, 9 November 1983), although the Saudi government flatly denied the allegations (*MEED*, 11 November; *BBC/SWB/ME*, 15 November 1983).

By the time a settlement was finally reached, it had become increasingly clear that Saudi Arabia had to settle for a minimal achievement of securing 'Arafat's safe departure from Tripoli. Sa'ud al-Faisal met Khaddam and Asad in Damascus at the end of November (*BBC/SWB/ME*, 22 and 24 November 1983) and obtained from the Syrian leadership an agreement on a 'permanent cease-fire', conditional on 'Arafat's expatriation (*MEED*, 25 November; *BBC/SWB/ME*, 26 November 1983). The Saudi Foreign Minister failed to secure further concessions from the Syrians on their acknowledgement of 'Arafat's role in future negotiations or their commitment to halt the intra-PLO mutiny against him (*MECS*, 1983–1984: 628).

The cease-fire, a face-saving gain for Riyadh, was in part attributed to international pressures to bring an end to the fighting. While Sa'ud al-Faisal was meeting Khaddam, the Soviet Foreign Minister, Andrei Gromyko, after receiving pro-'Arafat Farouq Qaddumi, issued a statement calling for a cease-fire. When Khaddam visited Moscow in mid-November, restraint was ordered by the superpower (Karsh, 1991: 154). The UN Security Council also adopted a resolution along the same line (*MEED,* 25 November 1983). Meanwhile, the Steadfastness Front members—South Yemen, Libya and Algeria—joined forces with Moscow to pressurise the Syrians (*MEI,* 25 November 1983); by then, Damascus had become ready for a compromise due to all the above reasons. Additionally, it was also concerned that a complete destruction of al-Fath would play into the hands of Israel and its Christian Lebanese allies (Picard, 2002: 133).

After 'Arafat's expatriation, Saudi reluctance to isolate Syria, thereby widening the Arab rift, dictated Riyadh's response to the opening of the PLO-Egyptian dialogue; in mid-January 1984, 'Arafat paid a historic visit to Cairo—hailed, at that time, 'as dramatic and as epoch-making as Sadat's tour to Jerusalem' (*MEI,* 13 January 1984)—ending over six years of a bitter hostility between the two parties. Although the groundbreaking reconciliation was very much in the interest of Saudi Arabia,[27] it withheld public support for the meeting, mainly out of consideration for Syrian disapproval of 'Arafat's initiative. When the PLO leader requested a meeting with King Fahd after his Cairo visit, Riyadh chose to turn down the request in awareness that full Syrian co-operation was indispensable in finding a solution to the Lebanese question, which took another sharp downward turn as follows.

### Riyadh between Damascus and Washington
### (January–March 1984)

Thus far, Syria's local superiority on the Lebanese ground and Moscow's commitment to rearm its Arab ally have been explored as key dynamics behind Riyadh's loss of grip on Damascus' decision-making. The story does not end here, however. A fundamental shift had taken place in the Arab regional balance of power since the immediate aftermath of the Fez II, when the Saudis were riding high, and this can be attributed to the US, the one actor—even the Syrians admitted—which could potentially deliver peace or war.

The Reagan administration's attitude to the Arabs in general and the Syrians in particular underwent significant changes since the time it launched the Reagan Plan for the Middle East. Although the underlying motivation behind the Plan's inception was to protest against the Israeli aggression in Lebanon, within a year, Washington came to abandon any semblance of a neutral mediator and swung to the pro-Israeli extreme. Its support did not end at political and economic support for Israeli policy, but rather extended to direct military invention in the interest of the Jewish state. This revision of US policy was a decisive factor in the decline of Riyadh's regional influence and prestige, as they were contingent on the ability to pressurise the superpower to deliver Israel to the negotiating table under terms acceptable to the Arabs. This partly explains why, as late as October 1983 when the Americans had long ceased to promote the Reagan Plan, Prince 'Abdallah was still alluding to it favourably as an initiative 'which prescribed to reinstate Palestinian rights' (Al-Nahar, 9 October 1983). Riyadh's hope was to be brutally betrayed.

America's hostile attitude was elevated decisively after the two suicide bombings of the Marine headquarters and the French battalion's centre on 24 October, killing 239 Marines and 56 French paratroopers (Al-Nahar, 25 October 1983; Picard, 2002: 126). The US administration accused Syria, as well as Iran, as being the masterminds behind the attack. In the following months, the US did not hesitate to conduct a direct military assault on Syrian positions in Lebanon. To rub salt into the wounds of Arab sensibility, Reagan concluded a new strategic co-operation agreement with Yitzhak Shamir on 29 November to replace the one suspended in December 1981 in the aftermath of the Israeli annexation of the Golan Heights. Although Riyadh headed Washington's Arab allies in criticising the agreement (MEED, 2 December; MEI, 9 December 1983), the US administration responded with a major air attack on Syrian positions around Beirut. Not only was it the first combat use of US aircraft in the Middle East, but it was also perceived in the Arab world as a co-ordinated US-Israeli strategy; the Israeli fighter bombers had attacked Syrian forces in central Lebanon less than 24 hours earlier (Petran, 1987: 333).

Such a blatant pro-Israeli policy undermined what meagre credibility the pro-Western Arab regimes had left. The new American aggression attack, which was designed to overwhelm the Syrians, ironically bolstered their prestige instead. The dynamic was succinctly summarised in MEI:

Everything the hard-line Syrians and their allies had said about the Americans and Israel seemed to be true, and the positions of the Arab moderates who have pinned their hopes and indeed fates on Washington began to look even more parlous...Despite Syria's erstwhile isolation and abiding unpopularity in the Arab world, the Arab moderates had no choice but to rally behind Assad. It is one thing for Israel to hit the Syrians—many Arab moderates would not be adverse to seeing Assad being cut down to size, though attacks on his forces just seem to pump him up further. But for the

Americans to get involved in direct hostilities with the Syrians is too dangerous an embarrassment for the pro-Western Arab regimes...With the Americans moving in their current direction, Syria becomes everything it claimed to be: the only real Arab bulwark standing against Israel's plans for the region the front line of defence for the Arab world as a whole (9 December 1983).

The politics of prestige and credibility aside, another local event sent a chill through the minds of the Arab moderates. On 12 December, Lebanon's Shi'i militant group, Islamic Jihad, claimed responsibility for a bomb explosion in Kuwait. It was a fresh reminder that Kuwait—and by extension the rest of the GCC—was firmly in the arena of the Lebanon and the Gulf war and that Asad appeared to hold a key to delineating the boundaries of these conflicts (*MEED*, 16 December; *Time*, 19 December 1983). This attack seemed to have played a distinct part in softening Saudi attitude towards Syria to that of appeasement (*MECS*, 1983–1984: 126); two days after the explosion, Sa'ud al-Faisal visited Asad to offer support in the Lebanese issue (*Al-Nahar*, 15 December 1983) and then held a tripartite meeting with Khaddam and Lebanese Foreign Minister Elie Salim (*Al-Nahar*, 15 December 1983). In a parallel development, the Arab League Secretary General formally announced on 21 December that the Riyadh Arab summit was rescheduled for 31 March 1984—much to Syria's satisfaction—only to be postponed 'indefinitely' two months later (*MECS*, 1983–1984: 126). A further blow to Saudi confidence in the Lebanese arena came on 17 January 1984 when the Saudi consul Hussain Farrash was abducted, allegedly by a Shi'i Lebanese (*New York Times*, 18 January; *BBC/SWB/ME*, 18 and 20 January 1984). He was to remain in custody for the next 16 months until 20 May 1985, when Sa'ud al-Faisal visited Tehran (Deeb, 1988: 181, 184n69). When he was eventually released, a message of gratitude from King Fahd was delivered to President Asad, indicating Damascus' involvement in the affair (*MEED*, 1 June 1985).

Meanwhile, the US Marines continued to be humiliated by the Syrians and their Lebanese allies. The strength of an army cannot always be measured by the actual number of troops, but rather by how many of them a country is prepared to lose. In Syria's case, the answer was 'as many as it takes', but the US was shattered of its confidence when some dozen Marines were killed and a few pilots captured (Seale, 1990: 416-417). By the end of January 1984, it appeared a matter of time before the traditionally Sunni quarter of West Beirut—the area from which Saudi Arabia's most loyal allies came—fell into the hands of Syria's Lebanese allies.

Thus, the Saudis embarked on its last attempt to piece together a security agreement on Lebanon by sending Hariri and Tuweijiri to Damascus,[28] but met with Syria's intransigence, oscillated to issuing unusually explicit criticism towards the US; Prince 'Abdallah received a US Round Table business delegation in Riyadh on 1 February, led by the former US Ambassador, John West. He called for the Marines' withdrawal from Lebanon and criticised the US for pursuing 'wrong policies' (Al-Nahar, 2 February 1984). On 7 February, the US Marines, together with the other multinational forces, began redeployment hastily and ingloriously (BBC/SWB/ME, 10 February 1984). The best the Saudis could try was to obtain minimal security consensus from the local factions for the post-evacuation phase. For this purpose, first Rafiq al-Hariri toured Damascus, Beirut and Larnaca (Al-Nahar, 12 February; BBC/SWB/ME, 13 and 15 February 1984), followed by Sa'ud al-Faisal. Sa'ud al-Faisal produced a draft agreement on internal stability but was met with opposition from Khaddam and Walid Junblat (Al-Nahar, 17-20 February 1984). When the failure of its initiative appeared inevitable, Riyadh reverted to denial—the Kingdom had 'not presented any particular plan' (Washington Post, 18 and 20 February 1984). Eventually, the more heavy-weight delegation had to come to Damascus: Crown Prince 'Abdallah accompanied by Bandar, Turki bin 'Abdallah and Hariri (Al-Nahar, 20 and 21 February 1984). Only after such flurry of diplomatic activities, a cease-fire agreement was reached on 24 February (Al-Nahar, 24 February; New York Times, 24 February 1984). Soon thereafter, Amin Jumayyil, abandoned first by Israel, and now by the US, had little option left but to convey to the Syrian leadership his intention to abrogate unilaterally the 17 May accord.[29] Just as the Accord's conclusion symbolised Asad's lowest ebb ten months ago, by the same token, its cancellation testified to Syria's renewed strength. When the Lausanne Lebanese peace conference was convened based on the new formula,[30] Khaddam, a considerably senior representation, dominated the proceeding while Saudi Arabia resigned itself to a peripheral role.[31]

### The Superpowers and Syrian-Saudi Relations

The Mountain War and the ensuing US Marines military clashes with Syria highlighted the superpower factor in Syrian-Saudi relations. Saudi closeness to Washington and Syria's alliance with Moscow did affect the bilateral relations, but not in a simplistic formula, which assumes that global superpower conflict could be exported to the periphery. Instead, the two Arab capitals attempted to 1) at times, capitalise on the other's tie with the hostile superpower when such a tie opened new channels of communication or 2) at other times, undermine the other's regional policy as an act of collaboration with the superpower's anti-Arab 'conspiracy', and by so doing, bully the other into revising the policy. Both Syria and Saudi Arabia attempted at different times to utilise each other's ties with Moscow and Washington respectively. If Syria or Saudi Arabia managed to persuade its superpower ally to adopt a policy more acceptable to the Arab audience, it could claim some political credits for the success, while failing to do so, by the same token, resulted in a loss of prestige.[32]

In Lebanon of the early 1980s, Saudi Arabia consistently failed even to appear as though it possessed any leverage over Washington's decision-making and was embarrassed by the American lack of sensitivity and consideration for its own sensibilities. When the Syrians realised that Riyadh was virtually powerless in modifying Washington's policy, they were quick to adopt the second option of discrediting the Saudis in this light. The Saudis, as a result, mostly succumbed to Syria and endorsed the latter's policy, in recognition that befriending the hard-liners in Damascus sheltered them from vicious reproach.

A comparison between the US military engagement in Lebanon and the Soviet invasion of Afghanistan offers fresh insight into the dynamics of superpower factor in Syrian-Saudi relations. Even though Syria's close alliance with Moscow came under severe criticisms in the wake of the Afghan invasion, Damascus was not compelled to distance itself from the superpower for fear of Muslim backlash or isolation in the Islamic world. In contrast, Washington's Lebanese operation threatened to tarnish Saudi Arabia's 'Arab' reputation to such an extent that the Kingdom quickly oscillated to a position that furthered the interests of the superpower's very enemies. While this contrast was largely a product of difference between the Syrian and Saudi states—in their foreign policy goals, decision-making styles, geo-political assets and historical conditions, it was also a testimony to the exceptionally binding power of Arabism in defining the acceptable code of diplomatic conduct.

## The Gulf War (October 1982–March 1984)

In the eighteen months under review in this chapter, the decline in Riyadh's regional leadership was most pronounced in the Gulf arena, despite the fact that ending the Iran-Iraq war remained its major foreign policy objective. When Syria endorsed the markedly anti-Iranian resolutions in Fez II in September 1982, hopes were initially raised high among the Gulf Arabs: Damascus could finally be disciplined into ending its support for Tehran. As seen in Chapter Three, such hopes were bluntly betrayed by Damascus, whose co-operation with the Shi'i regime, if anything, intensified in the following months.

Saudi Arabia persisted in its individual initiative to sponsor a *rapprochement* between Damascus and Baghdad, but when its high-profile mediation effort failed in January 1983, it opted for detachment from the issue. In the rest of the period under review, mediation campaigns were launched only through collective efforts with other GCC states, and at no point did it threaten Syria with its financial leverage to bring it into line with the majority Arab position. The economic aid from Riyadh to Damascus did seem to have declined during this period, but the Kingdom's overall economic down turn most probably had as much to do with it as any displeasure with the Syrian regional policy.[33] Saudi Arabia oil production level fell from about 10 million barrels a day in 1981 to about 2 million by September 1985, which, coupled with the decline in oil price, created a severe budget deficit (Abir, 1988: 179). To give an indication of Saudi Arabia's economic troubles, the Kingdom was said to have accumulated $24 billion deficit on current account by 1984, which increased to $30 billion the following year (Cordesman, 1987: 39). The collective approach to apply pressure on Syria achieved some success, but it was much overshadowed by the dramatic turn of events in Lebanon. It was not until April 1984—the beginning of the Tanker War and of frequent Western hostage taking in Lebanon—that the Gulf war became the central defining factor in the Syrian-Saudi tug-of-war. This section covers, therefore, a buildup towards the more dramatic next phase.

Syrian and Iraqi exchanges of hostile propaganda continued throughout 1982, and it was only in January of the following year that Riyadh attempted to sponsor an end to the vicious verbal exchanges.[34] Prince 'Abdallah's visit took place against the background of the Israeli-Lebanese Peace Treaty negotiations, but in view of the fact that he travelled to and from Damascus via Baghdad, it seems most plausible to assume that his paramount concern was in the Gulf issues (*Al-Nahar*, 16 and 17 January 1983). The economic burden of upholding Iraq was damaging to the faltering economies of the GCC states, and the Prince allegedly demanded Syria's neutrality in the war as well as the re-opening of the Iraqi oil pipeline (*MEI*, 4 February 1983). 'Abdallah was said to have offered a one-time payment of $2 billion in return (Hirschfeld, 1986: 115). The prompt departure of Syria's Foreign Minister 'Abd al-Halim Khaddam for Saudi Arabia, the very next day after the Asad-'Abdallah meeting, pointed to an inconclusiveness in the Saudi initiative (*Al-Nahar*, 16 and 17 January 1983). This tour by Khaddam also aimed at rallying support against Israel and the US on the Lebanese issue (*MEED*, 21 January; *Al-Nahar*, 16 January 1983). The absence of enthusiastic support from the Gulf Arabs on this pressing agenda in the Levant—at least from Syria's point of view most probably contributed to Damascus' uncompromising attitude towards Iraq.

After Damascus, 'Abdallah returned to the Kingdom via Baghdad, accompanying Iraq's Saddam Hussain. Rumours anticipated that Asad would follow suit (*Al-Nahar*, 19 January; *MEI*, 4 February 1983), but on the contrary, Syria responded to the Saudi initiative with a seemingly provocative defiance: the Syrian-Iranian-Libyan tripartite meeting of Foreign Ministers on 20–21 January (*BBC/SWB/ME*, 21 January 1983). The meeting concluded with a joint communiqué of fierce criticisms against Iraq and any party in favour of partial peace with Israel (*BBC/SWB/ME*, 25 January 1983), but this act of defiance was followed by a display of caution and sensitivity; the day after the tripartite meeting, Syrian Chief of Staff Hikmat al-Shihabi arrived in Riyadh, presumably to explain Syria's position (*BBC/SWB/ME*, 24 January 1983). The underlying motive may well have been to secure the financial flow; one source reported that Syria's foreign currency reserve was 'desperate', yet new construction projects were being announced (*MEED*, 4 February; cf. *Saut al-Ahrar*, 2 March 1983).

Syrian efforts to please both Saudi Arabia and Iran were clearly displayed in Information Minister Ahmad Iskandar Ahmad's tour to Tehran and Riyadh in early February (*Al-Nahar*, 8 February; *MEI*, 18 February 1983). This visit to Tehran and Jiddah was aimed at reassuring the Saudis that, with the Syrians' help, the Iranians could be dissuaded from expanding the war to the GCC states. The timing of the visit was significant, as the Iranians had started a major offensive against the Iraqis just before Ahmad Iskandar departed Tehran for Jiddah (*MEI*, 18 February 1983). If the Saudi press commentary were to be an index to governmental views, the Syrian Minister's visit did not mitigate Riyadh's disappointment with Syria; the day after Ahmad's arrival to meet King Fahd, an editorial in the Saudi daily *Al-Riyadh* criticised that those Arab leaders who had agreed to support Iraq at Fez should live up to their commitment as members of the Arab League (*BBC/SWB/ME*, 9 February 1983). Having failed consistently in its single-handed effort to sponsor a Damascus-Baghdad *rapprochement*, Saudi Arabia began to adopt a collective approach in their Gulf policy after Prince 'Abdallah's latest unsuccessful attempt.

Saudi Arabia was directly behind the convention of the Baghdad meeting of the Popular Islamic Conference (*Al-Mu'tamar al-Sha'bi al-Islami*) on 14–17 April 1983, in which some fifty leading '*ulama* in the Muslim world gathered to promote Iraq's Islamic credentials to counter the Iranians. The Conference was chaired by Ma'ruf al-Dawalibi, the ex-Syrian Prime Minister who fled to Saudi Arabia in the 1960s to become a royal adviser.[35] The Third Conference of the Arab Parliamentary Union also met in Baghdad the following month, and the very convention of these meetings constituted a diplomatic setback for Syria (Hirschfeld, 1986: 119). These collective pressures notwithstanding, Syrians stepped up their relations with Iran by signing further agreements on oil supply and banking (*MEED,* 5 August 1983). By the end of the year, analysts speculated that the amount of economic aid and subsidies from Tehran had offset any decline in the Arab aid. Sources claimed that the Iranian aid amounted to $1 billion a year while the Arab aid between $1 and 1.2 billion, of which Saudi Arabia accounted for some $0.8 billion (*Washington Post,* 29 December 1983; Djalili cited in Marschall, 1991: 86).

It is no surprise, therefore, that the GCC meetings produced little concrete measures against Syria's support for Iran (Hirschfeld, 1986: 119). The Council members did, however, make some co-ordinated efforts to dissuade Damascus. As the Iranian offensive intensified in the autumn of 1983, Kuwait and the United Arab Emirates launched mediation campaigns between Syria and Iraq, in mid-September (*BBC/SWB/ME,* 15 September 1983) and early October (*Al-Nahar,* 10 October; *Al-Safir,* 12 October 1983) respectively. These efforts were co-ordinated closely with Saudi Arabia, which was in the midst of diplomatic flurry on Lebanon. Also, in October 1983, the Iraqi and Syrian Foreign Ministers held direct talks in New York during the UN General Assembly session, in the presence of the Kuwaiti and Saudi Foreign Ministers (*MEI,* 28 October 1983; *MECS,* 1983–1984: 131). Yet, Syria, upon attending the ministerial meeting of OAPEC (Organisation of Arab Petroleum Exporting Countries), defiantly proclaimed that the reopening of the pipeline was not to be expected in the near future (*MEED,* 25 November 1983).

All the above efforts did little to change Syria's attitude towards the war until April 1984 when the battlefield was expanded to threaten the secure passage of the Straits of Hormuz, which also coincided with Syrian-Iranian disagreements over the Lebanese policy. In the next phase, Syria would concentrate its efforts on projecting itself as a sole 'mediator' between the Iranians and the Gulf Arabs, a strategy consistent with displaying its reservations on an expanded Iranian presence in Lebanon as well as on Iraqi soil.

## The Myth of 'Abdallah-Rif'at Connection: A succession crisis in Syria (November 1983–May 1984)

Based on the analyses thus far, there is no over-stating of the prominent role played by Prince 'Abdallah, the Commander of the National Guard, in Syrian-Saudi diplomatic contacts. Within the Saudi royal family, the Crown Prince has been known for his close relationship with the Syrian ruling establishment and was at times even criticised by his brothers for the excessive sympathy for Damascus.[36] His friendship, in particular, with

Rif'at al-Asad, the Syrian President's influential brother, had attracted much attention in newspaper reports and popular word-of-mouth anecdotes. Indeed, whenever Prince 'Abdallah visited Damascus, Rif'at was there at the airport to receive him.[37] The two are believed to be related by marriage to two sisters from the Shammar tribe, Prince 'Abdallah's maternal family line.[38] Countless rumours have spread on the joint business schemes between the two (e.g. *MECS*, 1982–1983, 800); more recently, the London-based satellite television channel Arab News Network (ANN), owned by Rif'at's son Sumir al-Asad, is said to have received substantial funding from 'Abdallah himself and Saudi entrepreneurs with close ties to the Prince.[39] Is there any truth in views, which ascribe the strong Syrian-Saudi relations to friendship between those two figures?

It is particularly appropriate to address this question in the analysis of Syrian-Saudi relations between September 1982 and March 1984. When President Asad suffered a potentially fatal heart failure in November 1983, Syrian domestic political scene entered a period of uncertainty and instability. Rif'at al-Asad, by then, had advanced his political position to become an extremely powerful figure, second only to his elder brother. He had established an independent power base in the elite military unit of the Defence Brigades, which numbered some 50,000 troops with the most sophisticated equipment of all Syrian military units. Exploiting the opportunity, presented by the President's illness, Rif'at plotted an internal coup to take over the regime. Rumours abound which suggest that Prince 'Abdallah was behind this scheme. Would Prince 'Abdallah actively participate in such a plot, and if yes, what would be the implications for Syrian-Saudi relations? This section will revisit the role of personal ties in the bilateral relations.

Rif'at had no qualms about publicising his intention to succeed his brother. He had called on the other major military and intelligence heavyweights to rally around him, while his men in the Defence Brigade hoisted his portraits on the streets of the capital as if to hail the new ruler.[40] The conflict subsided only after acute tension developed in late February 1984, when the Defence Brigades encircled the capital city and squared off with the Special Forces and the Presidential Guard, which remained loyal to the President. Eventually, the President made a surprising recovery, and the saga ended with Rif'at's nomination to a ceremonial role as one of the three Vice-Presidents—the other two assuming more substantial roles—only to be exiled to Europe later. When he was allowed back into Syria for a temporary visit later in the year, the permission was allegedly facilitated by 'Abdallah's plea to Hafiz al-Asad (*Washington Post*, 27 November 1984).

Some seasoned observers of Syrian affairs speculated that Saudi Arabia, and possibly even the United States, prompted Rif'at's mutiny (*MEI*, 6 April 1984; Sadiq, 1993: 215-218; Batatu, 1999: 233). One source goes so far as to claim that Crown Prince had promised Rif'at a financial package of $17 billion in the event of a successful take-over of the regime, in return for a major policy revision (personal communication, Aleppo, November 1999). This younger brother is known to have favoured reorientation of Syria's alignment from pro-Soviet to pro-US (Batatu, 1999: 233). He was rumoured to have had personal contacts with the Israeli government and was also known for closeness with Yasir 'Arafat as he disapproved of the anti-'Arafat rebellion (Ramet, 1990: 182; Raad, 1998: 162). In addition, he questioned the soundness of Syria's support for Iran in the Gulf war and promoted the introduction of a capitalist economic policy as opposed to the socialist ideals of the Ba'th Party (Sadiq, 1993: 213; *Financial Times*, 8 March 1984). Prince 'Abdallah allegedly made his offer conditional on implementation of all these policy changes in line with Saudi interests. In view of 'Abdallah's visit to Damascus in late February 1984 (*MEI*, 6 April 1984) at the height of the brothers' conflict, the speculation on his involvement could be plausible, but some flatly dismiss the likelihood as 'out of his ['Abdallah's] character' (personal communication, Riyadh, March 2002).

It is impossible for an outsider to assess the exact role of Prince 'Abdallah in all these developments. At best, all outsiders' views are no more than 'informed guess work', including this project's. Having spelled out this limitation, the 'informed guess' here is that Abdallah's promise of support is plausible, given the fact that it is in line with Saudi policy of attempting to maintain reasonable relations with all political forces—both the current rulers and their oppositions—in neighbouring countries. This policy not only allows Saudi Arabia to assume its favourite role as a mediator but also minimises the element of surprise should political instability next door result in a coup or a revolution. For instance, this is one of the reasons, in addition to the religious motive, behind its support for the Muslim Brotherhood, another reason being a modest leverage to discipline the existing Syrian regime. Thus, 'Abdallah's promise to Rif'at may have been a Saudi way of 'insurance' against a successful intra-family coup by Rif'at, and the Saudi leadership may have wanted to capitalise on such an eventuality by securing commitments to change Syria's regional policy. This, however, is not to say that 'Abdallah actively incited the mutiny, a point emphasised by the fact that there was no indication that Hafiz al-Asad's relationship with Prince 'Abdallah deteriorated following this period.

A variety of strategic interests and issues govern the Syrian-Saudi relations, in the background of which exist shared historical experiences and social interaction. Over the years, a web of close personal friendships between key individuals developed.[41] Nevertheless, there is no indication that such ties played a detectable influence in foreign policy decisions of either government, and this applies even to the 'Abdallah-Rif'at connection. When the tension between Princes 'Abdallah and Sultan heightened in 1978 and early 1979, it was expected that the Kingdom's foreign orientation would make a tangible shift towards a more pro-Arab nationalist, anti-American orientation in view of growing influence of the pro-'Abdallah camp (*MECS*, 1978–1979: 737-740). This did not happen, and so as the policy revision later when Prince 'Abdallah assumed the role of an acting head of state in place of ailing King Fahd.

This does not mean that analysis of such human contacts is an entirely wasted effort for outside observers. Against the background of shortage of documentation, which Saudi official travelled to Damascus on a given occasion, or which one delivered the message to Asad, for instance, offer limited clues on the direction of the talks. If Sa'ud al-Faisal or Bandar travelled to Damascus, in place of more senior 'Abdallah, it could be a face-saving gesture by the Saudis who were suspecting a stalemate in the negotiation. It is also the case that Syrians would find it more difficult to say 'No' to 'Abdallah than to the first two, so on crucial negotiations Saudis tended to play the 'Abdallah 'card'. Because details of Syrian-Saudi high-level meetings are never made public, even such an ambiguous indicator is of some modest use for observers (personal communication, Riyadh, March 2002).

If anything, personal links, such as 'Abdallah-Rif'at, are exemplary of the *mode* or *style* of diplomacy prevalent in the Arab region. As Chapter One's historical overview of Syrian-Saudi relations demonstrated, the politics of the region was as much about personalities, as political parties or pure ideologies. Add to that the fact that the same rulers have been the heads of states for an extended period of time—meeting same faces on various summits and conferences for decades—and the fact that these rulers enjoy highly centralised power, what should be diplomatic negotiations between government offices can acquire strong colouring of personal contacts. In the case of the Rif'at-'Abdallah tie, the link attracted particularly strong attention presumably because of Rif'at's flamboyant character and conduct,[42] and also because of the scandalous amount of cash involved in such conducts. Whether the two are indeed related through marriage or not, there is a risk of over-emphasising its significance in consolidating the friendship; this is particularly so, in view of the fact that both men have allegedly married more than a dozen women each.[43] In short, the personal ties between key political and business figures in Syrian-Saudi relations could be indicating a logical progression from—or the residue of—the traditional politics of the tribes, extending its scope across the Syrian desert to the Najd and beyond.

## Conclusion

L. Robinson asserted: '[t]he more successful Asad has been in pursuing his regional strategic ambitions, the more financial benefits, mainly in the form of Gulf Arab aid, have accrued' (1996: 50). When Asad's 'regional strategic ambitions' are interpreted to encompass all the questions ranging from the PLO, Lebanon, Iran, to the superpowers, Robinson's assertion confirms the documentation of this chapter. Although it is impossible to establish the exact amount of aid Saudi Arabia paid to Syria, most sources believe that the Kingdom contributed some $800 million each year to Syria as part of the Baghdad Summit commitment in the period under review. The figure reached roughly 80 percent of the total received by Syria under this framework (*MEED*, 6 January 1984). In addition, Riyadh was considered to have provided Damascus with more through secret bilateral deals, as was evident in the fact that reports on senior Saudi officials' visits to Damascus were often concluded by speculation over the dividends paid. If there were any decline in the sum, it had more to do with the downturn in the economy of oil producers in general rather than displeasure with Syria's regional policy—at least in the case of Saudi Arabia.

Syria made a remarkable comeback in the period under review—from subordination at Fez II to the symbolic abrogation of the 17 May agreement. This renewed strength was highlighted most vividly by the abrupt withdrawal of US Marines from the Lebanese coast. The political dynamics of Arabism drove Saudi Arabia to consensus-seeking, while Syria succeeded in gaining leverage by making this task deliberately difficult to achieve. In this sense, Arabism was still relevant not as a unifying factor, but as a point of reference for the Arab regimes to define a code of conduct, or differentiate between desirable and undesirable behaviours (*MECS*, 1982–1983: 223). For the Saudis, appearing to be in line with such a code of conduct constituted a key factor in regional and national security as they saw it. Indeed, much of their political manoeuvres of mediation and summoning of Arab summits were motivated by the need to maintain the façade—of being committed to the common Arab or Islamic cause and of having an independent agenda from Washington's influence.

Saudi aid to Syria is also understood in this regard. L. Robinson asserts that 'strategic rent' by nature cannot buy policy changes from the rent recipient such as Syria. Instead, its purpose lies in improvement of public image and domestic legitimacy (1996: 48). In other words, as long as Syria does not *publicly* humiliate Saudi Arabia, what the Kingdom 'can realistically hope for'— i.e. public display of solidarity—has been attained through the channelling of aid. Hence, the Syrians treat the Saudi officials with outwardly brotherly embraces but are in *private*, willing to pursue interests harmful to their 'donor'.

This chapter's analysis also disentangled the myth of personal connections, particularly at the leadership level, in defining Syrian-Saudi bilateral relations. The 'personalised' methods of conducting diplomacy may have been a strong feature in Arab politics in general, and some connections may have weighed heavier than others. That, however, is not to say that the friendship between leaders has provided sound basis for co-operation or key to understanding its anatomy.

In contrast, this chapter's analysis of the period between October 1982 and March 1984 pointed to the central role which the superpowers played in defining the power relationship between Damascus and Riyadh. Syria's reacquisition of prestige as a major regional player would not have been possible had the Soviets not re-stocked the Syrian military arsenal. The Saudis were less fortunate in winning the understanding from Washington on their own needs. When the US became a direct participant who took sides in the Lebanese conflict, it negatively affected the credibility of the pro-US Arab regimes, foremost the Saudis. The more the Syrians regained their confidence, the more the Saudis withdrew themselves into the back scene, unable to resolve the dilemma of needing to achieve incompatible objectives—to simultaneously please Washington and Damascus.

The factors which contributed to re-building Syria's strength were passing elements, however. Andropov, the most responsive Secretary General to Damascus' plea for arms to date, died in February 1984 to be replaced by a more sceptical successor, Chernenko. Asad's illness after November 1983 led to instability within the ruling circles. In Lebanon, Syria's limitation as a regional actor was exposed after March 1984, when it proved itself to be capable of obstructing others' policies but unable to implement its own solution. Lebanon again slid back to vicious cycles of civil war. In the next phase, the Syrians attempted to rely more on the Iran card than any other time to improve its standing, which often meant bargaining against the conservative Gulf Arabs led by Saudi Arabia.

# 5

# SYRIA'S VETO POWER VS. SAUDI QUEST FOR ARAB CONSENSUS
## With reference to the Gulf War
## (April 1984–August 1990)

In late April 1984, a Saudi oil tanker was set ablaze, midway between Bahrain and Kharg Island (*BBC/SWB/ME*, 27 April 1984). The initial report did not identify the origin of the missile which caused the damage, but it later transpired to have come from Iraq. Iran promptly adopted the same tactics, attacking any oil tanker that had loaded up in Iraq. This was the start of the so-called Tanker War in the Gulf, wherein the belligerents of the Iran-Iraq war expanded the scope of their conflict through indiscriminate attacks on vessels passing through the Straits of Hormuz. The immediate aim of this new strategy was to curb the enemy's oil income and, by extension, the injection of cash into its war efforts. Numerous Saudi- as well as Kuwaiti-owned tankers consequently fell victim to the attacks at the initial stage of the Tanker War (*BBC/SWB/ME*, 15 and 17 May 1984), spreading across the region fresh alarm at the expansion of conflict.

Until April 1984, Syrian-Saudi relations had played a dominant role in shaping key regional events, ranging from the conflict in Lebanon, the Arab-Israeli conflict, Egypt's position in the Arab world, and superpower involvement in Middle East conflicts. These issues had arguably occupied a higher priority in Syrian-Saudi diplomatic exchanges than the Iran-Iraq war for the simple reason that their potential to destabilise the region loomed ever so large. The logical outcome of this was that the analyses of Syrian-Saudi relations in the previous chapters have focused less on the Gulf. However, after April 1984, the arena of the Syrian-Saudi tug-of-war shifted mainly to the Gulf, the immediate backyard of Saudi Arabia, because of the intensification and expansion of the fighting, outshining the immediacy of other crises.

In comparison to the preceding years, there was a definite shift of Arab focus away from the Arab East to the Gulf. In the case of Lebanon, the conflict degenerated into a deeper quagmire after the US withdrawal, but Riyadh chose noticeably to withdraw from the diplomatic scene. Instead, at least from the Saudi point of view, the significance of the Lebanese conflict was increasingly pictured through the prism of the Gulf conflict or as an extension of Iranian aggression; militancy of pro-Iranian Lebanese elements began to target specifically those interests belonging to countries supportive of Iraq. A similar diminution of Arab interests was observed in the Arab-Israeli conflict—much to Syria's exasperation. The intransigence of the Israeli government and the failure of international and regional actors to present a workable solution to the conflict, despite active efforts to that end in the preceding years, contributed to the overshadowing of the conflict by vicious fighting in the Gulf.

Other factors which had previously preoccupied Syrian-Saudi debates, such as Egypt's readmission into the Arab mainstream and superpower interference in the Middle East, also began to owe much of their significance to their linkage to the Gulf war at the dawn of the Tanker War. The more the Iranians succeeded in the battlefronts, the more the majority Arabs, i.e. the camp led by Iraq's supporters, acknowledged the need to bring the weight of Egypt back into their side. This was the main context in which Iraq—originally the most outspoken critic of the Camp David accords—quickly embraced Egypt. After the humiliating US withdrawal from Lebanon, the next potential arena of overt superpower interference or confrontation was in the Gulf for numerous reasons: the Iranians had made it an integral part of their policy to hold American and other western hostages; the Arab Gulf states were seeking to stock their arsenals with advanced weaponry from the West; and the Soviet Union was closely keeping an eye on these developments through their hold on Afghanistan and through their enlarged presence in countries like Syria.

In these contexts, the outbreak of the Tanker War opened a new phase in Syrian-Saudi relations. In the first two years of the Tanker War, the moderate Arab states led by Saudi Arabia applied fresh pressure on Damascus to make use of its good offices with Tehran to mitigate the tension. This was the period in which Syria went out of its way to present itself as the only credible Arab actor with an influence over Tehran. It maximised its efforts to act as a go-between, thereby collecting rewards from both the moderate Arab states on the one hand, and Tehran on the other. Thus, the standard formula in Syrian-Saudi relations of sustaining co-operation *because of* their differences and *because of* their belonging to opposing networks of alignment—rather than *in spite of* them—was very much at work. Related to this point, the previous chapters have explored the binding disciplinary power of Arabism which conditioned Saudi Arabia to pursue Arab consensus on key regional issues, and this logic was also governing its policy on the Iran-Iraq war. The Kingdom's obsession with securing a unified Arab position on the war had the undesirable outcome of granting Syria a 'veto power' over Saudi policy and induced Saudi acquiescence to most Syrian wishes. The first section of this chapter examines, therefore, the pattern of Syrian-Saudi co-operation in the Gulf war based on Saudi reluctance to antagonise Syria.

Nevertheless, such an environment in which Syria could perform a fine-tuned balancing act did not last. During the last two years of the war (1986–1988), events on the battlegrounds and Syria's diplomatic and economic crises tipped the balance against its fortune, as will be discussed in the second part of this chapter. The end result was a reduction in Syria's ability to exercise the 'veto power' and to attract Saudi support for its pursuit of economic and diplomatic gains. Correspondingly, Saudi Arabia began to adopt a more assertive profile, at times even displaying readiness to disregard Syrian interests altogether, although it was a qualitatively different affair from its display of over-sized confidence in the earlier 'Saudi Era', wherein Riyadh sought to wear the mantle of Arab leadership. How, at long last, Riyadh managed to free itself from the Syrian 'shackle' and whether this new assertiveness indicated an emergence of a new, long-lasting pattern in bilateral relations were important questions, which, in turn, gave a clue to another more fundamental question—whether Arabism still played a role in shaping their foreign policies.

The final conclusion of this chapter, which covers the interim period between the first and the second Gulf crises, indicates that neither Riyadh's gradual distancing from Damascus nor the Iran-Iraq cease-fire brought an end to the narrative of Syrian-Saudi relations. It demonstrates that the end of the Gulf war instead brought back to the balance sheet all the aforementioned factors which had previously shaped Syrian-Saudi relations but were temporarily eclipsed by the Gulf war. The end result was that the two actors had to acknowledge once again each other's indispensability in the pursuit of their individual regional policies—testifying to the multi-faceted nature of their bilateral relations. As a final chapter of the detailed case study of Syrian-Saudi relations in the troubled years between 1978 and 1990, the following analyses will focus on the function of the Gulf factor in the dynamics of the bilateral relations.

### The Tanker War in the Gulf
### (August 1984–February 1986)

With the outbreak of the Tanker War and the subsequent intensification of the fighting, two trends pertaining to Damascus-Riyadh relations surfaced. The first was the centrality that the Gulf war began to occupy in their bilateral relations. All the other key questions appeared to merge into the developments in the Gulf, be they Lebanon, relations with the superpowers, Egypt's place in the region, or Arab solidarity. The second trend was the Arab moderates' renewed interest in Damascus' good offices with Tehran. Syria, accordingly, did its utmost to present itself as the *only* channel of communication with Tehran if not a restraining influence to the revolutionary regime (Chubin and Tripp, 1988: 183-185). Damascus attempted—and most of the time succeeded—to cash in on this fresh expectation through collecting rewards from both sides of the conflict. The first ten months of the Tanker War, therefore, represented most clearly how the conflict in the Gulf constituted one of the key shaping elements of Syrian-Saudi relations; one side of the equilibrium—in this case, Syria—could best market its potential value to the other party when their patterns of regional alignment were diametrically opposed.

However, from March 1985, Syria's ability to present itself as a sole mediator in the Gulf conflict was severely restricted. First, Egypt's return to inter-Arab political scene redefined the regional power balance against Syria's fortunes. Second, Iran's success in its military ventures rendered implausible Syria's claim to be a 'moderator', at least from the Gulf Arabs' standpoint. The more Iran took the upper hand in the conflict, the more tension built up in Syrian-Iranian relations—restricting Syria's ability to restrain Iran's militancy. Third, Damascus was further discredited by its inability—or what its critics considered as unwillingness—to bring an end to the Lebanese war and its role in exacerbating the intra-Palestinian conflict. All these developments severely deepened Syria's regional isolation, a negative ramification of which also surfaced in its faltering economy. The only consolation was that the Asad regime appeared to have extinguished most of the flames of internal dissent which had plagued Syrian domestic politics since the 1970s.

After March 1985, these new conditions pressed the Asad regime to redefine its strategy towards the Gulf. Instead of concentrating on the mediation efforts, it attempted to market its value by playing on the Saudi obsession with Arab consensus. Asad thus embarked on a diplomatic brinkmanship of reconciling himself just enough with his long-term Arab opponent, King Hussain, to dampen his paymasters' criticisms, without jeopardising his Tehran connection.

*Syrian Mediation (April 1984–February 1985)*

During the first ten months of the Tanker War, Syria undertook at least four notable mediation initiatives, in response to requests from the Arab moderate camp led by Saudi Arabia: 1) in late May 1985, 2) August–September 1985, 3) November–December 1985, and 4) January–early February 1986. The first took place immediately after the 19 May Tunis Arab Foreign Ministers' conference, which was convened in response to the tanker attacks but adopted a resolution only mildly condemning Iran. [1] Riyadh dispatched 'Abd al-'Aziz al-Tuweijiri to Damascus on 22 May to enlist Syrian intervention in dissuading Iran from threatening the safe passage of the Gulf waters (*MECS*, 1983–1984: 134, 628). The very next day, a Syrian delegation of high rank departed for Tehran, led by Vice-President 'Abd al-Halim Khaddam and Foreign Minister Faruq al-Shar' (*BBC/SWB/ME*, 24 May 1984). The two, according to Radio Damascus, reiterated Syria's opposition—and no doubt a position shared by Riyadh—to aggression on any Arab state not directly involved in the war and cautioned that such an expansion of the war would only invite Western intervention (*BBC/SWB/ME*, 25 May 1984). Then, the Syrian delegation made a short stopover in Jiddah on their return home from Tehran, in order to brief the Saudi leadership on the exchanges with the Iranians (*Al-Nahar*, 27 May 1984). The official statements reiterated an abstract expression of solidarity between Syria and Saudi Arabia (*MECS*, 1983–1984: 151n80), and the Syrian Arab News Agency reported that the two Ministers had discussed with King Fahd 'Syria's efforts to de-escalate tensions in the Gulf and to prevent an expansion of the Gulf war' (*Al-Nahar*, 27 May; *New York Times*, 27 May 1984).

In the first instance, the Iranians appeared pacified by the Syrians; following the departure of the two Syrian ministers, the Iranian Speaker of the *Majlis*, Hashemi Rafsanjani, issued a statement assuring that the war with Iraq would not be extended to other Arab Gulf states, albeit on condition that their assistance to Iraq was stopped.[2] Also on 25 May, at the United Nations, Iran pledged that it would not attack commercial ships in the Gulf if Iraq did not (*New York Times*, 27 May 1984). Concomitantly, the Iranian attacks on the tankers eased, and Syrian daily *Tishrin* went out of their way to publicise the success of their mission and proclaimed itself the defender of 'the Gulf's security and sovereignty' (26 May 1984 cited in *MECS*, 1983–1984: 151n79). A week later, Khaddam gave an interview in which he communicated to the Gulf countries Syria's commitment to assist them in defending themselves (*BBC/SWB/ME*, 4 June 1984). Nevertheless, the optimism emanating from this round of Syrian mediation abruptly came to a halt in the first week of June when an

Iranian aircraft entered Saudi aerial space and was promptly shot down by the AWACS stationed in the Kingdom.

Yet, the Syrians remained persistent. First, they appealed to Moscow to apply pressure on Iran to prevent escalation of violence in the Gulf.[3] Then, they attempted to soothe the Gulf Arabs through verbal assurances about Iran's limited aims. Foreign Minister Shar' proclaimed in late July:

> We and Iran have developed complete understanding on the need to avoid expanding the area of the Iran-Iraq war, on preventing the involvement of any Gulf state in this war, on rejecting US intervention in the region's affairs, and refraining from attacks on oil tankers in the Gulf if Iraq stops. The Iranians have emphasised that they have no ambitions against any inch of Arab territory (*BBC/SWB/ME*, 26 July 1984).

Defence Minister Mustafa Tulas re-emphasised the point by claiming that 'from Imam Khomeini personally' Syria had 'obtained assurances...that Iran would not violate the sovereignty of any Arab country' (*Al-Majallah*, 4 August 1984).

These statements provided the context in which the second round of Syrian mediation between the GCC and Iran materialised in early August. The Kuwaiti Deputy Prime Minister and Foreign Minister, Shaikh Sabah al-Ahmad al-Jabir allegedly met the Iranian Minister of Revolutionary Guards, Mohsen Rafiqdust in Damascus (*BBC/SWB/ME*, 6 August 1984). Since the AWACS incident in June, Iran had grown more responsive to such mediation;[4] it was a sign that Tehran was revising its Gulf policy towards moderation, based on fresh realisation that antagonising the non-combatant Gulf states was placing severe constraints on its own war efforts (Chubin and Tripp, 1988: 167-168). The following month, Syria again acted as a go-between, when a high-ranking Iranian delegation, comprising President Khamenei, Foreign Minister Velayati and Rafiqdust among others, visited the Syrian capital (*BBC/SWB/ME*, 8 September 1984). Saudi Crown Prince 'Abdallah followed (*Al-Nahar*, 16 and 17 September 1984), who had not been seen in Damascus for an unusually long period of seven months, since his high-profile effort to reconcile Damascus with Baghdad ended in a miserable failure. 'Abdallah was followed by Saudi ambassador to Washington Prince Bandar a few days later (*Al-Nahar*, 21 September 1984).

After these meetings, Rafsanjani allegedly launched a secret peace plan to ameliorate the Gulf states' anxiety. The message—transmitted via Damascus to Riyadh and on to Washington—indicated Iran's willingness to relinquish any say in the future composition of the Iraqi regime, provided that the Arab Gulf states would stop supporting the Iraqi regime (Caret, 1987; Marschall, 1991: 71). The plan did not produce a concrete result, but its main significance lay in the resulting establishment of direct communication channels between Tehran and Riyadh on the one hand, and Tehran and Washington on the other. These emerging channels were, in part, attributable to Damascus' diplomacy, but the Syrians were wary of further development of ties which circumvented Syria. They carefully monitored what was to become of this network, as was demonstrated later in Irangate and Damascus' vital role in uncovering the scandal.

The third round of Syrian mediation took place between November and December 1984, first in relation to the GCC Summit scheduled in late November, followed by a hijacking incident of a Kuwaiti airliner. 'Abd al-Halim Khaddam and Faruq al-Shar', the two faces representing Syria's diplomatic corps, had journeyed to Tehran before arriving in Riyadh on 19 November, on the eve of the GCC Summit in Kuwait (*Al-Nahar,* 20 November 1984; *MECS,* 1984–1985: 119). The tour materialised after Saudi envoy Rafiq al-Hariri's two visits to Damascus the previous week, in which he conveyed to the Syrian leadership the new GCC peace initiative to be proposed at the forthcoming summit. Hariri requested the Syrians to explore Tehran's viewpoints on the initiative, prior to the official issuance. Although Riyadh later refuted Syria's input to the GCC initiative,[5] the case was different when a hijacked Kuwaiti airliner landed in Iran a few weeks later. After the resolution of the crisis—during which Iranian Foreign Minister referred to Syria's help at work (*BBC/SWB/ME,* 10 December 1984), King Fahd sent a public message of gratitude to President Asad for his contribution (*Al-Nahar,* 13 December 1984).

The fourth round of Syrian mediation took place between late January and early February 1985. After the 27 January Syrian-Iranian-Libyan trilateral meeting of foreign ministers in Tehran (*BBC/SWB/ME,* 29 January 1985), Saudi Prince 'Abdallah arrived in Damascus (*Al-Safir,* 1 February 1985), followed by Kuwaiti Deputy Prime Minister and Foreign Minister Shaikh Sabah al-Ahmad al-Jabir (*BBC/SWB/ME,* 9 February 1985), to discuss yet another GCC sponsored peace initiative. Meanwhile, Syria's Khaddam promptly departed for Algiers to enlist support for Damascus' mediation efforts. These Arab efforts, however, yet again came to nil, due to an Iranian rebuff; Rafsanjani issued a statement a week after 'Abdallah's Damascus visit, scoffing at the idea of an Arab peace plan and refusing Arab mediation in any form, even by Hafiz al-Asad (*Al-Nahar,* 10 February 1985).

During the first phase of the Tanker War, Syria was generally successful in accruing material reward from both the Iranians on the one hand, and the Arab Gulf states on the other. The financial benefit was particularly crucial when Syria's economy was showing acute signs of strain, not unrelated to the Arab financiers' reluctance to fulfil the Baghdad summit agreement of subvention to frontline states.[6] When Khaddam and Shar', responding to the start of the Tanker War, made their first attempt at mediation in May 1984, the Iranian *Majlis* decided on a favourable economic package for Syria, including a new agreement on Iranian oil shipment and a debt-rescheduling, while the two ministers were still present in Tehran (*BBC/SWB/ME*, 25 May 1984; *MECS*, 1983–1984: 135). The oil deal with Iran was particularly crucial for the Syrian economy; it was estimated to cover 70 percent of the total crude oil refined at the Syrian port city of Baniyas (*MEED*, 20 April 1984).

Although the exact value of the cheques which Damascus picked up from the Gulf side would be impossible to establish, rumours of Saudi financial aid to Syria were prevalent in this period (e.g. *MEI*, 13 July 1984). Also, at least one symbolic reward from Saudi Arabia was publicly announced during Shar' and Khaddam's stopover in Jiddah on their way home from Tehran; King Fahd 'personally' made a religious donation worth 5,000,000 Riyals equivalent to $1.4 million (*BBC/SWB/ME*, 29 May; *MEED*, 1 June 1984). Other Gulf states followed suit. In July, the United Arab Emirates (UAE) was rumoured to have offered a donation in the form of oil supplies,[7] while in August Kuwait made a dramatic U-turn from its announcement only three months earlier that it would reduce its annual subvention to Syria from $556 million to $338 million (*MECS*, 1983–1984: 301). It allegedly pledged an extra $165 million for Damascus' role in securing Iran's promise to halt attacks on tankers (Marschall, 1991: 71). Furthermore, the Saudi Development Fund announced a new aid package of $179 million to Syria in October (*MEED*, 26 October 1984). This type of developmental aid package was common in the 1970s but had been virtually non-existent since.

The Tanker War was a mixed blessing for Syria, because on the one hand, it brought such a windfall opportunity to capitalise on requests for mediation, while on the other, it was the start of strains in Syrian-Iranian relations and of a return of Egypt to the Arab fold. Iran's aggression in the war alarmed Syria which consistently opposed the expansion of fighting to other neighbouring countries. Furthermore, other disagreements were accumulating between Damascus and Tehran. In Lebanon, after the short-lived success of the Lausanne Conference in March, the situation on the ground deteriorated sharply, and the conflict began to take on a new dimension—the growing interference of the Iranian Revolutionary Guards in Lebanese politics, cultivating their proxy, Hizbullah, which clashed periodically with Syrian and Amal forces.[8] The following years came to be known as a period of 'the war of camps' in Lebanon's civil war history.

Also, the Asad regime was beginning to be agitated by the behaviour of the Iranian pilgrims to the Shi'i holy shrine of Sa'ida Zainab in the outskirts of Damascus (*MEI*, 4 May 1984). The number of Iranian visitors had increased fifteen times between 1973 and 1984 when it recorded over 157,000 per annum (Marschall, 1991: 90); these pilgrims from time to time clashed with Syrian security forces as a result of their political demonstrations or attempts to impose their own social values onto Damascene streets.[9] Furthermore, even the emergence of a Saudi-Iranian direct communication link was not altogether a desirable scenario, if it meant that Damascus was going to be bypassed.

Saudi Arabia's new strategy was exactly that—to complement the Syrian channel with their direct contacts with Tehran. Several alarming incidents contributed to formulation of this new Saudi strategy. Aside from the Tanker War, which brought Saudi vessels into target of attacks, two separate incidents in Lebanon reminded the Saudi leadership that they were no bystanders to the conflict. In early June amidst reports of tanker attacks, a bomb exploded in front of the Saudi consulate in Beirut. Also, the Saudi embassy in Beirut was concurrently occupied by a militant Shi'i group for a short while in protest against 'Saudi Arabia's collaboration in the conspiracy against the Islamic Revolution in Iran' (*BBC/SWB/ME*, 9 June 1984). Another attack on the consular section of the Saudi embassy took place on 24 August, setting fire to the building (*BBC/SWB/ME*, 27 August 1984). In response to these attacks, Saudi diplomats were withdrawn from Lebanon, marking the end of active Saudi engagement in Lebanon's search for a cease-fire (*MEED*, 7 September 1984). These events were a reminder that the Gulf conflict had a far-reaching repercussion on the Kingdom's security, extending beyond the confines of the Gulf.[10]

Faced with the pressing need to respond to these threats and encouraged by signs of slight moderation in Iran's antagonism towards themselves, the Saudis began a direct dialogue with Tehran. The first reports on suspected Iran-GCC direct contacts began circulating around mid-June (e.g. *Washington Post*, 16 June 1984), followed by good-will announcements of a Saudi invitation to Rafsanjani and of an increase in the quota of Iranian pilgrims allowed in for the *Hajj*.[11] In September, an Iranian opposition source reported secret contacts between the two countries at the United Nations (*BBC/SWB/ME*, 29 September 1984). The Saudis' friendly gesture was reciprocated in early November 1984 when a hijacked Saudi aircraft was taken to Iran. The Iranian government co-operated to resolve the crisis (*BBC/SWB/ME*, 7 November 1984). These efforts to build a link culminated in the Iranian Minister of Energy's visit to the Kingdom, reciprocated by Sa'ud al-Faisal's unannounced visit to Tehran in May 1985—the first visit by a Saudi minister to Iran since the overthrow of the Shah.

### Syrian Brinkmanship against the Background of Egypt's Return (February 1985–February 1986)

The evolving Saudi-Iranian channel did not automatically reduce Syria's weight in Saudi strategic thinking, partly because regional factors other than the Iran-Iraq war came into play, attesting to the multi-dimensional nature of Syrian-Saudi relations. In a parallel and related development to the Gulf war, Egypt—which once withdrew itself into isolation—was gradually making a comeback in the Arab world. The two developments were closely inter-connected, because the majority Arab view began to seek after Egypt's political and military weight in the light of an emerging possibility of a comprehensive Iranian victory against 'Arab' Iraq. To give additional momentum to Saddam Hussain and Yasir 'Arafat's courtship of Egypt which had already begun earlier, King Hussain of Jordan made a historic announcement in September 1984 to resume diplomatic relations with Cairo (BBC/SWB/ME, 29 September 1984). Thus, the seed of Amman-Cairo-Baghdad (plus Yasir 'Arafat's faction of the PLO) co-operation was sown, culminating later in the Mubarak-Saddam-Hussain tripartite summit on 16 March 1985. The triangle was viciously attacked by Syria's Faruq al-Shar' as a 'pro-US' axis (BBC/SWB/ME, 12 November 1984) and unsurprisingly began to take on the appearance of an anti-Syrian bloc—a direction certain to deepen Syria's regional isolation (MECS, 1984–1985: 80).

Saudi reaction to the return of Egypt was characteristically mixed; on the one hand, Riyadh had been seeking such a development for years, but on the other hand, it was agitated by King Hussain's unilateral action, which was destined to antagonise Syria, and was, therefore, counter-productive to an Arab consensus—an item of exceptional value in Saudi foreign policy. Immediately after King Hussain's announcement, a Saudi official statement read: 'Saudi Arabia fully understands the importance of Egypt and its weight', but a welcoming remark was qualified by the need for an Arab summit endorsement before Egypt could be formally reinstated in the Arab League (BBC/SWB/ME, 29 September 1984). The convening of such a summit, like all the other proposals for regular and extraordinary summits in the previous two years, was once again blocked by Syrian objections, and Saudi Arabia refrained from pushing the issue further in the Arab arena. Instead, Egypt was invited to the December 1984 Islamic Conference Organisation (ICO) Foreign Ministers' meeting, in which a decision was reached to reinstate Egypt at the ICO Casablanca meeting the following month.[12] The

Kingdom's general approval of Egypt's return was hinted in statements by individual royal family members, [13] but as the Amman-Cairo-Baghdad tripartite alignment became consolidated, Riyadh found itself in a deeper dilemma—sandwiched between the need for Arab consensus, to which Syria held the key, and the desire to support those Arabs who shared important common interests with Riyadh and were also on the right side of Washington.

King Fahd's visit to Washington in February 1985—the first, after a few cancellations and postponements since the conclusion of the Egyptian-Israeli peace treaty—was a clear demonstration of the Saudi dilemma and the limitation of Riyadh's influence. On 11 February, only a few days before the visit, a new Jordanian-Palestinian agreement was signed between King Hussain and Yasir 'Arafat to co-ordinate their positions on a negotiated peace, including the formation of a joint delegation. The agreement was a challenge to Riyadh in its partial content—by contradicting the comprehensive approach enshrined in the 1982 Fez resolutions, which the Saudi leadership considered 'to be of the highest importance, were proud of having initiated them, and were constantly on the alert for moves that might threaten them by arousing strong opposition from one Arab country or another.'[14] When Egypt's Mubarak acted as midwife to the Hussain-'Arafat agreement, the challenge bore an element of personal competition over who could claim the mantel of Arab leadership, because King Fahd had personally played a well-publicised role in Fez. Now, upon his long-awaited visit to Washington, he had to convince Washington to broaden the scope of the peace talks to include the Syrians—more in line with the Fez approach and therefore, crucial for the survival of its spirit—and then later to undertake the most challenging task of selling the scheme to Damascus. Another goal in this visit was to win Washington's agreement to provide F-15 fighter planes to the Kingdom. The intensification of the Tanker War increased the real need for sophisticated weaponry, but perhaps as important was the fact that such a bounty would be seen as evidence of Riyadh's influence over the superpower, effecting tremendous boost to its prestige. The King's high-profile visit to the US capital could not have been a better occasion for such a symbolic achievement. As it turned out, when Reagan 'slammed the door, snubbed requests for $8.5 billion weapons supply and instead handed it to [Israel's] Shamir' (*MEI,* 22 February 1984), the consequences were deeply embarrassing for the Saudis.

Neither was the Kingdom going to have an easy ride on the subject of peace talks. Washington was ambiguous about the inclusion of the Golan and was increasingly frustrated by Saudi sensitivity to Syrian needs.

Immediately after the Fahd-Reagan summit meeting, Saudi ambassador to Washington Prince Bandar was dispatched to Damascus to discuss the summit meeting with Asad, especially on the subject of Hussain-'Arafat agreement (*Al-Nahar*, 18 February 1985). Bandar characterised his meetings in Damascus as 'brilliant' but no concrete achievement was made in terms of bringing Damascus closer to accepting the Jordanian-Palestinian formula.[15] Thus, although Riyadh's heart was, for the most part, with the agreement, Syrian objections to it hindered the Saudis from giving it tangible support. Egypt's increasingly prominent role in the region and Washington's indifference to Riyadh's sensitivity to regional influence and prestige also deprived the Saudis of any meaningful bargaining chip with the Syrians.

It was not only Saudi Arabia that was finding the tide running against it in the spring of 1985. For Syria, not only was Egypt's return to the centre stage of Arab politics threatening to marginalise Damascus' standing in the region, but there was also another problem in the Gulf; Iran's major offensive on the Iraqi marshlands in March 1985 had severely tarnished Syria's reputation as a self-proclaimed moderating influence on Tehran. After the Tunis Arab Foreign Ministers conference in late March, Shar' uncomfortably stressed 'the vital role played by Syria's good offices with Iran' (*BBC/SWB/ME*, 28 March 1985), and soon thereafter, went out of his way to convince the rulers of Saudi Arabia and Kuwait of Syria's efforts in attaining a cease-fire in the Gulf as he travelled to Riyadh on 2 April, then to Kuwait the following day (*Al-Nahar*, 3 April 1985). To make matters worse for the Syrians, against the background of growing mistrust about their intentions and credibility among the Arab audience, the Syrian-backed Amal militia besieged the Palestinian camps in Beirut soon after Israel withdrew into what it unilaterally declared as a 'security zone' in the south. The Amal attack generated waves of Arab (and Iranian) anger directed against Damascus, even from Libya, its long-term Steadfastness ally.[16] As if to send signals to Damascus that its role was becoming increasingly irrelevant, Sa'ud al-Faisal suddenly left on a state visit to Tehran on 18 May without prior consultation or even notification to the Syrians (*MEI*, 31 May 1985). Although no concrete agreement or improvement in bilateral relations was achieved in this visit, Hussain Farrash, the ex-Saudi consul kidnapped in Beirut sixteen months previously, was freed on this occasion (*BBC/SWB/ME*, 20 and 21 May 1985). Damascus was equally annoyed with the Iranians for pursuing direct contacts with the Saudis. This only rubbed salt into the wounds of a sharply deteriorating Syrian-Iranian relationship particularly after Iran's March offensive onto Iraqi soil.[17]

Syria responded aggressively to these diplomatic crises.[18] Even towards the Saudis—who were usually spared of explicit censure in Syrian propaganda—a rare outburst of frustration was displayed. When King Fahd publicly thanked Asad for his role in securing Farrash's release (*BBC/SWB/ME*, 22 May 1985), Asad, in his Damascus Television address to the men of religion, snubbed the suggestion that Syria was at all involved in the matter:

> Despite the fact that our relations with Saudi Arabia are good, our brothers there [in Saudi Arabia] could not believe that we were unable to return to them that Muslim Saudi diplomat, who was not a fighter. The kidnappers refused to hand over the Saudi diplomat. They [the Saudis] levelled accusations at us. (13 June cited in *BBC/SWB/ME*, 18 June 1985)

King Fahd retorted a few days later by criticising 'the Palestinian killings in an Arab country'—a thinly disguised reproach to Syria's behaviour in Lebanon (*BBC/SWB/ME*, 20 June 1985).

The 7 August 1985 Casablanca Arab emergency summit only fuelled angry exchanges. The Moroccan initiative to address the latest Palestinian infighting in Lebanon was immediately supported by Sa'ud al-Faisal, who announced that King Fahd himself would attend the meeting (*MECS, 1984–1985*: 601). Since the success of the meeting required Syrian co-operation—something which had been unavailable since Fez II and likely to be the case in view of the current agenda—Saudi Arabia made a low-key effort to lure Damascus into participating in the event. In contrast to the usual Saudi courtship of dispatching high-ranking officials to Damascus in such a situation, the only signal of enticement from Riyadh was an announcement of economic packages; firstly, *MEED* reported that Jiddah-based Islamic Development Bank had approved loans to Syria totalling $18.7 million (3 August 1985). Secondly, on 5 August, while Arab Foreign Ministers preparatory meeting for the Casablanca summit was in session without Syrian, Algerian, Lebanese and PDRY participation, a Saudi economic delegation arrived in Damascus (*Al-Nahar,* 6 August 1985). The following day, the Saudi Development Fund promised Syria a loan of 100 million riyals for the expansion of electricity stations projects (*Al-Nahar,* 7 August 1985).

The absence of diplomatic exchanges between Riyadh and Damascus prior to the summit perhaps indicated that Riyadh did not expect Syria to change its hard-line position whatever it did. Also, the Saudis were likely to have placed a slightly lesser importance on the summit which was not its own initiative.[19] When the summit did convene on 7 August without the participation of Syria and the Steadfastness Front members, it transpired that the Kingdom was represented by Crown Prince 'Abdallah instead of King Fahd, whose absence indicated the Saudis' wish to take part but also their reluctance to be too closely associated with an event that so antagonised Syria, which by extension exacerbated Arab polarisation (*MECS,* 1984–1985: 116, 601). Reflecting such reluctance to fuel the anger of Syria and its hard-line compatriots, the final communiqué (*BBC/SWB/ME,* 12 August 1985) was so mildly toned that 'Arafat accused the Gulf states of succumbing to Syria's blackmail (*MEI,* 23 August 1985). Furthermore, Egypt's readmission to the League was not even discussed, much to Damascus' satisfaction.

Saudi reluctance to bend under pressure from Syria was expressed only through media reports which had censured Syria's boycott as 'the absolutely unacceptable...imposition of views over the whole Arab nation' (*BBC/SWB/ME,* 12 August 1985). Saudi commentaries attacked Damascus' obstinacy as having 'no justification'. Another publication asked:

> Why is Syria reluctant to attend the summit? Is it worried that the summit might adopt a new resolution pertaining to Palestinian rights? Or is it anxious lest the summit condemn those who support the perpetuation of the Iraqi-Iranian war? (*MECS,* 1984–1985: 602).

As to the Syrians, their boycott, which successfully brought along the Steadfastness allies, allowed them to evade criticism on their regional policy, particularly on the Palestinians in Lebanon, but no less important, on the Gulf war—yet again, underlining their centrality in the Arab politics. The boycott apparently pleased the Iranians who had been anxious that the latest friction with the Damascus might give it an incentive to join the majority Arab camp and break off its alliance with Tehran; after the closure of the Casablanca summit, on 10 August, the Iranian *Majlis* announced a hefty reward for Syria—the renewal of an agreement to grant 6 million tonnes of crude oil, which was to expire on 20 March 1986 (*MECS,* 1984–1985: 652). When Damascus felt confident that it could continue to benefit from its alliance with Tehran without suffering much of a penalty from the Arab side, it defiantly hosted a Syrian-Iranian-Libyan tripartite meeting of Foreign Ministers on 24-25 August; the final communiqué harshly criticised the proceedings of the Casablanca summit 'which consisted of plots and attempts by the capitulationist Saddam-Mubarak-Hussain-'Arafat axis against the fateful Arab and Islamic causes' (*BBC/SWB/ME,* 27 August 1985).

Such a reconciliation with Iran and the conciliatory resolution of the Casablanca summit once again permitted Syria to tread the tightrope of collecting benefits from both sides of the confrontation, Iran and the pro-Iraqi Arabs. When the Casablanca summit established reconciliation committees to heal inter-Arab rifts, Damascus went along with the Saudi initiative to reconcile itself with Jordan—a dramatic turn of events in view of their hostile relations since the late 1970s. Crown Prince 'Abdallah, together with representatives from the Arab League Secretariat and Tunisia, arrived in Damascus on 10 September, moved on to Amman and Baghdad, and then returned to Syria on the 13th. [20] Although Asad allegedly agreed on a Syria-Jordan-Iraq mini-summit, this shuttle diplomacy only produced a bilateral meeting in Jiddah between Syrian and Jordanian Prime Ministers 'Abd al-Rauf al-Kasm and Zaid al-Rifa'i (*Al-Nahar*, 14 September 1985).

Like reports on most other Saudi mediation attempts, this one also was accompanied by allegations of financial incentives offered. A western source reported that upon agreeing to enter reconciliation talks, Syria was granted $ 600 million while Jordan was rewarded with a promise of free oil supplies for the rest of 1985 (*MECS*, 1984–1985: 117). Even the Kuwaitis, who had earlier suspended payments of their Baghdad summit subvention, decided to resume their contribution to Syria (*MEED*, 28 September 1985). More reports on financial aid followed in the subsequent few months (e.g., *Los Angeles Time*, 13 November; *Observer*, 1 December 1985) when Syrian and Jordanian representatives followed up on their achievements; high-level meetings were held in Riyadh and Amman in late October (*BBC/SWB/ME*, 24 October 1985) and then the Jordanian Prime Minister visited Damascus on 12-13 November (*Los Angeles Time*, 13 November 1985). Five days after this Damascus meeting, Khaddam visited Saudi Arabia to inform King Fahd of the progress (*Al-Nahar*, 19 November 1985). These contacts eventually led to King Hussain's historic visit to Damascus on 30-31 December 1985, the first since 1978.

Although rumours of covert financial enticement were strenuously denied by the Saudis (e.g. *BBC/SWB/ME*, 3 December 1985), at least two official Saudi development aid packages to Syria were publicly announced during the period of October-November 1985—a commitment becoming increasingly rarer in the preceding years. The day after Khaddam's departure from Riyadh, the Saudi Development Fund announced a $44 million loan (*Al-Safir*, 20 November; *Al-Nahar*, 20 November 1985). The announcement was followed by another one in the same month, this time from the Jiddah-based Islamic Development Bank to lend $ 11.3 million for jute bag imports to Syria (*MEED*, 30 November 1985).

It is, however, misleading to suggest that these windfalls were the sole or even primary motive behind Damascus and Amman's receptivity to Saudi-led mediation; the reconciliation was more a result of converging interests between the two capitals than of Saudi exercise of leverage[21]—notwithstanding Riyadh's publicised attempt to take credit for the success and Damascus' public appreciation of Saudi contribution.[22] For Syria, rebuilding of ties with Jordan entailed foiling the Jordanian-Palestinian agreement to peace talks and the emergence of an anti-Syrian bloc, orchestrated by Egypt, Iraq, and Jordan. Meanwhile, for Jordan, which was growing increasingly frustrated by the lack of progress in its negotiations with 'Arafat, the realignment with Damascus—by then, 'Arafat's sworn enemy—was the clearest warning signal to press for more flexibility from the Palestinian leader. Thus, Saudi mediation role, like many other Saudi efforts before, was confined to providing a framework or platform for the *rapprochement*. The fact that Riyadh made no such breakthrough with either the Syrian-Iraqi rift or the Syrian-PLO conflict testified to the limited efficacy of Saudi cash in producing fundamental changes to Damascus' policy.

As a rule, a push to one direction was followed by a pull to another in Asad's brinkmanship or the balancing act between the pro-Iraqi Arabs on the one hand and Syria's strategic ally, Iran, on the other. Between September 1985 and early 1986, almost every single positive response to Saudi-led mediation efforts was followed by a gesture to calm Tehran's anxiety and exasperation. The day after the first Kasm-Rifa'i meeting on 16 September 1985, Khaddam travelled to Tehran to reassure the Iranians that the Syrian-Iranian alliance was not endangered by the realignment. On 26 October, a few days after the Syrian-Jordanian high-level talks in Riyadh and Amman, the Syrian ambassador to Tehran reassured Iranian Foreign Minister Velayati that Syria's solidarity with Iran in the Gulf war was unwavering (*BBC/SWB/ME*, 24 October 1985). In one of these meetings, Tehran allegedly threatened to cancel its alliance with Syria if the overtures to Jordan were intended to be the first step towards a quest for a separate peace in the Camp David fashion (*MEI*, 20 December 1985). The results of Syrian efforts were mixed, indicating the difficulty of the balancing-act. Initially, the Iranians appeared to have bought the Syrian argument, when in early December, Kasm's three-day visit to Tehran resulted in a bilateral understanding on economic, trade and cultural issues, wherein Iran committed to continue the oil delivery to Syria (*MEED*, 7 December 1985). On 22 December, the Syrian-Iranian-Libyan tripartite meeting of Foreign Minister, the third in 1985, further reconfirmed their solidarity. However, in the same month, Iran suddenly halted the flow of oil, claiming that their installations on Kharg Island had been damaged by Iraqi bombardment; but the real cause was Syria's demands to reschedule its debt (*MECS*, 1984–1985: 121). Syria was allegedly $1.5 billion behind in payment, or in other words, it had not paid anything at all since the oil delivery agreement was concluded in 1981 (Kienle, 1990: 167-168).

During the first seven weeks of 1986, Syria maintained its feeble attempt to reassure its Arab critics that Iran had no ambitions to acquire Arab land and that Damascus' alliance with Tehran was instrumental in preventing the expansion of war to the Arab Gulf states;[23] the greatest blow to the credibility of such a statement came in mid-February, when Iran besieged Iraq's Faw port and oil installations, thereby bringing the threat of war ever closer to the GCC states. Immediate Riyadh-Damascus and Damascus-Tehran diplomatic contacts notwithstanding, [24] Saudi Arabia—and in essence, the whole of the GCC—became more overtly pro-Iraq with the seige of Faw as the turning point, while Syria's credibility as a moderator of Iranian expansionism was practically shattered (Chubin and Tripp, 1988: 167-168). Damascus and Riyadh were to readjust their policy towards each other accordingly, as will be discussed in the following section.

One of the remarkable phenomena of the period covered in this section—the first twenty-two months of the Tanker War—was Saudi Arabia's persistent adherence to the policy of keeping the United States out of the Gulf despite the acuteness of the security threats. The first American offer to have a physical presence in the Gulf was made as early as Carter's presidency. The offer was repeatedly reiterated following the AWACS incident and other tanker attacks, but Riyadh declined for fear of inviting superpower clashes in the region and accusations from fellow Arabs that its association with the superpower was too close to be legitimate. Also, Washington's closeness to Israel proved to be more than a psychological obstacle for Riyadh when pro-Israeli elements in the US government leaked the news of the US intention to station a Rapid Deployment Force in the Gulf. The disclosure was intended to embarrass and alienate the Saudis, thereby increasing their reluctance to seek even arms from Washington (*MEI,* 1 June 1984). Riyadh's studious attempt to leave a healthy distance with Washington, in turn, urged it to seek other options—most importantly the 'Arab' option—in resolving the Gulf crisis. Hence, Syria's value as an asset to Riyadh increased accordingly—a significant addition to Damascus' acknowledged influence over Lebanese and Palestinian issues, which were not entirely separate from the developments in the Gulf.

The end result was Syria's continued ability to hijack the Arab political agenda in the first stage of the Tanker War, thereby severely restricting Saudi Arabia's policy options, as succinctly summarised in *MECS*:

Despite the Saudis' obvious frustration, the fact of the matter was that Syria's position dictated much of Saudi foreign policy. They prevented Riyadh from convening a summit conference; they prevented King Fahd from attending the Casablanca summit; they obstructed a Saudi attempt to bring about a Syrian-Iraqi reconciliation which might have ended the Gulf war; they prevented the Saudis from giving clear-cut support to the Jordanian-PLO dialogue; they prevented them from supporting Egypt's return to the Arab ranks; they obstructed their attempt to end the split within al-Fath between 'Arafat and his rivals; and they prevented the emergence of a new Lebanon consistent with Saudi interests and priorities. *Thus, Syria did have something close to veto power over Saudi policies in the region.* (1984–1985: 602, emphasis added)

In the period after March 1986, however, this Saudi perception of the desirable US role in the Gulf was to undergo a dramatic revision, and with it, Syria's position in Saudi strategic thinking was also transformed.

### Internationalisation of the Iran-Iraq War and the Predicament of Syria and Saudi Arabia (February 1986–July 1988)

For Syria, the Iranian offensive on Iraq's Faw port and oil installations and the ensuing deterioration in its relations with Tehran coincided with difficulties on several different fronts outside the Gulf. Domestically, the economic recession had hit a crisis level by 1986, as the economy grew at an average rate of less than 1 percent per annum in the previous three years (Sukkar, 1994: 26-28). Its foreign currency reserves recorded an all-time low at $50 million, while skyrocketing trade deficits and inflation also indicated the enormity of the problem (Zisser, 2001: 39). The economic crisis was compounded by deterioration in internal security, epitomised in various bombing campaigns in Syria's major cities; for these incidents, Asad blamed Iraq, Israeli agents in Lebanon, the Muslim Brotherhood and the United States.[25] In Syria's immediate vicinity, sporadic military clashes with Israel in the latter half of 1985 culminated in the 19 November Israeli shooting of two Syrian Mig-23s over Syrian territory. In February 1986, Israeli fighter jets forced down a Libyan executive jet, on which a Syrian delegation headed by 'Abdallah al-Ahmar, the assistant secretary-general of the Ba'th Party, was making a homeward journey.[26] Thus, by the spring of 1986, Syria and Israel appeared to be on a deadly collision course. In Lebanon, Syria's ambition to impose its own order was suffering a serious setback as the precarious Shi'i, Druze and Maronite agreement pieced together under Syrian auspices on 28 December 1985 crumbled in less than a fortnight (Karsh, 1991: 164), and the so-called 'war of camps' continued with no prospect of a lasting cease-fire.[27] To further complicate matters, Syria's dominance of the

Lebanese scene was being increasingly challenged by the growing influence of Iran and the Hizbullah militants.

Moreover, Asad's alliance with Moscow was becoming progressively qualified, as the new head of state Mikhail Gorbachev, inaugurated in March 1985, initiated a profound shift in Soviet global and Middle East orientation. Although the diplomatic reorientation—coined as 'New Thinking'—was not implemented in practice until 1987 (Freedman, 1991: 206), Moscow's attempt to diversify contacts with a number of Middle East regional actors, including Israel, had been prevalent from the mid-1980s; the aim was to revise its Middle East policy's previous concentration on the alliance with Damascus. As early as June 1985 when the first Asad-Gorbachev summit meeting took place, the new Soviet leader reportedly expressed his reservation about assisting Asad's quest for 'strategic parity' with Israel,[28] although his categorical dismissal of the notion's relevance in the changing world came only in the April 1987 summit meeting.[29] The consequence was grave indeed for the Syrians, because the alliance with Moscow and forthcoming Soviet aid were a vital component of Syria's national security. It was also important for Syria's regional prestige to be able to impress its adversaries and friends alike with the strength of the Soviet Union's commitment to it—just as Saudi Arabia's prestige in the region somewhat fluctuated in accordance with its ability to influence Washington's decision-making (MECS, 1984-1985: 650).

The loosening of Syrian-Soviet ties happened at a time when Syria most needed the superpower backing to counter the new wave of international ostracism; although the Syrian government's involvement in kidnappings and organised intimidation had been suspected before, it became a target of concerted world-wide censure as a sponsor of international terrorism in the spring of 1986. At London's Heathrow Airport on 17 April, a bag of explosives was found by security guards before it made its way on to an El Al flight to Tel Aviv. The incident was soon thereafter linked to Nizar al-Hindawi, a Jordanian national who was found to have connections with Syrian intelligence. [30] Although no conclusive account of Syria's involvement is established, the end result was international condemnation—with Britain as a leading voice—against Syria's sponsorship of terrorism. When, six months later, Hindawi was found guilty at a British court, Margaret Thatcher's government broke off diplomatic relations with Damascus, the US and Canada recalled their ambassadors, and the European Community imposed limited sanctions. Also, bomb explosions in West Berlin in late March and early April of the same year were linked to the Syrian authorities (MECS, 1986: 620). In the eyes of the international community, these incidents seemed to be a mere tip of an iceberg; the on-going kidnappings of Westerners in Lebanon as well as decades of violence in the region, which had been conducted, for instance, by militant Palestinian groupings, all appeared in some way connected to the Asad regime.

In April 1986, the Syrian leadership had reasons to be genuinely anxious about an imminent military assault by the United States. On 15 April—two days before the El Al flight incident of Hindawi—the superpower had launched attacks on the Libyan cities of Bengazi and Tripoli, under the rationale of curbing Libya's sponsorship of international terrorism. From where Damascus stood, there seemed no reason why it would not be the next on the US hit list (*MECS*, 1986: 99). Cornered from all directions—internationally, regionally and economically—Damascus in the spring of 1986 needed to be particularly cautious with its handling of relations with Saudi Arabia if it were to avoid near-total diplomatic isolation.

Saudi Arabia was not much better off; the price of oil dropped in 1986 from some $25 a barrel to less than $10 in a space of four months, while the King lamented the diplomatic situation in neighbouring states: 'We are surrounded by the most critical conditions we have ever faced' (*MECS*, 1986: 543). The Kingdom's crisis was relatively more focused (than the dispersed nature of threats surrounding Syria) on the following entwined issues: 1) finding an end to the now seven-year long Iran-Iraq war; 2) devising a formula for Syrian-Iraqi *rapprochement* which would provide the basis for an end to the war; and 3) convening an Arab summit which had been postponed since 1983 due to inter-Arab rifts, most prominent of which was between Damascus and Baghdad. With Iran's occupation of the Faw peninsula as a turning point, Tehran's threats against Saudi Arabia became 'much more direct, unequivocal, and menacing than at any time since the beginning of the war' (*MECS*, 1986: 562). Although Iran paid some conciliatory diplomatic gestures to Riyadh during the following months,[31] it also markedly stepped up the propaganda campaign against the Kingdom, and its verbal threats were accompanied by attacks on Saudi oil tankers.

One of Tehran's main complaints was on the Saudi oil policy of flooding the market and forcing the world oil price down. This, the Iranians claimed, was a deliberate attempt to limit Iran's ability to sustain the war efforts and was, therefore, tantamount to a 'declaration of war' (*Al-Nahar*, 22 April 1986; Hunter, 1990: 107). Indeed, by 1986, Saudi aid for Iraq had expanded from strictly financial aid and construction of an Iraqi oil pipeline across the Kingdom—to substitute for the loss of the transport route via Syria—to a much larger scope. Together with Kuwait, it allegedly allowed their territory to be used for the transfer of war materials to Iraq, passed on information and intelligence gathered by AWACS, and permitted the Iraqi air force to use their territory as launch pads for operation against Iranian targets (*MECS,* 1986: 562; Hunter, 1990: 106). Thus, the spillover of the Gulf war was Saudi Arabia's core security concern in the wake of Iran's Faw operation.

As to Syrian-Saudi relations, the period under investigation in this section from the Faw (February 1986) to the Iran-Iraq cease-fire (July 1988) can be divided into two phases. During the first eighteen months, Riyadh continued its long-established quest for a regional diplomatic solution to the Iran-Iraq war—without involving outside global powers. Hence, Syria was still treated as a key to forming a unified Arab rank on the question as was in the previous period, and as a result, the overall pattern of Syrian-Saudi relations—in which they disagreed on almost every major policy issue in the region, but Riyadh remained anxious not to alienate Syria—did not change (*MECS,* 1986: 558). The difference, however, was in the Syrian regime's new show of flexibility on the Gulf policy, or in other words, its amenability to Saudi and Jordanian mediation efforts between Damascus and Baghdad. The change resulted primarily from Syria's acute economic and diplomatic crises, as detailed above, and the ineffectiveness of its policy of keeping its Iranian ally under control. These troubles did increase Damascus' dependency on Riyadh, particularly financially. As a result, the bilateral relations restored a more balanced equilibrium, reminiscent of the 1970s; in other words, Riyadh became more willing than in previous years to pursue policies that were not necessarily compatible with the Syrian position. Especially on the Gulf issues—*the* core concern for the Kingdom but not necessarily for Syria—Riyadh became more assertive, while Syria's co-operation in that arena was traded off against Riyadh's acquiescence in areas related to the Arab-Israeli conflict. Thus, yet again, the bilateral relations were sustained not due to overlap of interests but rather due to their differences, which produced a paradoxical compatibility.

The turning point in this relationship came in the form of the Mecca disturbance in late July 1987. Saudi foreign policy became even more assertive to the extent that it appeared to dismiss the relevance of Syria's position on this or that regional issue, and Syria in contrast turned more conciliatory than any other time since 1982. This change in the dynamics was demonstrated at the Amman summit, the first summit convened with full participation since the 1982 Fez II, and, therefore, will be analysed in length.

*Joint Saudi-Jordanian Mediation between the Two Ba'thist Regimes*

*(March 1986–July 1987)*

In the wake of the Faw incident, Saudi obsession with bringing an end to the Gulf war was translated into renewed diplomatic activism to achieve a Syrian-Iraqi *rapprochement* which would serve as a first step in creating a unified Arab front against Tehran. The remarkable consolidation—at least by Arab standards—of the Jordanian-Syrian reconciliation since the previous year gave the Saudi leadership an additional impetus and certain optimism to pursue the Iraqi channel as well. Together with Jordan's King Hussain, who was now well placed to act as a mediator, the Saudis exerted considerable efforts to achieve a breakthrough. Preparation for an Asad-Saddam meeting started in late April 1986, when Sa'ud al-Faisal visited Damascus.[32] The process was followed up by King Hussain who received Asad in Amman on 5 May and then shuttled between Baghdad and Damascus throughout the month. When Asad was next in Jordan at the end of the month, he was reported to have 'listened intently' to Hussain's plea for improved relations with Baghdad.[33] That Damascus remonstrated unusually harshly to the Iranians against the attacks on Kuwaiti and Saudi oil tankers was also an encouraging signal for Amman and Riyadh (*MECS*, 1986: 123). Meanwhile, Asad personally sent a message to Fahd reproaching Iran (Marschall, 1991: 73). A hopeful air surrounded the flurry of diplomatic activities, as a meeting of Syrian and Iraqi Foreign Ministers was scheduled to take place on 13 June at a point along the two countries' border—a monumental achievement had it materialised.

As the fighting in the Gulf continued to escalate, Syria adopted a twofold strategy: 1) continuing to market itself as a credible pacifier of Tehran's aggression[34] even though the claim was sounding increasingly hollow, and 2) showing measured responsiveness to the newly revitalised Arab reconciliation efforts in order to remedy its diplomatic isolation. In the first months after Faw, it was the latter half of the strategy that yielded considerable fruits not only from the Gulf Arab capitals but even Tehran. Since December 1985, when Iran decided to cease oil delivery to Syria, Syrian-Iranian relations had been at one of their lowest ebbs. Time was now ripe for Damascus to review its tactics and apply pressure on its long-term ally. That pressure seemed to have an instant effect. On 7 June, six days before the scheduled date of the Syrian-Iraqi meeting, Iran's Acting Foreign Minister Muhammad 'Ali Besharati arrived in Damascus where he received assurances that it was not Syria's intention to change its allegiance from Tehran. On that same day, oil delivery was resumed. When the Syrian-Iraqi meeting was indeed cancelled, the Syrians picked up another reward in the form of an Iranian promise to ease the pressure for debt repayment and to sell Syria 2.5 million tons of oil between October

1986 and March 1987 at discounted prices (*MECS*, 1986: 99). Furthermore, Tehran allegedly offered military co-operation in Lebanon, which had been another major source of friction between the two (Marschall, 1991: 73).

Syria's display of openness and flexibility to Arab overtures was well rewarded when its last minute cancellation of the meeting with Iraq occasioned no punishment or explicit criticism (*MECS*, 1986: 101), despite the grave disappointment it caused in Riyadh and Amman. Damascus even appeared to have been handsomely rewarded just for its interest in sitting at the negotiating table. Sources claimed that Saudi Arabia pledged a grant of anything between $300 million and $2 billion,[35] while other news reports suspected that the Kingdom had guaranteed an International Monetary Fund (IMF) loan to Syria amounting to $1 billion. Still others speculated that it was Syria's debt to Iran that the Saudis offered to pay for.[36] Whatever the sum might have been, at the very least, Syria could take comfort in the fact that the Kingdom continued to live up to its Baghdad Summit commitment in 1986, even when other Arab financiers had long forgone the obligation.[37]

The failure of the June efforts did not entirely dishearten the Saudi leadership, and four months later, it embarked on another attempt at reconciling Damascus with Baghdad. On 18 October, Crown Prince 'Abdallah made an unannounced visit to Damascus, the first since April 1985. The visit was publicised as in the framework of the Arab League's 'committee for clearing the Arab atmosphere' and his talks with Asad apparently dealt with Syrian-Iraqi *rapprochement* and the Saudi desire to convene the regular annual Arab summit in Riyadh. Press reports suspected that the Prince's entrance on the scene—rather than an official of a lower standing—indicated that reconciliation was within reach (*Al-Nahar*, 19 October 1986), as he made his way to Baghdad from Damascus the following day (*Al-Safir*, 20 October 1986). Again, no breakthrough was found, but yet again, no censure against Syria followed; this time, however, the Saudi reticence might have had much to do with its embarrassment over the uncovering of one of the most bewildering scandals in the 1980s—the US-Iranian arms-for-hostage deal, or the 'Irangate'—and Saudi Arabia's part in it, as will be outlined below.

When the 3 November issue of pro-Syrian Lebanese paper *al-Shira'* first disclosed to the world the secret US-Iran weapons deal, the timing indicated that it was perhaps a calculated Syrian act to embarrass its enemies and to discipline unruly allies, thereby easing the pressures on itself. This was because, for Damascus, things could not have turned much worse from October 1986 in terms of diplomatic ostracism and isolation: the Hindawi trial's ruling that month was detrimental to Syria's international reputation; Iran was showing little sign of easing its aggression towards the Arab Gulf states, and Damascus' policy was in no small part held responsible for it; Syrian-Iranian disagreements over Lebanon had culminated in the one-day kidnapping of the Syrian chargé d'affaires in Tehran in late October (*MECS,* 1986: 139); Lebanon was still a quagmire; and the Steadfastness Front had practically disintegrated, as South Yemen had been weakened by internal conflict and Algeria had begun distancing itself from Syria and Libya.

Irangate was, in short, a secret operation which involved US weapons sales to Iran via Israel, in return for release by Iran of some American hostages. Although Israel had been suspected of supplying Iran with US weapons from the start of the Gulf war (Seale, 1990: 483), the operation formally became the Reagan administration's defined policy around the summer of 1985 (Agha and Khalidi, 1995: 156-157). The transaction of the arms sales was funded in such a way that it would produce profits which the administration then used to fund the Contra rebels in Nicaragua—and this was where the Saudi role came in. A Saudi businessman and personal friend of King Fahd, Adnan Khasshogi, according to Aburish, 'was the father of this elaborate scheme' (1994: 269) but most sources are convinced that the Saudi leadership was more closely involved, despite their vehement public denial; 'Ali Musallam, a personal envoy of King Fahd, and Muhammad Ayas, the business manager of King Fahd's son Muhammad, either participated in the negotiations or played a key role in channelling royal family funds into the arms deal (*MECS,* 1986: 563). The result of its disclosure was Saudi loss of face with the Arab audience, and the sheer embarrassment was made doubly worse by the Israeli involvement in the deal. The Saudi role in the scheme, in spite of such a high risk, attested to its obsession with the Iranian threat and its ensuing desperation to establish any amicable contact with Tehran in order to mitigate its bellicosity.[38]

Saudi Arabia was, by all accounts, not the prime target of Syria's decision to uncover this chain of events, but it helped to moderate Saudi apprehension at Syria's regional policy,[39] and, at least indirectly, dissuaded it from convening the Riyadh Arab summit—postponed since 1982 mainly due to Syria's obstruction. Despite the major Iranian offensive against Basra from late 1986 to January 1987, which heightened Saudi anxiety more than ever, Riyadh and Damascus maintained somewhat cordial and mutually supportive relations until the summer of 1987.

In the first half of 1987, the two capitals first worked together for mutual interests at Kuwait's ICO summit meeting on 26–29 January. Rumours persisted that Saudi Arabia and the host country Kuwait bought Syria's participation for $ 500 million in order to ensure success of the meeting (*MECS*, 1987: 155), and Asad's presence at the conference did bring a significant gain; he encountered there for the first time Egypt's Husni Mubarak. The unofficial encounter, most probably prearranged by the Saudis and the Kuwaitis (*MECS*, 1987: 119), was surprisingly amicable, in stark contrast to their open hostility at the actual summit sessions, and the two leaders agreed on holding more talks in the future. The possibility of Egyptian-Syrian reconciliation raised Saudi hopes in remedying the Arab polarisation, which had plagued the Arab world since the late 1970s. For Syria, dialogue with Egypt presented a potential window of opportunity to rectify its acute regional and international isolation, but the decision to participate in the summit was at the same time a tremendous compromise; Syria was exposed to further criticism for its Gulf policy, and none of its Steadfastness allies joined ranks with it to give support. Furthermore, Asad was unable to stop the summit from explicitly criticising attacks on the Palestinian camps in Lebanon and Soviet aggression towards Afghanistan. With regard to its Iranian ally, which absented itself from the event altogether and pleaded with Syria to do the same, Asad's participation in the event added more problems to the already rocky alliance.

Although the price was thus not small, Asad's flexible attitude at the ICO summit paid off a month later in the Lebanese arena. On the eve of the ICO summit, and in the midst of negotiations between warring Lebanese factions, Rafiq al-Hariri, the familiar Saudi envoy on Lebanese issues, arrived in Damascus with a message from Fahd (*Al-Safir*, 24 January 1987). Although no details of the message were disclosed, Asad may have received a Saudi green light to use force once again to impose a *pax Syriana* onto the country, in return for Asad's co-operation at the Kuwaiti summit and promises of revising his Gulf policy. In February, shortly after the ICO summit, Syria began a massive military campaign with at least 7,000 troops rolling into West Beirut, the positions it had once evacuated in June 1982. The 35,000-strong Syrian forces clashed with Hizbullah fighters, claiming an unprecedented number of casualties, before they once again gained control of more than 60 percent of Lebanese territories later in the month. All this Syria managed with surprisingly little hostile reaction from the outside world. Elizabeth Picard, a seasoned observer of politics in the Arab East, explained it as international acknowledgement that only Damascus was potentially capable of introducing some semblance of order, and that even a Syrian one was preferable to the prevailing anarchy. In her words:

The silence of the international community at the new take over of Lebanon...modestly hid the deals proposed to General Assad: the

Soviets expected him to improve his relations with the PLO and Iraq; the Western powers expected him to have a positive influence on the terrorists and hostage-takers; and the Arabs expected him to make his Iranian ally listen to reason (2002: 134).

It was now Asad's turn to fulfil his side of the deal. On 22 April, on the eve of his visit to the USSR, one of King Fahd's sons, Prince Faisal, arrived in Damascus with a message from the King (*Al-Nahar,* 23 April 1987). On his way back from Moscow on the 27th, Asad met Saddam Hussain at a point near the Jordanian-Iraqi-Saudi common border, in the company of King Hussain and Crown Prince 'Abdallah (*Al-Nahar,* 5 May 1987). Although the result of the meeting was never officially announced, a significant degree of agreement was reached on issues such as mutual propaganda campaigns, support of opposition groups, allocation of Euphrates water and oil pipeline disputes—but not on Syria's alliance with Iran *per se.* The measure of success was also reflected in the number of follow-up meetings in the next two months between ministers and officials of the two countries.[40] Rumours of Saudi financial incentives offered to Syria again abounded, mostly in the form of free oil delivery to replace the Iranian supply (*Al-Nahar,* 9 May; *Al-Anwar,* 10 May 1987). A month later, the Kingdom offered Syria 100,000 tons of wheat to alleviate the effects of one of the worst droughts the country had known (*Al-Nahar,* 4 June 1987). On 28 July, reports were circulated that the Kingdom had further pledged $5 million to help Syria's hosting of the Mediterranean Games in Lattakia (al-Ladhaqiyyah) in September 1988—the biggest sporting event ever in the country (*Al-Anwar,* 28 July; *Al-Safir,* 28 July 1987). However, on that very day in late July, the Syrian-Iraqi thaw came to an abrupt end as Iraq shot down a Syrian Mig-21 fighter plane, flying over Iraqi air space, and captured the pilot (*MECS,* 1987: 122).

Syria's ability to capitalise on the overtures from the anti-Iranian Arab majority was a replay of the June 1986 Jordanian-Saudi mediation efforts. In response to the Asad-Hussain meeting, Tehran signed a new oil delivery agreement with Syria on 2 May without pressure to settle the outstanding debts first (*Financial Times,* 2 July 1987; *MECS,* 1987: 123). The Syrian-Iranian alliance gradually restored some health when additional economic agreements were signed in later months.

Thus, during much of 1986 and the first half of 1987, Syria and Saudi Arabia still differed on most regional issues, but the acuteness of troubles that both actors were facing had forced them into co-operation—albeit an uneasy one, sometimes facilitated by financial enticements, sometimes by a needling as in the Irangate disclosure. Saudi Arabia's co-operation with Syria's efforts to counter allegation of involvement in terrorism was exemplary of the co-operative relations. First, King Fahd offered to mediate between Damascus and the Western capitals (*MECS*, 1987: 610; Seale, 1991: 482). Second, when Asad attempted to justify Syria's position by drawing a distinction between 'terrorism' and 'war of liberation' and asserted that Syria's role in any act of violence was restricted to the latter, the Saudi ambassador to Damascus implicitly endorsed these lines by chairing the Arab committee on 'defining terrorism and differentiating between terrorism and the people's struggle' (*MECS*, 1987: 651). However, the newly discovered equilibrium of Syrian-Saudi co-operation, based on their *differences*, nearly disintegrated after July 1987 when the Saudis were pushed over the edge by Syria's Iranian ally and its patience with the dangerous status quo was exhausted.

### The Mecca Pilgrim Clashes and the 1987 Amman Summit: Turning Points towards the End of the War (July 1987–July 1988)

Since the 1979 Iranian Revolution, the new regime in Tehran had actively exploited the annual *Hajj* as a platform to demonstrate its political opinion against the Saudi regime and other 'enemies of Islam'. This strategy had been a source of bitter contest between Tehran and Riyadh in the early 1980s, but when the two capitals established a direct channel of communication, one of the first goodwill gestures, which the Iranians implemented, was to put a halt to the pilgrims' provocative political demonstrations. As a measure of calm prevailed, the Saudi government went so far as to increase the quota for the Iranian pilgrims to 150,000 in 1984.

The 150,000 Iranians of the 1987 *Hajj*, however, allegedly arrived with a specific aim of destabilising the Kingdom; according to an Israeli account, only 20 percent were genuine pilgrims, while remaining 25 percent was composed of Revolutionary Guards, 40 percent suicidal volunteer fighters, and 13 percent what the Iranians called members of 'the generation of the revolution' (*MECS*, 1987: 589). Though different versions of the event still prevail, the Saudis squarely placed responsibilities on the Iranians; in their version, it was the Iranians who, on 31 July, instigated mass riots in Mecca and violently clashed with the Saudi police and the National Guard reinforcements, causing hundreds of deaths. The Saudi authorities counted 402 deaths of which 275 were Iranian pilgrims, while Iran claimed that 400 Iranian pilgrims died (*MECS*, 1987: 173). Against the background of Tehran's call for the overthrow of Al-Sa'ud regime, the Mecca riots were followed by two massive explosions at oil installations in Ras Tanura probably by Shi'a Aramco workers affiliated to the Iranian *Da'wa* (Abir, 1988: 219-220) These events sharply reminded Saudi Arabia of its vulnerability in the face of Iranian threats and of the failure of its long-term efforts to find accommodation with Tehran through negotiations.

Syria, together with the UAE and Algeria, offered to mediate between Tehran and Riyadh, while Asad personally conveyed his regrets over the incident to King Fahd.[41] On 13 September, Khaddam met Fahd in Jiddah in this context, while Shar' travelled to Tehran a few days later to press Iran to ensure safe passage of vessels through the Gulf. However, the diplomatic initiative was clearly insufficient to pacify the Saudis, and pressure on Syria to review its Gulf policy was mounting. Aside from regular calls to all Arab states to severe ties with Iran, Sa'ud al-Faisal delivered a speech at the Tunis Arab Foreign Ministers meeting in August, containing an 'uncharacteristically strong' attack on Iran (*Chicago Tribune,* 24 August 1987). With obvious reference to Syria, he urged all Arab states to 'adopt a unified Arab position, because it is clear that Iran does not want to stop its war and wants to expose the whole region to the danger of foreign intervention' (*Financial Times,* 24 August 1987).

The event in Mecca in July 1987 was a turning point in the Iran-Iraq war because of the ensuing change in Saudi attitude towards Iran and also because that change led to direct US military involvement in the conflict—dramatically altering its course. As one senior Saudi official was quoted as saying after the riots: 'Events brought Saudi Arabia to the point where we have to show our teeth' (*New York Times,* 16 October 1987), indicating Saudi Arabia's departure from its traditional preference for low-keyed, reactive foreign policy with marked reluctance to take controversial initiatives. The Mecca events, as Khalidi and Agha note, had 'a significant galvanising effect on Saudi policy', making it 'stronger, more aggressive and generally more self-confident than before'. One of the manifestations of this new Saudi profile, they continue, was 'its new willingness to take sides on inter-Arab policy disputes, and to support a firmer line in dealing with regional conflicts' (1987–1988: 26). All these were to severely restrict Syria's ability to play maverick of Arab politics and to 'veto' Saudi regional policy. In addition, what is particularly important to stress here is that this confidence was 'buttressed by all-out US support in the Gulf,' rather than as a result of any self-born, internal sources of strength' (Khalidi and Agha, 1987–1988: 26). How did the US factor get introduced to the balance sheet? Examination of the US re-flagging of oil tankers and the November 1987 Amman Arab Summit help explain the dynamics at work.

The intensification of Iranian attacks on Arab tankers in 1986 began to have a costly material effect on Kuwait and Saudi Arabia's oil trade. In December 1986, Kuwait took an extreme step of requesting both the US and the USSR to seek the protection of the Kuwaiti tankers by reflagging a majority of them. When the two superpowers accepted the request, Kuwait first presented it as a purely commercial decision—and in the Soviet case, it was not inaccurate a description—but in effect, the US acceptance marked the beginning of its abrasive naval interference in the Gulf. The first US convoy sailed the reflagged tanker in late July, and by September, a special American military command established in the Gulf had directly carried out attacks against Iranian targets (*MECS*, 1987: 186-187) with 'behind-the-scenes' Saudi assistance (Khalidi and Agha, 1987–1988: 35). It was a matter of time that the US presence required land bases, there to stay over a long term. As Joffé, correctly predicted soon after the US vessels' arrival in the Gulf: 'In essence, the USA had, at a stroke acquired the permanent presence in the Gulf region which it had vainly sought ever since the Carter administration had proposed it in the wake of the Iranian Revolution' (1987–1988: 14). The Saudis had strenuously strove to avoid this scenario for almost a decade, partly for fear of turning the Gulf into a platform of superpower rivalry, but the changes taking place in the Kremlin under Gorbachev made this possibility remote. Another danger was in the negative impact that visible US military presence could produce on the legitimacy of the ruling regimes, but the prolongation of the Gulf war, coupled with the severe economic strains caused by the oil glut of the 1980s, pushed the Gulf regimes into the embrace of the US military umbrella more than they would have otherwise preferred (Joffé, 1987–1988: 12-13). In the short term, nevertheless, the Gulf Arabs derived much comfort and confidence from the mighty US military presence and its role in hindering Iran's advance on the Iraqi soil.

Riyadh's renewed confidence and assertiveness were most clearly manifest in the convening of the Amman Arab Summit in early November 1987, attributable to active Saudi-Jordanian initiatives. That the summit was successfully opened without falling victim to a key members' boycott[42] in itself amounted to a notable achievement by the driving forces behind the convention—in view of the fact that such a summit call had been serially shot down by Syria for some five consecutive years. In November 1987, Syria's diplomatic and economic troubles were so grave that it thought it no longer prudent to continue with its long-standing sabotaging tactic, which was wearing away the Arab majority's patience. Iran's military attack on Baghdad as the summit was convening only added to Syria's discomfort. Thus, the summit had a successful opening and, when a unanimously agreed final resolution was adopted, the atmosphere was euphoric (*MECS*, 1987: 133, 143-147); even outside observers hailed it as signifying an end to the long period of confusion and disarray in inter-Arab political relations and the emergence of political unanimity not seen since 1982 Fez II (Joffé, 1987–1988: 6).

The convention of the Amman Summit and its final resolutions promised to be a potential departure from the established pattern not only of inter-Arab relations in general but of Syrian-Saudi relations since 1978 in particular. The new Saudi assertiveness was openly displayed when they pressed issues which were sure to upset the Syrians, thereby foiling the latter's long-standing policy of playing 'spoiler' to Saudi policy, particularly in the context of Arab summit meetings. The summit was an expression of Saudi determination to devote the discussions to Gulf issues against the Syrian insistence on maintaining Israel as the priority case. When the resolution was unanimously adopted, its wording—the harshest condemnation of Iran's 'intransigence' to date—brought much satisfaction to Riyadh, although no immediate punitive measure was stipulated.[43] In this context, the Asad-Saddam meetings on 9–10 November as a starting point in Syrian-Iraqi *rapprochement* were the most tangible achievement for Jordan and Saudi Arabia; the long-term success of the summit itself, in turn, was to be judged by how much progress was made in thawing relations between the two Ba'thist regimes.

Another major accomplishment of the summit, which Saudi Arabia had previously shied away from pursuing, was Egypt's readmission to the Arab mainstream. Although Asad adamantly refused to accept its readmission to the Arab League, he conceded to the summit declaration that individual states were free to restore diplomatic relations with Egypt;[44] in effect, his concession annulled the Baghdad summit decision of collective sanctions against Cairo, a resolution Asad had dearly defended for almost a decade. Within hours, the UAE announced the restoration of relations and eight other states, including Saudi Arabia, followed suit shortly thereafter. This summit decision was destined to reappoint Egypt as a leading player in Arab politics with the effect of further weakening the minority bloc led by Syria. Asad, however, aware that he alone could not change this trend, decided to build on the Kuwait ICO summit meeting with Mubarak, to make a gesture of good-will albeit qualified, and to prevent the consolidation of an anti-Syrian Cairo-Baghdad axis.

Saudi Arabia's renewed confidence was manifest in another critical point in its relations with Syria—renewal of the Baghdad Summit aid commitment. The 10-year term of the 1978 agreement was about to expire, but the Kingdom resolutely showed its muscle by refusing to discuss the subject at all. Although the Arab oil states in November 1987 allegedly promised Syria a significant amount of financial aid on an individual basis (see below), the suspension of the Baghdad Summit aid sent a clear symbolic message—i.e. aid to Syria and other frontline states should no longer be considered an automatic obligation of oil-producing states, but instead the recipients must 'win' the aid through their services to common Arab interests. Furthermore, Saudi Arabia successfully prevented another Syrian-proposed topic from being discussed at the summit. No attention was paid to the Syrians' demand for a condemnation of the presence of US naval forces in the Gulf—a subject which used to have the effect of stirring considerable embarrassment among the Saudi leadership and other conservative Gulf Arabs in the previous years (*MECS*, 1987: 131).

Such demonstrations of Saudi willingness to contradict Syria's position notwithstanding, some reports deduced from Crown Prince 'Abdallah's participation in place of King Fahd that Syria still held a key to Saudi Arabia's Arab policy (e.g. *Washington Post*, 7 November 1987; *MECS*, 1987: 57, 596). According to this reading, the King's absence—the official reason for which was ill health—was a sign of Saudi reluctance to enter public confrontation with Syria on the aforementioned difficult issues.[45] Nonetheless, the Saudi decision to have 'Abdallah represent the country in this celebrated event was not just a sign of defensiveness but tactically a sound decision, too, in view of the fact that 'Abdallah had long enjoyed a special rapport with the Syrian leadership and had been playing for years an instrumental role in organising Syrian-Iraqi dialogue. Then what, if anything, did Saudi Arabia and Jordan concede to the Syrians to secure their participation and co-operation in the summit and to coax them into meeting the Iraqi delegation?

First, the Saudi aim of holding a summit solely dedicated to the Gulf issue had to be compromised upon Syria's insistence, which made its participation conditional on broadening the agenda to include the Arab-Israeli conflict (*MECS*, 1987: 128). Second, the conference meeting refrained from defining concrete measures of sanctions against Iran, and many Arab states continued to maintain diplomatic relations with Iran—including Saudi Arabia. Third, Syria could also take comfort in the fact that it successfully blocked Egypt's readmission to the Arab League, although it was almost fully rehabilitated. In such qualified respects, some concluded that the 'Syrian veto was still in effect' (*Chicago Tribune*, 12 November; *Mideast Markets*, 23 November 1987; *MECS*, 1987: 57). Also, innumerable sources spoke of massive financial inducements offered to Syria by Arab oil-producing states with some variation in figures, ranging from $2 billion to 'several billion' (*MECS*, 1987: 133). These pledges were apparently conditional on a substantial improvement in Syrian-Iraqi relations and Asad's endorsement of a resolution condemning Iran, because Saudi Arabia and Kuwait 'were in no mood to back Syria without return' (Lay, 1987–1988: 20).

Thus, at the Amman Summit, some evidence of continuity could be observed with regard to the Saudis' sensitivity to Syria's concerns, but the amount of concessions that Syria had to swallow was unprecedented, attesting to its diminishing regional influence. In any case, the summit's long-term implication could only be assessed by whether the achieved consensus was consolidated in the subsequent period. This was where Syria had previously held the key (Lay, 1987–1988: 22), but the fortunes had changed. After the closure of the summit, Faruq al-Shar' declared Syria's objection to the summit's condemnation of Iran and, within a week, travelled to Tehran to prove his point (*MECS*, 1987: 134). He did so in a fashion somewhat reminiscent of the Syrians' behaviour at the 1982 Fez II summit where it reluctantly consented to everything and then went off to Tehran the very next day and denied it all. This time, unlike in 1982, Syria's display of defiance only limited its own options; although Damascus actively campaigned to mediate between Iran and the Gulf Arabs particularly between December 1987 and January 1988 (*Al-Watan al-'Arabiyy*, 1 January; *Al-Nahar*, 23 January 1988; Lay, 1987–1988: 22; *MECS*, 1988: 152), such Syrian initiatives raised neither interest nor hope among the Arab majority. In the aftermath of the Amman Summit, the development of the Iran-Iraq war reduced Syria's value to the Gulf oil-producing states. Instead, the Gulf Arabs became more overtly hostile to Tehran, culminating in Saudi Arabia's severance of diplomatic ties on 26 April 1988 against the background of US attacks on Iranian targets. The war ended in August 1988, after Iran, burdened by the prolonged war, accepted the UN cease-fire proposal with neither prior consultation with nor notification to Damascus, testifying to the latter's diminished role in the Gulf (*New York Times*, 26 September 1988).

Until the final year of the Iran-Iraq war, Saudi Arabia's insistence on finding a regional solution to the conflict made Syria an indispensable player in Gulf politics, thereby making its Damascus connection valuable for the Kingdom. Based on this understanding, Riyadh invested much, financially and diplomatically, in avoiding Asad's displeasure for the first seven years of the war. This policy was apparently redefined after the Mecca incident in 1987, and when the war finally ended a year later, it had little to do with Damascus. Had Riyadh been over-investing in Syria's much exaggerated capacity? The short answer is arguably a 'no' for the simple reason that the significance of Syrian-Saudi relations in inter-Arab politics is a multifaceted one and does not lie solely in the Gulf arena. Although the Gulf war did somewhat dominate relations between 1984 and 1988, the end of the war reintroduced to the Syrian-Saudi dialogue other factors that had previously preoccupied the two regimes—Lebanon and the Arab-Israeli conflict—the significances of which were extensively discussed in Chapters Two to Four. Also, the fact that Saudi Arabia's need for Syrian co-operation in the Gulf was reduced, not by the strengthening of its own capabilities but by increasing its dependency on the US and Western Europe, indicated the dormant persistence of Saudi insecurity, and this factor was to bring back Syria's importance with the outbreak of another Gulf crisis in 1990. When the new strength was founded on such a precarious basis, the fundamental causes behind Saudi Arabia's need to find accommodation if not active co-operation with Syria had not diminished.

### Conclusion: Between the First and the Second Gulf Wars (July 1988–August 1990)

President Asad's uncharacteristically flexible attitude in towing the majority Arab line on many important issues at the Amman summit appeared to promise an end of an era in inter-Arab politics, characterised by polarisation during the best part of the 1980s. However, for those who envisaged the dawn of a new era whereby conformity and co-operation became the norm, it was to be a premature assessment of the Amman summit. The summit discussions, by excessively concentrating on the issue of the Gulf War, had unintended destabilising effects in the traditional centre of Arab politics—the Levant, and these ironical by-products of the summit decisions had important ramifications pertaining to Syrian-Saudi relations.

One of the most important developments following the Amman summit—and the one with the most profound implications for Arab politics to the present day—was the outbreak of a popular Palestinian uprising, the *intifada*, in December 1987 (Korany, 1991b: 321). When the Amman summit communiqué made no reference to support for the principle of Palestinian self-determination, let alone the possibility and/or desirability of achieving an independent Palestinian state on the West Bank and Gaza, the Palestinians on the Israeli-Occupied Territories believed that their concerns had been largely overlooked. Their despair at both the collective Arab effort to achieve an acceptable peace and at the competence of the exile-Palestinian political groupings (despite 'Arafat's representation in Amman) compelled these Palestinians to take matters into their own hands; in its first month, the uprising claimed the lives of more than thirty Palestinians, shot dead by the Israeli security forces or 'settlers' (Lay, 1987–1988: 16).

The outbreak of the *intifada* was a mixed blessing for Damascus. On the one hand, it rendered uncertain future Syrian control over the Palestinian debate. By the time the Algiers Arab summit closed in June 1988, the PLO had strengthened working co-operation with the Palestinians of the Occupied Territories and had consolidated its position as the authoritative and legitimate voice of the Palestinian cause. On the other hand, the

resurgence of the Arab-Israeli question to the forefront of the Arab
political debate, after a period of eclipse behind the Iran-Iraq war, was a
welcome opportunity for Asad (*New York Times,* 30 March 1988; Nasrallah,
1988: 50). When King Hussain disengaged Jordan from the West Bank in
the aftermath of the Algiers summit by suspending the West Bank
Development Plan and dissolving the lower house of the Jordanian
parliament, Syria's weight as a party in future negotiations for the
Arab-Israeli peace appeared to have increased (Windsor, 1988: 9); this was
particularly so in view of Israel's refusal (and the US' reluctance till late) to
hold negotiations with the PLO, another main party to the conflict. These
developments came as a reminder to Riyadh of Damascus' pivotal role in
the Arab-Israeli conflict which ensured its influence in wider regional
politics. Once again Riyadh was to be expected to pay considerable
attention and consideration to Syria's interests.

Another noticeable phenomenon at the Amman summit was the
marginalisation of the Lebanese conflict, despite the continually
deteriorating socio-economic situation in the country as a result of the
protracted civil war. When no financial aid was pledged and no special
committee was formed to address the dire situation, the implication was
that Lebanon was now 'allocated' to Syria (Khalidi and Agha, 1987–1988:
28-29). This new status of Lebanon in Arab politics was also a two-sided
gift to Damascus: on the one hand, it had given its enemies a new
platform to undertake effective anti-Syrian activities—as Iraq discovered
and exploited soon thereafter—but on the other, it firmly set the course
towards Syrian monopoly of the country's affairs. When the Iran-Iraq war
ended in the summer of 1988 and Riyadh's attention was focused once
again on the volatile situation in Lebanon, it was plain that the Saudis had
to enlist Syria's co-operation first.

Syria was thus, in a qualified way, back in the centre of Arab political
debate, but this was not to say that its deep-rooted predicament had been
rectified. The biggest threat to Syria in the summer of 1988 came from the
end of the Iran-Iraq war on terms that allowed Iraq to claim a victory.
Baghdad had emerged as a champion of the Arab cause, challenging
Damascus' claim to the title, and worse, set out to punish Syria for its
support of Iran during the eight-year war. This Iraq sought to achieve in
Lebanon by supporting anti-Syrian Maronite General Michel 'Awn who
laid a tremendous obstacle to Syria's objective to contain the fighting
under its domination. Furthermore, the troubled economy showed no sign
of recovery, while it had no effective method of breaking out from the
international isolation. The decline in the Soviet Union's status as a global
superpower and the growing reluctance on Moscow's part to be associated
with Damascus' security policy appeared to be an irreversible trend. Syria's

regional isolation was also accentuated by the fact that no subvention was pledged in the final statement of the June 1988 Algiers Arab summit for aiding the frontline states, despite the expiration of the Baghdad summit aid terms.[46]

Syria's dramatic return to the centre of Arab political stage came later upon Iraq's invasion of Kuwait in August 1990. The event marked the opening of a new era in Syrian-Saudi relations, in the Arab political order, and arguably even in what was termed 'the New World Order' (cf. Hinnebusch, 1993a; Quilliam, 1999). Even though Iraq's invasion did take President Asad by surprise, and even though the event was characterised as a god-sent opportunity for the Syrian leadership (e.g. Kienle, 1994: 385), Syria's comeback was not purely a product of a spur-of-the-moment, reactive policy decision; rather, during the two years between the Iran-Iraq cease-fire and the second Gulf crisis, Damascus had prepared itself for reorientation by adopting a new pragmatism on key questions—namely Lebanon, diplomatic relations with Egypt, and its attitude towards the American-led peace process. In the course of this policy realignment, Syria asserted its claim to be an able, albeit unruly, partner of Saudi Arabia in the latter's aspiration to construct a regional order with majority Arab consensus as a backbone. This was the recognition that Damascus had temporarily lost in the final year of the Iran-Iraq war.

By providing a brief analysis of the interim period between the two Gulf wars, this section—the conclusion of the final chapter of the case study—provides a recapitulation of the factors which acted as building blocks of their often reluctant or uneasy partnership. Since the 1978 Camp David the two countries had disagreed on almost all major policy questions, but in the last two years of the 1980s, either the two actors had come to reach a new level of accommodation or the issues of controversy themselves had subsided as will be discussed below. In due course, the two actors had begun to find more issues to agree on than to disagree by the time the new era of the 1990s had opened.

One of Hafiz al-Asad's main diplomatic reorientations in the mid-1980s was an establishment of warm relations with King Hussain of Jordan, his long-term archrival. This link to an Arab moderate together with his long-term connection with the Saudi leadership provided a springboard in improving relations with Egypt towards the end of the Iran-Iraq war. A further impetus towards this direction came when the end of the war resulted in an ever more hostile and powerful Iraq. From where Damascus stood, there was no other Arab power but Egypt that was capable of helping Syria counterbalance the Iraqi threat. When Mubarak was invited to the May 1989 Casablanca Arab summit, the Syrian-Egyptian reconciliation was complete, and it was formalised seven months later with the restoration of diplomatic ties. The process was guided and encouraged by both Saudi Arabia and Jordan,[47] and Syria allegedly attempted to collect some cash reward of $800 million for going along with their encouragement (*MECS*, 1988: 157; *Al-Qabas*, 10 January 1989). Although the reconciliation was concluded entirely on Egypt's term, it is difficult to ascertain whether Saudi inducement was essential to coaxing Syria into accepting the terms. When Syria's redefined goals had much to gain from the *rapprochement*, it may have been a pure convergence of Syrian and Saudi interests. Thus, one of the main sources of controversy in Syrian-Saudi relations from 1978—the question of Egypt's position in the Arab world, which, by implication, meant the principles of negotiated settlement with Israel—began to subside.

Asad engineered another diplomatic somersault when he showed responsiveness to a US call for an international conference on Middle East peace, encouraged in part by Saudi Arabia (*MECS*, 1988: 696). In March 1988, Washington launched the Shultz initiative in an effort to jump-start the peace process, responding to the spread of the *intifada* (Quandt, 1993: 379, 486-487). It was the most important diplomatic step taken by the Reagan administration on the Arab-Israeli conflict since the 1982 Reagan Plan. Although it did not attract much enthusiasm from any party, neither did Asad reject outright the new initiative, thereby taking a step towards a thaw in Syrian-US relations (Windsor, 1988: 8). In the final years of the Reagan administration, Washington finally came to acknowledge the indispensability of Syria in any comprehensive peace settlement. The Shultz initiative reflected the acknowledgement—a far cry from the Reagan Plan—which deliberately avoided the question of the Golan Heights. Furthermore, Asad's conciliatory attitude to the new US Middle East policy won tentative American support for its position in Lebanon, on which the two countries had been engaged in a close dialogue since 1988 (Windsor, 1988: 8; *MECS*, 1988: 738). In these regards, Syrian-US relations gradually improved in the months leading up to the 1990 second Gulf crisis, when the *rapprochement* was crowned by Syria's participation in the US-led multinational coalition.

The significance of the US factor in Syrian-Saudi relations was thus diluted, and the same could be said with regard to another superpower, the Soviet Union. Gorbachev's active courtship of the conservative Arab regimes, including the Saudis, attested to Moscow's new foreign policy orientation. Riyadh, in response, assisted Moscow in arranging negotiations between Soviet officials and the Afghan *Mujahidin* leaders (Vassiliev, 1998: 472-273). When the Soviets completed withdrawal of their forces from Afghanistan in February 1989, the last main obstacle to the normalisation of relations between Riyadh and Moscow was removed, leading to restoration of full diplomatic relations in September 1990.

In the immediate vicinity of the Arab region, Syrian and Saudi interests began to converge in some important respects. It was plain that Saudi Arabia was considerably annoyed when the Damascus-Tehran axis proved to be a long-term strategic alliance—rather than a tactical arrangement against the common enemy in Baghdad—and was upheld even in the aftermath of the war. However, when the alliance functioned to prevent Damascus' regional isolation, [48] Riyadh also began to see certain advantages in keeping Syria strong enough to counterbalance ever-powerful Iraq and to keep a check on Egypt's returning influence (*MECS*, 1989: 589). The Saudi notion of insecurity transformed into a perception of concrete threat when Iraq, Egypt, Yemen, and even Jordan—which had developed into a partner of Saudi Arabia on various key Arab issues—signed an agreement in February 1989 to form the Arab Co-operation Council (ACC), with no prior consultation with King Fahd, not to speak of President Asad. Saudi Arabia perceived it as a 'hostile encirclement' (Khaled bin Sultan, 1995: 157), as was plain from looking at a map, while Syria also had enough reason to suspect that the bloc was targeted against itself. Thus, even Syria's Gulf policy, or more precisely its alliance with Tehran, ceased to be a cause for Saudi embitterment. In fact, Khalid bin Sultan, Saudi commander of the multinational forces of Desert Storm and Assistant Minister of Defence, praised Asad's instrumental role in ensuring Iranian neutrality in the second Gulf crisis (1995: 180).

Consequently, most of the factors outlined in Chapter Two, which had been placing Syria and Saudi Arabia in the opposite camps in the regional divide of the post-Camp David era, were resolved or disintegrated in the late 1980s. There remained, however, one potentially explosive element: the Lebanese crisis. Lebanon was where Syria and Saudi Arabia continued to have the most profound disagreements in the period between July 1988 and August 1990. Nevertheless, when the joint-Syrian-Saudi effort (with US blessing) produced a formula to end a decade and a half-long civil war, it became the most vivid testimony to the effectiveness of their co-operation in shaping regional events. A month after the Iran-Iraq cease-fire, Lebanese President Amin Jumayyil's term expired, calling for a fresh election. When Syria failed to impose its favoured presidential candidate against the background of active Iraqi support for anti-Syrian Lebanese Christians, the country ended up with two separate governments and inched towards the danger of partition. King Fahd held Syria's obstinacy responsible for this renewed crisis and summoned Asad to Riyadh to discuss the matter in December 1988.[49] It was plain that his visit materialised in response to accumulating differences between the two capitals rather than as a result of greater co-ordination. However, it was also noteworthy that his sudden appearance in Riyadh markedly contrasted with the absence of such a visit since summer 1982, previous to which he was a frequent guest in the Saudi capital (see Chapters Two and Three). In view of the fact that the long absence overlapped with the period of greatest uneasiness in Syrian-Saudi relations, Asad's resumption of visits to the Kingdom in turn seemed to point to an improvement in the bilateral relations.

The tension in Lebanon reached a new crisis level in March 1989 when General 'Awn, with Iraqi aid, declared a 'war of liberation' against Syria, and the fighting immediately escalated, involving indiscriminate firing of rockets and artillery. In response, the Arab League, supported by the US, appointed a tripartite committee of Saudi Arabia, Morocco and Algeria to establish a cease-fire. When the committee at first issued a harsh criticism of Syria's policy, Damascus responded decisively to punish Riyadh; Syrian media broadcast news reports about unrest in the Eastern Province, serious frictions and tensions within the royal family, and deterioration in Fahd's health (MECS, 1989: 590). Shortly thereafter, the committee became much more accommodating towards Syria's role in the conflict, leading up to the Ta'if Accords in October 1989. The accords recognised Lebanon's 'special relationship' with Syria, stipulated many of the constitutional reforms that Syria had long sought (such as a more balanced system of sectarian representation in Parliament) and only loosely provided for Syria's troop withdrawal (Drysdale, 1993: 287). Although the implementation of the accords had to wait until Syria's final victory over 'Awn's forces while the world's attention was focused on Iraq's invasion of Kuwait, their principles were formally enshrined in the unequal Syrian-Lebanese Treaty of Brotherhood, Co-operation and Co-ordination of May 1991, confirming Syria's hegemony.

Syria's hostile propaganda campaign against the Kingdom aside, the Saudis and their tripartite committee partners were aware that Syria's 30,000 to 40,000 soldiers in Lebanon (as opposed to General 'Awn's 20,000), its web of alliances with militias, and the formidable intelligence network rendered it pointless to craft a cease-fire formula without Damascus' full backing. Also, the Saudis were said to have been unwilling to risk such a Syrian humiliation in Lebanon that would further inflate Iraqi prestige (Times, 28 August 1989). In view of these considerations, the Saudi leadership acknowledged the need to pay enough attention to Syria's interests. When negotiations at Ta'if encountered difficulties, Sa'ud al-Faisal hurried to Damascus for a two-day visit and secured minor concessions from the Syrians (Daily Telegraph, 23 October 1989). These contacts between Saudi Arabia and Syria again invited speculations that the former had paid as much as $17 billion to entice the latter into acceptance of the draft agreement (*Independent*, 31 October 1989). The new pattern of Saudi-Syrian accommodation in Lebanon was symbolised by the political role granted to Rafiq al-Hariri, Saudi Arabia's 'Lebanon-man', in post-civil war Lebanon under Syrian tutelage. His humanitarian organisation had been distributing tens of millions of aid to impoverished Lebanese families since the 1980s (e.g. *Al-Watan al-'Arabiyy,* 22 January 1988, 13 January 1989) while he expanded his business interests in the country and eventually bought his way into the office of Prime Minister.[50]

In this final chapter of the detailed study of Syrian-Saudi relations, the analysis focused on the dynamics in which Syria had much to gain from Saudi Arabia on the issue of the Gulf war (pressurising Iran and collecting financial gains), while Riyadh also somewhat suspiciously hoped for certain benefits from Damascus' influence over Tehran. Also, it was the Saudi obsession with attaining a co-ordinated *Arab* solution to the conflict which allowed Syria to exercise a veto power over Saudi policy, thereby deriving concessions from the Kingdom. Once again, this obsession was underpinned by the vital importance it placed on acquiring *Arab* legitimacy for its policies, attesting to the 'disciplinary' function of Arabism at work. Towards the end of the war, Syria's political differences with Iran were more prevalent, its ability to moderate Iranian bellicosity was proving to be increasingly limited, and its weakness was further exposed in the economic troubles and the international isolation. When the Saudis became disillusioned by Syria's performance and capabilities towards Iran, its political value in the Saudi eyes markedly decreased; in consequence, Saudi Arabia displayed an unprecedented level of assertiveness and willingness to stand up to the Syrian challenge. This chain of development attested to the paradoxical phenomenon by which the healthier the state of Syrian-Iranian relations, or in other words, the more Damascus contradicted Saudi policy aims, the more value Riyadh found in building amicable relations with Damascus.

To take the matter further, Saudi Arabia even appeared at times positively to welcome Syria's maverick behaviour. The Arab regional system since its inception had always found its members apprehensive of hegemonic domination by one member or the other. Thus, countries like Saudi Arabia derived certain comforts in the existence of checks and balances between key member states. Syria's long-standing policy of being deliberately difficult assigned it a counterbalancing role against the potential hegemonic ambitions of Iraq or Egypt, as has been discussed.

This work's main interest has been to explain the paradox of sustained co-operative relations between Syria and Saudi Arabia even at times of obvious differences and even of clashes of interest in almost every conceivable issue of Arab concern. With the end of the Gulf war and the

214 SYRIA AND SAUDI ARABIA

global realignment, these sources of disputes gradually subsided. When the 1990s opened, conditions had changed to such an extent that they found more convergence of interests. Syrian-Saudi co-operation then became more a logical choice than a paradox, albeit with some remnants of disagreements.

# CONCLUSION

The purpose of this study was first to analyse the paradox of Syrian-Saudi 'alliance'—how and why the two actors maintained an outwardly cordial relationship even at times of acute differences. The conclusions of preceding chapters have led to a rephrasing of the hypothesis; counter-intuitively, Damascus' need for close ties with Riyadh and vice versa increased *because of*—rather than *in spite of*—their differences. This curious phenomenon was explained in part by the existence of 'shared' or 'transnational' identities between the two countries—namely Arabism, Islam, and the unique entwinement of the two, contingent to which were certain common norms. Syria and Saudi Arabia both possessed the ability to significantly lower or raise the cost of each other's policy and to alter each other's regional prestige, and this ability emanated in no small part from their 'shared/transnational identities'.

The study's focus on the role of 'shared identities' does not rule out the explanatory power of other approaches to alliance or alignment formation, such as various forms of balance-of-power explanations, the economic factor in foreign policy decision-making, or the unique existence of social/personal ties across the Arab region. These explanations were particularly useful in understanding Syrian and Saudi decisions on specific issues at specific times. The study did, however, argue that the existence of 'shared identities' had played a decisive role in defining the aims and perimeters of these policy decisions. On the whole, the existence of 'shared identities' granted Syria not only financial dividends but, more importantly, disproportionate leverage over Saudi policy, due to its ability to mobilise the symbols of 'Arabism'. On the other hand, it severely constrained the Saudi leadership's policy aims and options. Pursuit of Arab/Islamic legitimacy in the regional arena became an aim in itself because of its linkage to prestige and credibility which in turn were connected to concrete security issues. It also imposed limits of what is 'permissible'—and what is not—for a legitimate Arab/Islamic regime to pursue as its policy.

Throughout the period under investigation, neither the Syrians nor the Saudis ever perceived the other party as central to their key regional or international concerns. As was mentioned in the very opening of this study, they have been *outside* each other's immediate spheres of interests and concerns—perhaps bar the unique period of 'the Struggle for Syria' when Saudi interest on control of Syria *itself* was relatively high. This aspect of their relationship—the non-overlapping spheres of interests—helped the two actors to avoid direct competition on the same turf.

In a similar vein, the fact that Syria's self-image as a fortress of Arab nationalism did not directly clash with the Saudis' self-proclaimed role as the defender of the Islamic faith helped the two countries to avoid competition, and in some instances, even complemented each other by giving ideological endorsement or approval to one another's policies. When Agha and Khalidi describe the durability of *Syrian-Iranian* relations in the following terms, the statement could stand fully even when replaced with *Syrian-Saudi* relations:

> The durability of the *Syrian-Iranian* relationship despite such apparently incompatible policies can be partly explained by the very disparate nature of the regimes themselves, and somewhat paradoxically, by their high degree of tolerance for each other...The ability to accommodate the other side thus stems from the mutual recognition that neither seeks to emulate the other or to compete with it on its own terms...Within this context common *Syrian-Iranian* priorities can be seen to be largely peripheral to either side's central strategic concerns. As such the potential for a serious conflict of interests between the two is minimized and the incentive to maintain the relationship is reinforced (1995: 119-122, emphasis added).

However, the above explanation, although profoundly elucidating, does not suffice to untangle the main puzzle of Syrian-Saudi relations: if one party's interest was so peripheral to the other's, why have Syria and Saudi Arabia held such an important key to the *realisation* of each other's policy goals? To give but a few examples, Syria had failed to impose its preponderance over Lebanon until Saudi diplomatic initiatives in the 1976 Riyadh summit and the 1979 Ta'if conference fully supported its attempts. Moreover, its goal of 'strategic parity' with Israel would have been laughably irrelevant and unrealistic, had Saudi Arabia not paid for a substantial part of Syria's arms imports and rescued it from balance of payments crises. On the other side of the equation, Syria also exercised a comparable degree of influence on Saudi policy; Riyadh desperately sought Syria's co-operation in neutralising the Iranians until the very last stage of the Iran-Iraq war. The sheer success of Syria's 'vetos' over the Kingdom's diplomatic initiatives in the Arab fora—e.g. the Fahd Plan—attested to the degree of Damascus' influence. Thus, each held a key to the success of the other's regional policies, or in other words, had the capacity either to lower the cost significantly or to lay detrimental obstacles in front of them. This 'key'—which could be used as either 'carrot' or 'stick'—made Syria and Saudi Arabia extremely cautious and attuned to the other side's needs particularly at times of sharpest disagreements. Hence, the outward appearance of the diplomatic relations was almost always 'brotherly embraces' and showering of 'praise for the Arab effort of Sister Syria/Saudi Arabia'—in stark contrast to the frequent exchanges of angry abuses between Damascus and other Arab capitals, particularly Egypt, Iraq and Jordan.

It is noteworthy that a few external conditions had elevated the importance of Syria and Saudi Arabia in each other's eyes in the immediate aftermath of Camp David. One was the strategic and political marginalisation of Egypt and Iraq in the late 1970s and 1980s which allowed Damascus and Riyadh, the hitherto second-rank capitals in the Arab hierarchy, to assume regional leadership and establish their own spheres of influence (Hinnebusch, 1991: 40; Lesch, A.M., 1995: 17). The low-key rivalry between the two poles was masked by the curious compatibility, reflecting their limited capabilities in comparison to, for instance, the overarching hegemony of Egypt under Gamal 'Abd al-Nasir. Second, the relationship with the two superpowers was also a significant variable in Syrian-Saudi bilateral relations. Visible closeness with Washington or Moscow has been a perpetual source of predicament for both Saudi Arabia and Syria. The link exposed the leaderships to criticism of corroboration with 'imperialists' or 'atheists'—a tainted reputation in the Arab nationalist or Islamic language. The Kingdom hoped its ties to Syria, the self-styled symbol of 'Arabism', would moderate such criticisms, while the latter also banked on its good relations with the self-appointed defender of Islam to do the same for itself. Thus, the two capitals were increasingly drawn towards co-operation because of their difference in access to the two global superpowers.

This study aimed to contribute to a wider debate of whether identities play a role in alliance-making. The conclusion came in support of the argument that identities and their ensuing norms and values should not be seen as exterior to state interests; instead, identities and interests are mutually informed and at times constitutive. It opens an argument that any 'ideas'—one form of which is identity—should be considered as a potential variable in foreign policy analyses. The argument was presented in this study through focusing on 'shared/transnational identities', because in the past century, Arab nationalism and Islam have arguably occupied a dominant place in Arab political discourse. Building on the finding of other works which concentrated on how Arab states, more often than not, engaged in hostility over the monopoly of Arab nationalist or Islamic languages, this study attempted to delineate conditions in which the 'sharing' of identities *can* at times lead to co-operation—in however reluctant a form.

Whether the theoretical conclusions reached in this study may be applied to other cases of alliance can be assessed only by further comparative studies. The speculation would be, perhaps not easily, at least not outside the Arab region. First of all, historical analyses are by de facto bound by the specific setting of the case addressed, and deductive generalisation risks simplification. Second, various authors have attested to the uniqueness of the Arab region with regard to national sentiments. For instance, Noble underlined the uniqueness of inter-Arab politics when he asserted that the existence of larger common identity, such as Arabism and Islam, 'gave rise to relations between Arab states which were qualitatively different from those in other regional systems' (1991: 55). In view of such uniqueness in the built-in characteristic of the region, it is unlikely that same assumptions hold true in analysing the potential emergence of 'transnational identities' across the Association of Southeast Asian Nations (ASEAN) states or the Organisation of African Unity (OAU) states, or even across the European Union.

At this point, it is important to recall that this study addressed the question of 'identity' or 'shared/transnational identity' as one of the normative variables which may influence foreign policy. The findings of this project should, therefore, go beyond the studies of the Middle East and contribute to broader discussions on the relationship between ideas and values on the one hand, and 'state interests' on the other. In such a respect, it stands in favour of examining seriously how such notions as 'human rights' or 'democracy' may have an impact on and be impacted by the shaping of 'state interests' and the foreign policy-making of a wide range of states.

### Aftermath: 1990 and beyond

The Iraqi invasion of Kuwait on 2 August 1990 and the subsequent Gulf War II between the Iraqi government and the US-led multinational coalition presented Syria with a fortuitous opportunity to consolidate its diplomatic reorientation, which had already been underway since 1988

(Drysdale, 1993; Eppel, 1993; Kienle, 1994). This diplomatic trend was new and old at the same time; it was new in that a radical restructuring of the international system at the global level—the demise of the bipolar system—compelled Syria to accept new conditions and rules of the game. However, at the Middle East regional level, it also involved a revisiting of some old themes; these had dominated most of the 1970s, but were temporarily eclipsed after 1978. As was the case with the 1970s, the era was now to a considerable extent characterised by the revival of the Damascus-Riyadh-Cairo axis, an active American involvement in the Arab-Israeli peace talks, and, with regard to the Levant, unchallenged Syrian preponderance in Lebanon. These were all developments that were materialised through Syria's siding with the multinational coalition in the war against Iraq. The period after 1990, by extension, created a setting for Syrian-Saudi relations similar to that in the mid-1970s; this was one in which the two countries' interests in key regional issues roughly overlapped. The logical outcome was resurgence of mutually beneficial co-operation and with a minimum degree of friction.

The well-publicised history of Syrian-US tension over the previous two decades notwithstanding, Hafiz al-Asad contributed Syrian army contingents to the US-led multinational coalition—a decision greatly appreciated and rewarded by the Saudis. During the crisis, the Syrian regime received a financial contribution of estimated $ 1-2 billion from Saudi Arabia and the Gulf states,[1] and reached a tacit understanding with the US[2] and Saudi Arabia to impose its unchallenged dominance over post-conflict Lebanon, which in turn consolidated Damascus' expanded regional and international role. From the viewpoint of *identity* in foreign policy, it is noteworthy that the justification for Syria's stand centred around four arguments, most of which invoked nationalist and Islamic themes: 1) Syrian forces would protect the *Holy Places*; 2) it was a *pan-Arab* act of preventing further polarisation of the Arab nation; 3) the stationing of the foreign forces would be for a limited amount of time, and the *Arab* forces must be ready to replace them; and 4) Asad had promised Fahd that Syria would help him defend his territory (Lesch, A.M., 1991: 41).

Saudi Arabia appreciated Syria's troop contribution, for all the reasons that accentuated the still powerful appeals of transnational identities in the Arab world. The value of Syrian troops, in the eyes of King Fahd who genuinely feared that his Kingdom was next on Saddam's hit-list (Goldberg, 1993: 127-128), lay less in the military aspect but as the symbolic political asset. Saudi Arabia's Khalid bin Sultan, commander of the coalition forces, praised Syria's role as indispensable to the coalition, 'because Asad's reputation as a stern Arab nationalist, dedicated to opposing Western and Israeli encroachments into the Arab homeland, helped legitimise the Coalition in the eyes of the Arab opinion' (Khaled bin Sultan, 1995: 180). Asad's stand helped to counterbalance Saddam's attempt to cast his war as an *Arab* one, he continues, by placing on the coalition 'the imprimatur of Arab solidarity and Arab nationalism' (1995: 231-237).

The major gain for Syria was its regional repositioning as a central actor in the newly emerging order, characterised by the revival of the Damascus-Riyadh-Cairo tripartite axis (Kienle, 1994: 386), and by extension, its rehabilitation in the wider international community. On 6 March 1991, the Damascus Declaration, or what came to be known as the '6+2' formula, was signed in Syria's capital, attesting to its reinstated status. In return for security co-operation, the formula stipulated the six Gulf Co-operation Council (GCC) member states' contribution to Syrian and Egyptian economic development. Mubarak-Fahd-Asad meetings and joint efforts, particularly on the Arab-Israeli peace talks, were frequent during the 1990s and beyond (e.g. *Al-Hayat*, 23 January; *Al-Ahram*, 5 June 1996; *Al-Ahrar*, 5 May 2000). Although interests in the Damascus Declaration as a security pact were not sustained for much more than a year, it functioned as an economic and political forum for years to come, upheld by the influence of the 'triangle'.[3]

Another reason why Saudi Arabia would pay close attention to Syria's wishes was the importance it continued to hold in the Gulf through its ties with Iran. Syrian-Iranian relations strengthened after Gulf War II, and the two countries signed a strategic accord in September 1991 (Eisenstadt, 1992: 38). Agha and Khalidi claim that the weight of the Damascus-Tehran axis gave a substantive leverage over Riyadh, because of its ability to perform a restraining role against future Iraqi aggression (1995: 85-88). The new century introduced other factors which overturned the regional order and completely disrupted the basis of previous assumptions—the 11 September 2001 attack, the 'war on terror' and the George W. Bush administration's aggressive anti-Syrian campaigns. Although it is outside the scope of this project to discuss what implications these recent momentous events would have for Syrian-Saudi relations, it is enough for its purpose to state that the Gulf remains an important area, one which compels Syria and Saudi Arabia to maintain a co-operative relationship with each other.

Through backing Syria's foreign policy positions, Saudi Arabia also played a prominent role in the 1990s Arab-Israeli peace talks, which were kick-started in Madrid and, by another terms, climaxed in Oslo. On one hand, Riyadh encouraged Damascus to move forward in the peace talks; the means used were the time-honoured ones of financial inducements.[4] On the other, Riyadh resolutely confined its own policy options to within the scope that Syria found acceptable. The Saudi stand against public dealings with Israel even after 1993 has been remarkable, considering that other Gulf states variably established economic ties with Israel, publicly received visiting Israeli delegations, or toyed with the possibility of normalisation. There was also a significant amount of pressure on Riyadh from Washington to follow in the footsteps of its neighbours. Riyadh's resoluteness can be explained partly in terms of the importance of Islam in the Saudi leadership's legitimacy claims, as exemplified in the King's self-styled role as 'a guardian of the Holy Places'. This has precluded the Kingdom from taking such a step until the status of East Jerusalem, home to the al-Aqsa Mosque, received a satisfactory resolution. At the very least, the Saudi leadership would have needed the cover of a peace treaty on the Syrian-Lebanese track—marking the final disbandment of the frontline state line-up—before it would find it prudent to take such a step.

It is noteworthy that the most important 'key' to the 'Saudi door' in Arab-Israeli negotiations rested in Syria's hands. This point of view was succinctly explored by Cobban, which merits a slightly long citation:

> Given the strategic weight of Saudi Arabia within the Middle East, Syria's ties with it…were often seen as one of the big stakes that the Syrian negotiators brought with them to the negotiating table—whether they were openly laid on the table or not. The Syrians liked to present themselves, however discreetly, as providing a crucial potential key with which Israel could one day unlock its hitherto blocked relationship with the rich Arab hinterland…this asset [of a key to good relations with Saudi Arabia] acquired more negotiating value [after the Labour Party came to power]. Eitan Haber, the longtime Rabin intimate who coordinated all the different tracks of the peace process on his old friend's behalf, has said that 'Yitzhak Rabin understood immediately that the Syrians are the key to a comprehensive peace, including with Saudi Arabia and with Iraq, even though he understood elsewhere in the world, the peace with the Palestinians would have most meaning. (1999: 35)

By mid-1996, the peace talks had entered a deadlock after the election of Binyamin Netanyahu to the Israeli Premiership. This was accompanied by a hardening of the US position towards Syria (Seale, 1996: 27-29). In this regard, Saudi Arabia again threw its weight behind Syria's major diplomatic victory at the June 1996 Cairo Arab Summit, whose communiqué warned against premature improvement of relations with Israel. In July of the following year, Prince 'Abdallah co-ordinated positions with the Syrian leadership and announced the Kingdom's boycott of the fourth post-Madrid economic forum, or the MENA (Middle East and North Africa) Conference, to be held in Qatar in November.[5] Despite US Secretary of State Madeleine Albright's active behind-the-scenes efforts to coax Arab participants into participation, the conference opened with the conspicuous absence of heavyweights like Cairo and Riyadh.[6] Thus, Syria and Saudi Arabia demonstrated substantial co-ordination.

Smoother relations between the two countries created a favourable situation for expanding spheres of co-operation on purely bilateral issues—something that was absent in the previous decades. When Syria embarked on a new economic liberalisation project, though more words than actions, Saudi Arabia became its largest benefactor. On 4 May 1991, the Syrian People's Assembly passed the Law for the Encouragement of Investment (Law No.10), aiming at attracting foreign capital. To facilitate the inflow of Saudi investment in particular, the Syrian-Saudi Council of Businessmen had been established; this occurred three days after the signing of the Damascus Declaration and two months before the passage of the Law on 9 March 1991 ('Brutukul Insha' Majlis Rijal al-A'mal al-Sa'udiy-al-Suriy', 9 March 1991). Against this backdrop, Saudis occupied the largest share among the foreign investors throughout the 1990s. According to Muhammad Saraqibi, Director of Investment Office at the Office of Prime Minister in Syria, they collectively invested some $1 billion per annum on average, or in other words, 13-14 percent of the total foreign investment at $ 8 billion (personal communications, Damascus, December 1999). Joint Syrian-Saudi companies began to spring up, one such example being Muhammad Haikal's Al-Sham Shipping Company (*MEED*, 30 January 1998). The most prominent example of a Saudi private investor is Prince Walid bin Talal. His $100 million investment on a Damascus Four Seasons hotel is a much talked-about venture (*MEED*, 23 January 1998). In 2000, the two countries prepared the grounds for establishing a free trade zone (*Al-Sharq al-Awsat*, 7 June 2000). In the same spirit, a Syrian-Saudi Higher Joint Committee (*al-Lajnah al-Sa'udiyyah al-Suriyyah al-'Ulya*) was formed in 1995 to oversee bilateral co-operation in a variety of fields, including explicit and formal political co-ordination. Under the chairmanship of the two foreign ministers, regular meetings of twice a year (one held in each capital) have taken place.[7]

In June 2000, Hafiz al-Asad died and left a legacy of his thirty year-long iron fisted rule to be inherited by his second son, Bashshar. The leadership change did not alter the course of Syrian-Saudi relations. Scores of condolences from Saudi princes were published, invariably expressing continued solidarity with the new leader.[8] Bashshar, in just over two months after taking over the presidency, announced that his first Arab tour would start with Saudi Arabia. It is worth recalling that his deceased older brother, Basil, also chose the Kingdom as destination of his first diplomatic mission in 1991 after assuming control of the Republican Guard (*al-Haras al-Jumhuri*) (Raad, 1998: 176). Bashshar declared that this tour, which included a stop in Egypt, was aimed at 'confirming Syria's adherence to the Arab triangle of Syria-Egypt-Saudi Arabia' (*Al-Hayat,* 20 August 2000). A year later, within a week after the event of 11 September 2001, Bashshar al-Asad visited Egypt, Yemen and Saudi Arabia to discuss appropriate Arab response to President George W. Bush's campaign against terrorism.[9] In the ensuing years, his administration's aggressive policy to promote 'democratisation' in the Middle East and the occupation of Iraq have further stigmatised Arabs and Muslims in general, and the two governments of Syria and Saudi Arabia in particular. In this new international political climate, Syria and Saudi Arabia are likely to find reasons to maintain their co-ordination and co-operation for the foreseeable future.

# NOTES

## Introduction

1. See, for instance, Hajj Hamad's book on Saudi Arabia (1996) whose cover page reads, 'No war without Egypt; no peace without Syria; no normalisation without Saudi Arabia'.
2. The two countries have not been bound by formal bilateral treaties, save the 1972 Economic and Trade Agreement, extended every year to the present day, and a minor agreement of co-operation in sports and youth affairs, signed on 8 January 1992 (*Al-Riyadh*, 11 June 2000). Also, security agreements between the two countries are often referred to, but they do not bear the conditions of formal bilateral treaties, as the details of the agreements are not made public, and these security agreements often fall under the wider umbrella of the Arab League security co-operation formulated by Ministers of Interior.
3. For the Saudi support for al-Fath, see Abu Talib (1992: 99). For Syria's relations with the PLO, see Brand (1990) and Batatu (1999: 287-322).

## Chapter One

1. In the early 1920s, during Ibn Sa'ud's raid against the Rashidi capital, Ha'il, Ibn Sha'lan—the shaikh of the Ruwala bedouin tribe—offered him assistance from the north (al-Rasheed, 1991: 64). Damascus remembers the glory of Ibn Sha'lan by naming one of its districts after him, whose magnificent old house stands there in decay today.
2. One slanderous account of the House of Saud suggests that he had 'specialised in the procurement of young blondes from his native Syria' (Aburish, 1994: 30).
3. See Little (1990: 52-55) for US involvement in the coup.
4. The Syrian and Saudi authorities denied any direct Saudi or Egyptian link to this organisation, but British and American observers had no doubt about it (Rathmell, 1995: 69-71; Seale, 1986: 98).
5. For an authoritative account of these developments, see Seale (1986).
6. The sectarian composition of Syria's population has stayed roughly the same in the post-independence period as follows: the Sunnis (69.0%), the 'Alawis (11.5%), the Druze (3.0%), Ismailis (1.5%), and the Christians (14.1 %) (van Dam, 1996: 1; cf. Khoury, 1987: 15).
7. Translation by al-Yassini (1983: 13) from 'Abd al-'Aziz bin Baz's publication with an indicative title, *Naqd al-Qawmiyyah al-'Arabiyyah 'ala Da'wa al-Islam wa al-Waqi'* (A Critique of Arab Nationalism Based on Islam and Reality).

8. At its inception, the Front consisted of five member parties—of Nasirist, communist and Arab Socialist Unionist inclinations—with the Ba'th occupying the majority in the cabinet and the People's Assembly, Syria's parliament, at all times.

9. Asad's alliance with the Damascene business community served as a cornerstone in defeating his Islamist opponents in the early 1980s (Kienle, 1994: Perthes, 1995).

10. For the full text of the Economic and Trade Agreement, see Damascus Chamber of Commerce (1999: 135-142).

11. See Kanovsky for figures (1983–1984: 284). When viewed in terms of share in Syria's total budgetary revenues, Arab financial aid increased from 4 percent in 1968–1972 to 31 percent in 1973-1976 (Kienle, 1990: 93). Saudi Arabia contributed to development projects in Syria as well. One of the examples was an establishment of a mixed-sector company for agriculture, the Syrian-Saudi Corporation for Industrial and Agricultural Investments, in August 1976. See the Corporation's publication on the agreement (1976).

12. See Winckler for several different estimated figures of Syrian workers in Saudi Arabia between 1970–1990 and the wage difference between Syria and Saudi Arabia for construction workers (1997: 108-110).

13. For instance, Aburish asserts: 'A good way to judge how angry Saudi Arabia behaves with a fellow Arab country is to examine how it limits the number of visas issued to its citizens to work in Saudi Arabia' (1994: 75).

14. Damascus pushed for this resolution to assert its rival claim as a representative of the Palestinian cause, while Riyadh was keen to secure autonomy for the PLO (Seale, 1990: 254).

15. See *Al-Nahar* for the communiqué text (18 January 1975).

16. In between those two meetings, a Saudi economic delegation was dispatched to Damascus and allegedly promised Syria a loan of some $219 million (*Al-Nahar*, 10 April 1975).

17. Quandt stresses the importance of over 200,000 Palestinians residing in the Kingdom (1981: 32-33). On the other hand, Yegnes claims that this was not the case because 'Saudi security services have long maintained rigid and close supervision over activities of the Palestinian community in the Kingdom.' Rather, the 'Saudi dynasty believes that the Palestinian threat lies in their dispersal and in their ability to foment violence in various places' like Jordan or Lebanon (1981: 109). This paper argues that although both are relevant explanations, neither is as crucial as the symbolic value of the Palestinian question in the competition for Arab legitimacy and prestige. See Chapter Three below for more on the role of Palestinian factor in Arab politics, especially the section on the Fahd Plan (August 1981–January 1982).

## Chapter Two

1. Saudi Arabia adhered to this policy as late as August 1978, a month before the Camp David agreement, by proposing to convene an Arab summit to facilitate reconciliation between the two capitals, the proposal promptly rejected by Damascus (*Al-Safir*, 5 August 1978). The subsequent visit to Damascus and Baghdad by Prince Turki al-Faisal, the head of the Saudi intelligence services, can be interpreted along the same line (*Al-Nahar*, 13 August 1978).

2. See *MECS* (1978–1979: 262-263) for the measures agreed upon.

3. For figures of contribution from and entitlements to other Arab states, see *MECS* (1978–1979: 217).

4. See Halliday (1990: 125). On 13 March 1979, Syria's Khaddam met King Khalid, Foreign Minister Sa'ud al-Faisal and Rashad Fira'un to discuss the Yemen conflict (*BBC/SWB/ME*, 15 March 1979).

5. For detailed discussion on the obstacles to the unity, see Kienle (1990: 144-147) and *Arab Report* (14 February 1979).

6. See *MECS* (1978–1979: 263-265) for its full-text.

7. For the similarities between the two movements, see Salamé (1985).

8. The signs of brewing discontent were also seen in events preceding the Grand Mosque incident. In March 1979, a coup d'état was allegedly planned by the Deputy Commander of the Air Force, 'Ali al-Bashir, and some one hundred officers and pilots (*MECS*, 1978–1979: 743). In October, Lebanese daily *Al-Safir* reported an existence of 'a large Islamic movement in Saudi Arabia', different from those responsible for the Grand Mosque seizure. This group was called the *Salafiyyin*, led by 'Abdallah Fahd al-Nafisi, a Cambridge-educated Kuwaiti (*BBC/SWB/ME*, 5 October 1979; Salamé, 1985: 16).

9. On Syria's relations with Imam Musa al-Sadr, see a brilliant chronicle of his life and his role in Lebanese politics by Ajami (1986). Ajami quotes Kramer's excellent summation of the emergence of Asad-Sadr connection: 'the regime of Hafiz al Asad needed quick religious legitimacy; the Shi'is of Lebanon, Musa al Sadr had decided, needed a powerful patron. Interest busily converged from every direction' (1986: 174).

10. Examples of Syria's support ranged from training of Iranian opposition activists in al-Fath and Amal camps in Lebanon to issuance of Syrian passports to anti-Shah dissidents (Marschall, 1991: 8-10).

11. By the time the Iran-Iraq war had erupted, Tehran referred to the group's activity as 'treacherous to the Islamic cause', because it was directed against the Syrian regime which stood against Zionism, the common enemy of Islam (Abd-Allah, 1983: 183).

12. See Hirschfeld (1986: 119). The exceptions to these Arab states were the Steadfastness Front members and the PLO which followed Syria's lead. The UAE and Oman also opted for maintaining some ties with Iran.

13. For the background of the Pan-Arab Charter, see Tripp (2000: 230-231). For the full text of the Charter, see *MECS* (1979–1980: 224-225).

14. The two countries signed a security agreement the previous year, although few tangible programmes had since been introduced at this stage. The *Washington Post* reported that the Saudi leadership had become wary of rising Iraqi political influence among prominent princes who despised the Kingdom's pro-American orientation (4 May 1980).

15. See *BBC/SWB/ME* (26 September 1980). Chubin and Tripp suspect that at least some of the Gulf states—Saudi Arabia and Kuwait in particular—were informed in advance of Iraq's intention to invade Iran (1988: 140, 163). Aburish goes much further, suggesting that the war was a joint Saddam-Saudi scheme with US encouragement. He claims: 'The negotiations between the Saudis and Saddam to find ways to face the common Iranian threat lasted a long time and in August 1980 they concluded a secret agreement whereby Saudi Arabia guaranteed to provide Iraq with "all the financial aid required to undertake all the necessary moves to protect its national honour"' (1994: 138).

16. On 25 September, President Asad had a phone conversation with King Khalid and King Hussein about the conflict (*BBC/SWB/ME*, 27 September 1980). Three days later, Faruq al-Shar', the Syrian Minister of State for Foreign

Affairs, met King Khalid (*BBC/SWB/ME*, 30 September 1980).

17. The doctrine was based on the conviction that if the Arabs were to extract a just settlement from Israel, it could only be done after the Soviets helped strengthening their military capability to reach a par with the opponent. See Khalidi and Agha (1991: 186-218) on the doctrine.

18. The figure for Soviet advisers counted more than in any other single developing country in the world. The number rose to some 7,000 in the early half of the 1980s (*Economist*, 26 January; *Washington Post*, 22 February 1980; Ramet, 1990: 205-206).

19. For an example of such a statement, *BBC/SWB/ME*, 11 June 1979. The view was expressed in the Saudi daily '*Ukkaz* at a time when the USSR attempted to pressurise the Palestinians to halt their military operations from South Lebanon against Israeli territory. Such a modification in the USSR's pro-PLO stance allegedly coincided with the signing of the second Strategic Arms Limitation Treaty (SALT-2) with the US. Another occasion on which Saudi Arabia warned against Moscow's sinister motives concerning the Arab-Israeli conflict came out as '*Ukkaz* reported Hafiz al-Asad's visit to Moscow in October 1979—possibly an implicit warning to caution Asad from going too far with strengthening his Soviet ties (*BBC/SWB/ME*, 17 October 1979).

20. For the background of the invasion, see R.O. Freedman (1991: 71-73).

21. For the details of upgraded Soviet military supplies, see *Washington Post* (22 and 28 February 1980), Qindil (1980b) and Karsh (1991: 123).

22. His dissident group, Union of the Peoples of the Arabian Peninsula, took credit even for the Grand Mosque incident in November 1979. Although this claim is contrary to the established account of the incident, he may have made indirect contribution to the rebellion. Some of the arms used by Juhaiman 'Utaiba's group, for instance, were smuggled into the country through trucks from Syria and Lebanon (*MEI*, 7 December 1979; *MECS*, 1979-1980: 687, 691). Nasir al-Sa'id was kidnapped in Beirut shortly after this Mecca incident, never to be seen again. The Saudi authority allegedly paid the PLO members in Lebanon $2 million to facilitate the operation (Aburish, 1994: 65).

23. There were, however, slight variations in the content of friendship and co-operation treaties, which Moscow concluded with numerous allies. For comparisons with the PDRY-USSR treaty, for instance, see Halliday (1990: 193-194).

24. For different categories of the USSR's bilateral treaties with its allies, see Karsh (1991: 28-30).

25. Until that point, Saudi citizens were able to visit Syria without an entry visa, and every summer, thousands of Saudi holidaymakers spent a few months in the country to escape from the heat (*Al-Nahar*, 7 and 16 July 1980).

26. *Al-Nahar* claims that this cancellation was a direct outcome of an improvement in Syrian-Saudi relations following Rif'at's visit to the Kingdom (16 July 1980).

27. Syria as well as North Yemen allegedly facilitated behind-the-scenes contacts between Saudi and Soviet officials in the late 1970s and the early 1980s. Riyadh, however, denied any such allegation (Bligh and Plant, 1982: 28).

28. Sa'ib Salam's family played a central role in Lebanese politics for generations (Ajami, 1986: 211-212).

29. Concomitantly, there was an explosion in a chemical factory near Khobar in Saudi Arabia only a day before the Beirut embassy incident (*BBC/SWB/ME*, 11 October 1980).

30. Baroudi is of Lebanese Christian origin, and the day after he issued this comment, he added that he had not been speaking as a representative of his native land (*Arab Report and Record*, 1-15 October 1978).

## Chapter Three

1. One interviewee emphasised that some of the Saudi funding was channelled specifically to the Brotherhood's women's association (*al-Qabisat*) and other civil activities (personal communication, Damascus, 1999).

2. See Seale (1986) and al-'Azm (1973). Another prominent figure among the five is Ma'mun al-Kuzbari, the first Syrian Prime Minister after Syria's secession from the UAR.

3. Usama bin Laden, the prime suspect of the 11 September 2001 attack on the United States, falls into this category. Born to a Yemeni father who later became a Saudi national and a Syrian mother, he married a Syrian cousin from his mother's side as the first wife (Fisk, 2001). Some sources assume that bin Laden supported the Syrian Muslim Brotherhood's campaign against the Asad regime (details of his involvement are not known) and that only after its near demise in 1982, he travelled to Afghanistan to fight the Russians (personal communications, Damascus, 1999). Others, however, doubt if bin Laden had any involvement in the Brotherhood campaign (e.g. Aoyama, personal communication, Tokyo, September 2002).

4. One Syrian source claims that Shaikh 'Abd al-'Aziz bin Baz, the Grand Mufti of Saudi Arabia, issued a *fatwa* in 1980 in favour of an Islamic revolution in Syria (personal communication, Aleppo, November 1999). No other source has been available on the question.

5. According to *Al-Safir*, (4 August 1979), Muslim Brotherhood leaders from a number of Arab and Muslim countries met in a hotel near London's Heathrow airport in July 1979, in the presence of Kamal Adham, former chief of Saudi intelligence, originally from northern Syria. See also *BBC/SWB/ME* (17 April 1980) for another such conference.

6. On the Shi'a organisations, see Darraj and Barut (1999: 581-601).

7. The Saudi Communists periodically issued from Damascus statements criticising the Saudi regime (e.g. Radio Damascus, 12 June 1982 cited in *MECS*, 1981-1982: 248; *BBC/SWB/ME*, 1 March 1983 and 22 June 1984). On Saudi Communists, see al-Qahtani, (1988); Salamé, (1993: 596-597); *Arab Report* (9 May 1979).

8. An example is Saudi aid to the co-founder of the Ba'th Party, Salah al-Din Bitar. In the late 1970s, he allegedly published with Gulf funding an anti-Asad regime periodical, *al-Ihya' al-'Arabi,* and pressed the Saudi government to cut off aid to Syria (Seale, 1990: 330).

9. According to this report, Asad had surprised Hussein by complaining that Saudi Arabia was paying millions to the Muslim Brotherhood and the Sunnis in Syria. The report put the number of Sunnis detained in Syria at 25,000 and alleged that Asad had refused to listen to a Saudi message demanding their release (*Arab Report,* 5 September 1979).

10. Information Minister Muhammad 'Abduh Yamani claimed that the 'report is groundless and Saudi Arabia does not interfere in the internal affairs of other states' (*Al-Safir,* 2 March 1982).

11. Abu Ghuddah is another example of those Syrians who were exiled to Saudi Arabia under the Ba'thi rule in the 1960s. He resided in the Kingdom from

1965, lecturing at Saudi universities until his return to Syria in 1995.

12. See Safran (1988: 324). For the final resolutions, see *MECS* (1980–1981: 277-280).

13. According to *MEED* (12 December 1980), however, this announcement was in direct response to the Soviet pressure. It was not until after the Israeli annexation of the Golan in December 1981 that the oil flow actually began.

14. The US wished to make the supply of AWACS conditional on Saudi co-operation in the Lebanese area, i.e. applying pressure on Syria for restraint and inducing Damascus to co-operate with Philip Habib's mission. See *International Herald Tribune* (19 May 1981).

15. See his interview in *BBC/SWB/ME* (22 May 1981). Asad did not specify in this interview that his figure was a monthly estimate, but it can be inferred from his assertion that the Arab aid only covered 10 percent of the actual cost, which was quoted at $100 million.

16. For instance, Saudi Oil Minister Ahmad Zaki Yamani said in a television interview in Washington on 19 April: 'the Israelis are a threat much greater than the Soviet threat' ('Documentation: Saudi Arabia and the Gulf', 1981: 184).

17. See Kazziha (1990: 307). He goes on to say that the Palestine item remained the top of the agenda for Saudi Arabia and the Gulf states, as it not only improved the Saudi image among the Arabs but, more importantly, contributed to enhancing domestic social cohesion (1990: 310).

18. The announcement of the plan coincided with Sadat's visit to Washington, where he was pressurising Washington to revive the Camp David peace process. Such timing Fahd chose for his announcement is an indication of his intention to take over Egypt's leadership in pursuing peace in the region. Hence, the plan received a hostile comment from Sadat who criticised it as presenting 'nothing new' (*BBC/SWB/ME*, 11 August 1981).

19. He further dismissed Muhammad al-Tall's endorsement of the plan as no more than an expression of 'a personal position'. (*Al-Safir*, 16 October 1981).

20. Damascus left it to the press to criticise the deal, although the Kingdom was not mentioned by name. For instance, *Tishrin*'s editorial read that some Arabs 'still depend on the US' and 'have not learned the lesson of Sadat's death' (cited in *New York Times*, 30 October 1981).

21. See *MEI* (11 December 1981). Some lip service was paid during the meeting regarding the prospect of a Soviet role, but the Plan was not formally amended to reflect it.

22. South Yemen was inexplicably represented by President Ali Nasir Muhammad (*Washington Post*, 26 November 1981), possibly to express defiance to the Iraqi regime, whose relations with Aden were at the lowest ebb.

23. See Robin Wright in *Observer* (10 January 1982). The Syrian Minister of Information, Ahmad Iskandar Ahmad, praised the Gulf aid: 'We are satisfied with our brothers' assistance' (*BBC/SWB/ME*, 11 January 1982).

24. See *New York Times* (3 January 1982). Also, Syrian and Saudi diplomats have co-ordinated their efforts in defending Damascus' position at the 6 January UN Security Council session on Israel's annexation of the Golan ('Un nouvel axe Damas-Ryad', 20 January 1982).

25. Hirschfeld claims that 'Syrian support for Iran, though not the prime reason, created an additional motive for the establishment of the GCC' (1986: 119), presumably because it increased the weight of Iranian threat.

26. Iran denounced the Syrian Muslim Brotherhood movement as 'treacherous to the Islamic cause' (Abd-Allah, 1983: 183). The reason given was because the Brotherhood's operation was directed against the regime which stood against Zionism, the foremost enemy of Islam (Marschall, 1991: 14; Agha and Khalidi, 1995: 13; Hunter, 1993: 209).

27. Some accounts dispute this view. Abd-Allah claims that in early March 1982, less than a month after the Hama incident, the Saudi charge d'affaires in Damascus handed 'Abd al-Halim Khaddam a check for £10 million (1983: 194 citing *Al-Fajr al-Jadid*, 6 March 1982). Hirschfeld also stressed that the 7 March GCC meetings 'took pains to avoid attacks on Syria' (1986: 118), but the claim is unsubstantiated.

28. For details of the invasion, see Rabinovich, (1985: 121-152) and Fisk (1990: 199-281).

29. *MEED* (11 June 1982) asserts that Syria's feeble response to the invasion outraged the Gulf states, but such an outrage was not outwardly expressed. If there was any indication of Saudi disappointment with Syria's performance, perhaps it is noteworthy that Fahd-Asad phone conversation did not take place until 9 June, three days into the invasion (*BBC/SWB/ME*, 11 June 1982).

30. See Fisk (1990: 268-269). For Fahd's strongly worded warning against the Israeli destruction of Beirut, see *Al-Nahar* (20 June 82). It was announced at the Royal Court (*diwan*) following his meeting with Syrian Foreign Minister Khaddam on a visit to the Kingdom.

31. Syrian media occasionally complained of the 'rich countries' or 'reactionary and pro-American regimes' but no explicit attack against Saudi Arabia was broadcast (*MECS*, 1981-1982: 248, 860).

32. See the *New York Times* (14 June 1982). The prompt succession of Prince Fahd did not cause any disruption or instability in the Saudi regime, as Fahd had been acting as the *de facto* head of state in most spheres of policy-making throughout Khalid's reign.

33. The report substantiates the figure by claiming that US $ 14 billion was the sum that Syria owed to the Soviet Union for Damascus' latest purchase of wheat (*BBC/SWB/ME*, 13 July 1982).

34. Prior to the summit, President Reagan had requested President Asad to open the Syrian border to the Palestinian fighters, according to the Beirut home service report on 15 July. Asad rejected the proposal and instead demanded an Israeli withdrawal from Lebanon (*BBC/SWB/ME*, 17 July 1982).

35. Khaddam stressed upon his return from Washington: 'Syria's stand is clear, constant and principled on refusing to accept the Palestinian fighters' (*BBC/SWB/ME*, 23 July 1982; cf. *MEI*, 30 July 1982).

36. See Aruri, Moughrabi and Stork for the full text of 'The Reagan Plan for the Middle East' (1983: 79-84) and its analyses (1983: 53-72).

37. See *MECS* (1982-1983: 819). Aruri, Moughrabi and Stork suggest that Israel's outright rejection was within the Reagan Administration's calculated strategy, in which the Arab governments would be more inclined to accept the Plan due to Begin's rejection (1983: 73).

38. In public, King Fahd unequivocally denied the Kingdom's intention to submit 'any specific proposal or idea' at the coming summit, calling instead for 'joint Arab action' (*BBC/SWB/ME*, 1 September 1982; *New York Times*, 31 August 1982).

39. See Agha and Khalidi (1995: 53-54) for a good comparison of Syria's calculations in Fez I and II.

40. Karsh objects to accounts which assess Moscow's behaviour during the month of June 1982 as 'virtual inaction', claiming that its military aid to Syria consisted of the same ingredients as in previous wars (1988: 66-70). Most other accounts stress the Soviets' lack of involvement (e.g. Roberts, C.A. 1983: 154-156; Ross, 1990).

41. For the text, see *MECS* (1981–1982: 270).

42. In private, Iskandar also reassured the Iranians not to be concerned, since Syria was expecting little implementation of the Fez agreement in the first place. Iran in turn downplayed its attacks against the summit and particularly Syria's role in it. For the contrasting Iranian reactions to Fez I and II, see Agha and Khalidi (1995: 52-55).

43. For Asad, a mere mention of Syrian withdrawal was a tough point to swallow; he put the summit to test on its fourth day when Lebanon was on the agenda (*Newsweek*, 20 September 1982).

44. See Mordechai Gazit in *MECS* (1981–1982: 206; 1982–1983: 166). Karsh supports this view by claiming that 'at the Fez summit of Arab leaders in September 1982, Syria obstructed Saudi attempts to bridge the gap between the Reagan Plan and the Arab position on a settlement' (1988: 72).

45. For comparison of the phraseology of Fez I and II proposals on Middle East peace, see *MEI* (17 September 1982).

### Chapter Four

1. For an argument that Saudi Arabia and other rich Arab moderates could have implemented a greater financial blow to the US economy by targeting specific areas, yet failed to use such a leverage at the time of the invasion, see Aruri, Moughrabi and Stork, (1983: 79-84) and Wright (1982: 13-14).

2. He went on to say that the Arab world was now left in 'full of debris of a collapsing era,' in which the Arabs thought they could compensate for the military imbalance in the Arab-Israeli equation with their oil, money and political leverage in the West (*Washington Post*, 25 November 1984).

3. For President Asad's speech on the subject, see *BBC/SWB/ME* (23 November 1982). The speech was delivered immediately after Lebanese President Amin Jumayyil's visit to Saudi Arabia—his first overseas trip since taking office following his brother Bashir's assassination (*Al-Majallah*, 20–26 November 1982)—in which he discussed the withdrawal of all foreign forces from Lebanon, including the Syrians (*BBC/SWB/ME*, 17 November 1982).

4. See *Al-Mustaqbal* (16 October 1982). The Saudi *al-Madinah al-Munawwarah* reported that King Fahd was to visit Damascus in late December (6 December 1982), but no such visit took place. The report was also compounded by speculation that the Kingdom had begun supplying, or was preparing to supply a multi-billion dollar loan for Syria (*MEED*, 17 December 1982; *MECS*, 1982–1983: 812).

5. However, it is noteworthy that the Soviets resisted Syria's desire to upgrade the Friendship Treaty to a defence pact, and also categorically rejected a suggestion that its commitment in the Treaty extended to Lebanese territories (Karsh, 1991: 147-148).

6. Saudi daily *Al-Jazirah* (2 May 1983) criticised Syria's dominance over some factions of the PLO in the following terms: 'certain hands are covertly and overtly meddling in Palestinian affairs and certain Palestinian factors still link

their decisions to certain Arab capitals, which do not care about higher Palestinian [or] ...Arab interests' (cited in *MECS*, 1982–1983: 756).

7. In the words of Rabinovich: 'Israel's plans for Lebanon were based to a large degree on Bashir Jumayyil personally' (1985: 154).

8. On 18 April, a truck packed with explosives killed sixty including seventeen Americans. Washington believed that behind the incident were Iranian hands with Syrian complicity (Seale, 1990: 406).

9. Quoted in Seale (1990: 406), who himself called the treaty 'an astonishing straitjacket on Lebanon's sovereignty' (1990: 409).

10. See *MEI* (27 May 1983) for more details of the Memorandum.

11. On Saudi objection to the Lebanese-Israeli treaty, see *Al-Nahar* (30 December 1982) and *MECS* (1982–1983: 755). On Saudi-Lebanese disagreement over reconstruction aid for Lebanon and trade ban on Israeli-occupied Lebanon, see *MEI* (18 March; 29 April 1983) and Petran (1987: 302-310).

12. When Syria's Khaddam visited Riyadh to meet King Fahd and Prince 'Abdallah on 25 April (*Al-Nahar,* 26 April 1983), rumours circulated that the Kingdom had resumed financial support for Syria (*MEED,* 29 April 1983). *MEED* also reported that Kuwait reinvigorated its financial assistance to Syria (11 March 1983).

13. When the official negotiation first opened, Radio Riyadh report suggested that Washington should understand better what 'the Syrian brothers' were seeking (14 December 1982 cited in *MECS*, 1982–1983: 758).

14. On the meeting, see Seale, (1990: 408). Khaddam was in Riyadh two weeks before on 24 April to co-ordinate its strategy with Saudi Arabia (*Al-Nahar,* 26 April 1983).

15. *MEI* highlights Bandar's prominent role as Reagan's preferred intermediary in communication with the Arab leaders, eclipsing the role of the US embassy in Saudi Arabia (19 August 1983). Bandar's appointment was part of King Fahd's larger scheme in the intra-royal family power struggle to consolidate his Sudairi clan's dominance. Bandar's father Sultan being Fahd's full brother, his appointment was to provide the King with a direct link to Washington, bypassing Sa'ud al-Faisal's Foreign Office (Abir, 1988: 184-188).

16. See *New York Times* for the abduction (22 July 1983) and for Dodge's message of gratitude to Asad (24 July 1983). According to Seale, Syrian agents physically rescued Dodge from Tehran (1990: 412).

17. See *Al-Nahar* on the visit (1 August 1983). It was also aimed at calming Syria's sensitivity towards Saudi contacts with the US; in the 29 July issue, it was published that a committee had been formed consisting of Bandar, Robert McFarlane and Wadi Haddad (a Palestinian advisor to Amin Jumayyil on security matters) in order to resolve the Lebanese-Syrian tension. The Saudi Information Minister's spokesman issued a statement denying the allegation (*BBC/SWB/ME*, 1 August; *MEED,* 5 August 1983).

18. The Israelis began to wonder why they should confront the Lebanese Druze, and by so doing, alienate their own Druze community, for an increasingly questionable alliance with Maronite groups (Rabinovich, 1985: 157).

19. For a sympathetic analysis of Saudi mediation efforts, see Abu Talib (1984).

20. Rafiq al-Hariri was born in 1944 in Sidon, Lebanon and moved to Saudi Arabia in 1965. There he found his own construction company, Saudi Oger, which became one of the fastest growing companies, thanks to the mid-1970s construction boom in the Kingdom. He acquired Saudi citizenship, but returned to post-Ta'if Lebanon for a political career (*MEED,* 13 November

1981), holding the office of prime minister from 1992 to 1998 and from 2000 to 2004. His assassination in February 2005 triggered Lebanese and international outcries against Syrian presence in Lebanon, resulting in the official pullout of Syrian forces. The event allegedly caused a strain in Syrian-Saudi relations in its immediate aftermath, but Prince Abdullah expressed 'support for Syria' three months later during his regional tour which took him to Sharm al-Shaikh, Damascus and Amman (*Daily Star,* 9 May 2005).

21. For chronological details of the visits, see 'Al-Qissah al-Kamilah li-l-Wisatah al-Sa'udiyyah' (1983: 24-26). When the first visit of the two ended in a stalemate, 'Ali al-Sha'ir arrived in Damascus the next day (21 September) for further consultation with the Syrian leadership (*BBC/SWB/ME,* 23 September 1983).

22. Compare the Syrian demands at Bandar's 20 September Damascus visit (*Al-Nahar,* 21 September; *MEED,* 23 September 1983) with the final agreement reached on 25 September (Saudi Press Agency, 26 September; *BBC/SWB/ME,* 27 September 1983).

23. See *MEED* (23 September 1983) for allegation levelled by US officials and *BBC/SWB/ME* (28 September 1983) for that by the pro-Phalangist (anti-Syrian) Radio Free Lebanon.

24. See Bandar's speech (*Al-Nahar,* 28 and 30 September 1983) and Sa'ud al-Faisal's speech a few days later at the UN General Assembly (*Al-Nahar,* 4 October 1983). Bandar differentiated between Syrian and Israeli presence and also supported Syria's objection to the international peace-keeping force in Lebanon. Such differentiation was not merely an apologetic change in tactics for the benefit of the Syrians, but to an extent, in line with genuine Lebanese sentiment at that time. Picard claims that the Syrian army, 'though loathed, was never as totally foreign' as the Israeli presence (2002: 132).

25. On 9 October, Khalid al-Hassan, a Kuwait-based al-Fath moderate, arrived in Jiddah and then was flown into Damascus by the Kingdom's private jet for a six-hour meeting with Asad (*MEI,* 28 October 1983).

26. See *MEI* (28 October 1983) for the Baghdad aid and the Riyadh summit. In 1983, Syria had received little of the official Arab aid, and the most serious threat came from Kuwait, whose National Assembly on 8 November called for a suspension of aid still outstanding for 1983 and for all of 1984. The assembly's vote was not binding, and like the earlier threat to halt Kuwaiti payment for the ADF, the purpose here was foremost to send Damascus a warning signal (*MEED,* 18 November 1983).

27. 'Arafat's Cairo visit took place only a few days before the convention of the ICO summit in Casablanca, wherein Saudi Arabia masterminded the campaign to invite Egypt back in. The summit proceedings again highlighted the Kingdom's dilemma; an Egyptian delegation helped King Fahd absent himself from a number of meetings so as not to antagonise the Syrians and Libyans too directly on the question. The King chose to abstain rather than vote in favour of Egypt's readmission and completely omitted the issue from his post-summit statement. As for Syria, represented by Khaddam, stormed out of the conference room as the vote was being counted (*MEED,* 27 January 1984; *MECS,* 1983–1984: 128-129).

28. In the meantime, Donald Rumsfeld, Reagan's special envoy, was on standby to visit Damascus, anticipating positive achievement in the Saudi initiative (*BBC/SWB/ME,* 28 January; *Al-Nahar,* 30 January 1984).

29. Fahd congratulated Asad on the occasion: 'This cancellation is a great victory

for the Arab homeland as a whole' (*Al-Nahar*, 7 March 1984).

30. Walid Junblat and Amal leader Nabih Birri both objected to the formula, claiming that nothing short of Jumayyil's resignation would be an agreeable precondition for the conference, but Asad had pressured them to strike a deal at that time. *MEI* thus concludes that Asad had established even in Christian minds that 'he can deliver his side of the bargain by reining in the opposition forces' (9 March 1984).

31. Saudi Arabia was represented by a somewhat junior figure of Muhammad Ibrahim Mas'udi, the Minister of State, who confined himself to discussing economic aid schemes for the reconstruction (*Al-Nahar*, 7 March 1984; Deeb, 1988a: 181).

32. In the Mountain War, the Saudi mediation efforts bore some fruits only after the fighting had passed its peak and the frontlines had been redrawn. By then, a presence of a mediator became convenient for all actors involved, and the Saudis were readily available to perform the role (*MECS*, 1982–1983: 755).

33. This assessment (*MECS*, 1982–1983: 745) seems convincing in view of the fact that Saudi Arabia's economic downturn was translated into overall lower aid commitments even to the close allies, such as Iraq and Jordan (*Washington Post*, 30 January 1983; Brand, 1994: 110-111). Meir estimates that there was a 41 percent decline in OAPEC aid to Jordan between 1981 and 1983, while the figure for Syria was smaller at 30.5 percent decline (cited in Cordesman, 1987: 48n22).

34. A Saudi source announced in December 1982 that Fahd would shortly visit Damascus (*MEED*, 17 December 1982), but such a visit by the King himself did not take place. Rumours circulated towards the end of 1982 that the Kingdom had begun supplying, or was preparing to supply, a multi-billion dollar loan for Syria (*MECS*, 1982–1983: 812).

35. For his role in the Popular Islamic Conference, see *MECS* (1982–1983: 244) and for his personal effort in reconciling Iraq with Syria, see *BBC/SWB/ME* (26 April 1983).

36. Such a criticism is raised strongly when there is an intra-royal family power struggle (*MECS*, 1982-1983: 745). Particularly pronounced was 'Abdallah vs. Sultan rivalry in the wake of King Khalid's reign. See various issues of *MECS*. 'Abdallah's close relationship with Syria was at times viewed by his rival half-brothers as a mark of pro-Soviet inclination.

37. See various issues of *Al-Nahar* as cited thus far on 'Abdallah's visits to Damascus. Salih 'Adaymah, ex-Defence Brigade and Rif'at's loyal follower, also refers to the special relationship in his chronicle (1992).

38. In view of reports in *MEI* (6 April 1984), *MECS* (1982–1983: 800) and the *Washington Post* (27 November 1984), this marital connection seems an accepted fact, although one source close to the ruling circle of the Syrian regime categorically denied the existence of such a tie. According to this source, the rumour might have originated from the fact that one of Crown Prince Abdullah's ex-wives was of Syrian origin with a maiden name, Fustuq (personal communication by e-mail, 05 February 2002).

39. See Greenwood (1998), *Gulf States Newsletter* (4 May 1998) and Raad (1998: 167-168). According to Raad, the ANN broadcast an extensive coverage of Prince 'Abdallah's meeting with Rif'at in June 1997 as if it was a meeting between two heads of states. The ANN's media advisor, Zubaidah Muqabil, was promptly arrested in Damascus in the following month.

40. For detailed accounts of 'the brothers' war'—to use Patrick Seale's

terminology—see Drysdale (1985: 246-250), Batatu (1999: 232-237) and Seale (1990: 421-440).

41. Such human networks exist not only in the highest echelon but in all walks of society. The Syrian Defence Minister, Mustafa Tulas is said to have married his daughter into the 'Ujjahs, a successful Saudi business family of Syrian origin. Prince Walid bin Talal's business interest in Syria and Lebanon is allegedly facilitated by the fact that his mother is of a Lebanese origin. According to Raad, in 1998, he made a $100 million investment in Syria (1998: 37). *MEED* states that his investment on the Four Seasons Hotel was in total some $95 million (23 January 1998). The Prince was warmly welcomed by Asad upon his visit to Damascus in May of that year. In an earlier era, Queen Ifat, King Faisal's wife who bore him Prince Sa'ud al-Faisal among others, claimed her origin from a prominent Ottoman family from the Syrian region. It seems to be a consensus that Syrian and Lebanese women make popular wives among Saudi men, and as such, inter-marriage has been widely practised (personal communications, Damascus, 1999).

42. A popular rumour in Syria went that whenever 'Abdallah visited Damascus, Rif'at prepared a tent with attractive women and other pleasures of life on the peak of Mount Qasiyun and the two enjoyed their evenings until dawn. Incidentally, public access to the highest point of this mountain, which overlooks the city, is prohibited because of the military facilities there (personal communications, Damascus, 1999).

43. According to one source, Prince 'Abdallah married three Syrian women in total (personal communication, Aleppo, February 1999).

## Chapter Five

1. For the resolution and Sa'ud al-Faisal's conference speech, in which he appealed to Iran to cease attacks on the tankers, see *BBC/SWB/ME* (21 May 1984).

2. See the *New York Times* for the statement (27 May 1984). Indeed, the Arab Gulf states were thought to have provided Iraq with about $35 billion in aid at this stage (*New York Times*, 26 May 1984). When more Iraqi naval attacks followed Rafsanjani's statement, Iran clarified its position on the Arab Gulf states' role in the conflict; in Tehran's view, the aid given to Iraq by those countries made them 'directly responsible' for the crisis (*BBC/SWB/ME*, 28 May 1984).

3. Immediately after Rif'at al-Asad visited Moscow in the first week of June 1984, a high-level Soviet-Iranian contact took place, the first since Tehran expelled eighteen Soviet diplomats and purged the local communist party over a year ago (*New York Times*, 9 June 1984).

4. In contrast to earlier hostility to any mediation effort, Iranian press commented favourably on 'changing Saudi attitudes' toward the Gulf issues, as Rafsanjani accepted the Kingdom's invitation to visit Mecca on a pilgrimage (*BBC/SWB/ME*, 19 July 1984).

5. Sa'ud al-Faisal was unequivocal that there was 'no connection between the Syrians' visit [to Tehran] and the Gulf initiative' (*Al-Mustaqbal*, 1 December 1984).

6. *MEI* (25 January 1985) and *the Economist* (26 January 1985) both refer to Syria's economic stagnation of 1984 and attribute it to the fact that no more than 40 percent of the approximately $2 billion annual Arab pledge—the Saudi share—was paid into its treasury. *MEED* (6 January 1984) and *MEI* (4

May 1984) speculate that the figure for 1983 was also approximately the same. Another notable cause of Syria's economic troubles was its continued presence in Lebanon which cost the treasury some $250,000 per day—explaining the high defence spending at 58 percent of total annual budget (*MEED*, 20 April and 14 December 1984).

7. Abu Dhabi promptly denied the allegation which was originally reported in *Al-Watan al-'Arabiyy* (*BBC/SWB/ME*, 7 July 1984).

8. At one point, the tension grew to such that Syria expelled six hundred Revolutionary Guards from the Biqa' valley (*MECS*, 1984–1985: 698).

9. In 1983, upon US ex-President Jimmy Carter's visit to Damascus, an Iranian pilgrim cried out 'Death to America', as he hoisted Imam Khomeini's poster. Other pilgrims demanded the closure of bars in Damascus and withdrawal of 'unethical' films from the shop counters and cinemas (*MEED*, 25 March 1983; Marschall, 1991: 93).

10. Kostiner described the collaboration between different Shi'i forces in the Gulf and in Lebanon: 'The Arab Gulf, then, had become an arena for Shi'i radicals of many outside nationalities—Iranian, Iraqi and Lebanese' (1987: 183).

11. The increase—from 105,000 to 150,000—was no small step for Riyadh to take, in view of the fact that political demonstrations by the Iranian pilgrims had been a significant source of friction between the two governments (*Washington Post*, 28 July 1984). After the violent clash between the pilgrims and the Saudi security forces during the 1987 *Hajj*, the quota was reduced to 45,000.

12. Delegates from Syria, Iran and Libya walked out after the vote was counted in favour of Egypt (*New York Times*, 19 December 1984).

13. Sa'ud al-Faisal was quoted: 'We welcome Egypt back. It is in Arab interest to unify ranks' (*Al-Mustaqbal*, 1 December 1984). Prince Talal went further in his interview with Egyptian daily *Al-Ahram* by expressing his wishes 'to see a unanimous decision at the next Arab summit on the restoration of Arab relations with Egypt' because there were 'no Arabs without Egypt' (cited in *BBC/SWB/ME*, 7 January 1985).

14. The assessment goes on to read: 'and Syria in particular' (*MECS*, 1984–1985: 79).

15. Bandar departed Damascus and travelled via Iraq and Jordan before stopping in Riyadh (*Al-Safir*, 19 February 1985). Asad also expressed satisfaction with his meeting with Bandar (*BBC/SWB/ME*, 19 February 1985). The discussion continued when US assistant Secretary of State Richard Murphy travelled to Damascus to meet Khaddam and Asad and then continued on to meet Fahd in late April 1985; but again, no understanding was reached between the parties (*BBC/SWB/ME*, 24 April 1985).

16. See *MECS* (1984–1985: 112). The Kuwaiti parliamentary debate in the following months, for instance, expressed its strongest opposition to aid for Syria and censure of its policy on Lebanon and the Gulf war. It decided on cuts to aid for the frontline states (*MEED*, 5 July; *MEI*, 26 July 1985). However, it is noteworthy that the Kuwait-based Arab Fund for Economic and Social Development did agree to a loan of $10 million for work to upgrade the Damascus water system (*MEED*, 20 July 1985).

17. Other major disagreements were over Lebanon. Iran and its Lebanese Shi'i allies were strongly opposed to Syrian and Amal policy of disarming the Palestinians. Iran also preferred Shaikh Muhammad Fadlallah to take the Amal leadership over from Syrian-backed Nabih Birri. The fact that the Islamic

Republic News Agency of Iran first reported the 31 July bomb explosions that occurred in front of Syria's Interior Ministry indicated the depth of the Syrian-Iranian rift (*MEED,* 3 August 1985).

18. Towards Kuwait, for instance, a presumably government-initiated—as all demonstrations were in Syria—anti-Kuwaiti demonstration was held in front of its embassy in Damascus on 10 June (*MEED,* 15 June 1985).

19. The only Syrian-Saudi meeting held in this period was during Khaddam's meeting with Fahd when he visited Ta'if on 16 July (*Al-Nahar,* 17 July 1985)

20. On his tour, see *Al-Nahar* (11 September 1985). Simultaneously, ex-Saudi ambassador to Lebanon Ahmad al-Kuhaimi met Shar' to be appointed the new ambassador to Damascus. Furthermore, Prince Talal bin 'Abd al-'Aziz had just departed Damascus the day before Prince 'Abdallah's arrival, after completing his three-day visit to the Syrian capital (*Al-Nahar,* 10 September 1985).

21. For this assessment and the Syrian and Jordanian motives behind their engagement in negotiation, see a sound argument in *MECS* (1984–1985: 601).

22. A commentary in *Al-Riyadh* read: 'The normalisation of the situation between Syria and Jordan is the natural outcome of the policies carried out by the Saudi leadership in general, and Crown Prince 'Abdallah in particular' (29 May 1986 cited in *MECS,* 1985–1986: 80, 557).

23. See, for instance, Faruq al-Shar''s statement in Kuwaiti News Agency (29 January 1986 cited in *MECS,* 1986: 616) and Asad's interview with Kuwaiti *al-Qabas,* cited in *BBC/SWB/ME* (27 January 1986).

24. Sa'ud al-Faisal met Asad in Damascus on 22 February and travelled on to Baghdad, while Asad also received an envoy from the Iranian Foreign Ministry. A delegation from Kuwait preceded Sa'ud al-Faisal's visit to Damascus (*Al-Nahar,* 23 and 24 February 1986).

25. The 16 March 1986 bomb explosion in central Damascus was followed by a series of explosions a month later, recording some 150 deaths (*MECS,* 1986: 608-611). This was in spite of President's approval rate of 99.97 percent for his third seven-year term in February (Seale, 1990: 473-474)

26. According to Zisser, Syria's instigation of the Hindawi scheme in April 1986 (see below) was in revenge of this Israeli interception (2001: 42). Zisser also claims that the only reason why Israel intercepted the flight was because it mistakenly thought that the plane was carrying the al-Fath leader, Abu Jihad (Khalil al-Wazir). The plane was allowed to continue its journey after the identities of the passengers were established. Seale's account disagrees (1990: 473-474). See below.

27. There were active diplomatic exchanges between Damascus and Riyadh in response to this crisis in Lebanon. Khaddam visited Riyadh on 15 January, and the following day, Asad received Sa'ud al-Faisal (*Al-Nahar,* 16 and 17 January 1986). The issue was discussed again in February, when the Saudi Foreign Minister visited the Syrian capital in the aftermath of Iran's siege of the Faw peninsula (*Al-Nahar,* 24 February 1986).

28. According to P. Seale, Asad's first words to his aides as he walked out of the meeting were: 'We must now look for another option' (personal communication, London, May 1998).

29. See Karsh for the full text of Gorbachev's speech at dinner for Asad on 24 April 1987 (1991: 217-220).

30. See Seale for details; he implies that many of these terrorism-related accusations levelled against Damascus were in fact products of Israel's plot to

frame Syria (1990: 475-482).

31. Most probably in response to the November 1985 GCC summit communiqué, the most balanced ever adopted on the Iran-Iraq conflict, Velayati made a visit to Riyadh in December 1986 (*MEI,* 20 December 1985; Hunter, 1990: 107). At least three more such Iranian delegations visited the Kingdom during 1986.

32. See *Al-Nahar* (22 April 1986). The very next day, on 22 April, Syrian Minister of Economy Muhammad al-'Amadi was in the Kingdom, received by 'Abdallah and Saudi Minister of Commerce (*Al-Nahar,* 23 April 1986).

33. See *Al-Nahar* (27 May 1986), which also reported that Saudi Arabia was firmly behind these Jordanian diplomatic activities. Hussein promptly departed for Baghdad after his meeting with Asad.

34. Syrian Foreign Minister Faruq al-Shar' was in Ta'if on 14 May after his meeting with his Iranian counterpart in Tehran. A week later, Vice-President Khaddam also made an unannounced visit to the Saudi summer capital and was received by 'Abdallah and Fahd. For the two visits, see *Al-Nahar* (15 and 23 May 1986).

35. 'Diplomatic sources in Paris' were attributed to the lower figure (*Al-Nahar,* 14 June 1986) and 'Jordanian officials' for the higher one (*Wall Street Journal,* 1 July 1986).

36. See *MECS* (1986: 99, 558). These allegations were invariably discounted by the Saudis. With regard to the IMF loan, there is no record that Syria formally applied for such a loan, the primary reason behind which was to protect its independence in economic policy-making.

37. *Al-Safir* (14 August 1986) reported that Saudi Arabia had pledged $180 million to Syria in the framework of aid to the frontline states.

38. Apart from the involvement in the Iran-Contra affair, the Saudis were concomitantly reported to have shipped large amounts of refined petroleum products to Iran in return for Tehran's curbing of support for the Shi'a oppositions in the Kingdom (*MECS,* 1986: 106).

39. Neither Syria nor Saudi Arabia made public comments about the other's role in the scandal or the uncovering of it. There was no change in the outwardly friendly relationship, and at the end of November 1986, Saudi Interior Minister Prince Na'if arrived in Damascus for a five-day visit and signed with his Syrian counterpart a security co-operation agreement (*Al-Nahar,* 27 and 28 November; *Al-Safir,* 1 December 1986). The exact details of the agreement are unknown.

40. See *MECS* (1987: 121-122). After the Mecca incident (see below) there was a rumour of delay in delivery of Saudi financial assistance to Syria, although the Saudi Finance Ministry sources discounted it (*Al-Nahar,* 17 August 1987).

41. Asad also held a meeting with the visiting Iranian deputy foreign minister and promised to contact Saudi Arabia to arrange for the delivery of the Iranian bodies (*MECS,* 1987: 646).

42. Among the Steadfastness camp, or 'the Arab minorities', Libya's Qadhdhafi refused to participate in the summit, but his absence had little impact on the summit course, testifying to the centrality of Syria (and Asad) in inter-Arab politics in comparison.

43. This was partly attributed to objections not only from Syria but also from Libya, Oman, Qatar and the UAE, which maintained reasonable relations with the Iranians (*MECS,* 1978: 133).

44. Asad stated that restoration of diplomatic ties with Egypt was 'a sovereign matter to be decided by each state in accordance with its constitution and law'

(Lay, 1987-1988: 19).

45. One may recall 'Abdallah's substitution for Fahd's absence at the 7 August 1985 Casablanca Arab emergency summit. On that occasion, it was indeed Fahd's reluctance to honour with his presence a summit event that was boycotted by Asad. The difference between Casablanca and Amman is that Asad attended the latter.

46. According to *MECS, Al-Siyasah*, (4 July 1988) stated that aid levels were fixed at 250 million per annum for Syria and $150 million for Jordan (1988: 148). Even if this new sum were indeed promised, the figure suggests a steep reduction in commitments from the original agreement in Baghdad ten years ago. *MECS* also highlighted the overall decline in *official* Arab aid to Syria from the estimated figure of $1.06 billion in 1985 to $800 million in 1986, $600 million in 1987, and $500 million in 1988 (1988: 733). Lawson quoted an even more drastic decline in the aid figure, at less than $80 million in 1988 (1996: 133). Although the degree of reduction is thus unclear, there is unanimous agreement that there was a substantial decrease. For more statistical data on Arab aid to Syria, consult van der Boogaerde (1991).

47. For Saudi mediation efforts, see reports on Crown Prince 'Abdallah's visit to Damascus from 6 January 1989 (*Al-Qabas,* 6 January 1989; *Al-Sharq al-Awsat,* 7 January 1989; and especially, *Al-Ra'y al-'Amm,* 7 January 1989). *Al-Qabas* suggested that just days before the Casablanca Arab summit, Mubarak and Asad met in Riyadh (4 May 1989).

48. Saudi Arabia's Prince 'Abdallah also acted as mediator in Syrian-Moroccan reconciliation in January 1989 (*Al-Diyar,* 10 January; *Al-Usbu',* 11 January 1989). Syria had unilaterally severed relations in 1986. Riyadh also encouraged reconciliation between Damascus-PLO and Damascus-Baghdad, but these did not yield as concrete a result.

49. His visit to Riyadh coincided with that by Usama al-Baz, Egypt's first under-secretary of state on foreign affairs (*MECS,* 1988: 696; *Al-Qabas,* 14 December 1988). Syrian-Egyptian reconciliation, therefore, may also have been discussed.

50. At the time of writing, Syria has been censured by the international community as the hand behind his assassination in February 2005. As the investigations into his murder, including that by the UN, are ongoing, it is outside the scope of this project to assess the precise implications in the context of Syrian-Saudi relations.

## Conclusion

1. The lower figure is quoted in Kienle (1994: 387), and the higher one in Drysdale (1993: 283). Eisenstadt claims that Soviet arms transfers to Syria worth $ 650 million was financed by the Gulf states after the war (1992: 37).

2. Aoyama alleges that the US traded its acquiescence for Syria's commitment to embark on economic liberalisation, an outcome of which was *al-infitah* of the 1990s (1998: 2). Furthermore, according to Seale, Asad extracted promises from the Bush administration that it would concentrate its Middle East policy on the Arab-Israeli issue once the conflict with Iraq was resolved and that the new American initiative would be based on the UN resolutions 242 and 338, in accordance with Damascus' long-standing official position (1996: 31-32).

3. See Agha and Khalidi (1995: 30-31). In late June 1997, Syria convened a Damascus Declaration Foreign Ministers economic forum to discuss establishment of a common market. To give support to this event, Prince

'Abdallah was in Damascus and Beirut for the duration of the conference (*Gulf States Newsletter,* 14 July 1997).

4. By 1994, Syria had once again begun to receive 25 percent of Arab aid (Perthes, 1995: 64-65).

5. Syria, a long-term rejectionist of MENA since the first meeting in Casablanca, saw its participation as tantamount to acceptance of Israel's occupation. Saudi Arabia joined efforts with Syria in urging other Arab states to follow suit (*MEI,* 11 July 1997;*Gulf States Newsletter,* 14 July 1997).

6. Among the Arab states, Oman, Kuwait, Yemen, Jordan and Tunisia sent delegations (*MEI,* 5 December 1997).

7. The minutes of the eighth meeting held in Riyadh on 15–16 February 2000 are available at http://www.arabicnews.com/ (28 February 2000). For earlier meetings, see *Al-Hayat* (21 June 1995) and *Al-Ahram* (29 June 1995).

8. See Prince Salman's statement (*Al-Riyadh,* 13 June 2000), Sa'ud al-Faisal's (*Al-Sharq al-Awsat,* 14 June 2000) and Prince Sultan's (*Al-Hayat,* 11 June 2000). Prince 'Abdallah, who attended the funeral expressed his support for Bashshar (*Al-Ahram al-Masa'i,* 15 June 2000) and delivered the same message from King Fahd (*Al-Hawadith,* 14-23 June 2000).

9. Upon his return, Bashshar al-Asad urged the UN to distinguish between terrorism and legitimate resistance to foreign occupation (*MEI,* 28 September 2001)—a language remarkably identical to that of his father's after the Hindawi affairs.

# BIBLIOGRAPHY

## BOOKS, ARTICLES AND CHAPTERS

'Abd Allah, Anwar (1995), *Al-'Ulamah wa al-'Arsh: Thunaiyyah al-Sultah fi al-Sa'udiyyah* (The Men of Religion and the Throne: The Duality of Authority in Saudi Arabia), London: al-Rafid li-l-Nashr wa al-Tawzi'.

Abdallah, Ibrahim Saad Eddine (1988), 'Migration as a Factor Conditioning State Economic Control and Financial Policy Options', Giacomo Luciani and Ghassan Salamé, eds., *The Politics of Arab Integration*, London: Croom Helm.

Abd-Allah, Umar F. (1983), *The Islamic Struggle in Syria*, Berkeley: Mizan Press.

Abir, Mordechai (1988), *Saudi Arabia in the Oil Era: Regime and Elites; Conflict and Collaboration*, London and Sydney: Croom Helm.

Abukhalil, Asad (1990), 'Syria and the Shiites: Al-Asad's Policy in Lebanon', *Third World Quarterly*, 12 (2), April.

—— (1994), 'Syria and the Arab-Israeli Conflict', *Current History*, 93 (580), February.

Aburish, Saïd K. (1994), *The Rise, Corruption and Coming Fall of the House of Saud*, London: Bloomsbury.

Abu Talib, Hasan (1984), 'Al-Wisatah al-Sa'udiyyah wa al-Azmat al-'Arabiyyah' (Saudi Mediation and the Arab Crises), *Al-Siyasah al-Dawliyyah*, January.

—— (1992), *Al-Mamlakah al-Sa'udiyyah wa Dhilal al-Quds* (The Saudi Kingdom and the Shadows of Jerusalem), Beirut/Cairo: al-Maktabat al-Thaqafiyyah/Sina lil-Nashr.

Acharya, Amitav (1992), 'Regionalism and Regime Security in the Third World: Comparing the Origins of the ASEAN and the GCC', Brian L. Job, ed., *The Insecurity Dilemma: National Security of Third World States*, Boulder and London: Lynne Rienner.

'Adaymah, Salih (1992), *Tahlil Rif'at al-Asad: Maqulah fi Hikmat al-Siyasat wa Siyasat al-Hikmah* (An Analysis of Rif'at al-Asad: A Thesis on the Wisdom of Politics and the Politics of Wisdom), Paris.

Agha, Hussein J. and Ahmad S. Khalidi (1995), *Syria and Iran: Rivalry and Cooperation*, London: Pinter/the Royal Institute of International Affairs.

Ajami, Fouad (1978/1979), 'The End of Pan-Arabism', *Foreign Affairs*, 57 (2), Winter.

—— (1986), *The Vanished Imam: Musa al-Sadr and the Shia of Lebanon*, London: I.B. Tauris.

—— (1992), *The Arab Predicament: Arab Political Thought and Practice Since 1967*, New

York: Cambridge University Press.

Amin, Samir (1978), *The Arab Nation,* Michael Pallis, trans., London: Zed Press.

Amirahmadi, Hooshang, and Nader Entessar (1993), 'Iranian-Arab Relations in Transition', Hooshang Amirahmadi and Nader Entessar, eds., *Iran and the Arab World,* London: Macmillan.

—— (1993), 'Iran and the Persian Gulf Crisis', Hooshang Amirahmadi and Nader Entessar, eds., *Iran and the Arab World,* London: Macmillan.

Anderson, Benedict (1983), *Imagined Communities: Reflections on the Origins and Spread of Nationalism,* London: Verso.

Anthony, John Duke (1982), 'Aspects of Saudi Arabia's Relations with the Other Gulf States', Tim Niblock, ed., *State, Society and Economy in Saudi Arabia,* London: Croom Helm.

—— (1984), 'The Gulf Cooperation Council', Robert G. Darius, John W. Amos, and Ralph H. Magnus, eds., *Gulf Security into the 1980s,* Stanford: Hoover Institution Press.

Armanazi, Ghayth N. (1993), 'Syrian Foreign Policy at the Crossroads: Continuity and Change in the Post-Gulf War Era', Youssef M. Choueiri, ed., *State and Society in Syria and Lebanon,* Exeter: University of Exeter press.

Aruri, Naseer, Fouad Moughrabi and Joe Stork (1983), *Reagan and the Middle East,* Belmont: Association of Arab-American University Graduates (AAUG).

Asad, Talal and Roger Owen, eds. (1983), *Sociology of "Developing Societies": The Middle East,* London: Macmillan.

Avi-Ran, Reuven (1991), *The Syrian Involvement in Lebanon since 1975,* Boulder, San Francisco and Oxford: Westview.

Ayoob, Mohammed (1994), 'Security in the Third World: Searching for the Core Variable', Norman A. Graham, *Seeking Security and Development: The Impact of Military Spending and Arms Transfers,* Boulder and London: Lynne Rienner.

—— (1995), *The Third World Security Predicament,* Boulder and London: Lynne Rienner.

Ayubi, Nazih N. (1995), *Over-stating the Arab State: Politics and Society in the Middle East,* London and New York: I.B. Tauris.

Azar, Edward E. and Chung-in Moon, eds. (1988), *National Security in the Third World: The Management of Internal and External Threats,* Aldershot: Edward Elgar.

al-'Azm, Khalid (1973), *Mudhakkirat Khalid al-'Azm* (The Memoirs of Khalid al-'Azm), vol.1-3, Beirut: al-Dar al-Muttahidah lil-Nashr.

al-'Azmah, Bashir (1991), *Jil al-Hazimah—min al-Dhakirah / Mudhakkirat* (The Era of Defeat—as Recollected: Memoirs), Beirut: Riad el-Rayyes Books.

'Azmah Samitah bayna al-Sa'udiyyah wa Suriyya: 'Amaliyyah Sirriyyah Yudabbiru-ha A'da' al-Usrah al-Malikah ma' Dimashq wa 'Adan' (A Dormant Crisis between Saudi Arabia and Syria: the Enemies of the Ruling Family Plot a Covert Operation with Damascus and Aden")(1980), *Akhir Sa'ah,* 20 February.

Bailey, Clinton (1987), 'Lebanon's Shi'is After the 1982 War', Martin Kramer, ed., *Shi'ism, Resistance and Revolution,* Boulder: Westview.

Bakhash, Shaul (1990), 'Iran's Relations with Israel, Syria and Lebanon', Miron Rezun, ed., *Iran at the Crossroads: Global Relations in a Turbulent Decade,* Boulder: Westview.

Bannerman, M. Graeme (1979), 'Saudi Arabia', P. Edward Haley and Lewis W. Snider eds., *Lebanon in Crisis: Participants and Issues,* Syracuse: Syracuse University Press.

Barakat, Halim (1993), *The Arab World: Society, Culture, and State,* Berkeley, Los Angeles, and London: University of California Press.

Baram, Amatzia, and Barry Rubin, eds. (1993), *Iraq's Road to War,* London: Macmillan.

Barnett, Michael N. (1998), *Dialogues in Arab Politics: Negotiations in Regional Order,* New York: Columbia University Press.

Bar-Siman-Tov, Yaacov (1983), *Linkage Politics in the Middle East: Syria between Domestic and External Conflict, 1961-1970,* Boulder: Westview.

Batatu, Hanna (1981), 'Some Observations on the Social Roots of Syria's Ruling Military Group and the Causes for Its Dominance,' *The Middle East Journal,* 35(3), Summer.

—— (1982), 'Syria's Muslim Brethren', *MERIP Reports,* 12(9)/No.110, November-December.

—— (1999), *Syria's Peasantry, the Descendants of Its Lesser Rural Notables, and Their Politics,* Princeton: Princeton University Press.

Beblawi, Hazem (1987), 'The Rentier State in the Arab World,' Hazem Beblawi and Giacomo Luciani, eds., *The Rentier State,* London: Croom Helm.

—— (El-Beblawi) (1982), 'The Predicament of the Arab Gulf Oil States: Individual Gains and Collective Losses', Malcolm H. Kerr and El Sayed Yassin, eds., *Rich and Poor States in the Middle East: Egypt and the New Arab Order,* Boulder: Westview.

Ben-Dor, Gabriel (1977), 'Political Culture Approach to Middle East Politics', *The International Journal of Middle East Studies,* 8.

Binder, Leonard (1967), 'The Tragedy of Syria', *World Politics,* 19(3), April.

Bligh, Alexander and Steven E Plant (1982), 'Saudi Moderation in Oil and Foreign Policies in the Post-AWACS-Sale Period', *Middle East Review,* 14(3-4), Spring-Summer.

Bloom, William (1993), *Personal Identity, National Identity and International Relations,* Cambridge: Cambridge University Press.

Brand, Laurie (1990), 'Asad's Syria and the PLO: Coincidence or Conflict of Interests?' *Journal of South Asian and Middle Eastern Studies,* 14(2), Winter.

—— (1994), *Jordan's Inter-Arab Relations: The Political Economy of Alliance Making,* New York: Columbia University Press.

Brown, L. Carl (1984), *International Politics and the Middle East: Old Rules, Dangerous Game,* London: I.B.Tauris.

—— (2001), *Diplomacy in the Middle East: The International Relations of Regional and Outside Powers,* London: I.B.Tauris.

Buchau, James (1982), 'Secular and Religious Oppositions in Saudi Arabia', Tim Niblock, ed., *State, Society, and the Economy in Saudi Arabia,* London: Croom Helm.

Buzan, Barry (1991), *People, States and Fear: An Agenda for International Security Studies in the Post-Cold War Era,* New York and London: Harvester Wheatsheaf.

Calabrese, John (1990), 'Iran II: The Damascus Connection', *The World Today,* 46(10).

Caret, Charles (1987), 'Iran/Syrie: L'Alliance contre-Nature', *Politique Étrangère,* February.

Carter, J.R.L. (1984), *Merchant Families of Saudi Arabia,* 2nd ed., London: Scorpion Books.

Chalala, Elie (1988), 'Syria's Support of Iran in the Gulf War: The Role of Structural Change and the Emergence of a Relatively Strong State', *Journal of Arab Affairs,* 7(2).

Chaudhry, Kiren Aziz (1992), 'Economic Liberalization in Oil-exporting Countries: Iraq and Saudi Arabia', Iliya Harik and Denis J. Sullivan, eds.,

*Privatization and Liberalization in the Middle East*, Bloomington and Indianapolis: Indiana University Press.

Choueiri, Y. (1987), 'Two Histories of Syria and the Demise of Syrian Patriotism', *Middle Eastern Studies*, 23(4), October.

—— ed. (1993), *State and Society in Syria and Lebanon*, Exeter: University of Exeter Press.

Chelkowski, Peter J., and Robert J. Pranger, eds. (1988), *Ideology and Power in the Middle East: Studies in Honor of George Lenczowski*, Durham and London: Duke University Press.

Chubin, Shahram, and Charles Tripp (1988), *Iran and Iraq at War*, London: I.B.Tauris.

—— (1989), 'Iran and the War: From Stalemate to Ceasefire', Miron Rezun, ed., *Iran at the Crossroads: Global Relations in a Turbulent Decade*, Boulder: Westview.

—— and Charles Tripp (1996), 'Iran-Saudi Arabia Relations and Regional Order' (Adelphi Paper 304), London: IISS.

Cobban, Helena (1991a), *The Superpowers and the Syrian-Israeli Conflict: Beyond Crisis Management?*, New York: The Center for Strategic and International Studies.

—— (1991b), 'The Nature of Soviet-Syrian Link under Asad and under Gorbachev', Richard T. Antoun Quataert, eds., *Syria: Society, Culture and Policy*, Albany: State University of New York Press.

—— (1999), *The Israeli-Syrian Peace Talks: 1991-96 and Beyond*, Washington, DC: United States Institute of Peace Press.

Cordesman, Anthony H. (1987), *Western Strategic Interests in Saudi Arabia*, London, Sydney and Wolfeboro: Croom Helm.

—— (1997), *Saudi Arabia: Guarding the Desert Kingdom*, Boulder: Westview.

van Dam, Nikolaos (1978), 'Sectarian and Regional Factionalism in the Syrian Political Elite', *The Middle East Journal*, 32(2), Spring.

—— (1983), 'Minorities and Political Elites in Iraq and Syria', Talal Asad and Roger Owen, eds., *Sociology of "Developing Societies": The Middle East*, London: Macmillan.

—— (1996), *The Struggle for Power in Syria: Politics and Society under Asad and the Ba'th Party*, London and New York: I.B. Tauris.

Darraj, Faisal and Jamal Barut, eds. (1999), *Al-Ahzab wa al-Harakat wa al-Jama'at al-Islamiyyah* (The Islamic Parties, Movements and Groups), vol.2, Damascus: The Arab Centre for Strategic Studies.

David, Steven R. (1991), 'Explaining Third World Alignment', *World Politics*, 43(2), January.

Dawisha, Adeed I. (1979), 'Internal Values and External Threats: The Making of Saudi Foreign Policy', *Orbis*, 23(1), Spring.

—— (1980), *Syria and the Lebanese Crisis*, London: Macmillan.

—— ed. (1983), *Islam in Foreign Policy*, Cambridge: Cambridge University Press.

—— (1984), 'Saudi Arabia's Search for Security', Charles Tripp, ed., *Regional Security in the Middle East*, (Adelphi Library 8), Aldershot/London: Gower/IISS.

—— and I. William Zartman, eds. (1988), *Beyond Coercion: The Durability of the Arab State*, London and New York: Croom Helm.

—— (1990), 'Arab Regimes: Legitimacy and Foreign Policies', Giacomo Luciani, ed., *The Arab State*, London: Routledge.

Deeb, Marius (1988a), 'Saudi Arabian Policy toward Lebanon since 1975', Halim Barakat, ed., *Toward a Viable Lebanon*, London and Sydney: Croom Helm.

—— (1988b), 'Shia Movements in Lebanon: Their Formation, Ideology, Social Basis, and Links with Iran and Syria', *Third World Quarterly*, 10(2), April.

Devlin, John F. (1983), *Syria: Modern State in an Ancient Land*, Boulder/London: Westview/Croom Helm.

—— (1984), 'Syrian Policy', Robert O. Freedman, ed., *The Middle East since Camp David*, Boulder and London: Westview.

Diab, M. Zuhair (1994), 'Have Syria and Israel Opted for Peace?', *Middle East Policy*, 3(2), July.

Dickey, Christopher (1987), 'Assad and His Allies: Irreconcilable Differences?', *Foreign Affairs*,66(1).

'Documentation: Saudi Arabia and the Gulf' (1981), *Survival*, XXIII (4), July/August.

Drysdale, Alastair (1982), 'The Asad Regime and Its Troubles', *MERIP Reports*, 12(9)/No.110, November-December.

—— (1985), 'The Succession Question in Syria', *The Middle East Journal*, 39(2), Spring.

—— and Raymond Hinnebusch (1991), *Syria and the Middle East Peace Process*, New York: Council on Foreign Relations.

—— (1993), 'Syria since 1988: From Crisis to Opportunity', Robert O. Freedman, ed., *The Middle East after Iraq's Invasion of Kuwait*, Gainsville: University Press of Florida.

van Dusen, Michael H. (1972), 'Political Integration and Regionalism in Syria,' *The Middle East Journal*, 26(2), Spring.

—— (1975), 'Syria: Downfall of a Traditional Elite', Frank Tachau ed., *Political Elites of Political Development in the Middle East*, New York: Halsted Press.

Efrat, Moshe (1991), 'The Soviet Union and the Syrian Military-Economic Dimension: A *Realpolitik* Perspective,' Moshe Efrat and Jacob Bercovitch, eds., *Superpowers and the Client States in the Middle East: The Imbalance of Influence*, London and New York: Routledge.

Ehteshami, Anoushiravan (1996), 'Defence and Security Policies of Syria in a Changing Regional Environment', *International Relations*, 8 (1), April.

—— and Raymond A. Hinnebusch (1997), *Syria and Iran: Middle Powers in a Penetrated Regional System*, London and New York: Routledge.

Eilts, Hermann Frederick (1988), 'Saudi Arabia: Traditionalism versus Modernism—A Royal Dilemma?', Peter J. Chelkowski and Robert J. Pranger, eds., *Ideology and Power in the Middle East: Studies in Honor of George Lenczowski*, Durham: Duke University Press.

Eisenstadt, Michael (1992), *Arming for Peace? Syria's Elusive Quest for "Strategic Parity"*, Washington, DC; The Washington Institute for Near East Policy.

Eppel, Michael (1993), 'Syria: Iraq's Radical Nemesis', Amatzia Baram and Barry Rubin, eds., *Iraq's Road to War*, London: Macmillan.

Evron, Yair (1987), *War and Intervention in Lebanon: The Israeli-Syrian Deterrence Dialogue*, London and Sydney: Croom Helm.

Faksh, Mahmud A. (1984), 'The Alawi Community of Syria: A New Dominant Political Force,' *The Middle East Studies*, 20(2), April.

—— (1993), 'Asad's Westward Turn: Implications for Syria', *Middle East Policy*, 2(3).

Fisk, Robert (1990), *Pity the Nation: Lebanon at War*, London: Andre Deutsch.

—— (2001), 'Osama bin Laden: The Godfather of Terror?', *The Independent*, 15 September.

Freedman, Lawrence, and Efraim Karsh (1993), *The Gulf Conflict 1990-1991: Diplomacy and War in the New World Order*, London and Boston: Faber and Faber.

Freedman, Robert O. (1991a), 'The Soviet Union and Syria: A Case Study of Soviet Policy', Moshe Efrat and Jacob Bercovitch, eds., *Superpowers and Client States in the Middle East: The Imbalance of Influence,* London and New York: Routledge.

—— (1991b), *Moscow and the Middle East: Soviet Policy since the Invasion of Afghanistan,* Cambridge: Cambridge University Press,.

Gause III, F. Gregory (1990), *Saudi-Yemeni Relations: Domestic Structures and Foreign Influence,* New York: Columbia University Press.

—— (1994), *Oil Monarchies: Domestic and Security Challenges in the Arab Gulf States,* New York: Council on Foreign Relations.

Golan, Galia, and Itamar Rabinovich (1979), 'The Soviet Union and Syria: The Limits of Co-operation', Yaacov Ro'i, ed., *The Limits to Power: Soviet Policy in the Middle East,* London: Croom Helm.

—— (1990), *Soviet Policies in the Middle East: From World War II to Gorbachev,* Cambridge: Cambridge University Press

Goldberg, Jacob (1986), *The Foreign Policies of Saudi Arabia: The Formative Years, 1902-1918,* Cambridge and London: Harvard University Press.

—— (1993), 'Saudi Arabia: The Bank Vault Next Door', Amatzia Baram and Barry Rubin, eds., *Iraq's Road to War,* London: Macmillan.

Golub, David B. (1985), 'When Oil and Politics Mix: Saudi Oil Policy, 1973-1985' (Harvard Middle East Papers Modern Series no.4), Cambridge: CMES, Harvard University.

Gordon, David C. (1983), *The Republic of Lebanon: Nation in Jeopardy,* Boulder: Westview.

Greenwood, Frances (1998), 'Syrian Politics by Satellite', *Middle East International,* 13 March.

Gubser, Peter (1979), 'Minorities in Power: The Alawites of Syria,' R.D. McLaurin, ed., *The Political Role of Minority Groups in the Middle East,* New York: Praeger.

Haim, Sylvia G., (1976) ed., *Arab Nationalism: An Anthology,* Berkeley: University of California Press.

Hajj Hamad, Muhammad Abu al-Qasim (1996), *Al-Saudiyyah: Qadar al-Muwajahah al-Masiyiriyyah wa Khasa'is al-Takwiyin (Saudi Arabia: Destiny of the Decisive Confrontation and Characteristics of the Formation),* British West Indies: International Studies and Research Bureau.

Halliday, Fred (1979), *Arabia without Sultans,* London and New York: Penguin Books.

—— (1982), 'A Curious and Close Liaison: Saudi Arabia's Relations with the United States' Tim Niblock, ed., *State, Society, and the Economy in Saudi Arabia,* London: Croom Helm.

—— (1987-1988), 'Gorbachev and the "Arab Syndrome": Soviet Policy in the Middle East', *Arab Affairs,* 1(5), Winter.

—— (1988a), 'The Gulf in International Affairs: Independence and After,' B.R. Pridham, ed., *The Arab Gulf and the Arab World,* London: Croom Helm.

—— and Hamza Alavi, eds. (1988b), *State and Ideology in the Middle East and Pakistan,* London: Macmillan.

—— (1990), *Revolution and Foreign Policy: The Case of South Yemen 1967-1987,* Cambridge: Cambridge University Press.

Hamzeh, A. Nizar (1993), 'Lebanon's Hizbullah: From Islamic Revolution to Parliamentary Accommodation', *Third World Quarterly,* 14(2), April.

Hasou, Tawfig Y. (1985), *The Struggle for the Arab World: Egypt's Nasser and the Arab League,* London: Kegan Paul Inc.

Heikal, Mohamed (1975), *The Road to Ramadan: The Inside Story of How the Arabs Prepared for and Almost Won the October War of 1973,* London: Collins.

Heller, Mark, and Nadav Safran (1985), 'The New Middle Class and Regime Stability in Saudi Arabia' (Harvard Middle East Papers Modern Series no.3), Cambridge: CMES, Harvard University.

Helms, Christine Moss (1981), *The Cohesion of Saudi Arabia: Evolution of Political Identity,* London: Croom Helm.

Henderson, Simon (1995), *After King Fahd: Succession in Saudi Arabia,* 2nd ed., Washington, DC: The Washington Institute for Near East Policy.

Heydemann, Steven (1999), *Authoritarianism in Syria: Institutions and Social Conflict 1946-1970,* Ithaca and London: Cornell University Press.

Hinnebusch, Raymond A. (1982a), 'The Islamic Movement in Syria: Sectarian Conflict and Urban Rebellion in an Authoritarian-Populist Regime,' Ali E. Hillal Dessouki, ed., *Islamic Resurgence in the Arab World,* New York: Praeger.

—— (1982b), 'Syria under the Ba'th: State Formation in a Fragmented Society,' *Arab Studies Quarterly,* 4(3).

—— (1988), 'Syria', Shireen T. Hunter, ed., *The Politics of Islamic Revivalism: Diversity and Unity,* Bloomington: Indiana University Press.

—— (1989), *Peasant and Bureaucracy in Ba'thist Syria: The Political Economy of Rural Development,* Boulder: Westview.

—— (1990), *Authoritarian Power and State Formation in Ba'thist Syria: Army, Party, and Peasant,* Boulder: Westview.

—— (1991), 'Revisionist Dreams, Realist Strategies: The Foreign Policy of Syria', Bahgat Korany and Ali E. Hillal Dessouki, eds., *The Foreign Policies of Arab States: The Challenge of Change,* 2nd rev. ed., Boulder: Westview.

—— (1993a), 'Asad's Syria and the New World Order: The Struggle for Regime Survival', *Middle East Policy,* 2(1).

—— (1993b), 'State and Civil Society in Syria,' *The Middle East Journal,* 47(2), Spring.

—— (1995a), 'The Political Economy of Economic Liberalization in Syria', *International Journal of Middle East Studies,* 27.

—— (1995b), 'Syria: The Politics of Peace and Regime Survival', *Middle East Policy,* 3(4), April.

—— (2001), *Syria: Revolution from Above,* London: Routledge.

—— and Anoushiravan Ehteshami, eds. (2002), *The Foreign Policies of Middle East States,* Boulder and London: Lynne Rienner.

Hirschfeld, Yair (1986), 'The Odd Couple: Ba'athist Syria and Khomeini's Iran", Moshe Ma'oz and Avner Yaniv, eds., *Syria under Assad: Domestic Constraints and Regional Risks,* London and Sydney: Croom Helm.

Hitti, Nassif (1993), 'Lebanon in Iran's Foreign Policy: Opportunities and Constraints', Hooshang Amirahmadi and Nader Entessar eds., *Iran and the Arab World,* London: Macmillan.

Al-Hizb al-Shuyu'iyy fi al-Sa'udiyyah (Communist Party in Saudi Arabia) (1980), *Ahdath Nufimbir (Mahram) 1979 fi al-Sa'udiyyah* (The Events of November 1979 in Saudi Arabia), n.p.: Manshurat al-Hizb al-Shuyu'iyy fi al-Sa'udiyyah, June.

Holden, David and Richard Johns (1981), *The House of Saud,* London and Sydney: Pan Books.

Hollis, Martin, and Steve Smith (1990), *Explaining and Understanding International Relations,* Oxford: Clarendon Press.

Hollis, Rosemary (1995), '"Whatever Happened to the Damascus Declaration?": Evolving Security Structures in the Gulf', M. Jane Davis, ed., *Politics and*

*International Relations in the Middle East,* Aldershot: Edward Elgar.

Hopwood, Derek (1988), *Syria 1945-1986: Politics and Society,* London: Unwin Hyman.

Hourani A. H. (1947), *Minorities in the Arab World,* London, New York and Toronto: Oxford University Press.

—— (Albert) (1970), *Arabic Thought in the Liberal Age, 1789-1939,* London: Oxford University Press.

Hudson, Michael C. (1977), *Arab Politics: The Search for Legitimacy,* New Haven and London: Yale University Press.

—— (1983), 'The Islamic Factor in Syrian and Iraqi Politics', James P. Piscatori, ed., *Islam in the Political Process,* New York and Cambridge: Cambridge University Press.

Hunter, Shireen (1990), 'Iran and the Arab World', Miron Rezun, ed., *Iran at the Crossroads: Global Relations in a Turbulent Decade,* Boulder: Westview.

—— (1991), 'The Gulf Cooperation Council: Security in the Era Following the Iran-Contra Affair', Robert O. Freedman, ed., *The Middle East from the Iran-Contra Affair to the Intifada,* Syracuse: Syracuse University Press.

—— (1993), 'Iran and Syria: From Hostility to Limited Alliance', Hooshang Amirahmadi and Nader Entessar, eds., *Iran and the Arab World,* London: Macmillan.

Ismael, Tareq Y., and Jacqueline S. Ismael (1991a), *Politics and Government in the Middle East and North Africa,* Miami: Florida International University Press.

—— (1991b), *International Relations of the Middle East: A Study in World Politics,* Syracuse: Syracuse University Press.

al-Ja'fari, Bashshar (1987), *Al-Siyasah al-Kharijiyyah, al-Suriyyah, 1946-1982* (Syrian Foreign Policy, 1946-1982), Damascus: Dar al-Tulas lil-Dirasat wa al-Tarjamah wa al-Nashr.

Jankowski, James, and Israel Gershoni, eds. (1997), *Rethinking Nationalism in the Middle East,* New York: Columbia University Press.

Job, Brian L. (1992), 'The Insecurity Dilemma: National, Regime, and State Securities in the Third World', Brian L. Job, ed., *The Insecurity Dilemma: National Security of Third World States,* Boulder and London: Lynne Rienner.

Joffé, George (1987-1988), 'The Amman Summit: The Underlying Reality', *Arab Affairs,* 5, Winter.

Kanovsky, Eliyahu (1983-1984), 'What's Behind Syria's Current Economic Problems?', *Middle East Contemporary Survey (MECS),* vol.8.

Karpat, Kemal H., ed. (1968), *Political and Social Thought in the Contemporary Middle East,* London: Praeger.

Karsh, Efraim (1988), *The Soviet Union and Syria: The Asad Years,* London and New York: the Royal Institute of International Affairs/Routledge.

—— (1989), 'A Marriage of Convenience: The Soviet Union and Asad's Syria', *The Jerusalem Journal of International Relations,* 11(4).

—— (1991), *Soviet Policy towards Syria since 1970,* London: Macmillan.

Kazziha, Walid (1990), 'The Impact of Palestine on Arab Politics,' Giacomo Luciani, ed., *The Arab State,* London: Routledge.

Kechichian, Joseph A. (1993), 'The Impact of American Policies on Iranian-Arab Relations', Hooshang Amirahmadi and Nader Entessar, eds., *Iran and the Arab World,* London: Macmillan.

—— (1999), 'Trends in Saudi National Security', *The Middle East Journal,* 53(2), Spring.

Kedourie, Elie (1984), 'A New International Disorder,' Hedley Bull and Adam

Watson, eds., *The Expansion of International Society,* Oxford: Clarendon Press.

Kerr, Malcolm (1971), *The Arab Cold War: Gamal 'Abd al-Nasir and His Rivals, 1958-1970,* 3rd ed., London: Oxford University Press.

—— and El Sayed Yassin, eds. (1982), *Rich and Poor States in the Middle East: Egypt and the New Arab Order,* Boulder: Westview.

Khaled bin Sultan (HRH General) (1995), *Desert Warrior: A Personal View of the Gulf War by the Joint Forces Commander,* New York: HaperCollins.

Khalidi, Ahmad and Husain Agha (1987-1988), 'The Amman Summit: A New Arab Political Map', *Arab Affairs,* 5, Winter.

—— (Khalidi, Ahmed S. and Hussein Agha) (1991), 'The Syrian Doctrine of Strategic Parity', Judith Kipper and Harold H. Saunders, eds., *The Middle East in Global Perspective,* Boulder: Westview.

Khoury, Philip S. (1987), *Syria and the French Mandate: The Politics of Arab Nationalism 1920-1945,* London: I.B. Tauris.

—— and Joseph Kostiner eds. (1990), *Tribes and State Formation in the Middle East,* Berkeley, Los Angeles and Oxford: University of California Press.

Kienle, Eberhard (1990), *Ba'th v. Ba'th: The Conflict Between Syria and Iraq 1968-1989,* London: I.B.Tauris.

—— (1993), 'The Limits of Fertile Crescent Unity: Iraqi Policies towards Syria since 1945', Derek Hopwood, Habib Ishow. T. Koszinowski, eds., *Iraq: Power and Society,* Reading: Ithaca Press.

—— ed. (1994a), *Contemporary Syria: Liberalization between Cold War and Cold Peace,* London: British Academic Press.

—— (1994b), 'Syria, the Kuwait War, and the New World Order', Tareq Y. Ismael and Jacqueline S. Ismael, eds., *The Gulf War and the New World Order: International Relations of the Middle East,* Gainesville: University Press of Florida.

—— (1995), 'Arab Unity Schemes Revisited: Interest, Identity, and Policy in Syria and Egypt,' *International Journal of Middle East Studies,* 27.

Kimura, Yoshihiro (1983), *Gendai Higashi Arabu-no Seiji Kouzou* (The Political Structure of the Contemporary Arab East), Tokyo: The Institute of Developing Economies.

Knudsen, Erik L. (1996), 'United States-Syrian Diplomatic Relations: The Downward Spiral of Mutual Political Hostility (1970-1994)', *Journal of South Asaidn and Middle Eastern Studies,* 19(4), Summer.

Korany, Bahgat (1987), 'Alien and Besieged Yet Here to Stay: The Contradiction of the Arab Territorial State', Ghassan Salamé, ed., *The Foundations of the Arab State,* London: Croom Helm.

—— and Ali E. Hillal Dessouki, eds. (1991a), *The Foreign Policies of Arab States: The Challenge of Change,* 2nd rev. ed., Boulder: Westview.

—— (1991b), 'Defending the Faith amid Change: The Foreign Policy of Saudi Arabia', Bahgat Korany and Ali E. Hillal Dessouki, eds., *The Foreign Policies of Arab States: The Challenge of Change,* 2nd rev. ed., Boulder: Westview.

—— et al., eds. (1993), *The Many Faces of National Security in the Arab World,* London: Macmillan.

Kostiner, Joseph (1987), 'Shi'i Unrest in the Gulf', Martin Kramer ed., *Shi'ism, Resistance and Revolution,* Boulder: Westview.

—— (1990), 'Transforming Dualities: Tribe and State Formation in Saudi Arabia', Philip S. Khoury and Joseph Kostiner, eds., *Tribes and State Formation in the Middle East,* Berkeley, Los Angeles and Oxford: University of California Press.

Kramer, Martin (1987), 'Syria's Alawis and Shi'Ism', Martin Kramer ed., *Shi'ism, Resistance and Revolution,* Boulder: Westview.

Lacey, Robert (1982), *The Kingdom*, pbk ed., London: Fontana/Collins.
Lackner, Helen (1978), *A House Built on Sand: A Political Economy of Saudi Arabia*, London: Ithaca Press.
Lancaster, William (1981), *The Rwala Bedouin Today*, Cambridge: Cambridge University Press.
Lapid, Yosef (1994), 'Theorizing the "National" in International Relations Theory: Reflections on Nationalism and Neorealism,' Friedrich Kratochwil and Edward D. Mansfield, eds., *International Organization: A Reader*, New York: Harper Collins.
Laqueur, Walter Z. (1961), *Communism and Nationalism in the Middle East*, London: Routledge and Kegan Paul.
Lawrence Freedman (1993), 'The Gulf War and the New World Order', James Gow, ed., *Iraq, the Gulf Conflict and the World Community*, London: Brassey's.
Lawson, Fred H. (1982), 'Social Bases for the Hamah Revolt', *MERIP Reports*, 12(9)/No.110, November-December.
—— (1992), 'External versus Internal Pressures for Liberalization in Syria and Iraq', *Journal of Arab Affairs*, 11(1).
—— (1994), 'Domestic Transformation and Foreign Steadfastness in Contemporary Syria', *The Middle East Journal*, 48(1), Winter.
—— (1996), *Why Syria Goes to War: Thirty Years of Confrontation*, Ithaca: Cornell University Press.
Lay, David (1987-1988), 'The Amman Summit: A Turning Point?', *Arab Affairs*, 5, Winter.
Leca, Jean (1990), 'Social Structure and Political Stability: Comparative Evidence from the Algerian, Syrian and Iraqi Cases,' Giacomo Luciani, ed., *The Arab States*, London: Routledge.
Lees, Brian (1980), *A Handbook of the Al Sa'ud Ruling Family of Saudi Arabia*, London: Royal Genealogies.
Lesch, Ann M. (1995), *Inter-Arab Relations in the Post-Peace Era*, (The Emirates Occasional Papers), Abu Dhabi: The Emirates Center for Strategic Studies and Research.
—— (Ann Mosely) (1991), 'Contrasting Reactions to the Persian Gulf Crisis: Egypt, Syria, Jordan, and the Palestinians', *The Middle East Journal*, 45(1), Winter.
Lesch, David W. (1992), *Syria and the United States: Eisenhower's Cold War in the Middle East*, Boulder, San Francisco and Oxford: Westview.
Levey, Zach (1988), 'The Rearming of Syria and Rehabilitation of Soviet Credibility: October 1982 to May 1983', *The Jerusalem Journal of International Relations*, 10(4).
Little, Douglas (1990), 'Cold War and Covert Action: The United States and Syria, 1945-1958', *The Middle East Journal*, 44(1), Winter.
Lobmeyer, Hans Günter (1991), 'Islamic Ideology and Secular Discourse: The Islamists of Syria', *Orient*, 32(3).
—— (1994), '*Al-dimuqratiyya hiyya al-hall?* The Syrian Opposition at the End of the Asad Era', Eberhard Kienle, ed., *Contemporary Syria: Liberalization between Cold War and Cold Peace*, London: British Academic Press.
—— (1995), *Opposition und Widerstand in Syrien* (Opposition and Resistance in Syria), Hamburg: Deutsches Orient-Institut.
Longuenesse, Elisabeth (1979), 'The Class Nature of the State in Syria: Contribution to an Analysis', *MERIP Reports*, 9(4)/No.77, May.
—— (1985), 'The Syrian Working Class Today', *MERIP Reports*, 15(6)/No.134, July-August.

Luciani, Giacomo and Ghassan Salamé, eds. (1988), *The Politics of Arab Integration*, New York: Croom Helm.

—— (1990a), 'Allocation vs. Production States: A Theoretical Framework,' Giacomo Luciani, ed., *The Arab State*, London: Routledge.

—— and Ghassan Salamé (1990b), 'The Politics of Arab Integration,' Giacomo Luciani, ed., *The Arab State*, London: Routledge.

McLaurin, R.D., ed. (1979), *The Political Role of Minority Groups in the Middle East*, New York: Praeger.

Maddy-Weitznman, Bruce (1981), 'The Fragmentation of Arab Politics: Inter-Arab Affairs since the Afghanistan Invasion', *Orbis*, 25(2), Summer.

Ma'oz, Moshe, (1972), 'Attempts at Creating a Political Community in Modern Syria,' *The Middle East Journal*, 26(4), Autumn.

—— and Avner Yaniv, eds. (1986), *Syria under Assad: Domestic Constraints and Regional Risks*, London and Sydney, Croom Helm.

—— (1992), 'Syrian-Israeli Relations and the Middle East Process', *The Jerusalem Journal of International Relations*, 14 (3).

—— et al., eds. (1999), *Modern Syria: From Ottoman Rule to Pivotal Role in the Middle East*, Brighton: Sussex Academic Press.

Mayall, James (1990), *Nationalism and International Society*, Cambridge: Cambridge University Press.

Middle East Watch (1991), *Syria Unmasked: The Suppression of Human Rights by the Asad Regime*, New Haven: Yale University Press.

Migdal, Joel S. (1988), *Strong Societies and Weak States: State-Society Relations and State Capabilities in the Third World*, Princeton: Princeton University Press.

Milani, Mohsen M. (1994), *The Making of Iran's Islamic Revolution: From Monarchy to Islamic Republic*, 2nd ed., Boulder: Westview.

Moussalli, Ahmad S. (2000), 'The Geopolitics of Syrian-Iraqi Relations', *Middle East Policy*, 7(4), October.

Munadhdhamah al-Thawrah al-Islamiyyah fi al-Jazirah al-'Arabiyyah (1981), *Intifadah al-Mintaqah al-Sharqiyyah, 1400 Hijriyyah/1979 Miladiyyah* (The Uprising of the Eastern Province, 1979), n.p.: Munadhdhamah al-Thawrah al-Islamiyyah fi al-Jazirah al-'Arabiyyah.

Muslih, Muhammad (1993), 'The Golan: Israel, Syria, and Strategic Calculations,' *The Middle East Journal*, 47(4), Autumn.

Nasrallah, Fida (1988), 'Ceasefire in the Gulf: The New Geopolitical Balance', *Arab Affairs*, 1(7), Summer/Autumn.

—— (1994), 'Syria after Ta'if: Lebanon and the Lebanese in Syrian Politics', Eberhard Kienle, ed., *Contemporary Syria: Liberalization between Cold War and Cold Peace*, London: British Academic Press.

Niblock, Tim, ed. (1982), *State, Society, and the Economy in Saudi Arabia*, London: Croom Helm.

Noble, Paul C. (1991), 'The Arab System: Pressures Constraints, and Opportunities', Bahgat Korany and Ali E. Hillal Dessouki, eds., *The Foreign Policies of Arab States: The Challenge of Change*, 2nd rev. ed., Boulder: Westview.

Nonneman, Gerd (1988), *Development, Administration and Aid in the Middle East*, London and New York: Routledge.

Norton, Augustus Richard (1987a), 'The Origins and Resurgence of Amal', Martin Kramer ed., *Shi'ism, Resistance and Revolution*, Boulder: Westview.

—— (1987b), *Amal and the Shi'a: Struggle for the Soul of Lebanon*, Austin: University of Texas Press.

Olmert, Joseph (1987), 'The Shi'is and the Lebanese State', Martin Kramer, ed.,

*Shi'ism, Resistance and Revolution,* Boulder: Westview.

—— (Yosef) (1990), 'Iranian-Syrian Relations: Between Islam and Realpolitik', David Menashri, ed., *The Iranian Revolution and the Muslim World,* Boulder, CO: Westview.

Owen, Roger (1992), *State, Power and Politics in the Making of the Modern Middle East,* London and New York: Routledge.

Pappe, Ilan (1993), 'A Modus Vivendi Challenged: The Arabs in Israel and the Gulf War', Amatzia Baram and Barry Rubin, eds., *Iraq's Road to War,* London: Macmillan.

Perthes, Volker (1992), 'The Syrian Economy in the 1980s', *The Middle East Journal,* 46(1), Winter.

—— (1993), 'Incremental Change in Syria', *Current History,* 92(570), January.

—— (1995), *The Political Economy of Syria under Asad,* London: I.B. Tauris.

Peterson, Erik R. (1988), *The Gulf Cooperation Council: Search for Unity in a Dynamic Region,* Boulder and London: Westview.

Petran, Tabitha (1972), *Syria,* London: Ernest Benn.

—— (1987), *The Struggle over Lebanon,* New York: Monthly Review Press.

Picard, Elizabeth (2002), *Lebanon: A Shattered Country,* New York and London: Holmes & Meier.

Pipes, Daniel (1986), 'Syria: The Cuba of the Middle East?', *Commentary,* July.

—— (1990), *Greater Syria: The History of an Ambition,* New York and Oxford: Oxford University Press

—— (1991), *Damascus Courts the West: Syrian Politics, 1989-1991,* Washington, DC: Washington Institute for Near East Policy.

Piscatori, James (1983a), 'Ideological Politics in Sa'udi Arabia', James Piscatori, ed., *Islam in the Political Process,* New York and Cambridge: Cambridge University Press.

—— (1983b), 'Islamic Values and National Interest: The Foreign Policy of Saudi Arabia,' Adeed I. Dawisha, ed., *Islam in Foreign Policy,* Cambridge: Cambridge University Press.

Porter, Bruce D. (1984), *The USSR in Third World Conflicts: Soviet Arms and Diplomacy in Local Wars,* Cambridge: Cambridge University Press.

Porter, R.S. (1988), 'Gulf Aid and Investment in the Arab World,' B.R. Pridham, ed., *The Arab Gulf and the Arab World,* London: Croom Helm.

Pridham, B.R., ed. (1988), *The Arab Gulf and the Arab World,* London: Croom Helm.

al-Qahtani, Fahd (1988a), *Shuyu'iyyun fi al-Sa'udiyyah: Dirasah fi al-'Alaqat al-Sufiyatiyyah al-Sa'udiyyah 1902-1988* (Communists in Saudi Arabia: a Study of Saudi-Soviet Relations 1902-1988), London: al-Safa li-l-Nashr wa al-Tawzi'.

—— (1988b), *Sira' al-Ajniha fi al-'Ailah al-Sa'udiyyah: Dirasah fi al-Nidham al-Siyasi wa Ta'assus al-Dawlah* (The Struggle of the Factions in the Saudi Royal Family: A Study of the Political System and the Foundation of the State), London: al-Safa li-l-Nashr wa al-Tawzi'.

Qindil, Muhammad Wajdi (1980a), 'Madha Hadatha fi al-Sa'udiyyah?: Isharat al-Khatar al-Ahmar fi Adan...ila Aina?' (What happened in Saudi Arabia?: Signs of the Red Peril in Aden ... to Where?), *Akhir Sa'ah,* 23 January.

—— (1980b), 'Asrar Mihwar "Kabul-Dimashq-Adan"' (The Secrets of "Kabul-Damascus-Aden" Axis), *Akhir Sa'ah,* 13 February.

—— (1980c), 'Hadhihi al-Wahdah: Safqah...li-Hisab Man?' (This Unity: A Deal...at Whose Cost?), *Akhir Sa'ah,* 17 September.

—— (1980d), 'Madha Wara' al-Khilafat bayna Suriyya wa al-Sa'udiyyah?' (What's behind the Disagreements between Syria and Saudi Arabia?), *Akhir Sa'ah,* 26 November.

—— (1980e), 'Khafaya Mu'tamar 'Amman: Ma'ziq al-Munadhdhamah bayna Suriyya wa al-Sa'udiyyah' (The Secret Affairs of the Amman Summit: The PLO's Dilemma between Syria and Saudi Arabia), *Akhir Sa'ah,* 03 December.

—— (1980f), 'La'bah Suriyya 'ala Hudud al-Urdun: Li-madha Insahabat al Hushud? Wa Ma Huwa al-Thaman?' (The Syrian Game on the Jordanian Border: Why Did It Withdraw? And What is the Cost?), *Akhir Sa'ah,* 17 December.

'Al-Qissah al-Kamilah li-l-Wisatah al-Sa'udiyyah' (The Full Story of Saudi Mediation) (1983), *al-Mustaqbal,* 24 September.

Quandt, William B. (1982), *Saudi Arabia in the 1980s: Foreign Policy, Security and Oil,* Washington, DC: The Brookings Institution.

—— (1986), *Camp David: Peace Making and Politics,* Washington, DC: The Brookings Institution.

—— (1993), *Peace Process: American Diplomacy and the Arab-Israeli Conflict since 1967,* Washington, DC/Berkeley: The Brookings Institution/University of California Press.

Quilliam, Neil (1999), *Syria and the New World Order,* Reading: Ithaca Press.

Rabinovich, Itamar (1972), *Syria under the Ba'th 1964-1966: The Army-Party Symbiosis,* New York: Halsted Press.

—— (1982), 'The Foreign Policy of Syria', *Survival,* 24(4), July/August.

—— (1984), 'The Foreign Policies of Syria: Goals, Capabilities, Constraints, and Options', Charles Tripp, ed., *Regional Security in the Middle East,* London: IISS.

—— (1985), *The War for Lebanon, 1970-1985,* Ithaca and London: Cornell University Press.

—— (1986), 'The Changing Prism: Syrian Policy in Lebanon as a Mirror, an Issue and as Instrument', Moshe Ma'oz and Avner Yaniv, eds., *Syria under Assad: Domestic Constraints and Regional Risks,* London: Croom Helm.

—— (1998), *The Brink of Peace: The Israeli-Syrian Negotiations,* Princeton: Princeton University Press.

Ramazani, Rouhollah K. (1986), *Revolutionary Iran: Challenge and Response in the Middle East,* Baltimore and London: Johns Hopkins University Press.

Ramet, Pedro (1986), 'The Soviet-Syrian Relationship', *Problems of Communism,* September-October.

—— (1990), *The Soviet–Syrian Relationship since 1955: A Troubled Alliance,* Boulder, San Francisco and Oxford: Westview.

Ranstorp, Magnus (1997), *Hizb'allah in Lebanon: The Politics of the Western Hostage Crisis,* New York: St. Martin's Press.

al-Rasheed, Madawi (1997), *Politics in an Arabian Oasis: The Rashidis of Saudi Arabia,* London and New York: I.B. Tauris.

Rathmell, Andrew (1995), *Secret War in the Middle East: The Covert Struggle for Syria, 1949-1961,* London and New York: Tauris Academic Studies (I.B.Tauris).

el-Rayyes, Riad N. (1988), 'Arab Nationalism and the Gulf', B.R. Pridham, ed., *The Arab Gulf and the Arab World,* London: Croom Helm.

—— (al-Rayyis, Riyadh Najib) (1998), *Riyah al-Shimal: al-Sa'udiyyah wa al-Khalij wa al-'Arab fi 'Alam al-Tis'ayinat* (Northern Wind: Saudi Arabia, the Gulf and the Arabs in the 1990s), Beirut: Riad el-Rayyes Books.

Reich, Bernard (1984), *The United States and Israel: Influence in the Special Relationship,* New York: Praeger.

Riad, Mahmoud (1981), *The Struggle for Peace in the Middle East,* London: Quartet

Books.

—— (Riyadh, Mahmud) (1986a), *Mudhakkirat Mahmud Riyadh, Juz' al-Thani: al-Amn al-Qawmi al-'Arabiyy…bayna al-Injaz wa al-Fashl* (The Memoirs of Mahmoud Riad, Part 2: The Arab National Security…between Accomplishment and Failure), Cairo: Dar al-Mustaqbal al-'Arabiyy.

—— (Riyadh, Mahmud) (1986b), *Mudhakkirat Mahmud Riyadh, Juz' al-Thalith: Amrika wa al'Arab* (The Memoirs of Mahmoud Riad, Part 3: America and the Arabs), Cairo: Dar al-Mustaqbal al-'Arabiyy.

—— (Riyadh, Mahmud) (1992), *Mudhakkirat Mahmud Riyadh, 1948-1978: al-Bahth 'An al-Salam…wa al-Sira' fi al-Sharq al-Awsat* (The Memoirs of Mahmoud Riad, 1948-1978: The Search for Peace…and the Struggle in the Middle East), 3rd ed., Cairo: Dar al-Mustaqbal al-'Arabiyy.

Richards, Alan, and John Waterbury (1990), *A Political Economy of the Middle East: State, Class, and Economic Development*, Boulder: Westview.

Roberts, Cynthia A. (1983), 'Soviet Arms-Transfer Policy and the Decision to Upgrade Syrian Air Defences', *Survival*, 25(4), July/August.

Roberts, David (1987), *The Ba'th and the Creation of Modern Syria*, London and Sydney: Croom Helm.

—— (1991), 'The USSR in Syrian Perspective: Political Design and Pragmatic Practices', Moshe Efrat and Jacob Bercovitch, eds., *Superpowers and the Client States in the Middle East: The Imbalance of Influence*, London and New York: Routledge.

Robinson, Glenn E. (1998), 'Elite Cohesion, Regime Succession and Political Instability in Syria', *Middle East Policy*, 5(4), January.

Robinson, Jeffrey (1988), *Yamani: The Inside Story*, London: Fontana.

Robinson, Leonard (1996), 'Rentierism and Foreign Policy in Syria', *Arab Studies Journal*, 4(1), Spring.

Ross, Dennis (1990), 'Soviet Behavior toward the Lebanon War, 1982-84', George W. Breslaner, ed., *Soviet Strategy in the Middle East*, Boston: Unwin Hyman.

Rugh, William (1973), 'Emergence of a New Middle Class in Saudi Arabia', *The Middle East Journal*, 27(1), Winter.

Sabbagh, Mazin Yusuf (1997), *Liqa' al-Nusur: al-Qahirah—Dimashq…'Alaqah Mitamayyizah* (The Encounter of the Eagles: Cairo—Damascus…A Distinguished Relationship), Cairo and Beirut: Dar al-Shuruq.

Sadiq, Mahmud (1993), *Hiwar hawla Suriyyah* (A Dialogue on Syria), London: Dar 'Ukadh.

Sadowski, Yahya (1985), 'Cadres, Guns and Money: The Eighth Regional Congress of the Syrian Ba'th', *MERIP Reports*, 15(6)/No.134, July-August.

—— (1988), 'Ba'thist Ethics and the Spirit of State Capitalism,' Peter J. Chelkowski, and Robert J. Pranger, eds., *Ideology and Power in the Middle East: Studies in Honor of George Lenczowski*, Durham and London: Duke University Press,.

—— (1991), 'Arab Economies after the Gulf War: Power, Poverty, and Petrodollars', *Middle East Report*, 21(3)/No.170, May-June.

—— (2002), 'The Evolution of Political Identity in Syria', Shibley Telhami and Michael Barnett, eds., *Identity and Foreign Policy in the Middle East*, Ithaca and London: Cornell University Press.

Safran, Nadav (1988), *Saudi Arabia: The Ceaseless Quest for Security*, Ithaca and London: Cornell University Press.

al-Sa'id, Nasir, *Tarikh Al-Sa'ud* (The History of the House of Saud), Manshurat Ittihad Sha'b al-Jazirrah al-'Arabiyyah, n.p., n.d.

Saideman, Stephen (2002), 'Thinking Theoretically about Identity and Foreign Policy', Shibley Telhami and Michael Barnett, eds., *Identity and Foreign Policy in the Middle East,* Ithaca and London: Cornell University Press.

Salamé, Ghassan (Salamah, Ghassan) (1980), *Al-Siyasah al-Kharijiyyah al-Sa'udiyyah mundhu 'Am 1945: Dirasah fi al-'Alaqat al-Duwaliyyah* (Saudi Foreign Policy since 1945: A Study in International Relations), Beirut: Ma'had al-Inma' al-'Arabi.

—— (1981), 'Saudi Arabia: Development and Dependence', *The Jerusalem Quarterly,* 20, Summer.

—— (1988a), 'Integration in the Arab World: The Institutional Framework,' Giacomo Luciani and Ghassan Salamé, eds., *The Politics of Arab Integration,* London: Croom Helm.

—— (1988b), 'Perceived Threats and Perceived Loyalties', B.R. Pridham, ed., *The Arab Gulf and the Arab World,* London, New York and Sydney: Croom Helm.

—— (1990), '"Strong"' and "Weak" States: A Qualified Return to the *Muqaddimah*', Giacomo Luciani, ed., *The Arab State,* London: Routledge.

—— (1993), 'Political Power and the Saudi State', Albert Hourani, Philip S. Khoury and Mary C. Wilson, eds., *The Modern Middle East: A Reader,* London and New York: I.B. Tauris.

—— (1994), *Democracy without Democrats?: The Renewal of Politics in the Muslim World,* London and New York: I.B.Tauris.

Salem, Paul (1994), *Bitter Legacy: Ideology and Politics in the Arab World,* Syracuse: Syracuse University Press.

Salibi, Kamal (1988), *A House of Many Mansions: The History of Lebanon Reconsidered,* London: I.B.Tauris.

Sayigh, Yazid (1982), 'The Roots of Syrian-PLO Differences', *Middle East International,* 29 October.

Seale, Patrick (1986), *The Struggle for Syria: A Study of Post-War Arab Politics 1945-1958,* 2nd ed., London: I.B.Tauris.

—— (1990), *Asad of Syria: The Struggle for the Middle East,* Berkeley, Los Angeles and London: University of California Press.

—— (1993), *Abu Nidal: A Gun for Hire,* London: Random House.

—— (1996) with Linda Butler, 'Asad's Regional Strategy and the Challenge from Netanyahu', *Journal of Palestine Studies,* 26 (1), Autumn.

Sigler, John (1989), 'The Legacy of the Iran-Iraq War', Miron Rezun, ed., *Iran at the Crossroads: Global Relations in a Turbulent Decade,* Boulder: Westview.

Snider, Lewis W. (1979a), 'Inter-Arab Relations', P. Edward Haley and Lewis W. Snider eds., *Lebanon in Crisis: Participants and Issues,* Syracuse: Syracuse University Press.

—— (1979b), 'Minorities and Political Power in the Middle East,' R.D. McLaurin, ed., *The Political Role of Minority Groups in the Middle East,* New York: Praeger.

Stanley, Bruce (1990), 'Drawing from the Well: Syria in the Persian Gulf', *Journal of South Asian and Middle Eastern Studies,* 14(2), Winter.

Sukkar, Nabil (1994), 'The Crisis of 1986 and Syria's Plan for Reform', Eberhard Kienle, ed., *Contemporary Syria: Liberalization between Cold War and Cold Peace,* London: British Academic Press.

Taylor, Alan R. (1982), *The Arab Balance of Power,* Syracuse: Syracuse University Press.

Telhami, Shibley and Michael Barnett, eds. (2002), *Identity and Foreign Policy in the Middle East,* Ithaca and London: Cornell University Press.

Tibi, Bassam (1990a), *Arab Nationalism: A Critical Enquiry,* Marion Farouk-Sluglett and Peter Sluglett, trans. and ed., London: Macmillan.

—— (1990b), 'The Simultaneity of the Unsimultaneous: Old Tribes and Imposed Nation-States in the Modern Middle East,' Philip S. Khoury and Joseph Kostiner eds., *Tribes and State Formation in the Middle East*, Berkeley: University of California Press.

Tripp, Charles (1992), 'The Gulf States and Iraq,' *Survival*, 34(3), Autumn.

—— (1993), 'The Iran-Iraq War and the Iraqi State', Derek Hopwood, Habib Ishow. T. Koszinowski, eds., *Iraq: Power and Society*, Reading: Ithaca Press.

—— (2000), *A History of Iraq*, Cambridge: Cambridge University Press.

'Un nouvel axe Damas-Ryad' (1982), *Jeune Afrique*, 20 January.

Vassiliev, Alexei (1998), *The History of Saudi Arabia*, London: Saqi Books.

Vaziri, Haleh (1992), 'Iran's Involvement in Lebanon: Polarization and Radicalization of Militant Islamic Movements', *Journal of South Asian and Middle East Studies*, 16(2), Winter.

Walt, Stephen M. (1987), *The Origins of Alliances*, Ithaca and London: Cornell University Press.

Wedeen, Lisa (1999), *Ambiguities of Domination: Politics, Rhetoric, and Symbols in Contemporary Syria*, Chicago and London: University of Chicago Press.

Wenner, Manfred (1975), 'Saudi Arabia: Survival of Traditional Elites', Frank Tachau, ed., *Political Elites and Political Development in the Middle East*, New York: Halsted Press.

Wilson, Peter W. and Douglas F. Graham (1994), *Saudi Arabia: The Coming Storm*, Armonk: M.E.Sharpe.

Windsor, Philip (1988), 'The Continuing Intifada: Regional and Strategic Implications of the Uprising', *Arab Affairs*, 1(7), Summer/Autumn.

Winckler, Onn (1997), 'Syrian Migration to the Arab Oil-Producing Countries', *Middle Eastern Studies*, 33(1), January.

Wright, Claudia (1982), 'Will the Arabs Cash Their Cheques?', *New Statesman*, 30 July.

al-Yassini, Ayman (1985), *Religion and State in the Kingdom of Saudi Arabia*, Boulder and London: Westview.

Yegnes, Tamar (1981), 'Saudi Arabia and the Peace Process', *The Jerusalem Quarterly*, 18, Winter.

Zisser, Eyal (2001), *Asad's Legacy: Syria in Transition*, London: Hurst & Co.

—— (1998), 'Appearance and Reality: Syria's Decisionmaking Structure', *Middle East Review of International Affairs (MERIA)*, 2(2), May.

—— (1994), 'Syria: the Renewed Struggle over the Succession', *The World Today*, July.

### THESES, DISSERTATIONS AND CONFERENCE PAPERS

Aoyama, Hiroyuki (1998), 'Suimenka-no "Wahei" Koushou: 1990-nendai-no Aru=Asado Seiken-to Shiria-Musurimu Douhoudan' (Subsurface "Peace" Talks: Al-Asad Regime and the Syrian Muslim Brotherhood in the 1990s), (unpublished thesis for the partial fulfilment of the doctoral curriculum by course work), Tokyo: Hitotsubashi University, January.

Marschall, Christin (1991), 'Syria, Iran, and the Changing Middle East Order: The Syro-Iranian Alliance 1979-1988,' (unpublished M.Phil thesis), Oxford: St. Antony's College, Oxford University.

Raad, Walid R. (1998), 'Internal Changes in Post-Cold War Syria' (unpublished MA thesis), Beirut: Lebanese American University, June.

Salamé, Ghassan (1985), 'Islam and Politics in Saudi Arabia', (paper presented to the conference on 'Islam and Politics in the contemporary Muslim World'

organised by the Center for Middle Eastern Studies, Harvard University), 15-16
October.
al-Yassini, Ayman (1983), 'Religion and Foreign Policy in Saudi Arabia' (CDAS
discussion papers no.2), Montreal: CDAS, McGill University, March.

## NEWSPAPERS, PRESS RELEASE AND MAGAZINES

*Al-Ahali* (Cairo)
*Al-Ahram* and *al-Ahram al-Masa'i* (Cairo)
*Al-Ahrar* (Cairo)
*Akhir Sa'ah* (Cairo)
*Al-'Amal* (Beirut)
*Al-Anwar* (Beirut)
*Arab Report* (London)
*Arab Report and Record* (London)
*Business Week* (New York)
*BBC/SWB/ME (British Broadcasting Corporation: Summary of World Broadcasts, Part 4:
the Middle East and Africa)* (London)
*Chicago Tribune* (Chicago)
*Al-Diyar* (Beirut)
*Daily Star (Beirut)*
*Daily Telegraph* (London)
*The Economist* (London)
*The Financial Times* (London)
*The Guardian* (London)
*Gulf States Newsletter*
*Al-Hawadith* (London and Beirut)
*The Independent* (London)
*International Herald Tribune* (Paris and Zurich)
*Al-Liwa'* (Amman)
*Los Angeles Times* (Los Angeles)
*Al-Majallah* (London)
*MECS (Middle East Contemporary Survey)* (New York and London)
*MEED (Middle East Economic Digest)* (London)
*MEI (Middle East International)* (London)
*Mideast Markets* (London)
*Al-Mustaqbal* (Paris)
*Al-Nahar* (Beirut)
*Newsweek* (New York)
*The New York Times* (New York)
*The Observer* (London)
*Al-Qabas* (Kuwait)
*Al-Ra'y* (Amman)
*Al-Ra'y al-'Amm* (Kuwait)
*Al-Riyadh* (Riyadh)
*Al-Safir* (Beirut)
Saudi Press Agency
*Sawt al-Ahrar*
*Al-Sharq al-Awsat* (London)
*Time* (New York)
*Times* (London)
*Tishrin* (Damascus)

*Ukkaz* (Jiddah)
*Al-Usbu'* (Cairo)
*The Wall Street Journal* (New York)
*The Washington Post* (Washington, D.C.)

## OFFICIAL DOCUMENTS AND STATISTICAL RECORDS

Arab Monetary Fund (1992), Economics and Technical Department, *Foreign Trade of Arab Countries 1981-1991,* vol.10, n.p.

'Brutukul Insha' Majlis Rijal al-A'mal al-Sa'udiy-al-Suriy' (Protocol on the Establishment of the Syrian-Saudi Council of Businessmen) (1991), Damascus, 9 March.

van der Boogaerde, Pierre (1991), *Financial Assistance from Arab Countries and Arab Regional Institutions* (occasional paper no.87), Washington, DC: IMF, September.

Damascus Chamber of Commerce (*Ghurfah Tijarah Dimashq*) (1999), *Al-Ittifaqiyyat al-Tijariyyah bayna Suriyyah wa al-Duwal al-'Arabiyyah* (Trade Agreements between Syria and the Arab States), Damascus: Damascus Chamber of Commerce.

*Dustur al-Jumhuriyyah al-'Arabiyyah al-Suriyyah* (The Constitution of the Syrian Arab Republic) (1973), Damascus.

Syrian-Saudi Corporation for Industrial and Agricultural Investments (SIACO (1976); *al-Sharikah al-Suriyyah al-Sa'udiyyah li-l-Istithmarat al-Sina'iyyah wa al-Zira'iyyah*), 'Ittifaqiyyah Ta'sis al-Sharikah wa Nidhami-ha al-Asasi' (Agreement on the Establishment of the Syrian-Saudi Corporation for Industrial and Agricultural Investments and Its Basic Organisation), Damascus.

Syrian Arab Republic, Central Bureau of Statistics, *Foreign Trade Statistics,* Damascus, various issues (annual publication).

Syrian Arab Republic, Central Bureau of Statistics, *Statistical Abstracts,* Damascus, various issues (annual publication).

# INDEX

17 May agreement
(Lebanese-Israeli) 141, 143,
145-152, 154-158, 165, 173,
232n11
al-Sha'ir, 'Ali 84, 142, 150, 152,
161, 233n21
Shamir, Yitzhak 163, 185
Shammar tribe 4, 170
al-Shar', Faruq 114, 117, 179,
180-182, 184, 186, 202, 206,
226n16, 237n20, 237n23,
238n34
Shi'a 63, 79, 84, 119, 124, 152, 154,
159, 164, 166, 183, 192, 226n9,
236n10, 236n17; in Saudi
Arabia 30, 32, 61, 62, 67, 72, 93,
201, 228n6, 238n38
al-Shihabi, Hikmat 168
al-Shishakli, Adib 20, 21
Shultz, George 145, 146, 148, 153,
210
Sinai II 41-43, 45
South Yemen, see People's
Democratic Republic of
Yemen (PDRY)
Soviet Union (the USSR) 15, 23-
25, 37, 66, 67, 73, 87, 103, 129,
135, 142, 155, 176, 193, 203,
209-211, 227n19, 227n23,
227n24, 229n21; and Iran, 61,
63, 122, 235n3; and Saudi
Arabia 2, 37, 42, 50-58, 67-72,
111-114, 126, 142, 147, 149,
150, 227n27, 229n16; and Syria,
2, 25, 28, 31, 51-54, 67-77, 90,
91, 100-104, 110-112, 117, 118,
122, 133, 137-143, 147, 150,
156, 159-162, 171, 174, 180,
193, 200, 227n18, 227n19,
227n21, 229n13, 230n33,
231n5, 239n1; see also
Afghanistan, Soviet invasion
of; Treaty of Friendship and
Co-operation (Syrian-Soviet)
Steadfastness and Confrontation

Front, see Front of
Steadfastness and
Confrontation
'strategic parity' 67, 113, 133, 193,
216
Sudan 53, 81, 95, 99
Sultan (bin 'Abd al-'Aziz al-Sa'ud),
Prince 37, 149, 158, 172,
232n15, 234n36, 240n8
Sunnis 17, 35, 63, 78, 79, 91, 94,
129, 146, 159, 164, 224n6,
228n9
surface-to-air missiles (SAM) 103,
143
Syria 17-21, 28-32, 47, 192-194;
and Arab-Israeli peace 42, 112,
132, 221; and Egypt 15, 16,
20-28, 45-49, 58, 73, 126, 128,
134, 199, 210, 223, 238n44,
238n49; and Iran 2, 59, 63-65,
96, 120-123, 133, 135, 140, 145,
166-169, 171, 186-191, 196-198,
200, 206, 220, 226n10, 230n26,
231n42, 236n17; and Jordan, see
Jordan, relations with Syria;
and Libya 65; and the
Palestinians 2, 18, 44, 45, 80,
115, 129-133, 144, 145,
154-156, 160-162, 178, 185-191,
194, 207, 208, 230n34, 230n35;
and the Soviet Union, see Soviet
Union and Syria; and the
United States 25, 71, 92, 103,
126, 149, 150-154, 163-167,
171, 192-194, 210, 219, 221,
224n3; conflict with Israel, see
Israel, conflict with Syria;
policy towards Lebanon 44, 50,
79, 80, 125, 126, 146, 152-154,
199-200 see also Lebanon and
Syria; position in the Arab
world 15-17, 36, 60, 64, 96-97,
120, 137, 139-141, 178-182,
186, 206; support for Saudi
oppositions 93-94;

and Saudi Arabia 23-26, 33, 38,
41, 47, 51-57, 72, 76, 89,
102-105, 113, 121, 127, 142,
149, 155-157, 162-165, 185,
186, 191, 207, 229n14, 231n1,
232n15; and Syria 25, 71, 92,
103, 126, 149, 150-154,
163-167, 171, 192-194, 210,
219, 221, 224n3; in Lebanon
145-166, 173-176, 212
'Utaiba, Juhaiman 62, 227n22

Vance, Cyrus 53
Velayati, 'Ali Akbar 180, 190,
238n31
Voice of the Arabian Peninsula 32,
37

Wahhabism and Wahhabis 2, 15
Walid (bin Talal bin 'Abd al-'Aziz
al-Sa'ud), Prince 222, 235n41
Weinberger, Casper 121, 149
World Islamic League 30

Yasin, Yusuf 19, 22
Yemen 27, 29-32, 34, 37, 46, 55,
56, 64, 78, 159, 223, 226n4,
228n3, 240n6
Yemen Arab Republic (YAR;
North Yemen) 32, 53, 55, 56,
67, 95, 131, 161, 211, 227n27
see also Yemen

al-Zaim, Colonel Husni 20
Zionism 226n11, 230n26